the
social
sciences
in the
looking
glass

the social sciences in the looking glass

edited by didier fassin
& george steinmetz

*STUDIES IN THE
PRODUCTION
OF KNOWLEDGE*

DUKE UNIVERSITY PRESS durham & london 2023

Project Editor: Bird Williams
Designed by Aimee C. Harrison
Typeset in Portrait Text and SangBleu Kingdom by
Westchester Publishing Services

Library of Congress Cataloging-in-Publication Data
Names: Fassin, Didier, editor. | Steinmetz, George, [date]- editor.
Title: The social sciences in the looking glass : studies in the
production of knowledge / edited by Didier Fassin and George
Steinmetz.
Description: Durham : Duke University Press, 2023. |
Includes bibliographical references and index.
Identifiers: LCCN 2022041006 (print)
LCCN 2022041007 (ebook)
ISBN 9781478019459 (paperback)
ISBN 9781478016823 (hardcover)
ISBN 9781478024095 (ebook)
Subjects: LCSH: Social sciences. | Social sciences—Philosophy. |
Social sciences and history. | BISAC: SOCIAL SCIENCE /
Anthropology / Cultural & Social | SOCIAL SCIENCE / Sociology /
General
Classification: LCC H61 .S5935 2023 (print) | LCC H61 (ebook) |
DCC 300.1—dc23/eng/20221223
LC record available at https://lccn.loc.gov/2022041006
LC ebook record available at https://lccn.loc.gov/2022041007

Cover art: Diego Velázquez, *Las Meninas*, 1656-1657. Oil on
canvas, 10.4 ft. × 9.1 ft. Source: Wikimedia Commons.

CONTENTS

part three. exploring borders and boundaries

introduction

Toward a Social Science
of the Social Sciences

DIDIER FASSIN AND
GEORGE STEINMETZ

One cannot talk about such an object without exposing oneself to a permanent mirror effect: every word that can be uttered about scientific practice can be turned back on the person who utters it. Far from fearing this mirror—or boomerang—effect, in taking science as the object of my analysis I am deliberately aiming to expose myself, and all those who write about the social world, to a generalized reflexivity.
—PIERRE BOURDIEU, *SCIENCE OF SCIENCE AND REFLEXIVITY*

OVER THE PAST HUNDRED YEARS, social scientists have conducted research on multiple social worlds of science and technology, even developing a prolific subdiscipline. But remarkably, their interest, which has covered a wide range of disciplines and practices, from physics to biology, from laboratories to scientific controversies, has largely avoided a similar exploration of their own knowledge and practice. Indeed, the history of science, and later the social studies of science, broadly speaking, have been primarily focused, since the creation of the journals *Isis* and *Osiris* in the early twentieth century, on the natural sciences. In recent decades, however, historians, sociologists, anthropologists, and others have begun to examine various aspects of the social sciences, including their politics and ideologies, their epistemologies and methods, their institutionalization and professionalization, their national development and colonial expansion, their heterogeneous globalization and local contestations, and their public presence and role in society (e.g., Scott and Keates 2001; Porter and Ross 2003; Steinmetz 2005; vom Bruch, Gerhardt, and Pawliczek 2006; Fassin and Bensa 2008; Backhouse and Fontaine 2010; Danell, Larsson, and Wisselgren 2013; Rollet and Nabonnaud 2013; Backhouse and Fontaine 2014; Randeria and Wittrock 2019). Strikingly, this trend has been concomitant with a reconfiguration of the scientific landscape in which the social sciences are inscribed, a reshaping of their borders with neighboring fields such as literary studies and cognitive science, to take extreme examples, and a radical questioning of their very foundations, by feminist, postcolonial and posthumanist studies, as well as, from a symmetrical viewpoint, by so-called analytical approaches (e.g., Connell 2007; Joas and Klein 2010; Moyn and Sartori 2013; Kennedy 2015; Fassin 2017). It is therefore an interesting and challenging time to engage in what could be called a "social science of the social sciences." The object of this volume is to offer current social scientific perspectives (defined broadly) on this reflexive moment in which the social sciences begin to examine themselves in the mirror or looking glass—hence our volume's title.

As was famously formulated by Norbert Elias, the originality of the social sciences within the wider scientific field is that the observer and the observed belong to the same category, even when the latter is described in terms of professions, networks, ethnic groups, religious practices, or social fields: both are human beings. In contrast, in the natural sciences, the two are distinct, as human beings study black holes, tectonic plates, algae, genomes, or bosons. It is therefore easier for historians and sociologists of the natural sciences to distance themselves from their object of study. Not that natural scientists are entirely dispassionate in their research: the controversies around climate change are a reminder of how emotional certain topics may be. But in general, they are more committed to their discipline than to their object as such. On the contrary, social scientists are always caught in a tension between involvement and detachment, especially when their research deals with questions that have a moral or political dimension.[1] Working on abortion, inequality, democracy, terrorism, crime, or debt entails some form of personal "involvement," which can be referred to as belief, value, conviction, prejudice, ideology, or subjectivity, even when scholars feel committed to scientific "detachment," using surveys, statistics, models, theories, or fieldwork to approach objectivity. It might even be argued that the more they try to achieve perfect detachment the more they are blind to their own involvement.

The project of a social science of the social sciences heightens this tension. It supposes that human beings study human beings who are themselves studying human beings. It should therefore not be a surprise that social scientists would have been reluctant to conduct such program, which renders detachment even more difficult and involvement even more hazardous. This reluctance should indeed be understood in light of the fact that research on the social sciences is inscribed in the same social space to which the researcher belongs. The ethnography, sociology, or history of a given domain of the social sciences supposes an investigation among colleagues, or scientific "ancestors," or, at least, within a scientific space characterized by competition and rivalry, friendships and allegiances, anxieties of influence, and inherited ideas of obscure provenance. These complications come at a cost for the student of this domain. Yet how could we defend the idea of a critical social science when the only area that would escape our inquiry would be precisely our own disciplines? Like others before us,[2] we therefore call, in this book, for a critical epistemology that applies to the social sciences the same principles and rigorous methods that are used to study other sciences as well as the other domains of social life beyond science.

This critical epistemology takes various methodological forms and can adopt diverse theoretical frameworks. In a time when, as the coronavirus pandemic has shown, sciences in general and the social sciences in particular are disputed, we have privileged in this volume a discussion respectful of epistemological diversity and attentive to distinct theoretical foundations. It is our endeavor here to bring together multiple scientific traditions—history of science, intellectual history, sociology of knowledge, political sociology, cultural anthropology—so as to illustrate the richness and diversity of the research being conducted in an emerging domain, rather than proposing or imposing a unitary paradigm—a temptation that has sometimes led to unfruitful disputes and divisions in the social studies of the other, "exact" sciences. This being said, we must acknowledge that the very foundation of our collective endeavor—the critical reflexivity of the social sciences, expressed through the metaphor of the looking glass in the title—has a clear affinity with the historical sociology of knowledge developed by Pierre Bourdieu and his colleagues, of which it is possible to find variable degrees of presence across the chapters. All of us consider that the social sciences tend to be constituted as fields and institutions and are embedded in national contexts and inscribed in historical moments, and that they can therefore not be apprehended without taking into account these multiple dimensions. All of us agree that it is important to study social scientific practices in relation to both the form and content of the research produced and to study social scientists' positionality not only from an intellectual but also from a social and political perspective. These elementary principles are however freely applied by each author.

The social science of the social sciences and the humanities emerges at an interesting juncture for these disciplines, and from this viewpoint, it is without doubt timely. On the one hand, these arenas have come increasingly under fire from several directions, particularly political and scientific ones. In the political realm, social science has been attacked on three fronts. First, neoliberal criticism judges them unproductive, considering that the only useful social sciences are those that contribute to the wealth of nations. Second, authoritarian criticism deems them too critical, especially in their analysis of power relations and hidden interests. Third, an ad hoc criticism that has recently flourished on both sides of the Atlantic accuses the social sciences of finding excuses for deviance and crime, because they analyze the structural causes underlying these phenomena. In the scientific domain, they have been attacked by two important currents composed of two distinct sets of disciplines that nevertheless share a similar vision of science, according to which science can only talk about facts that can be established through empirical evidence, allowing us to formulate objective and verifiable truths. The first set of critiques comprises mainstream economics, much political science, and large segments of sociology, using modelization and mathematical formalization, quantification, and experimental designs grounded in rational-actor theory. The second set encompasses cognitive sciences broadly speaking, including experimental psychology, analytic philosophy, evolutionary theory, and neuroimaging, which have in common strong universalistic claims about the functioning of the brain and its implications for social life. The former represents a form of social science positivism inherited from the twentieth century but with increasingly potent tools. The latter illustrates a form of neopositivism of the twenty-first century mobilizing increasingly sophisticated technologies from the life sciences. Beyond their differences, these strands tend to question inductive, interpretive, qualitative, and critical social sciences as unscientific, ideological, or flawed.

At the same time, these latter approaches have experienced in the past decades a renewal and enrichment of their objects, approaches, methods, theories, and one might even say: paradigms. The scope of interest among social scientists has expanded beyond human beings to the study of animals, nature, life, infrastructures, cyborgs, and the planet. Feminist studies, race studies, and postcolonial and decolonial studies have shaken well-established approaches to social knowledge in all domains. Political scientists and legal scholars have begun to practice forms of ethnography. Just as artificial intelligence has become a method for some, it is also now an object of study for others. In sociology, actor-network theory (ANT) coexists with the new institutionalism and the social field approach, while cultural and historical sociology flourishes aside economic sociology. In anthropology, ontological, structuralist, historical, neo-Marxist, and neo-Foucauldian strands cohabit in conflictive but often productive ways. In philosophy, the divide between analytic and continental branches remains, but with some bridges being built between them. In sum, there is no homogenous field of social sciences and humanities but a bountiful and turbulent intellectual space of analysis and reflection about human beings and beyond.

It is at this juncture that we inscribe our book, as a "defense and illustration" of a critical social science, to paraphrase Joachim Du Bellay's famous sixteenth-century essay on language and poetry. Beyond their diversity of themes and contexts, the common thread of the book's contributions is a critical approach to the politics and practices of the social sciences. This does not simply mean that it is critical of social science, as with works that uncover the history of eugenics, counterinsurgency research, colonial social science, or social science under authoritarian regimes (e.g., Strauss 1952, 22–37; Klingemann 1992; Kojenikov 1999; Carson 2007; Rohde 2013; Steinmetz 2013, 2022; Mastnak 2015; Morcillo Laiz 2016; van Eekelen 2016). It means above all that this reading of the social sciences can contribute critically to the politics and practice of social science itself, and beyond that, to the understanding of social processes. In particular, it can unveil the hidden genesis of currently accepted concepts and languages; disinter forgotten works that remain valuable in the present; and question the foundations of our thinking about societies and about the specific place occupied by human beings in our comprehension of the world. And since the social sciences are thoroughly entangled in the social facts they describe and analyze, only by singling out the former can we understand why our world looks the way it does.

Such critical endeavor is significantly facilitated in this volume by two elements. First, the confrontation between authors from various social sciences allows for a multiplication of perspectives, while it is more frequent to have scholars from a single discipline represented.[3] The chapters have for their object history, sociology, anthropology, legal studies, cognitive sciences, animal studies, and religious studies, and in some cases, interdisciplinary spaces or the social sciences as a whole. Second, the geographical scope of the chapters covers five continents and the movements of ideas, scholars, and scientific resources among them, whereas many existing studies have focused on a single country or on nation-state comparisons.[4] Our scope thus generates two complementary results. On the one hand, the examination of similarities and differences between national traditions from various continents leads to a critique of the epistemological and conceptual self-evidences of the social sciences. On the other hand, the study of the internationalization, globalization, and hegemonization of theories and methods underscores the dynamics of encounters, exchanges, appropriations, and contestations in various historical periods.

Our collective work is the result of a one-year collaboration. Indeed, an international group of scholars from across continents as well as disciplines of the social sciences and humanities gathered at the School of Social Science of the Institute for Advanced Study during the academic year 2017–18 to explore a variety of topics such as the constitution and transformation of scientific fields, their national specificities and asymmetric forms of internationalization, their material and epistemological conditions of production, the crises and controversies they go through, and the relationships they have with society at large. Our book is thus the outcome of regular exchanges and multiple interactions generated by this long-term residence.

THE VOLUME IS DIVIDED into three parts, exploring successively the temporal, spatial, and liminal dimensions of the social sciences. The first section deals with the making of disciplines from a historical perspective, combining theoretical, epistemological, and material angles. Indeed, these disciplines as we know them today are the product of social, political, financial, and intellectual contexts. The chapters therefore bring together studies of the evolution of the history of the social sciences, the ambiguous role of private donors, the emergence of scientific concepts, the interactions among neighboring disciplinary fields, and the reassessment of methodological approaches. The second section examines how the social sciences are shaped by national contexts and affected by supranational institutions and global transformations. They are thus analyzed in the contexts of postwar socialist Poland, in Japan at the time of the 1968 protests, and in India during the long period following its independence, as well as under the constraints of European programs and in the unequal conditions of world competition. The third section explores the connections of the social sciences with bordering disciplines and knowledge constellations. More specifically, the chapters focus on the influence of the critical humanities and subaltern studies, the frictions between the social and cognitive sciences, the debates on animal cultures, and the infinite expansion of the social scientific field beyond the human.

Opening the first part with an extensive review of the corresponding literature, George Steinmetz argues that the history of the social sciences has not been a smooth and linear one but has evolved via major theoretical jolts, which he calls "concept-quakes" in reference to Friedrich Nietzsche's phrase. The first shift was the move from the classical history of sciences to the Marxist understanding of science as being intimately connected with its socioeconomic context. The second caesura was the invention of the sociology of knowledge, which looked beyond the capitalist contexts of knowledge emphasized in Marxist accounts to include everything from the state to religion. The sociology of knowledge, largely the heir of idealism, gave rise to a sociology of science that was attentive to historical and cultural contexts while also informed by content-oriented approaches, thus combining externalist and internalist readings of science. Several different strands appeared after the sociology of knowledge, including the Mertonian sociology of science, the French historical school of epistemology, and the cluster of approaches known as science and technology studies (STS), the sociology of scientific knowledge (SSK), and ANT. With respect to the *social* sciences, however, the third shock was the passage from the social studies of science, dominated by the ANT developed by Bruno Latour, to the historical sociology of the social sciences, which received a decisive impulse through Pierre Bourdieu's field theory. Steinmetz argues that several of the tenets of ANT and science and technology studies can be internalized by a neo-Bourdieusian field theoretic approach, while others are incompatible. The range and depth of knowledge generated by studies of social science using Bourdieu's approach is the best indicator of its usefulness.

Rarely able to finance themselves through the market, the social sciences rely on public and private funding to exist. Focusing on the contribution of the Rockefeller Foundation in the development of international relations at the Colegio de México during the time of the Cold War, Álvaro Morcillo Laiz analyzes the role of philanthropy in the development of the social sciences. To do so, he uses the method of the counterfactuals, imagining what would have happened in the absence of this private patronage. This allows Morcillo Laiz to argue against "internalists," who believe that scientists follow their own intellectual logic independently of the support they receive. In the case examined here, the Rockefeller Foundation was decisive: first, in allowing the Center for International Studies to flourish, while the Center for Social

Studies, deprived of such funding, ended up closing; and second, in separating international relations from political science in Mexico. Beyond this specific example, it is undeniable that major private foundations from the United States have played a significant role in the fate of the social sciences in Latin America and beyond (Turner and Turner 1990; Tournès 2010; Krige and Rausch 2012).

Like money, ideas and the words that represent them circulate across space and time. Using as a case in point the notion of "creativity," which is overwhelmingly present today in the public sphere as well as the scientific domain, Bregje van Eekelen shows that such concepts have a history from which much is to be learned. Thus, the theme of creativity appeared in the United States at the heart of the industrial and military complexes in the middle of the twentieth century, that is, in a time of intense competition with the Soviet Union in terms of economic influence and the armaments race. But beyond these immediate strategic implications, creativity was also regarded more broadly as an alternative to the utilitarian approaches predominant in the economic and bureaucratic realms at the time. Indeed, brainstorming seemed more exciting and promising than traditional methods for generating innovations in the system of production. Creativity soon became a keyword at the interface of the corporate and academic worlds, with the enlisting of social scientists to legitimize it as a concept via the multiplication of "creativity studies" and "creativity experts." It would be wrong however to view the social life of such concepts as linear, since there have been numerous variations and inflections in the meanings, connotations, and uses of the word.

The same can be said of theories, as shown by Carel Smith in his analysis of the critique of legal theory and legal practice by the social sciences. The dominant view within legal studies has been for more than one hundred years that law was a rule-governed activity, either in its European form, "legalism," or in its US variation, "case law method." However, at the beginning of the twentieth century, this dogma was questioned by the Free Law Movement in Europe and by Legal Realism in the United States, which considered that judging resorts to forms of knowledge that exist beyond the system of rules and that involve politics. The social sciences therefore became an indispensable complement to legal scholarship, and were used to unveil the hidden ideologies behind adjudication. The balancing of interests came to be viewed as an attempt to take into account the conflicting viewpoints involved in any case. Such "social scientific" approaches were in turn criticized as irrational by scholars who continue to see law as a self-sufficient discipline. Beyond the specific example, the outcome of this battle shows that deductive reasoning continues to be understood as the neutral and universal "gold standard" in science, whereas other forms of reasoning, which are context-sensitive, always remain second best from a positivist perspective.

Yet the formation of social science is very much dependent on the contexts of its genesis as Amín Pérez shows in his consideration of the fieldwork conducted by Pierre Bourdieu with Abdelmalek Sayad in Algeria at the time of the war of independence. This research was pivotal in the later development of the Bourdieu's thinking. In this troubled context, ethnography, pragmatically combined with interviews, census, mapping, and photography, allowed Bourdieu to refine his analysis of social change and his critique of domination. It also made him realize, through a comparison of his personal experience and his early works in Béarn, that peasants on both sides of the Mediterranean were facing some similar issues and were responding to them in analogous ways. Moreover, the political tensions and military conflict at that time made Bourdieu acutely conscious of the inherent commitment of scholarship, thus avoiding both "academism" and "revolutionarism," and providing instead a practice faithful to the principles of science while not eluding social responsibility.

In the second part, several national and historical contexts come under scrutiny. Using the case study of the University of Łodz, Agata Zysiak analyzes the fate of sociology after the Second World War under the Communist regime. Following the interwar period of institutionalization of the new discipline with towering figures such as Florian Znaniecki, the postwar period was one of Soviet-style reform in academia, according to which higher education had to be oriented toward the advent of state socialism. Characterized as "bourgeois" despite its progressive engagement for the most part, classical sociology was banned from universities and replaced by forms of knowledge more closely aligned with the Stalinist project. Interestingly, however, the disappearance of sociology from academia was mostly nominal, as former sociologists created, or found refuge in, departments with different names and continued their research and, more broadly, their professional activities in universities. The discipline thus demonstrated its resilience even under ideological and political hardships, which explains why it had less difficulty than was the case in other Eastern and Central European countries to recover during the post-Stalinist thaw. Thus, while Polish sociology shares certain features with sociology emerging from the rest of the Soviet bloc, it is also unique in its strong identity and its capacity to withstand.

In the case of Indian anthropologists, there is an apparent paradox, since they have long avoided a reality that was overwhelming society: violence. As the Partition was accompanied by extreme brutalization, as Sikh and Muslim minorities were assaulted, as Naxalites were rebelling, anthropologists, in the tradition of their colonial predecessors, remained focused on tribal groups and the caste system, traditional themes that also constituted the main interest of their British and French colleagues. As Chitralekha argues, the anthropology of violence became a major theme of research some time later, notably with Veena Das, who examined the painful legacies of the Partition; Dipankar Gupta, who explored the militancy of the Sikhs; and Rabindra Ray and Bela Bhatia, who analyzed the Naxalite revolt, among others. Working on these contentious topics was not without risks for their authors, she reminds us. In the present context of exacerbated nationalism, social scientists who do so are exposed to threats and sanctions.

The development of the social sciences in Japan, as recounted by Miriam Kingsberg Kadia, has been no less influenced by their inscription in the national history and also by their transnational conversation with the United States. During the first half of the twentieth century, Japanese social scientists increasingly participated in Western-dominated international networks, a trend that was not reversed by the defeat of Japan and its occupation by the United States military. But the positivist orientation of Japanese researchers left them impervious to the flourishing of critical thinking in the West, whether in relation to the imperialist dark side of their own history or regarding the problems of their own society. The student movement of 1968 led to substantial transformations, particularly with the replacement of the older scholars by a younger generation. Paradoxically, however, many among the latter embraced the conservative idea of Japanese exceptionalism linked to an essentialization of the nation and its culture, which was only abandoned recently with the decline of the Japanese economy.

Moving to a supranational level, that of the European Union, Kristoffer Kropp shows that, contrary to expectations, apparently transnational research instruments may in fact be very locally produced, thus reflecting parochial ideas. Such is the case of the European Values Study, an important moral and political survey designed for the most part by members of two Catholic universities, one in Belgium, the other in the Netherlands, with a conservative agenda based on the idea that European Christian values were being corroded by individualization. Catholic sociology had connections with Christian Democratic parties, and under the veil of its apparent neutral approach, the opinion poll on European values essentially promoted certain moral and political ideas. With time, the survey was modified in an effort to give it a more solid theoretical basis and scientific credibility, but its religious legacy and conservative affinities never entirely disappeared. Far from depoliticizing the social sciences by removing possible nationalist excesses, supranational institutions can thus repoliticize them in other ways.

Moving one step further, Johan Heilbron examines the meaning and implications of the globalization of the social sciences. Cautioning against a Western and presentist perspective, he reminds us that since antiquity there have been multiple centers of production of knowledge and numerous forms of circulation among them. Concentrating on the specificity of the recent period, Heilbron argues that it is characterized by a shift from the "international" level, marked by the creation of disciplinary associations, to the "global" level, with a more systematic interconnection across the planet facilitated by new media of communication. But far from the hopes of democratization raised by this evolution, Heilbron shows that the core-periphery structure remains and has become even stronger, as revealed by the mapping of citations. Euro-American dominance continues, even if it is challenged here and there by scholarship from the periphery. Moreover, the expansion of transnational circulation has not reduced but rather augmented the hegemony of the United States. For example, the American Sociological Association has three times more members than the International Sociological Association. In the end, instead of enriching the social sciences, their globalization is weakening the weakest among social scientific cultures by impoverishing local knowledge, imposing dominant models, and debilitating public presence. The universalizing of a single scientific language and the homogenizing of publication norms marginalize other modes of expression and reflection. This realist analysis invites social scientists to a engage in a more critical reflexivity on their own practice.

Introducing the third part, Jean-Louis Fabiani wonders precisely whether such critical forms of reflexivity do not often come from outside the social sciences. Mentioning Michel Foucault, Judith Butler, and Edward Said, among many others, he suggests that philosophers, literary scholars, and postcolonial and gender students have shaken the self-evidences of social sciences in past decades. To address this bold question, Fabiani presents three configurations of knowledge, each corresponding to a particular structuration of agents, positions, objects, concepts, methods and social practices in a given moment. Focusing on the French social scientific arena, he examines the making of critical sociology in the 1960s, the triple heritage of Georges Canguilhem, and the critique of the critique of Orientalism. While each case is singular, all of them call for a recognition of the external influence of critical humanities on the social sciences.

From that perspective, India has been one of the most interesting sites of renewal of the social sciences. As analyzed by Peter D. Thomas, subaltern studies has recovered the voices and experiences of subaltern groups, particularly peasants. The influence of this approach has reached far beyond the domain of South Asian studies, opening up new research programs sensitive to oppression and domination as well as to resistance and consciousness. But as Thomas demonstrates, this exceptionally fertile movement, initiated by Ranajit Guha, has not entirely done justice to what had been its intellectual inspiration: Antonio Gramsci's theory of subalternity. Returning to this source via a fresh reading of the latter's works allows us to account for the greater complexity and present relevance of the concept. From this perspective, subalterns are neither positioned against nor outside hegemony or the state; subalternity is the complement of the hegemonic and an integral part of the modern state. This opens new ways of considering subalterns not from the viewpoint of their exclusion, in Partha Chatterjee's words, or incapacity, as argued by Gayatri Spivak, but as one of the realizations of the condition of citizens. Returning to Gramsci thus revives the promise of subaltern studies.

The chapter by John Lardas Modern examines the cognitive science of religion, an extension of an evolutionist theory according to which animals have an adaptive inclination to presume the presence of intelligent agents such as predators even when they are not visible, therefore adopting a behavior of prudence. This capacity of "agent detection" is a survival strategy also among humans, leading them to imagine ghosts, spirits, and gods, according to the anthropologist Pascal Boyer. Religion thus represents an "evolutionary advantage," with humans thinking of these supernatural beings in anthropomorphic terms, yet also as being endowed with superpowers. This model is subsequently mobilized to apprehend the resurgence of religious fundamentalism and combat jihadist terrorism on the basis of a cognitive understanding of their "apparently absurd beliefs." By inscribing religion in the brain, cognitive science therefore annihilates not only its spiritual experience but also its sociological and anthropological interpretation.

With primate sociology, it is the very human subject of the social sciences that disappears. As Nicolas Langlitz notes, this is a particularly fascinating domain, since primate sociology is situated at the interface of the natural and social sciences—indeed, it questions the very existence of this divide. Thus, the discipline's "prosocial turn," which affirmed the preeminence of solidarity and cooperation over selfishness and competition, was essential not only for the understanding of animal life but also for the establishment of common ground between animals and humans. Yet, as shown by the dispute between a comparative psychologist, Michael Tomasello, and a field primatologist, Christophe Boesch, who belong to the same institution, the debate is still ongoing. It continues between those who consider, like Tomasello, that altruism is what ultimately distinguishes apes and humans, and those like Boesch, who think that both species are capable of sharing and caring. The disagreement is both ideological and methodological, since one of the researchers works in the confined conditions of a lab while the other studies primates in their natural forest environment.

The most recent critique of the social sciences, posthumanism, is also the most deliberately radical, since it undermines the foundations not only of the social sciences but also of what is sometimes designated more broadly as the human sciences so as to include the humanities. Although it is an extraordinarily heterogeneous movement, in which little commonality can be found between the idea of the extension of the human via biological mutations, bodily prosthesis, or artificial intelligence, and the defense of the nonhuman world, be it animals, plants, nature, objects, or the planet, the core of posthumanism, according to Didier Fassin, has two components. First, it is a rejection of anthropocentrism, understood as both an epistemological and a moral critique of the centrality and superiority of human beings. Second, it is a dismissal of a series of dichotomies that have nourished a long tradition of thinking, such as subject/object, self/other, culture/nature, or mind/body. While it has been initially developed within literary, gender, and animal studies as well as within philosophy, anthropology is a latecomer to what is designated as its "ontological turn." Within a particularly complex and disparate field, it is possible to distinguish a soft posthumanism, whose ethical dimension invites humans to care for nonhumans, and a hard posthumanism, which renounces the principle of a common humanity or even speculates a dehumanized world. In both cases, the ambitious posthumanist project is at risk of relinquishing history and politics at the very moment when their importance has to be recognized to address the numerous threats that human beings, the most vulnerable in particular, are facing.

There are thus many reasons why a reflexive and critical—but sympathetic—inquiry into the social sciences is not only important but also timely. The world is rapidly changing, with deepening inequalities, political uncertainties, demographic instabilities, and environmental perils, as well as ever more invasive forms of surveillance and subject formation, which renders the sorts of critical knowledge produced by the social sciences all the more essential. It is just as essential that scholars continue to investigate the ways in which social science emerges from and sometimes contributes to social pathologies. The social sciences have once again come under internal and external pressures—from cognitive sciences broadly speaking and from reinvigorated positivist social sciences as well as from politicians who reject the very idea of studying, analyzing, interpreting, or explaining human social existence. As the scientization of the social proceeds apace, in multiple new forms, it remains as crucial as ever to understand the scientific as well as the social aspects of this relationship, which calls for the critical awareness that can be provided by a social science of the social sciences.

Notes

The Institute for Advanced Study has generously provided the space and time to develop the fecund and friendly exchanges from which this volume stems. In particular, we want to thank Donne Petito, for having facilitated our work all year long; Laura McCune, for organizing our final workshop; and Munirah Bishop, for her careful copyediting of the manuscript. The two anonymous reviewers have provided invaluable comments that have been critical to the revision of the manuscript, and we are grateful to them for their engagement with our collective work as well as to Kenneth Wissoker for his early expression of interest in it.

1   See Elias 1956. According to Elias (1956, 227), involvement and detachment "seem preferable to others which like 'subjective' and 'objective' suggest a static and unbridgeable divide between two entities 'subject' and 'object.'... A philosopher once said, 'If Paul speaks of Peter he tells us more about Paul than about Peter.' One can say, by way of comment, that in speaking of Peter he is always telling us something about himself as well as about Peter. One would call this approach 'involved' as long as his own characteristics, the characteristics of the perceiver, overshadow those of the perceived. If Paul's propositions begin to tell more about Peter than about himself the balance begins to turn in favor of detachment."

2   Foundational studies by Wagner and his collaborators (Wagner 1990; Wagner et al. 1991), focused on relations between the social sciences and states or policy-making.

3   Camic, Gross, and Lamont (2011), for example, has sociologists as editors and as the majority of its contributors. It is more common to focus on a single discipline—e.g., Stocking 1968; Fabiani 1988; Mirowski 1989; Park Turner and Turner 1990; Hands 2001; Calhoun 2007; Herman 2009; Heilbron 2015; Dayé and Moebius 2015.

4   For studies of the human and social sciences that break with methodological nationalism, see Pollak 1979; Gerhardt 2007; Heilbron, Guilhot, and Jeanpierre 2008; Steinmetz 2010; Pérez 2015; Baring 2016; Boldyrev and Kirtchik 2016; Kropp 2017.

References

Backhouse, Roger E., and Philippe Fontaine, eds. 2010. *The History of the Social Sciences since 1945*. Cambridge: Cambridge University Press.

Backhouse, Roger E., and Philippe Fontaine, eds. 2014. *A Historiography of the Modern Social Sciences*. Cambridge: Cambridge University Press.

Baring, Edward. 2016. "Ideas on the Move: Context in Transnational Intellectual History." *Journal of the History of Ideas* 77, no. 4: 567-87.

Boldyrev, Ivan, and Olessia Kirtchik. 2016. "On (Im)permeabilities: Social and Human Sciences on Both Sides of the 'Iron Curtain.'" *History of the Human Sciences* 29: 3-12.

Calhoun, Craig, ed. 2007. *Sociology in America: A History*. Chicago: University of Chicago Press.

Camic, Charles, Neil Gross, and Michèle Lamont, eds. 2011. *Social Knowledge in the Making*. Chicago: University of Chicago Press.

Carson, John. 2007. *The Measure of Merit: Talents, Intelligence, and Inequality in the French and American Republics, 1750-1940*. Princeton, NJ: Princeton University Press.

Connell, Raewyn. 2007. *Southern Theory*. Cambridge: Polity.

Danell, Rickard, Anna Larsson, and Per Wisselgren, eds. 2013. *Social Science in Context: Historical, Sociological, and Global Perspectives*. Lund: Nordic Academic Press.

Dayé, Christian, and Stephan Moebius. 2015. *Soziologiegeschichte: Wege und Ziele*. Berlin: Suhrkamp Taschenbuch Wissenschaft.

Elias, Norbert. 1956. "Problems of Involvement and Detachment." *British Journal of Sociology* 7, no. 3: 226-52.

Fabiani, Jean-Louis. 1988. *Les philosophes de la République*. Paris: Éditions de Minuit.

Fassin, Didier, ed. 2017. *If Truth Be Told: The Politics of Public Ethnography*. Durham, NC: Duke University Press.

Fassin, Didier, and Alban Bensa, eds. 2008. *Les politiques de l'enquête: Épreuves ethnographiques*. Paris: La Découverte.

Gerhardt, Uta. 2007. *Denken der Demokratie: Die Soziologie im atlantischen Transfer des Besatzungsregimes*. Stuttgart: Franz Steiner Verlag.

Gilman, Nils. 2003. *Mandarins of the Future: Modernization Theory in Cold War America*. Baltimore, MD: Johns Hopkins University Press.

Hands, Wade D. 2001. *Reflection without Rules: Economic Methodology and Contemporary Science Theory*. Cambridge: Cambridge University Press.

Heilbron, Johan. 1995. *The Rise of Social Theory*. Cambridge: Polity.

Heilbron, Johan. 2015. *French Sociology*. Ithaca, NY: Cornell University Press.

Heilbron, Johan, Nicolas Guilhot, and Laurent Jeanpierre. 2008. "Toward a Transnational History of the Social Sciences." *Journal of the History of the Behavioral Sciences* 44: 146-60.

Herman, Ellen. 2009. *The Romance of American Psychology: Political Culture in the Age of Experts*. Berkeley: University of California Press.

Joas, Hans, and Barbro Klein, eds. 2010. *The Benefit of Broad Horizons: Intellectual and Institutional Preconditions for a Global Social Science.* Leiden: Brill.

Kennedy, Michael. 2015. *Globalizing Knowledge: Intellectuals, Universities, and Publics in Transformation.* Stanford, CA: Stanford University Press.

Klingemann, Carsten. 1992. "Social-Scientific Experts—No Ideologues: Sociology and Social Research in the Third Reich." In *Sociology Responds to Fascism,* edited by S. P. Turner and D. Käsler, 127–54. London: Sage.

Knöbl, Wolfgang. 2001. *Spielräume der Modernisierung: Das Ende der Eindeutigkeit.* Weilerswist: Velbrück Wissenschaft.

Kojenikov, A. 1999. "Dialogues about Knowledge and Power in Totalitarian Political Culture." *Historical Studies in the Physical and Biological Sciences* 30: 227–47.

Krige, John, and Helke Rausch, eds. 2012. *American Foundations and the Coproduction of World Order in the Twentieth Century.* Göttingen: Vandenhoeck and Ruprecht.

Kropp, Kristoffer. 2017. "The Cases of the European Value Study and the European Social Survey—European Constellations of Social Science Knowledge Production." *Serendipities: Journal for the Sociology and History of the Social Sciences* 2, no. 1: 50–68.

Mastnak, Tomaž. 2015. "Hobbes in Kiel, 1938: From Ferdinand Tonnies to Carl Schmitt." *History of European Ideas* 41, no. 7: 966–91.

Mirowski, Philip. 1989. *More Heat Than Light: Economics as Social Physics, Physics as Nature's Economics.* Cambridge: Cambridge University Press.

Morcillo Laiz, Álvaro. 2016. "La dominación filantrópica: La Rockefeller Foundation, El Colegio de México, el Instituto di Tella, y las ciencias sociales en español (1938–1973)." In *Max Weber en Iberoamérica: Nuevas interpretaciones, estudios empíricos y recepción,* edited by Álvaro Morcillo Laiz and Eduardo Weisz, 573–606. Mexico City: Fondo de Cultura Económica y CIDE.

Moyn, Samuel, and Andrew Sartori, eds. 2013. *Global Intellectual History.* New York: Columbia University Press.

Park Turner, Stephen, and Jonathan H. Turner. 1990. *The Impossible Science: An Institutional Analysis of American Sociology.* Newbury Park: Sage.

Pérez, Amín. 2015. "Rendre le social plus politique: Guerre coloniale, immigration et pratiques sociologiques d'Abdelmalek Sayad et de Pierre Bourdieu." PhD diss., EHESS.

Pollak, Michael. 1979. "Paul F. Lazarsfeld, fondateur d'une multinationale scientifique." *Actes de la recherche en sciences sociales* 25, no. 1: 45–59.

Porter, Theodore, and Dorothy Ross, eds. 2003. *The Cambridge History of Science,* vol. 7: *The Modern Social Sciences.* Cambridge: Cambridge University Press.

Randeria, Shalini, and Björn Wittrock, eds. 2019. *Social Science at the Crossroads.* Leiden: Brill, Annals of the International Institute of Sociology.

Robin, Ron. 2001. *The Making of the Cold War Enemy: Culture and Politics in the Military-Intellectual Complex.* Princeton, NJ: Princeton University Press.

Rohde, Joy. 2013. *Armed with Expertise: The Militarization of American Social Research during the Cold War.* Ithaca, NY: Cornell University Press.

Rollet, Laurent, and Philippe Nabonnaud, eds. 2013. *Les uns et les autres: Biographies et prosopographies en histoire des sciences.* Nancy: Presses Universitaires de Nancy.

Scott, Joan, and Debra Keates, eds. 2001. *Schools of Thought: Twenty-Five Years of Interpretive Social Science.* Princeton, NJ: Princeton University Press.

Steinmetz, George. 2005. *The Politics of Method in the Human Sciences: Positivism and Its Epistemological Others.* Durham, NC: Duke University Press.

Steinmetz, George. 2010. "Ideas in Exile: Refugees from Nazi Germany and the Failure to Transplant Historical Sociology into the United States." *International Journal of Politics, Culture, and Society* 23, no. 1: 1–27.

Steinmetz, George, ed. 2013. *Sociology and Empire: The Imperial Entanglements of a Discipline.* Durham, NC: Duke University Press.

Steinmetz, George. 2022. *The Colonial Origins of Modern Social Thought: French Sociology and the Overseas Empire.* Princeton: Princeton University Press.

Stocking, George W., Jr. 1968. *Race, Culture, and Evolution: Essays in the History of Anthropology.* New York: Free Press.

Strauss, Leo. 1952. *Persecution and the Art of Writing.* Glencoe, IL: Free Press.

Tournès, Ludovic. 2010. *L'argent de l'influence: Les fondations américaines et leurs réseaux européens.* Paris: Autrement.

van Eekelen, Bregje. 2016. "Brainstorming und das verkörperte Wissen: Eine Ökonomie der Ideen in Amerika während des Zweiten Weltkriegs." In *Designing Thinking: Angewandte Imagination und Kreativität um 1960,* edited by Claudia Mareis and Margarete Pratschke, 75–103. Munich: Wilhelm Fink Verlag.

vom Bruch, Rüdiger, Uta Gerhardt, and Aleksandra Pawliczek, eds. 2006. *Kontinuitäten und Diskontinuitäten in der Wissenschaftsgeschichte des 20. Jahrhunderts.* Stuttgart: Steiner.

Wagner, Peter. 1990. *Sozialwissenschaften und Staat: Frankreich, Italien, Deutschland 1870–1980.* New York: Campus Verlag.

Wagner, Peter, Carol Hirschon Weiss, Björn Wittrock, and Hellmut Wollmann, eds. 1991. *Social Sciences and Modern States: National Experiences and Theoretical Crossroads.* Cambridge: Cambridge University Press.

Wisselgren, Per. 2015. *The Social Scientific Gaze: The Social Question and the Rise of Academic Social Science in Sweden.* Farnham, UK: Ashgate.

disciplines
in the making

PART ONE

From the History of
Science to the
Historical Sociology
of Social Science

concept-
quake

GEORGE STEINMETZ

History *must* itself resolve the problem of history, knowledge *must* turn its sting
against itself.—FRIEDRICH NIETZSCHE, *VOM NUTZEN UND NACHTHEIL DER HISTORIE
FÜR DAS LEBEN*

The social history of social science, so long as it is also considered a science of the
unconscious . . . is one of the most powerful means of distancing oneself from . . . the
grip of an incorporated past which survives into the present.—PIERRE BOURDIEU,
"A LECTURE ON THE LECTURE"

All sociology worthy of its name is "historical sociology."—C. WRIGHT MILLS,
THE SOCIOLOGICAL IMAGINATION

THE HISTORY OF THE SCIENCES has slowly given rise to a historical sociology of the social sciences. There are now professional associations for
the history of the social sciences, dedicated journals in English, German,
and French, and a growing body of monographs, taking various forms: individual biographies; studies of schools, institutions, generations, and subfields;
international comparisons and transnational studies; and handbooks and
edited collections like the present one. Yet one should not imagine that this

is a well-established area of study. The emergence of the practice of study-ing the social sciences historically and sociologically was the result not of a quasi-natural evolutionary process but of a series of conceptual ruptures, or concept-quakes.[1] These intellectual turning points have reconfigured the contextual preconditions that shape historical writing on the social sciences.

This chapter will use these concept-quakes as a starting point for asking a set of historical, theoretical, and philosophical questions about writing on the history of social science. When and how did the history of social science emerge? How have analysts explained the genesis, development, forms, and contents of the social sciences? What political, ethical, and metascientific goals have scholars pursued in writing the history of social science? And what are the ultimate contributions, the promises, of this research?

First I briefly examine the evolution of writing on the history of the natu-ral sciences.[2] I then turn to the emergence of more contextual and ultimately sociological approaches to the history of science. Several clues pointing in this direction already emerged in the writing of Hegel and Marx, whose ideas, taken together, constitute the *first* concept-quake.

The next important development occurred in the first half of the twenti-eth century with the invention of the sociology of knowledge. This is the *sec-ond* concept-quake. The sociology of knowledge looked beyond the capitalist contexts of knowledge emphasized in Marxist accounts to include everything from the state to religion. Relations between society and knowledge were analyzed as reciprocal rather than unidirectional ones.

The main reason for the backlash against the sociology of knowledge among American sociologists and postwar German sociologists was the per-ceived threat to absolute ethical values and objective scientific truth. The early writing of the American sociologist of science Robert K. Merton was linked to his antifascist democratic politics (Hollinger 1996), and while Merton was open to some Marxist ideas, he was also at the center of the negative response to the sociology of knowledge more generally. Merton's own work after World War II became narrower, less historical, and more focused on the "middle-range" level, as it adapted itself to professional academic sociol-ogy (Sica 2010). The social scientific response to the sociology of knowledge was the development of a "Mertonian" sociology of science (Barber 1990, 11), which avoided the dangers of relativism, explaining the *contents* of science sociologically by focusing on scientists' values and "institutionalized arrange-ments," competition and stratification, evaluations and awards, and publica-tions and citations, and adopted methods of citation analysis and "content analysis"—reducing texts to data (Merton 1977, 22–23).

The *third* concept-quake was the emergence of a historical sociology of the social sciences that took seriously the analysis of texts and intertextuality as well as their social contexts, at all scales of analysis. This program was actually announced in 1959 by Merton, who now presented a framework for the "comparative investigation of sociology in its social contexts" (Merton 1959, 22) that integrated textual analysis ("the historical filiation of ideas considered in their own right"); the immediate sites of knowledge production ("the social processes relating the men of science"), and macro-level contexts ("the structure of the society in which it is being developed"). Not coincidentally, Merton's Columbia University colleague C. Wright Mills had been examining the sociology of US sociology in various publications, culminating in *The Sociological Imagination,* which was also published in 1959. There Mills moved from first exploring sociologists' ideas and mapping the polarized intellectual structure of the disciplinary field, to a meso-level analysis of educational and scientific institutions, culminating in discussion of macro-level structures, including informal US imperialism, that were shaping social science. The genie was now out of the bottle: social science could be analyzed historically and sociologically in ways that combined all of the aspects that previous writers had sorted into the intellectual histories and the so-called internal and external contexts of science, overcoming that distinction.

The next section discusses several strands of writing on the history of social science that have appeared since this third caesura. In studies of ancient Greek thought, European Marxism, and American sociology, Merton's neo-Marxist student Alvin Gouldner (1965, 1970, 1980) integrated the three analytic levels that Merton had discussed in 1959. A different approach to the historical sociology of social science emerged from the French historical school of epistemology (Bachelard, Koyré, Canguilhem). A third set of approaches grew out of, and in reaction against, the Mertonian sociology of science: science and technology studies (STS), the sociology of scientific knowledge (SSK), and actor-network theory (ANT). The useful elements of these latter approaches, I will argue, can be integrated with Bourdieu's field-theoretical approach, while their problematic aspects should be jettisoned, including tendencies toward ontological empiricism, an epistemological stance of anticontextualism, and a normative stance of axiological neutrality that opposes critique and fails to seriously engage with issues of methodological reflexivity.[3]

I then discuss of the Bourdieusian historical sociology of the social sciences, which represents the most recent concept-quake. This Bourdieu-inspired research integrates (1) intellectual history, with close attention to texts and intertexuality; (2) a theoretically more adequate and realistic framework for analyzing the meso-level realm of scientific fields; and (3) the full array of macro-level or "external" contexts impinging on scientific fields. This perspective is far from static and is better characterized as "neo-Bourdieusian." In the spirit of this essay, the Bourdieu-inspired research certainly cannot be described as the final telos of the intellectual history described here. Yet it offers the best current response to the aporias of social theory (structure vs. agency, social change vs. social reproduction, rational vs. irrational explanations of action, explanation vs interpretation, etc.), while simultaneously placing the history of sociology at the center of its understanding of scientific reflexivity.

The last part of the chapter discusses four additional uses of the history of social science, in addition to reflexive vigilance (Bourdieu 2022): (1) disciplinary anamnesis; (2) illuminating historical transitions; (3) understanding the conditions for the flourishing of knowledge, including social science; and (4) explaining modern social processes that are codetermined by social science.

The Development of the History of Science

The historiography of science is an "ancient pursuit" that was "born as the history of ancient science," specifically mathematics and medicine (Daston 2001, 6842; Zhmud 2006). This history of science remained part of science itself through the nineteenth century, and it was mostly written by scientists themselves. Until well into the twentieth century, most of this writing was triumphal and progressivist (L. Laudan 1977), taking the form of a grand narrative whose dramatis personae were scientific men of genius. The earliest histories of science grew out of *heurematography*, the study of *protoi heuretai*—scientific and technical inventors and discoverers (Zhmud 2006). Members of the Peripatetic school wrote histories of the sciences, closely following "Aristotle's favorite idea of all arts and sciences as gradually approximating to perfection," and carrying out a program he set in motion in the last decade of his life (Zhmud 2006, 15, 140). There was a shift in the postclassical era from the study of "who discovered what" and "the invention of various sciences" to "the transmission of knowledge from one people (or author) to another," but this orientation was still compatible with a cumulative view of science (Zhmud 2006, 149, 297). Histories of science in the Renaissance took the form of genealogical histories and biographies of scientists. Jean Bodin's *Methodus* (1576) offered a history of science rooted in belief in the progress of knowledge

(Keller 1950, 237–39). The earlier history of *protoi heuretai* resurfaced as the study of the *ars inveniendi* (Leibniz, cited in Kragh 1987, 5).

The history of science in the Age of Enlightenment was "unequivocally depicted as the history of progress" and "was not in a position to recognize science as a proper historical phenomenon" (Kragh 1987, 4, 6). Some authors in the French Enlightenment and some Scottish moral philosophers were "aware that a wide range of social, economic, and political factors shape . . . human consciousness," but this "did not result in a more systematic examination" of the contextual questions that were at the center of later historical sociological thinking on the subject (Stehr and Meja 2005, 2). An exemplary Enlightenment work is Condorcet's *Esquisse d'un tableau historique des progrès de l'esprit humain* (1795), a history of science intended to demonstrate reason's power to transform society. Condorcet saw historical progress "as an essentially unilinear, incremental process, dependent upon the steady accumulation and ordering of knowledge," with new technologies leading to advances in knowledge and the dismantling of prejudices (Baker 1975, 375). Fontenelle (1790, 42) was similarly confident that "there is an order that regulates our progress." Savérien explained that he had expunged from his *History of the Progress of the Human Spirit in the Exact Sciences* all of the scientific errors committed by earlier scholars in order to focus attention on those who had "contributed to the veritable progress of Science," since "what is more splendid, in effect, than a chain of immutable and eternal truths!" (1766, 1: vii–viii). Priestley wrote around the same time that he adhered to the rule in writing the history of science "to take no notice of the mistakes" (1775, xi). This tradition continued into the twentieth century, when the English mathematician and philosopher Alfred North Whitehead intoned that a "science which hesitates to forget its founders is lost" (1917, 115).

Many historians argue that science proper—science "as we now know it"—is "an endeavor born of the nineteenth century" (Dear 2012, 197), and the same can be said of histories of science as "distinct from scientific publications" (Daston 2001, 6842). There was a marked increase in the number of histories of science published in the 1800s as compared to the previous century (see table 1.1). According to one estimate, "over a thousand substantial histories of science" were published before 1913 (R. Laudan 1993, 1). The narrative of science as surging inexorably forward continued to dominate most works during the nineteenth century, which were written in the frameworks of French positivism or English Whig historiography (McEvoy 1997; Yeo 1991).

Table 1.1. Books on History of Sciences in All Languages

MATH	1700–1799	204
	1800–1899	770
	1900–1999	7,119
MEDICINE	1700–1799	1,065
	1800–1899	2,538
	1900–1999	19,699
PHYSICS	1700–1799	106
	1800–1899	430
	1900–1999	4,819

Source: WorldCat, www.worldcat.org, accessed August 4, 2022

Two of the most influential nineteenth-century influential historians of science, offering very different interpretations of that same progressive history, were Auguste Comte and William Whewell. The British polymath Whewell greatly admired Kantian philosophy, which pushed his thinking away from a more sociological analysis of science. He regarded past science "as a story of heroic individuals—usually great *men*—wresting secrets from Nature" (Yeo 1993, 5). As for Comte, he was a "prophet of progress," for whom the highest forms of progress were situated in the realm of science and morality (Pickering 2009, 356). According to Comte, "On ne connait pas complètement une science, tant qu'on n'en sait pas l'histoire" (1852, 66). Comte argued that the sciences all developed following an invariable Law of Three Stages (1855, 25):

> From the study of the development of human intelligence, in all directions, and through all times, the discovery arises of a great fundamental law, to which it is necessarily subject, and which has a solid foundation of proof, both in the facts of our organization and in our historical experience. The law is this:—that each of our leading conceptions—each branch of our knowledge—passes successively through three different theoretical conditions: the Theological, or fictitious; the Metaphysical, or abstract; and the Scientific, or positive.

For Comte, the sciences were arranged in a hierarchy, differing in terms of their decreasing generality and the increasing complexity of their corresponding objects. "Each science depended on the preceding one and prepared

the way for the one that came after" (Pickering 2009, 420). Comte also anticipated a period in which scientific development would be managed by political
power, one in which sociology, as the most complex science situated at the
pinnacle of the hierarchy, would play a central role in directing the lower sciences. Insofar as Comte argued for relations of mutual dependence between
specific types of knowledge and specific forms of social structure (Znaniecki
1940, 2), he resembled Hegel (see below) and anticipated the later sociology
of science.

Ernst Mach, Paul Tannery, and George Sarton are transition figures
between these nineteenth-century historians of science and the twentieth century. Mach believed that the study of "the rejected and transient
thoughts" of scientists could be "very important and very instructive," as it
"not only promotes the understanding of that which now is, but also brings
new possibilities before us, showing that which exists to be in great measure
conventional and accidental" (quoted in Kragh 1987, 10). At the same time,
Mach subordinated his historiography to his philosophy of science, which
was one of the building blocks for twentieth-century epistemological positivism (Steinmetz 2005). The French mathematician Tannery established "the
vision of an *histoire générale des sciences* that should be not merely the separate
histories of the particular sciences but a history of scientific thought studied
in the context of society and ideas" (Crombie 1963, 1). Sarton played a key role
in establishing the history of science as a discipline by creating the journals
Isis and *Osiris*. His own approach was primarily internalist and progressivist,
but Sarton mentioned some "economic and social factors," albeit in "a subordinate role" and as having "no deep influence on the life of science" (Frängsmyr 1973, 106; Kragh 1987, 18).

While these nineteenth-century historians did not leave the production
of natural science completely untheorized, neither did they propose fully
contextualizing accounts. There is an important exception to this rule in
the nineteenth century, however, and it was located in the historiography of
the *human* sciences—the specifically, the history of philosophy—as pioneered
by Hegel.

The First Concept-Quake: Contextual Readings
of Science by Hegel and Marx

Hegel and Marx were perhaps the first to approach knowledge and science,
especially the human and social sciences, in a thoroughly contextualizing manner. Hegel *rehistoricized* the sciences, including philosophy itself

(Jaeschke 1993). Hegel lectured more frequently on the history of philosophy than any other topic. Clearly, these lectures were aimed at justifying Hegel's own system and at legitimating philosophy in general. In those respects they were nothing new in methodological terms. After all, others before Hegel had tackled the history of philosophy, including Stanley (1656), Brückner (1791), and Kantians such as Tiedemann (1794) and Tennemann ([1816] 1832). In its main aspects, however, Hegel's approach was completely novel. For Hegel, the history of philosophy paralleled world history itself, as "the medium of the development of the world spirit" (Jaeschke 1993, xvi). Hegel argued that each generation received all that each past generation had produced in science and in intellectual activity" as "an heirloom." All of this was then "changed, [as] the material worked upon" was "both enriched and preserved at the same time" in dialectical fashion (Hegel 1995, 1:3). Every past philosophy therefore "has been and still is necessary," and "thus, none have passed away, but all are affirmatively contained as elements in a whole" (Hegel 1995, 1:37). Philosophers needed to study "the essential ideas of philosophers in the past" because they "are all too prone to forget the origins and context of their own doctrines" (Beiser 1995, xxvii, xxviii). In sum, "the course of history does not show us the Becoming of things foreign to us, but the Becoming of ourselves and of our own knowledge" (Hegel 1995, 1:4). Contrary to views that wanted to discard past science or study it only to understand the source of errors, Hegel argued that knowledge of scientific history was an essential part of (scientific) self-consciousness.

This line of reasoning still bore some resemblance to Kant's vision of the history of philosophy as a chronicle of the progress of reason itself, but Hegel broke with Kant in insisting that each philosophical school had to be understood on its own terms and "in the context of its own time, as the self-awareness of the ideals and values of its age" (Beiser 1995, xv): "There is a definite Philosophy which arises among a people, and the definite character of the standpoint of thought is the same character which permeates all the other historical sides of the spirit of the people" (Hegel 1995, 1:53). One should not assume that one's own "principles are somehow natural, divine, eternal, or innate, when they are in fact only the product of a specific time and place, the self-awareness of the values and ideals of a specific culture" (Beiser 1995, xxvii). Hegel's contextualism was different from twentieth-century versions. He was *not* arguing that "political history, forms of government, art and religion" were "related to Philosophy as its causes"; rather, he was saying that they had the "same common root" as philosophy, namely, the *Weltgeist* or spirit of the time (Hegel 1995, 1:54).

Hegel's historicist approach was emulated by German historians of other disciplines, who began to examine their own past "for its own sake, to see events in context, and to fathom the deeper motives for actions" (Beiser 1995, xi). In this respect, the German history of science partly diverged from the British and French versions in the nineteenth century. The book series *Geschichte der Wissenschaften in Deutschland* published studies of the history of political science (Bluntschli 1864), legal science (Stintzing 1880–1910), and other humanities and social science disciplines. Many of these books followed a conventional approach, focusing on the key doctrines, discoveries, and personalities, without making an effort to connect them to social contexts. Yet a few authors pursued a more "Hegelian" line. As Lindenfeld (1997, 162) points out, the "number of lectures on the history of economic thought" increased sharply in Germany in the wake of the 1848 Revolution. Wilhelm Roscher, a founder of the historical school of economics, explored the relations between economic thought and politics, arguing that Fichte's entire philosophy, including his economics, "bore the unmistakable imprint of the democratic-revolutionary era"—that is, the French Revolution (Roscher 1874, 639).

The most famous Left Hegelian, Karl Marx, presented an analysis of science that veered between an Enlightenment-style vision of science marching inevitably forward and a proto-sociological approach. Like Condorcet, Cuvier, and d'Alembert, Marx frequently suggested that science develops autonomously and is not shaped in fundamental ways by its social and historical contexts. This is true even if those contexts provide necessary support for science. The progression of science is congealed in the "forces of production," which undergird the epochal rise and fall of entire class structures and superstructures. This is the essence of Marx's thesis of the "primacy of the productive forces" (G. A. Cohen 2001, chap. 6). The forces of production—and therefore science itself—are the opposite of epiphenomenal. They are the unmoved mover, the unstoppable conatus of history.

Alongside this dramatic heightening of the Enlightenment glorification of science, however, Marx allowed that natural science was socially determined in several different ways. First, as a form of thought, science has to be influenced by material social relations, since "the ideal is nothing but the material world reflected in the mind of man, and translated into forms of thought" (Marx 1976, 102). Second, capitalist social relations cause technology to advance dynamically by speeding up cycles of accumulation and generating new needs. Capitalism therefore stimulates science above and beyond any putative human baseline orientation toward material improvement (G. A. Cohen 2001; Mulkay 1979, 5). Third, Marx's theory of history suggests that social structures can sometimes *fetter* the advance of technology, and presumably science as well. Technology's advance is hobbled at particular historical junctures by class relations; this leads to revolutionary ruptures and the replacement of old class relations with new ones (Marx, in Marx and Engels 1978, 3–6). A fourth way in which social context encroaches on science involves the translation of science into technological applications. In *Capital* Marx writes in general terms about the "separation of the intellectual powers of production from the manual labour, and the conversion of those powers into the might of capital over labour," a process that is "finally completed by modern industry erected on the foundation of machinery." The "special skill of each individual insignificant factory operative vanishes as an infinitesimal quantity before the science . . . embodied in the factory mechanism," which embodies the power of the "master" (Marx and Engels 1978: 409). Later Marxists developed these ideas into theories of the separation of science from technology (Hessen [1931] 2009; Zilsel 1942), a separation taking dramatic forms such as automation, Taylorism, operations research, numerically controlled machine tools, and digital surveillance capitalism (Noble 2011; Zuboff 2019).[4] Marx thus acknowledged in various ways that science and technology were, in fact, shaped by social factors.

It is equally important that Marx follows Hegel in analyzing the human sciences "sociologically." Here too Marx sometimes expresses a more conventional view of the human sciences as eventually converging with the natural sciences, like Wilson (1998) and other advocates of "consilience." Yet this idea is contradicted at numerous points in Marx's writings, which can be mined for a rudimentary sociology of social knowledge and an antinaturalistic philosophy of science.[5] According to Marx and Engels, the history of ideas cannot be "torn away from the facts and the practical development fundamental to them" but is grounded in modes of production, in the "real premises . . . [and] real individuals, their activity and the material conditions under which they live" (Marx and Engels 1978, 167, 149). Intellectuals in general belong to the ruling class, they argue, but there is a "division of mental and material labour" *within* the bourgeoisie, such that "inside this class one part appears as the thinkers of the class (its active, conceptive ideologists, who make the perfecting of the illusion of the class about itself their chief source of livelihood), while the others . . . have less time to make up illusions and ideas about themselves" (Marx and Engels 1978, 173). The "individuals composing the ruling class," therefore, "rule also as thinkers, as producers of ideas" (Marx and Engels 1978, 173). Academic intellectuals are mainly producers of "ideology"—that is, representations in which "men and their circumstances" are not described accurately but "appear upside-down as in a *camera obscura*" (Marx and Engels 1978, 154). The historians in each epoch "*share the illusion of that epoch*" (Marx and Engels 1978, 165). Engels described socialist theory itself as "a reflex, in thought," of the fundamental "conflict between productive forces and modes of production," although this was an exceptional form of thought that somehow escaped distortion, inversion, and illusion (Engels 1910, 97). Accurate social knowledge is therefore possible, given the proper political orientation or social positionality—an argument developed further by Lukács and later by feminist standpoint theory (Harding 2003) and postcolonial theory (Agblémagnon 1965).

Marx and Engels therefore argue in various writings for the existential connections between science and the social conditions in which it arises. These connections do not need to take the form of mirroring or reflection but may take less direct forms. They suggest several ways in which science may *fail* to correspond to the mode of production or class relations. First, the cleavage between capitalists and ideologists within the ruling class may sometimes "develop into a certain opposition and hostility" (Marx and Engels 1978, 173). Second, philosophy sometimes registers *emerging* contradictions between social relations and "existing forces of production." Philosophical ideas sometimes *compensate* for social realities rather than simply legitimating or mirroring them. In Germany, "mental developments" such as young Hegelianism "serve as a substitute for the lack of historical development" (Marx and Engels 1978, 169). Such anticipatory philosophy may also arise when social relations inside one nation come into contradiction with "the practice of other nations" (Marx and Engels 1978, 159). This argument points to Marx's effort to situate intellectual production in multiscalar geospaces that encompass local, national, and international levels. In the afterword to the second edition of *Capital,* Marx connects national and historical variations in economic theory to differing contexts of social class formation and struggle, and suggests that the international migration of ideas can lead to disjunctures between ideas and their immediate social context (Marx 1976, 95–98). A third hypothesis concerns the relative autonomy of cultural production. Near the end of his life, Engels hypothesized that some forms of culture were more autonomous from capitalism than others, writing, "The further removed is the sphere we happen to be [in] from the economic sphere and the closer to the purely abstract, ideological sphere, the more likely shall we be to find evidence of the fortuitous in its development, the more irregular will be the curve it describes."[6]

Social theorists have tended to reject Marx's theory of ideology as tying culture, politics, and science too closely to political economics. At the same time, however, Marx and Engels followed in Hegel's footsteps in pouring the foundations for a sociology of social science. They did this by arguing that social thought is shaped by social determinants, and that it evolves in international as well as national and local arenas, and that it can be compensatory, anticipatory, legitimating, or relatively autonomous of social reality. It is not surprising, then, that Karl Mannheim, J. D. Bernal, Edgar Zilsel, Joseph Needham, and other pioneers of the historical sociology of knowledge and science traced their intellectual lineage to Marx. As Robert Merton wrote in 1949, "Marxism is the storm-center of *Wissenssoziologie*" (1949b, 462)—shortly before he turned against Marxism, at least in print.

The Second Concept-Quake: *Wissenssoziologie* (the Sociology of Knowledge)

Hegel and Marx provoked the first concept-quake by adumbrating a contextual, historicist account of science, social science, and thought. They were not alone in the nineteenth century, however. Other signs of a critical approach to science saw the light of day, especially in Central Europe. One source of this critique was the intellectual radicalization of German idealism and Romanticism in response to the Napoleonic Wars. This movement was analyzed by Karl Mannheim in his brilliant habilitation thesis on conservatism (Mannheim 1926) as having nourished a spectrum of philosophies skeptical of universalism, rationalism, and the Enlightenment. The previous section discussed the manner in which Hegel combined an account of the progress of philosophy-qua-reason with a historicizing view of influence of historical and geographic contexts on philosophical ideas. Nietzsche also contributed to the idea of a sociology of knowledge. Nietzsche's supposed irrationalism is linked to his early criticism of science as a threat to culture and his ethical and epistemological perspectivalism. At the same time, Nietzsche represents a continuation of Marx, insofar as his works endeavor to identify "the historical and social roots from which particular perspectives, ideas, and interests emerge" (Payne 2019, 204).

Skepticism about science reached a crescendo in the years before and after World War I, permeating the arts, philosophy, and politics. According to Gaston Bachelard, there was a "devalorization of objective and rational life" in interwar Europe more generally, "which . . . declare[d] science to be bankrupt" ([1938] 2002, 186). The apocalyptic industrial carnage of World War I, and the crises that followed in central Europe—hyperinflation, the collapse of empires, mass statelessness, the rise of fascism—fed this rising fire.

Stefan George, the charismatic figure whose intellectual circle in Weimar Germany included one of the founders of the sociology of knowledge, Max Scheler, proclaimed that "there is no path leading from me to science" ("Von mir aus führt kein Weg zur Wissenschaft"; Salin 1948, 256; Breuer 2012, 1168). The dominant intellectual tendency in Weimar Germany "was a neoromantic, existentialist, 'philosophy of life,' reveling in crisis and characterized by antagonism toward analytical rationality generally and toward the exact sciences and their technical applications particularly" (Forman 1971, 4). German sociology, the discipline in which contextual approaches to analyzing knowledge and science were best represented, understood itself as a "science of crisis," or *Krisenwissenschaft* (Frisby [1983] 1992, 107ff.; Weiß 1995).

The sociology of knowledge represents the second concept-quake in the emergence of a historical sociology of social science.[7] Scheler presented himself as an anti-Marxist, but as Bukharin noted, Scheler in fact borrowed "a number" of his "basic principles" from Marxism (1931, 17n13). Although Scheler "flatly repudiates all forms of sociologism," Merton noted that he also "indicates that different types of knowledge are bound up with particular forms of groups," including social classes (Merton 1949b, 472). In his famous book *Ressentiment* ([1912] 1972), for example, Scheler argued that we may find that "a particular literary work" (or work of social science) "is the product of a deeply rooted *resentment* that the author has for certain social strata" but that we must then seek to "discover the sociological genesis of this resentment within the system of social stratification with which the author found himself confronted" (De Gré 1941, 111). Scheler argued that "even some quite formal types of thought and valuation vary according to social class" (Scheler 1926: 204–5). Among the thought forms that took opposing forms among lower and upper classes, Scheler counted pragmatism versus intellectualism, milieu-theoretical thought versus nativist thought, and an optimistic view of the future combined with pessimistic retrospection versus a pessimistic view of the future combined with optimistic retrospection of the "good old days" (Scheler 1926, 204–5). Finally, Scheler argued that modern science emerged from the combination of "two social strata that were originally separate": a group of educated upper classes involved in "free contemplation" and another "class of people who have rationally accumulated the experiences of work and craftsmanship" (Scheler 1925, 142). This thesis about the origins of science was subsequently repeated by a number of Marxists, including Zilsel, usually without attribution.[8]

The aim of the sociology of knowledge, according to Karl Mannheim, was to trace the connections between "the social position of given groups and their manner of interpreting the world." It was significant that Mannheim defined this perspective as taking both the *forms* and *contents* of knowledge as its objects and that he was interested in the reciprocal relations between knowledge and the social world. Mannheim credited Marx with the "uncovering" (*Enthüllung*) of the class interests behind ideologies and analyzing culture's reification (*Verdinglichung*) under capitalism (Mannheim [1929] 1959, 277, 309–10).[9] Mannheim credited Nietzsche with ascribing "certain modes of thought" to aristocratic and democratic cultures and analyzing certain ideas as instruments of a will to power (Mannheim [1929] 1959, 310). A third influence on Mannheim was the Budapest "Sunday Circle," also known as the Lukács group, whose discussions during World War I circled around the idea of how knowledge depended on social position (Kettler 1971, 37; Karádi and Vezér 1985; Gluck 1985; Gabel 1991). Mannheim went beyond Lukács and Hungarian Marxism, however, in attending to the role of "generations, status groups, sects, occupational groups, schools, etc.," alongside capitalism and social classes (Mannheim [1929] 1959, 276). He also went beyond most Marxists in refusing to draw a sharp distinction between science and ideology, and in explicitly analyzing the social determinants and applications of social science (but see Lukács 1954).

What was the place of science in Mannheim's sociology of knowledge? Merton claimed that most students of *Wissenssoziologie*, including Mannheim, "neglected the analysis of the more firmly established disciplines" and exempted "the 'exact sciences'... from existential determination" (Merton 1937, 494; 1949b, 470).[10] Yet Mannheim was also accused of making the opposite mistake, namely, arguing that "even scientific thought, and especially in the social sciences," is "inescapably bound up with and 'corresponding' to the social position of the thinker" (von Schelting 1936, 665). This challenge to the objectivity of scientific truth was anathema to most American sociologists and post-1945 German sociologists, and the mini-struggle over Mannheim and the sociology of knowledge constituted an early front in sociology's perennial *Positivismusstreit*.[11] Yet this critique of Mannheim conflated the *philosophy of science*, which distinguishes between better and worse scientific practices, and the *sociology of science*, which seeks to explain the evolution of actually existing science. Mannheim had taken courses with Heinrich Rickert, the leading thinker of the German Southwest neo-Kantian school, for whom the distinction between the human and natural sciences was a central theme (Maquet 1951, 19; Oakes 1987; Köhnke 1991). Mannheim agreed in distinguishing epistemologically between the natural and the human sciences. He does not claim that the exact sciences are completely immune from social determination, although he allows that they progress over time, in contrast to the "cultural sciences."[12] But these are separate issues: even natural science may be shaped in its empirical development by social factors. Most relevant in the present context is the fact that Mannheim anticipated Foucault's critiques of discipline and governmentality by discussing (in *Man and Society in an Age of Reconstruction*) the ways in which various human and social sciences (pragmatism, behaviorism, psychoanalysis) were being deployed to shape social behavior (Mannheim [1935] 1951).

The first fully sociological account of natural science was presented by Émile Durkheim. In *Elementary Forms of the Religious Life* (1912), Durkheim traced the basic epistemological categories of modern thought, including scientific thought, such as time, space, number, cause, and force, to religious social practices and structures. Durkheim also argued that "modern science was an eminently social thing . . . because it was the product of an extensive cooperation . . . [and because] it involves methods and techniques that are the product of tradition and impose upon workers an authority comparable to that which is invested by legal rules and morals" (Durkheim 1910, 44).[13] This Durkheimian foundation of a *sociologie de la connaissance* can be traced through the works by Halbwachs on collective memory, Granet on the relations between Chinese social structure and the structures of Chinese thought (*La pensée chinoise*), Lévi-Straussian structuralism (*La pensée sauvage*). A full-fledged *sociologie de la connaissance* came into existence in Francophone sociology after 1945 (Maquet 1951; Bastide 1967), while a Francophone *sociologie de la science* had to wait even a bit longer (Pestre 1995; Lamy and Saint-Martin 2015).

Some of the earliest sustained efforts to create a sociology of natural science were carried out by Marxists. The "classic programmatic texts of Marxist historiography of science" are associated with the Soviet delegation to the second International Congress of the History of Science and Technology in London in 1931. The Soviet Union "was the first country in the world to create an institute or university department for the study of the history of science and technology"—the Commission on the History of Knowledge at the Soviet Academy of Sciences (Graham 1993, 137; David-Fox 2016). The commission was initially headed by Vladimir Vernadskii, a non-Marxist geochemist who focused on political and social conditions and religious factors in explaining scientific change while also paying attention to individual genius, as in traditional approaches (Graham 1993, 138). In 1930, Nikolai Bukharin became head of the commission, now renamed Institute for the History of Science and Technology. Bukharin headed the Soviet delegation to the London conference in 1931. There he argued that both the natural and social sciences are "heavily mediated by social, economic, and political factors, and therefore cannot be separated from the society in which [they emerge]" (Graham 1993, 140). Rejecting any empiricist philosophy of science, Bukharin insisted that "epistemological Robinson Crusoes are just as much out of place as Robinson Crusoes were in the atomistic social science of the eighteenth century," adding that "historically there is no absolutely unmixed individual sensation, beyond . . . beyond the individual as the *product* of society." Science should be understood as "practical activity," *scientific cognition* as "the practice of material labour continued in particular forms (natural science), of administration and the class struggle (the social sciences)" (Bukharin 1931, 2–3). The relation between theory and applied science corresponded to the division between mental and manual labor in society; the difference between the natural and social sciences is the difference between seeking "causal theoretical series (*Naturgesetz*, law) and teleological, normative series (rules, system of rules, prescriptions)." At the same time, the "pure" sciences "are not 'pure,' since the *selection of an object* is determined by aims which are practical in the long run—and this, in its turn, can and must be considered from the standpoint of the causal *regularity* of social development" (Bukharin 1931, 14). Bukharin's preliminary comments are important insofar as they combine history, sociology, and philosophy of science, interpret science as a practical and material activity, and range freely over the putative borders between social and natural science, exploring their differences and similarities.

An even more innovative contribution to the 1931 conference was the paper on "the social and economic roots of Newton's 'Principia'" by the physicist and historian of science Boris Hessen. This is one of foundational papers in the "externalist" analysis of science (Hessen [1931] 2009; Graham 1985). Hessen echoed Bukharin in attacking the cult of genius in older histories of science and argued that the main scientific problems tackled by physics in Newton's age were determined by the demands of production, warfare, and transportation: "The development of productive forces set science a series of practical tasks and made an imperative demand for their accomplishment." This does not mean that demands were translated directly into science, however, but that scientific goals were specified through *the study of existing technology*. Theoretical mechanisms were developed by studying practical mechanics (Freudenthal and McLaughlin 2009, 11). Hessen argues that "where 17th century scientists could not draw on an existing technology . . . the corresponding disciplines of physics . . . did not develop" (Freudenthal and McLaughlin 2009, 3). Hessen also attended to the social class relations and struggles that were relevant to science, including the movement of elites into science and the merging of the mechanical and liberal arts. Only "primitive" historical materialism, Hessen argued, would insist that economic factors are the sole determinants; also crucial are "political, juridical, philosophical theories, religious beliefs" (Hessen [1931] 2009, 27). Hessen argued further that the class compromise at the time of the Glorious Revolution led Newton to shy away "from fully endorsing the mechanization of the world picture," leading him to adapt "his concept of matter so as to be able to introduce God into the material world" (Freudenthal and McLaughlin 2009, 3).

Other Marxists began to analyze the social determinants of science. Cambridge scientist J. D. Bernal launched a frontal assault on *internalist* theories of science in his *Social Function of Science* (1939). Bernal's encyclopedic postwar *Science in History* expanded its purview to encompass the social sciences, which took up most of the concluding volume. Although he was less familiar with the social sciences, Bernal's basic thesis had sweeping implications, which agreed with Mannheim: the "relations between science [including social science] and society are fully reciprocal" (Bernal 1954, 1233). The journal *Science and Society*, created in 1936, was "dedicated to the growth of Marxian scholarship." In the first issue, the editors announced their interest in work that "illuminates the interdependence of science and society." One of the articles in that issue by the Dutch mathematician Dirk J. Struik argued that a "sociological stain" shaped the development of even the purest forms of mathematics (1942, 64). The Marxist economist Henryk Grossmann turned to the history of science as part of a critique of Franz Borkenau's account of the emergence of the modern mechanistic worldview in his book *Der Übergang vom feudalen zum bürgerlichen Weltbild* (1934). Like Boris Hessen, Grossman argued that "constructing, working with, and observing machines had made it possible to set aside some of the concrete appearances of physical phenomena—complicated by different kinds of motion and friction, for example—to identify abstract mechanical work" and generate a theory of mechanics (R. Kuhn 2009, 248). Edgar Zilsel (1942) elaborated on the arguments of Scheler, Hessen, and Grossman, arguing that modern science was born when elite social prejudices against manual labor began to weaken, permitting scholars who were trained to think methodically and rationally to adopt the craftsmen's experimental methods and causal thinking patterns. British scientist Joseph Needham began his multivolume project *Science and Civilisation in China* in 1948 by asking why China had surpassed other parts of the world in technical innovation for fifteen hundred years, with "scores of Chinese innovations" being "transmitted to the West," but yet "failed to make the breakthrough to experimental and mathematical science and hence to the Industrial Revolution" (Blue 1998, 198; Finlay 2000, 267, 279). Needham's answers included Marxist and non-Marxist factors. By panning out to a global and comparative perspective, Needham forced even his critics to operate on the terrain of "sociological" accounts of scientific differences (e.g., Sivin 1982). In 1946, Needham teamed up with UNESCO's first general director, Julian Huxley, to create the International Union of the History and Philosophy of Science, which was centered around a commission for the history of the social relations of science run by a group of Marxist scientists (Maurel 2010, 166).

During the early Cold War, when the sociology and history of science were getting under way, such Marxist treatments of science were often criticized in the United States on crudely political grounds. The Princeton historian Charles Gillispie attacked Marxist historians of science for expressing ideas that he found "shocking," such as attributing the "growth of science not too difficult, abstract thought about nature" but rather to factors such as "the rise of strong monarchies and the growth of capitalism!" (1957, 176). Of course, political objections were expressed on both sides of the Iron Curtain. The Soviet Institute of the History of Science and Technology between 1945 and 1988 "displayed continuing trauma" over the fate of Bukharin and Hessen, who had both been executed by Stalin, "by staying away from discussions of the social and political context of science" altogether (Graham 1993, 142). This was cruel irony, as Hessen's effort to demonstrate the social forces shaping Newton's views had been partially intended to protect "the core of modern science from ideological attack" (Graham 1993, 149). In the more recent period, Pierre Bourdieu's arguments for the social determination of science combined with his defense of scientific autonomy similarly evoke a mixture of anger and confusion among his critics on the left and the right that is reminiscent of Cold War polemics and of the earlier attacks on Mannheim. But we are getting ahead of ourselves. . . .

A *non-Marxist* historical sociology of *natural science* emerged between the wars. Ludwik Fleck, a medical worker and researcher in Lviv, published *Genesis and Development of a Scientific Fact* in German in 1935 (Fleck [1935] 1979). Fleck focused on the internal relations and beliefs within scientific communities, an approach that made a strong impression on Thomas Kuhn ([1962] 1970). Fleck's key concepts were *thought style* (*Denkstil*) and *thought collective* (*Denkkollektiv*). His focus was on historically dynamic interactions between an esoteric circle of experts and the exoteric circle of the wider society. Fleck's ability to ignore the Cold War polarization between "internalist" and "externalist" accounts of science seemed to illustrate the thesis that "marginal men participating in diverse thought collectives can create something new from the conflict" (Trenn 1979, iii). Fleck's ideas were later redeployed by Thomas Kuhn.

Several other non-Marxist sociologists, including Robert Merton, moved into the study of science between the 1930s and 1960s, although none of them fully embraced the "idea that scientific knowledge is socially constructed in the strong sense"—that is, in terms of the *contents* of science (Restivo and Dowty 2008, 636). Merton apprenticed himself at Harvard in the 1930s to the methodologically conservative Sarton (Nichols 2010, 78). The chair of the sociology department at the time was Pitirim A. Sorokin, whose work on the sociology of knowledge was an idiosyncratic blend of empiricist cultural sociology and metahistorical theory (Sorkin 1937–41). Merton's doctoral thesis, "Science, Technology and Society in Seventeenth-Century England" (1938), was fully "sociological" in a dual sense. The first part redeployed Weber's Protestant ethic thesis in explaining the rise of science in seventeenth-century England as a product of Puritanism. Merton argued that while the "congeniality of the Puritan and the scientific temper partly explains the increased tempo of scientific activity during the later seventeenth century," this did not account "for the particular foci of scientific and technologic investigation" (1938, 496). Merton provided an answer to this question about the foci of science in the second half of the book, which dealt with economic and military influences on science and technology. Merton acknowledged his debt to Boris Hessen here and in his first published article on "Science and Military Technique" (1935, 204; 1938, 501n24). Merton later calculated that "nine out of every ten discussions of [his] book . . . have centered on just one part of it, the one dealing with the interrelations between Puritanism and . . . science," but that "more space in the monograph" was "devoted to the hypotheses about economic and military influences" on science ([1970] 1973, 177).

The replacement of *Wissenssoziologie* by the sociology of science in the United States was a function of most American sociologists' general skepticism about "relativism" and threats to scientific objectivity and of the Cold War retreat from anything tainted by Marxism. Mannheim's antipositivism and his avant-garde Central European hypermodernity, with its rejection of general ideas of progress and tolerance of difference, were rebarbative to most American sociologists. As Alan Sica writes, Merton's project was first to convert *Wissenssoziologie* into "an Americanized 'sociology of knowledge,'" and then to "turn against" it, "and in so doing, to spoil the potential reception of Mannheim's ideas in the United States" (2010, 164, 175). Merton warned in 1952 that any investigation of "the connections between sciences and society constitute[d] a subject matter which ha[d] become tarnished for academic sociologists who know that it is close to the heart of Marxist sociology" (Merton 1952, 15). Merton also saw the sociology of knowledge as a poor fit with the "Big Science" beloved of his "bosom pal Lazarsfeld" (Sica 2010, 178, 180). As Shapin (1995, 291) observed, until 1970, "it was a truth almost universally acknowledged that there might be a legitimate sociological understanding of scientific error, of 'the blind alleys entered by science,' of the state of scientific institutionalization, and, perhaps, of the overall dynamics of scientific foci, but that there could be no such thing as a sociology of authentically scientific knowledge." Henrika Kuklick pointed out that the "notion of a general scientific method was premised on a distinction central to the philosophy of science in the 1930s—between the context of discovery and the context of justification. According to this formulation, sociological analysis can explain scientists' choices of research problems, which are conditioned by sociohistorical factors, but is irrelevant to judgment of research results, which are evaluated by universal criteria" (Kuklick 1983, 291). Chall (1958, 288), echoing Mannheim, suggested that the sorts of self-doubt that gave rise to a sociology of knowledge in Weimar Germany were missing in the United States, since it was economically so much more prosperous (see below).

By the 1960s, the sociology of knowledge had been thoroughly repressed, repudiated, or transformed into attitude surveys. It was replaced by a calming *sociology of science* that was compatible with empiricism, quantitative methods, and axiological neutrality, that avoided any sulfurous odors of Marxism or relativism and that focused not so much on science as on *scientists*—"their career patterns, work organization, patrons, and professed values" (Kuklick 1983, 291). In 1949, the Harvard historian of science James Conant discussed the "interconnection between science and society about which so much has been said in recent years by our Marxist friends"—just at a moment when such friendships were being shredded by McCarthyism (Conant 1947, 18). As an alternative to Marxism, Conant promoted local case studies of scientific research, which were best suited to demonstrate "the evolution of new conceptual schemes as a result of experimentation" (Conant 1947, 19). The Cold War was thus at the origin of a sociology of science that tended to lower its gaze modestly to the scale of the laboratory while bracketing wider contexts (Fuller 2000). During the 1950s, the US Social Science Research Council created a Committee on the History of Science that included sociologists. The American Academy of Arts and Sciences and the American

Council of Learned Societies began to organize science studies (Shryock 1956). The only remaining proponents of the Mannheim-style *sociology of knowledge* in US sociology were émigrés such as Peter L. Berger, Lewis Coser, Werner Stark, and Kurt Wolff, whose institutional marginality and *geisteswissenschaftliche* (human sciences) orientations created additional barriers to acceptance (Steinmetz 2010). And the American setting had its effects even on some of these latter-day Mannheimians. The widely-circulated book *Sociological Theory* by Lewis Coser and Bernard Rosenberg, which went through five revisions between 1957 and 1989, featured a long chapter on "Sociology of Knowledge" in the first and second editions (Coser and Rosenberg 1957), but this chapter disappeared completely in later editions, and the phrase "sociology of knowledge" was barely mentioned—even though Coser continued to operate as a Mannheimian "sociology of knowledge virtuoso" (C. Fleck 2013, 962) in books like his *Men of Ideas* (Coser 1965).

In Germany, the disappearance of *Wissenssoziologie* was a function, first, of the destruction of German sociology after 1933 (and Austrian sociology following the Nazi annexation) and of the intense hostility to Mannheim on the antisemitic right (Curtius 1932; Eschmann 1934) (Klingemann 2000). The postwar hegemony of US sociology and US power in general in the West played a role, as did Marxist rejections of "irrationalist" currents of German thought in the East. Weimar traditions were subjected after 1945 to a combination of "historical amnesia and epistemological critique" (Acham 1995, 291). The "Americanizing" first generation of postwar West German sociologists experienced "massive pressure to distance themselves from German intellectual history," which was believed to be closely tied to the German *Sonderweg*, or special path, that supposedly led to Nazism (Klingemann 2009, 262; Steinmetz 1997). In the case of the sociology of knowledge, this poisoned thought had been written mainly by Jewish sociologists. Nonetheless, it was now "good form to keep the older German sociology at arm's length" (Tenbruck 1979, 79; Kruse 1998), just as it was considered indiscreet for sociologists to examine the Nazi past in general and Nazism within the sociology discipline in particular (Käsler 2002, 166; Steinmetz 2017a, 489). Johannes Weyer (1986, 88–89) referred to this posture among postwar German sociologists as a program of "*not* coming to terms with the past" (*Vergangenheits[nicht-] bewältigung*).[14] The exiled historical sociologists who were still alive in the United States and United Kingdom were ignored by most West German sociologists. One "young Turk" in West German sociology at the time, Dietrich Rueschemeyer, sneered at Karl Mannheim's "historicist hypotheses" that could never be "operationalized in a form appropriate to industrial-style research."

Rueschemeyer recommended replacing Mannheim and Scheler's approach with laboratory research on "small groups"—a fad in American social psychology at the time.[15] Another young German sociologist, Heinz Maus, whose career had started with attacks on Mannheim during the Nazi era, continued to argue after 1945 that the intellectual path leading from Hegel, Romanticism, and Rickert to the historical sociology and epistemology of the Weimar era had been an intellectual dead end.[16] Marxists joined in the attack, accusing *Wissenssoziologie* of value relativism and political irrationalism (Lukács 1954). German-speaking sociologists only began the process of disinterring their discipline's Nazi past (Klingemann 1996, 2009) and restoring severed connections to Weimar *Wissenssoziologie* (e.g., Meja and Stehr 1982; Endreß 2001) in the 1980s (see below).

Thomas Kuhn is the other key figure in this intellectual transition from the sociology of knowledge to the sociology of science (Fuller 2000). Kuhn's 1957 book on the Copernican Revolution was still closer to Mannheim in considering a variety of "externalist" causes, including the beginning of the era of "voyages and explorations," the "Moslem invasion" of Europe, and intellectual developments in the Reformation and Renaissance such as humanism, Neoplatonic philosophy, and the intensified testing of inherited Aristotelian ideas by scholasticism (Kuhn 1957, chap. 4). Kuhn's more famous *Structure of Social Revolutions* ([1962] 1970), however, backed away from wider contextualizing factors, limiting its attention to the scale of scientific communities. As George Stocking (1965, 214) noted at the time, *Structure* was "imperfectly historicist in its focus on the inner development of science to the deliberate neglect of external social, economic, and intellectual conditions" (see Fuller 2000). Kuhn's contributions were nonetheless crucial insofar as they recuperated and reformulated certain postulates of the Weimar-era sociology of knowledge. He replaced the image of science "aiming for an ultimate theory of reality" with a less linear view of social scientific development, and showed that the sciences were like the humanities and social sciences in being "constituted as communities and traditions that periodically were subject to ideological strife" (Fuller 1994, 93, 82).

The Third Concept-Quake: From Social Studies
of Science to the Historical Sociology of Social Science

The third concept-quake is marked by the emergence of a full-fledged, explicit historical sociology of the social sciences. Hegel and Marx are crucial antecedents, and their ideas are preserved in these formulations in terms of a dialectical *Aufhebung*. Merton is an important transition figure here as well. Although Merton's sociology of science did not typically focus on the social sciences, Merton did not completely exempt his own discipline from sociological treatment. In fact, Merton laid out a compelling agenda for the "comparative investigation of sociology in its social contexts" in 1959 (Merton 1959, 22). Here Merton suggested that a field such as sociology could be "examined under three aspects: as the historical filiation of ideas considered in their own right; as affected by the structure of the society in which it is being developed; and as affected by the social processes relating the men of science themselves" (Merton 1959, 22). The first aspect pointed to the use of intellectual history, in contrast to the avoidance of close readings of texts in standard "Mertonian" research. The second aspect pointed to Hegel, Marxism, and the more expansive social contexts mobilized in the classical sociology of knowledge. The third aspect pointed toward approaches to studying science that were associated with the meso-level of scientific production: Ludwik Fleck's "thought community," Merton's own "thought community," Kuhn's paradigmatic "scientific groups," Crane's "invisible colleges" (1972), and more recently, Bourdieu's acutely defined theory of internally stratified, conflictual "scientific fields."

The same year that Merton published his programmatic statement on the sociology of social science, his Columbia University colleague C. Wright Mills published a book that showed how such an analysis might actually be carried out: *The Sociological Imagination*. Mills embraced Mannheim's "intricate and subtle" thought. Mills developed a complex account of the structural division of American sociology between the poles of "grand theory" and "abstracted empiricism" (Mills 1959, 6). The latter was characterized by the "zealous search for 'laws' presumably comparable to those imagined to be found by natural scientists" (Mills 1959, 18); by an exclusive focus on contemporary, not historical events; on events that "repeat themselves rather than those which occur only once;" and on the United States, to the exclusion of the rest of the world. Abstracted empiricism represented a sociology that had realigned itself toward an audience of *clients* rather than *publics*. The main goal of this form of social science was "the prediction and control of human behavior" (Mills 1959, 18, 156, 61, 102, 113). Second, Mills reconstructed Merton's "mid-range" processes taking place among the "men of science": their careers, cliques, growing administrative power, relations to foundations, and roles as "consultants of the corporation, army, and state, and . . . advertising" (Mills 1959, 102–3). Finally, Mills zoomed out to consider the macrostructures of American society that shaped sociologists' ontological and epistemological assumptions. Here Mills returned to the themes in his other writings: imperialism, capitalism, bureau-cracy, and the American "supersociety" (Mills 1958, 30, 115–16).

In the late 1950s and early 1960s, therefore, the idea that the social sciences could be studied sociologically by paying attention to historical contexts, "meso-level" dynamics, and close readings of texts began to gain traction. Although the Mannheimian version of the sociology of knowledge continued to be dismissed by "Mertonian" sociologists of science (e.g., Crane 1972, 5), some US-based sociologists began to present research in the Mannheimian mold, often without labeling it as such. All of these neo-Mannheimians had personal or intellectual connections to the Weimar sociological circles that had spawned the sociology of knowledge between 1910 and 1933. Bendix emi-grated from Germany in 1938 at the age of twenty-two, and all of his postsec-ondary studies were at the University of Chicago; but he wrote extensively on German sociological traditions, including in his 1943 MA thesis (Bendix 1943). Berger was an Austrian-born sociologist who received his PhD in 1954 from the New School, which was the main refuge of émigré Weimar social scientists in the United States. Luckmann was born in a German-speaking family in Yugoslavia in 1927, studied in Austria, and moved to the United States after World War II, where he also studied at the New School. In 1967, Berger and Luckmann published *The Social Construction of Reality*, whose subtitle is *A Treatise in the Sociology of Knowledge*. Coser fled Berlin in 1933 at the age of twenty and did not enroll as a graduate student in sociology in the United States until the 1950s. Like Bendix, Coser's work circled around the sociology of knowledge traditions that were coursing through German intellectual life at the moment of his exile (C. Fleck 2013). Mills studied and coauthored some of his first publications with the exiled German sociologist Hans Gerth, a student of Mannheim's. Stark was an Austrian-born sociologist who earned his doctorate at Hamburg in 1934 in political science with a thesis on eco-nomic history, and then taught in sociology departments in Britain and the United States (Das 1981). Wolff attended lectures by Mannheim in Frankfurt, went into exile in 1933, moved to the United States in 1945, and became a sociology professor, translator of Mannheim, and specialist in the sociology of knowledge. In short, none of these sociologists inculcated their earliest scientific "domain assumptions" (Gouldner) 1970) within standard American postwar sociology, and none seem to have formed strong *ego ideals* patterned on leading American sociologists such as Robert Park before the war or Talcott Parsons afterward.[17]

Alvin Gouldner's work exemplified this rediscovery of the sociology of knowledge. In *Enter Plato*, Gouldner set out to understand how Athenian society and culture "gave rise to and shaped Plato's *social* theory" (1965, 4)—a project parallel to Hessen's and Needham's. Gouldner did not rely strictly on internalist or externalist approaches; rather, he articulated a range of causal factors operating at differing distances from the site of intellectual production. Gouldner's *Coming Crisis of Western Sociology* (1970) analyzed the role of "internal" factors (Parsonian "positivism" and its dissolution) and external ones (the global countercultural revolt) in producing the supposed "crisis" of the discipline. Here Gouldner introduced the idea that scientists' experientially based *background assumptions* shape the development of theory by making them "resonate" emotionally with certain ideas and not others. These assumptions do not "rest on evidence" but are *affectively* laden, because they are inculcated early in socialization (Gouldner 1970, 35; Steinmetz and Chae 2002). Gouldner's *Coming Crisis* seemed to argue *performatively* that the history of sociology was another product of the critical crescendo he was diagnosing.

The French history of social science had a second source alongside the Durkheimian foundations: the historical school of epistemology, or *épistemologie française*, represented by Bachelard, Koyré, Canguilhem, and Foucault (Bitbol and Gayon 2015). This movement helped to push the history of science beyond the exact sciences and to include the human and social sciences in its purview. It gave rise to two traditions, one philosophical (associated with Foucault), the other sociological (associated with Bourdieu). Canguilhem served as *directeur de thèse* for both Foucault and Bourdieu (although Bourdieu switched to Aron as adviser and never completed his doctoral thesis). Canguilhem succeeded Bachelard as director of the Institut d'Histoire des Sciences et des Techniques in 1955 (Gayon 2016). In his *éloge* to Bachelard, Canguilhem described him as "renewing so profoundly the meaning of the history of science, wrenching it out of its situation (until then a subaltern one), and promoting it to a philosophical discipline of the first order" (Canguilhem 1968, 186). Bachelard's intellectual innovations powered the rising interest in the history and philosophy of science. According to Bachelard, the scientific fact cannot be accessed or assembled from empirical sense data but has to be "conquered, constructed, and confirmed" via an epistemological break with spontaneous perceptions and common sense (Bourdieu, Chamboredon, and Passeron [1968] 1991, 11). Bachelard rejected notions of continuous progress or a singular "scientific revolution," proposing the idea of continuous historical "ruptures" in scientific evolution (Bachelard [1938] 2002). Bachelard and Koyré introduced the idea, made famous in the English-speaking world by Thomas Kuhn, that there was not a single "Scientific Revolution" in the seventeenth century but rather many "minuscule versions" applied "to many other episodes in the history of science" (Daston 2016, 117). Bachelard was at the origin of the concept of "epistemological break," made famous by Althusser. Errors and obstacles were as important for the history of science as successful discoveries (Balibar 1978). Deeply influenced by psychoanalysis and Freud's writings about his own creative process, Bachelard identified an array of blockages to scientific knowledge rooted in unconscious emotions, including scientists' anxieties about social status (Bachelard [1938] 2002, 54). All of these ideas were crucial for the antiempiricist, constructivist, sociological approach to science that came to be associated with Bourdieu, and for the discontinuist approach to history (Grimoult 2003, 146–248) attributed to Foucault and Kuhn.

In addition to these insights into the workings of science in general, Koyré, Bachelard, and Canguilhem were interested in the human and social sciences, unlike earlier generations of French philosophers. As Fabiani notes, Canguilhem's definition of the history of science had the decisive effect of opening up a new field of objects—specifically, the "non-noble" disciplines in the social sciences. Koyré's article on Panofsky "helped raise interest for this work in France" (Fabiani 1989, 123–24). Psychology was the human science closest to philosophy in France (Paltrinieri 2016), and Canguilhem presented several analyses of its history (Canguilhem 1943, 1958). Foucault's historical studies of the human sciences also started with psychology (Foucault 1954). *Les mots et les choses* (1966) had drawbacks that are aptly summarized by Wittrock, Heilbron, and Magnusson: "Foucault not only eliminated the producers of the . . . discourses from his analysis, but he showed no interest in the actual process of discursive production, ignored its social and political conditions, and refrained from asking how and why epistemic change occurs." They add: "Foucault's "central proposition that man as a subject of science was invented only at the end of the eighteenth century has found little support" (Wittrock, Heilbron, and Magnusson 1998, 7). Nonetheless, *Les mots et les choses* helped to broaden the aperture to encompass the human or social sciences in general.

The social and human sciences had finally stepped onto center stage as objects of serious historical scrutiny. They were being analyzed theoretically and historically for the first time since Hegel's lectures on the history of philosophy and the stillborn historiography of the human sciences that Hegel inspired in nineteenth-century Germany. The third concept-quake was expressed in a number of sustained, contextualizing historical studies of social science in the 1960s that focused on psychology and anthropology. The *Journal of the History of the Behavioral Sciences* (1965–) initially carried a preponderance of articles on psychology. Anthropology was the next object of serious historical enquiry, with George W. Stocking Jr.'s *Race, Culture, and Evolution* (1968) and his edited series in the history of anthropology; Jacques Berque's essays on anthropology, sociology, and history of the Maghreb (collected in Berque 2001); and Talal Asad's *Anthropology and the Colonial Encounter* (1973), followed by a vast outpouring of work. The history of economics, which had been the first social science to receive serious treatment, reemerged in this period, with journals such as *History of Political Economy* (1969–present). The journal *History of Sociology* (1978–87) came to be edited by Alan Sica, one of the few US sociologists with expertise on the Weimar sociological milieu. The journal's contributing editors included the German refugee sociologist Werner Cahnmann and the Max Weber specialists Lawrence Scaff and Richard Swedburg, along with most of the full-time practitioners of the history of sociology in the United States at the time.

Several important theoretical and methodological programs for a historical sociology of social science emerged in the wake of the interventions by Mills and Gouldner. First, there were sophisticated neo-Marxist approaches to the history of social knowledge, starting with Goldmann ([1955] 2016) and culminating in Therborn's history of Marxism and sociology (1976). A second intervention was the *intertextual* approach to the history of ideas and intellectual history associated with the Cambridge school (Skinner 1969; Whatmore 2016).[18] Third was a body of work known under the acronyms STS, SSK, and ANT, discussed below. A fourth body of literature is associated with Peter Wagner and Björn Wittrock, and their international group of collaborators. Wagner and Wittrock advocated an approach to the sociology of social science that would "overcome the dichotomies of externalism and internalism as well as of micro- and macro-accounts, while bringing historicity back in, in a manner which is sensitive to particularities, yet does not shy away from the theoretical commitment." They proposed a theory of agency that avoided "behaviorist" and utilitarian, rational-choice approaches, and a philosophy of science that avoided "scientism" and "relativism," pointing to Bhaskar's Critical Realism as a better philosophical basis (Wagner and Wittrock 1991, 332). Finally, they suggested that Bourdieu's field theoretical approach was highly compatible with their own work.

It would be impossible even to try to categorize all of the work on the history and sociology of social science that has appeared since this period. The list of works on a single discipline such as anthropology or economics would fill pages, and there are many works that explore science, including social science, from nondisciplinary angles, focusing on methods such as statistics (Porter 1986), ideas such as objectivity (Daston and Galison 2007), techniques such as observation (Daston and Lunbeck 2011), historical periods such as the Cold War (Erickson et al. 2013), interdisciplinary formations such as colonial science (Singaravélou 2011; Tilley 2011; Steinmetz 2023), institutions like the US National Science Foundation (Solovey 2020), or specific universities, departments, and research institutes (e.g., Schumaker 2001). Indeed, one goal of this volume is to provide a working bibliography for this sprawling interdisciplinary and international arena, especially since the annual bibliographies published by *Isis*, the leading journal of the history of science, include just a tiny portion of the ongoing work on the history of the social sciences.

Explaining Variations in Interest in the History of Social Science

One of the obvious questions raised by the foregoing discussion is how we can explain the emergence of the historical sociology of social science. This chapter is not a historical sociology of social science but an intellectual history of writing on social science. Given the temporal and geographic scope covered here, it is impossible to explore the full range of reasons for the larger and smaller conceptual ruptures I have discussed thus far. I will provide two examples of such an account, however, in order to illustrate the lineaments of a historical sociology of social science: (1) the rise of the sociology of knowledge approach in Third Republic France and Weimar Germany and its failure to take root in the United States; and (2) the differential timing and foci of the rise of research on the *history of sociology* in France, Germany, and the United States.

Mannheim himself suggested an answer to the first question, concerning the social conditions propitious to a sociology of knowledge. As Merton summarizes Mannheim, it is "only in a highly differentiated society, characterized by high social mobility and democratization, that the confrontation of incompatible and mutually unintelligible universes of discourse leads to relativism. The sociology of knowledge could itself arise only in such a society where, with the emergence of new and the destruction of old basic values, the very foundations on which an opponent's beliefs rest are challenged" (Merton 1937, 500). Merton continues:

> With increasing social conflict, differences in the values, attitudes and modes of thought of groups develop to the point where the orientation which these groups previously had in common is overshadowed by in-

compatible differences. Not only do there develop different universes of discourse, but the existence of any one universe challenges the validity and legitimacy of the others. The coexistence of these conflicting perspectives and interpretations within the same society leads to an active and reciprocal *distrust* between groups. Within a context of distrust, one no longer inquires into the content of beliefs and assertions to determine whether they are valid or not, one no longer confronts the assertions with relevant evidence, but introduces an entirely new question: how does it happen that these views are maintained? Thought becomes functionalized; it is interpreted in terms of its psychological or economic or social or racial sources and functions. In general, this type of functionalizing occurs when statements are doubted, when they appear so palpably implausible or absurd or biased that one need no longer examine the evidence for or against the statement but only the grounds for it being asserted at all. Such alien statements are "explained by" or "imputed to" special interests, unwitting motives, distorted perspectives, social position, etc.... Not only ideological analysis and *Wissenssoziologie*, but also psycho-analysis, Marxism, semanticism, propaganda analysis, Paretanism and, to some extent, functional analysis have, despite their other differences, a similar outlook on the role of ideas. On the one hand, there is the realm of verbalization and ideas (ideologies, rationalizations, emotive expressions, distortions, folklore, derivations), all of which are viewed as expressive or derivative or deceptive (of self and others), all of which are functionally related to some substratum. On the other hand are the previously conceived substrata (relations of production, social position, basic impulses, psychological conflict, interests and sentiments, interpersonal relations, and residues). (Merton 1949b, 511–12)

If the United States in the middle third of the twentieth century was a "highly differentiated society, characterized by high social mobility and democratization," what, then, explains the failure of the sociology of knowledge? Chall suggested a modification of the hypothesis: "The sociology of knowledge flowers when conflicting perspectives and interpretations occur in a society" *and* "when such a society is economically inactive" (1958, 287). But if that were enough, we should expect the sociology of knowledge to reemerge in present-day America, characterized as it is by a Weimar Republic–style proliferation of ideological friend-enemy configurations and incommensurable worldviews. There is a third, more "internal" factor, relating to intellectual history and "the different concerns and language of social researchers" (Chall 1958, 287). The fact that German and French sociologists developed the sociology of knowledge was directly linked to their familiarity with Kantian discussions of the determination of thought by categories—a priori categories in Kant, socially derived categories in the thinking of neo-Kantian Heinrich Rickert (Bruun 2007, 65), Durkheim ([1912] 1915), and Bourdieu (1984). This background has been missing in the United States, given the perennial lack of philosophical interest among sociologists and the hostility to epistemological discussion.

What about the emergence of the historical sociology of sociology? I have already discussed the intellectual antecedents for this movement, starting with the ancient history of science, through Hegel and Marx in the nineteenth century, through to the twentieth-century sociology of knowledge and science. But these resources were available to anyone who cared to engage them. Their sheer presence cannot explain why there was a turn to historicizing the social sciences at differing moments in the United States (1950s–60s), France (1960s–70s), and Germany (1920s–30s and 1970s–80s). Without making any claim to provide a complete comparative account, we can briefly sketch some of the main components that would need to go into such an explanation.

In the United States, many of the founders of sociology, such as Albion Small, were in fact obsessed with writing the discipline's prehistory. Their work was partly motivated by the desire for disciplinary legitimation and struggles with competing paradigms. However, the first of these motives—seeking disciplinary legitimacy—had largely evaporated during the triumphal years of post–World War II disciplinary self-confidence and international hegemony (Steinmetz 2005), even if there were still squabbles between different theoretical schools. Nonetheless, American sociological leaders still felt a need to promote their approach internationally, especially in Europe, and one of the weapons in this scientific struggle was disciplinary history. During the 1960s, Paul Lazarsfeld encouraged sociology graduate students at Columbia University to carry out studies of European sociology with an emphasis on recovering indigenous empirical and quantitative traditions that could be supported against the currently dominant theoretical positions. This resonated with the goals of American foundations' "postwar Marshall Plan" in the social sciences, whose aim was to "reinforce conceptual and technical standardization and to thereby to eliminate national differences in the production of social science" (Pollak 1979 57). The version of the history of sociology that accompanied this program was premised on a simple "sequential view that social science is a triumphantly advancing mode of social knowledge" (Wagner, Weiss, et al. 1991, 28). The modernization theorist

Daniel Lerner understood sociology as progressing inexorably along with societal development (Merton and Lerner 1951; Lerner 1959). This vision of the history of sociology marked a massive regression in thinking about how to write the history of science, a throwback to a pre-Hegelian era.

Gouldner's *The Coming Crisis of Western Sociology* seems to fit with a view of the history of sociology emerging as a product of disillusionment with dominant paradigms and ideologies at the end of the 1960s. There was a brief efflorescence of publications on the *sociology of sociology* after 1970. Yet Mills and Gouldner had no real followers in writing the history of sociology. In 1973, Merton republished his preface to Barber's 1952 book *Science and the Social Order* under the title "The Neglect of the Sociology of Science."

That said, a handful of American specialists became active in writing the history of sociology in the coming decades. At the end of the twentieth century, Charles Camic bemoaned the lack of interest in the history of sociology even among historical sociologists (1997, 229). The same is largely true of specialists in the sociology of science, who continued to focus almost entirely on the exact and natural sciences. One roster of this truly invisible college is the list of editors of the short-lived *Journal of the History of Sociology*, which had an almost clandestine existence between 1978 and 1987. Even today, the history of sociology section of the American Sociological Association issues regular warnings that its membership is in danger of falling below the threshold required to keep sections going. There is no dedicated English-language journal for the history of sociology in the United States. Many studies labeled "history of social science" continue to confuse "genuine historical investigation" with "the search for 'utilizable sociological theory'" and seek "not to understand the thought of the past so much as to criticize the writings of all previous ages from a 'presentist' standpoint and to seek for any useful principles which may be still valid in today's systematics" (I. B. Cohen 1994, xv). There are probably no more than two dozen full-time specialists in the history of social science in the United States today, and fewer than a dozen specialists in US sociology. Participants in the US sociology field are still discouraged from engaging in critical research on the discipline itself, which is variously described as irrelevant, since ideas at best "merely reflect the social order, and play no role as determinants of social action" (Kuklick 1983, 294), or as a form of *Nestbeschmutzung* or navel-gazing "me-search," or perhaps as "a pathology of scientificity."[19] In sum, the history of sociology seems to have suffered largely the same fate as the earlier sociology of knowledge, at least in the United States.

In Germany and Austria, by contrast, the history of social science has become a small but well established subfield over the last four decades. Interest began to rise in the 1970s (Ludz 1972; Lüschen 1979) and gathered momentum in the 1980s, when research began to focus on recovering the repressed history of the social sciences in Nazi Germany and the work of German social scientists driven into exile. Two writers pointed out at the time that German sociology was "starting to reconceptualize the traditional form of disciplinary history *sociologically* as a reflexive approach to its own past" (Hülsdunker and Schellhase 1986b, 9). This process was aided by the fact that former Nazis were finally retiring from West German universities, including sociology departments.[20] Pathbreaking studies were published by Käsler (1984), Lepenies (1988), Klingemann (1996, 2009), and others (Schauer 2017). The sociology of knowledge may have been repressed in Germany, but it had not been entirely erased, and it continued to haunt the collective social scientific imagination. The interest in unearthing the histories of Nazism sometimes intersected with the sociology of knowledge (Endreß 2001). These factors, taken together, meant that the history of sociology has become a less peripheral topic in Germany than in the United States. A large literature has consolidated during the past two decades (see Moebius and Ploder 2017–19 for an overview). Much of it has moved beyond the earlier emphasis on the Weimar and Nazi eras, and has become more comparative and international in focus (e.g., Wagner 1990, 2001; Moebius 2006; Gerhardt 2007; C. Fleck 2011; Dayé 2020).

This brings us to French writing on the history of social science, which had been shaped by the above-mentioned *épistemologie française* and more recently by Bourdieu's theory of practice, habitus, symbolic capital, social fields, and reflexivity. The history of the social sciences, including sociology, has become a sizable subfield, organized around a number of vital journals.[21] One writer noticed in 1997 that French sociologists "now seem to be infatuated" with the history of sociology (Hirschhorn 1997, 5). The same has occurred in the history profession, where "historical research on the social sciences and their use in society" has become an "established branch of historical studies" (Raphael 2012, 41).[22] This can be traced partly to interactions between historians and sociologists around the journal *Annales* and interactions between historians and sociologists around Bourdieu (Steinmetz 2017a).

Science Studies and the Historical Sociology of Social Science

Before turning to Bourdieu we should briefly discuss science studies, a label used here to signal science and technology studies (STS), sociology of scientific knowledge (SSK), ANT, and related approaches. These emerged as alternatives to the Mertonian sociology of science and have also come to be seen as an alternative to Bourdieu's approach.[23] However, these approaches have rarely analyzed *social* scientific production. In certain respects they are fully compatible with Bourdieusian sociology of science. In other respects they have problematic implications for the sociology of social science.

Many of the tenets of science studies repeat arguments from the sociology of knowledge and the earlier history of science. Like the Marxist historians of science, science studies does not focus on "great men" and rejects a sharp division between technology and science, arguing that the influences between science and technology are reciprocal. Also like the Marxists, *Wissenssoziologie*, and most intellectual historians, science studies pays attention both to the contents and formal aspects of knowledge and to organizational and institutional sites and some social determinants (Gieryn 2018). Like the French epistemologists, science studies is interested in scientific errors, failures, and dead ends as well as successes, and it portrays scientific history as a highly discontinuous process. Like Foucault and the Cambridge school and many other historians, science studies has been interested in discourse analysis and in tracking semiotic filiations. All of this reflects the emergence of structuralism, semiotics, and discourse analysis since the 1960s (Dosse 1997).

The most novel aspect of science studies is its dogged focus on *micro-level* practices, interactions in scientific laboratories, and networks. Yet this focus does not translate well into studies of the humanities and social sciences. After being pressured for more than a century to become more quantitative and technicist, and to emulate a stereotypical image of the natural sciences, most research in the human sciences still does not take place in laboratories, rely on collective teams or elaborate technologies, or take a statistical form.[24]

Science studies approaches are of questionable value for the sociology of social science in several respects. One is the widespread insistence on a rigorous empiricism, a refusal to brook any conception of ontological depth or layering, or of ontological *emergence*.[25] The move to encompass human and nonhuman actors and their networked connections in a single, flat ontological level undermines the raison d'être of the social sciences, which is the ontological *emergence* of practice and social structure from underlying biological and physical realities. Erasing the distinction between human and nonhuman reopens the floodgates to the forms of scientistic naturalism that philosophers of science long worked to dismantle, from Weber and Rickert through to Bachelard, Bourdieu, and Bhaskar. These moves align science studies with an empiricism-qua-"actualism" that is strongly associated with social scientific positivism and antithetical to any realist or even realistic social science (Steinmetz 1998, 2005).

Science studies also perpetuates various elements of the earlier repudiation of *Wissenssoziologie*. Latour's emphatic rejection of contextual explanation ("context stinks"; Latour 2005, 148) recalls the earlier narrowing of the sociology of science to more proximate scientific and academic contexts. Latour's perspective is often understood as a critical or defiant one, despite the fact that Latour explicitly rejects "critical" social science (Fassin 2017) and claims to "have found a way to free the sciences from politics" (Latour 1999, 22). Latour attacks intellectuals' main defenses against political heteronomization by refusing to defend the autonomy of the scientific field (Steinmetz 2018). Far from critical, most STS writing is explicitly conservative insofar as it strikes a "studiously descriptive stance to the sciences it studies," sending the message that "science normally is as it ought to be" (Fuller 2007, 20). In criticizing Marxist approaches for their class reductionism, Latourian science studies abandons efforts to analyze the "structural bases for conflict" or the idea that "capacities of actors are often shaped by structures" that exist prior to their entry into a particular scientific science or that are located outside that scene (Albert and Kleinman 2011, 265).

That said, network analysis and the attention to scientific activity taking place outside structured fields can be fruitfully integrated into the Bourdieusian sociology of science.

The Historical Sociology of Social Science
as Social Scientific Reflexivity

The historical sociology of social science received a huge impetus from the practice-theoretical sociology of Pierre Bourdieu, whose group began tackling social scientific knowledge practices in the 1970s.[26] This work is distinctive in several ways. It takes seriously the idea that science *may* be organized into social fields (although it may also exist in unfielded sectors of social space). Fields are arenas organized around a specific type of social practice; they are internally divided, and riven by open or latent struggles around the distribution of specific symbolic resources. Fields may be relatively autonomous, that is, partially bounded and demarcated from their outside, but they are also subjected to and imbedded within environing social fields and spaces, and their autonomy may be erased under certain circumstances (Bourdieu 2004, 45–55). The resources that actors accumulate outside a given field are rarely irrelevant to practices within the field, but neither can these resources be immediately deployed without adaptation to the rules of the specific game. Certain ideas and norms tend to be taken for granted by all participants in a given field, constituting its *illusio*. The preexisting habitus (internalized bodily and mental dispositions) with which an actor enters a new field tends to be transformed into a field-specific form, even while retaining traces of its origin.

There are several key differences between this approach and the Mertonian, Kuhnian, and Latourian sociologies of science. First is the focus on divisions, conflicts, and inequalities of power and resources within science. The contrast could not be more dramatic with Merton's scientific ethos of "communism" or Kuhn's picture of consensus followed by periodic ruptures and reconvergence around a new unifying paradigm. Second, the Bourdieusian sociology of knowledge pays close attention to the *contents* of cultural *works* and to the practices of cultural *producers*. This work is alive to radical transformations of scientific fields, including their rise and demise, and to intersections and resonances among different fields (Steinmetz 2011, 2017a). Given the historicism of Bourdieu's work, his intensive interactions with historians, combined with his insistence on rigorous empirical research, it is not surprising that the Bourdieusian sociology of science tends to work intensively with primary documents and historical archives. Since fields can never be assumed to be spatially continuous with the nation-state, but often have a smaller or larger geopolitical footprint, the Bourdieusian sociology of knowledge always begins by determining a given field's spatial coordinates, in order to understand the circulation of ideas, objects, and actors within that field or between different fields (Bourdieu 1999; Steinmetz 2017a; Heilbron this volume). And because the central concept in Bourdieu's social theory is *practice* (Bourdieu 1977; Heilbron and Steinmetz 2018), studies of science inspired by Bourdieu tend to focus on scientific research practices (Heilbron 2011), exactly like the ANT/STS version of the sociology of science.

A crucial aspect of this work goes to the heart of the question of the *justifications* for the history of social science. Bourdieu hypothesizes that texts are defined by an interaction between (1) an author's habitus, reconstructed sociogenetically over biographical time; (2) the author's positions in specific, relevant fields, and the history of those fields, which explains the space of positions in a field at a given moment in time; and (3) the author's moves, or "position-taking," in those fields. Since this model of the production of texts encompasses social scientific texts, it follows that the social scientist needs to confront the problem of providing "an account of social reality that can explain how the theorist could come to have such an account" (Fuller 1995, 161). In other words, Bourdieu argues that social science requires a specific form of *reflexivity*. But what is this form?

Scientific reflexivity involves two main cognitive ruptures or breaks. The first entails a rupture with the practices under study. There is no reason to believe that actors necessarily understand the logic of their own action, and the sociologist therefore cannot base her analysis on actors' self-descriptions, as in Schütz or Garfinkel (Bourdieu 1977, 1–30). Rather than accepting actors' own descriptions of their action as the last word or taking them at face value, their practices are "objectified" by defining, categorizing, and redescribing them—by rendering them into language, statistics, charts and diagrams, photographs and films, or any other mode. In contrast to structuralism, however, Bourdieu rejects the idea that social structures directly explain action. The causal impact of social structures is mediated through habitus, which generates practices thorough processes of strategic, regulated improvisation. The objectification of practices via structuralism or quantitative analysis can therefore only be a first step in objectification. A second break is required: a break with the analyst's own spontaneous scientific categories—the concepts, techniques, and theories used to objectify the practices being studied. Social scientists need to hesitate before blindly adopting the instruments, theories, and concepts they find ready at hand. In order to "objectify" their own "objectifications," researchers need to objectify the scientific world in which they are taking part. They need to reflect on what they are doing when they do social science, which assumptions they unwillingly enact and which implicit understandings they may unwittingly reproduce. In the case of social science, this entails writing a genealogical history of the specific scientific field being studied, of adjoining scientific and nonscientific fields, and of the fields of power that surround science—up to the moment of the social investigation (Bourdieu 2004; Singh 2019).[27] The historical sociology of social science is therefore at the very heart of scientific reflexivity.

The study of individuals is part of Bourdieu's sociology as well as his approach to reflexivity. On the one hand, biography, or the sociological analysis of an individual, is ideally suited to exploring the interaction between habitus, field/social space, and practices/moves/texts, as Bourdieu demonstrated in his books on Flaubert (1996) and Manet (2017).[28] At the same time, the researcher may need to situate herself within the fields of her own activity, perhaps in the form of an autoanalysis (e.g., Bourdieu 2007). This approach to reflexivity is completely different from confessional-style approaches, as in "I am writing as an X or speaking as a Y." While the scientist's individual properties shape their work, the confessional approach overlooks the fact that the social properties of individuals that are relevant for shaping their practice within a given field may not be the same properties governing practices outside the field, in the field of power or social space in general. The scientific researcher's habitus is typically shaped and reshaped by the field of knowledge and the historical sociology of that field.

Modernization theory in Cold War America can provide an illustration of this approach. I might begin such an investigation with the puzzling fact that there has been more historical research on modernization theory than most other forms of social science. It is both familiar and seemingly "historical"— that is, outdated—perhaps suggesting that it continues to unwittingly structure sociological conceptions in the present (Tenbruck 1992; Steinmetz 2021). I would try to reconstruct the genesis of the fields in which I am located. This entire chapter has tried to sketch some of the lineaments of such an analysis. I would ask where this sort of research is located within American academia, what role it played and continues to play, perhaps in the form of shadows and traces of concepts and theories. Asking about my own position might entail looking for the sociobiographical reasons for my interests in modernization theory and genesis of my constructions of the concepts being used by the social scientists under study.

I would then need to reconstruct modernization theory itself in all of its textual and practical forms (books, conferences, publications, laboratories), and in its historical, disciplinary, and political homes—US science departments, institutes, foundations, branches of the US state and military, and overseas sites of implementation. Attention to the actual production of modernization theory may require movement beyond academic sites to nonacademic ones, and attention to the fact that the latter have a relative autonomy and that implementation always differs from policy, which differs from policy science. I would need to situate scholarly and political groups and individual modernization theorists and implementers within these fields. I might whether ask there was a subfield of modernization studies, and about its location and its relational standing vis-à-vis the main social scientific disciplines. I might then reconstruct the sociogenesis of the individuals who played dominant and dominated positions in these fields. This would lead me to study their social properties and life courses—family origins, education, career, and so on. Finally, I would reconstruct "third-order constructions," asking how modernization theorists conceived of the subjectivity of putatively traditional and modern communities, and of these subjects' constructions of the subjectivity of others. A case study of a figure like Daniel Lerner or Walt Rostow might be especially enlightening (see Knöbl 2001).

Ideally this entire set of reconstructions would also yield a picture of the reciprocal relations between modernization theory and the practices this theory was attempting to reshape, as well as other practices (Berque [1947]

2001; Cullather 2002). But as we argued in the introduction to this book, applied social science often fails to produce its intended outcomes (Franklin 2016) and has unexpected ramifications.

Other Uses of the History of Social Science

There are some additional epistemological, political, and ethical reasons for doing this kind of work. One is *disciplinary anamnesis*. Some past sociologists and theories are simply brushed aside as obsolete; others are actively resisted or even censored. Still others are repressed, in the full psychoanalytic meaning of that term.[29] Nazi-era sociology was "forgotten" for almost four decades by the vast majority of West German sociologists. Around half of the French sociologists worked in overseas colonies between the late 1930s and the mid-1960s, and some of the core concepts in French social thought emerged from this colonial context (Steinmetz 2020). Yet the secondary literature on the history of the sociological discipline and on specific sociological subfields completely ignores (or "forgets") this colonial engagement for reasons I have examined elsewhere (Steinmetz 2023). The refugee sociologists from Nazi Germany were largely ignored in the United States and United Kingdom. Research using the ideas of Karl Marx was excluded from professional social science in the Cold War US and postwar West Germany, and Durkheim and Weber were widely dismissed as outmoded as compared to American-style social science in France and Germany, respectively, after 1945. The first reference to Gramsci in an East German sociological publication was in 1988, a year before the collapse of that state (Peter 1991, 40).

A second contribution of this work is that transitions to the present may have been perceived more clearly at the onset of historical processes, especially observers with a foot in two different social worlds and worldviews. The societies colonized by Europe were completely remade by conquest and imperial rule, which makes descriptions from the periods before colonization or in colonialism's earlier phases especially valuable. Similarly, processes of individualization, secularization, and capitalism become more invisible as they become universal, entering common sense and the taken-for-granted (Peter 2001). We may be particularly interested in observations made by earlier social scientists, because of the categories they used to make sense of their experience, which may allow us to come closer in fusing our hermeneutic horizon with theirs, as Gadamer would say.

Third, the history of social science can contribute to a realistic understanding of the conditions for the *flourishing* of knowledge, including social science (Steinmetz 2017a). Conversely, the history of social science sometimes sheds light on the decadence of social science. In my analysis of interactions between historians and sociologists in France and Germany during the twentieth century (Steinmetz 2017a), I was able to identify three axes of variation within interdisciplinary practices: (1) symmetry, or equal participation by the parties, versus asymmetry; (2) processual, dialogic, recursive, and open-ended interactions, versus an orientation toward discrete outputs; (3) autonomy of intellectual production within a given field or sphere, versus heteronomy, that is, its subsumption under the interests of external political or economic powers. I discovered that the more generative forms of interdisciplinarity occurred where interactions had the following features: (1) the two parties were equal in power, or symmetrical; (2) the interacting groups were motivated by autonomous intellectual problems, rather than by external compulsion, cajoling, or influence; (3) where interaction allowed a fusion of perspectives, rather than being organized around a division of labor between disciplines.

A fourth raison d'être of the history of social science relates to the permeation of reality by social science. Of course, the consubstantiality of (or reciprocal relations between) social knowledge and social reality was a premise of Mannheim's original sociology of knowledge (Northrop 1951, xv). Giddens (1991, 2) suggests that social science in particular represents a reflexive monitoring of society[30] and argues that "the conceptual innovations and empirical discoveries of social scientists routinely 'disappear' back into the environment of events they describe, thereby in principle reconstituting it." Modernity is therefore "inseparable from *the constitutive role of social science,* and reflection upon social life more generally, which routinely orders and reorders both the intimate and more impersonal aspects of the lives people lead" (Giddens 1989, 252; see also Mandler 2019). This is one of many "looping" or feedback effects between knowledge and the realities it describes (Hacking 1999). The social sciences constitute social policies, educational systems, foreign affairs, and other political practices deliberately and unintentionally (Steinmetz 2004, 2007).

Historians of social science are thus able to shed light on the very construction of the world by social science. Even if we are interested in explaining social processes that ostensibly have nothing to do with intellectual or social scientific production, we may have to carry out intellectual or scientific histories in order to produce an adequate social scientific explanation. This is yet another way in which the history of social science is an indispensable part of sociological methodology in general. It is an approach that all social researchers need to master, regardless of their subject matter. This is true even if "scientific discourse on society exists alongside other," nonscientific discourses (Wagner and Wittrock 1991, 334), which also constitute whatever practices we are studying.

It is important to distinguish between the *intentional* application of social science to policy, or to the construction of social worlds, and the much broader range of *unintentional* effects of social science on worlds beyond its borders (Steinmetz 2004, 2020). Social science has been deliberately deployed to guide policies ranging from eugenics to social insurance, labor market policies, poverty relief, and schemes intended to "nudge" individuals toward preferred behaviors. Well-documented examples of deliberate social scientific policy-making include Cameralism and demography, Keynesian economics, psychological Taylorism in industry, and modernization theory and theories of "colonial development," which informed postwar projects of land reform, dam building, and the agrarian "Green Revolution" (Knöbl 2001; Robin 2001; Cullather 2002; Gilman 2003; Steinmetz 2017b).

Social science also shapes social practices in a myriad of unintentional ways (Steinmetz 2004). Social processes and events are sometimes codetermined by social scientific discourses that ostensibly have little to do with them. I tried to uncover some of the hidden causal chains explaining colonial policy in my book *The Devil's Handwriting*. I found that the ethnographic and civilizational accounts of European travelers, missionaries, and amateur ethnographers set the basic parameters of formal German colonial policies, even if this was not the conscious intent of those accounts, and even if they were generated years, sometimes decades or even centuries before colonial conquest. The history of social knowledge was a crucial component of the explanation of colonial genocide in German Namibia and of the partial breakdown of the rule of colonial difference in German Qingdao. This does not mean that we can redeploy such findings directly in an effort to prevent genocide or encourage civilizational exchange in other times and places. There is no social scientific recipe for "genocide prevention." It does, however, point to *some* conditions that have been conducive to these outcomes in the past, and therefore provides some guidance in the present.

Conclusion

The historical sociology of social science may seem to be poorly anchored in existing scientific disciplines and intellectual communities. It touches on the intellectual history and sociology of ideas and intellectuals, the philosophy and sociology of knowledge and science, on subfields like cultural anthropology and cultural sociology, and on entire disciplines such as literary criticism. However, this interstitial and interdisciplinary location can also prove to be advantageous, especially in the early stages of the formation of a new object of study. Without a clearly bounded disciplinary field or subfield in Bourdieu's sense, it is more difficult for specific groups to dominate this space. This is a potentially productive form of semimarginality, like that of Ludwik Fleck, and one that we might want to distinguish from the extreme *margins* of intellectual and social scientific space (Pérez 2022). This may be an ideal situation for the early stages of formulating a new intellectual agenda. The very irrelevancy of the historical sociology of social science to the main competing agendas in these fields of knowledge allows it to escape notice and to avoid the pressure to conform to *presentism, positivism, policy relevance*, and *pragmatism* that hover drone-like overhead. Since most modern social practices are permeated by social scientific concepts, the historical sociology of social science can claim to be a necessary part of much social scientific inquiry. As the centerpiece of scientific self-reflexivity, the historical sociology of social science can claim to be a necessary part of *all* social scientific inquiry.

Notes

For comments on earlier versions of this article I am grateful to the participants in the 2017–19 IAS theme seminar on the social sciences, the November IAS 2018 meeting, the October 2019 comparative-history workshop at Northwestern University, Department of Sociology, and several anonymous reviewers. Particular thanks to Didier Fassin, Johan Heilbron, and Ann Orloff for their suggestions at different points.

1　In Nietzsche (1874, 107). Some translators change Nietzsche's coinage *Begriffsbeben* into "earthquake of ideas," erasing his juxtaposition in the same sentence with the word *Erdbeben* (earthquake).

2　The boundaries separating the natural and social sciences, and separating both from the humanities, vary across time and space, as do the names of these metacategories (Diemer 1968; I. B. Cohen 1994; Feuerhahn 2020).

3　Although Steve Woolgar has long insisted on the need to analyze the observers of scientific activity along with scientists themselves (Latour and Woolgar 1979, 27–33; Woolgar and Ashmore 1988), and criticized the "lack of reflexive sensitivity" in SST (Woolgar 1991, 21), the literature on the sociology of science/technology is still strikingly "lacking in reflexive practices" (Collyer 2011, 320), particularly regarding the *sociological* form of reflexivity, in which the researcher tries to explain the conditions of possibility of her own account.

4　While recent science studies sometimes simply reject any hard distinction between pure science and its technological applications, this is a step backward with respect to these Marxist discussions, which analyze the variations in the boundary and the methods of translation.

5 For a non-naturalistic Marxist philosophy of science, see Bhaskar and Callinicos 2003; Brown, Fleetwood, and Roberts 2002. Marx's posthumous *Theories of Surplus Value* (*Theorien über den Mehrwert*) is a *history* of economic theories but lacks a *sociology* of economic knowledge.

6 Letter, Engels to W. Borgius, January 25, 1894, in Marx 1975, 50: 264–67.

7 Other contributors to the early sociology of knowledge not discussed here include Hans Freyer, Ernst Grünwald, Paul Honigsheim, Wilhelm Jerusalem, Siegfried Landshut, Siegfried Marck, Alexander von Schelting, Georg Simmel, and Alfred Weber.

8 F. J. Moore, author of a book on the history of chemistry, had already made a similar observation before Scheler: "The Greek Philosophers . . . had no first-hand knowledge of chemical transformations. Their social position kept them out of touch with those who might have given them practical information, and the whole atmosphere of the age discredited experiment as it discredited manual labor. Pure thought was alone held worthy of the philosopher" (Moore 1918, 2).

9 Some writers attempt to cast epistemological and political aspersions on the crucial scientific practice of uncovering hidden or conceptual causes or factors in accounting for empirical phenomena. In discussions of the sociology of knowledge, this empiricist gesture sometimes works by shifting the meaning of Mannheim's term *Enthüllung* by translating it as "unmasking" (which would be closer to *entmasken* in German) or "unveiling" (which would be *entschleiern* in German). A more straightforward translation of *Enthüllung* is "uncovering." This translating game allows Baehr (2019)—repeating insinuations made by Boltanski (2012)—to characterize the entire sociology of knowledge approach as a "conspiratorial" and "paranoid" activity. Von Schelting (1936, 667) proposed "debunking" as a less charged English translation of *Enthüllung*.

10 David Bloor repeated Merton's misleading charge (Kaiser 1998).

11 In addition to Merton 1937, 1949a, 1949b, and von Schelting 1936, see Speier 1938; and Dahlke 1940.

12 The relevant passage in *Ideology and Utopia* is subtle: while the "simple relationship between an earlier incomplete period and a later complete period of knowledge may to a large extent be appropriate for the exact sciences" compared to the "cultural sciences," this does not mean that the historical evolution of discovery and invention is unaffected by social factors (Mannheim [1929] 1959, 271). Merton distorts Mannheim's argument by summarizing it as a claim that "formal knowledge" (i.e., science) is "unaffected by the social or historical situation" (Merton 1949a, 253).

13 Durkheim's influence on subsequent investigations of the social roots of knowledge was recognized by Grünwald (1934, 17–20).

14 This is a play on the word describing the official postwar West German program of *Vergangenheitsbewältigung* or "coming to terms with the [Nazi] past."

15 Rueschemeyer 1958; Kuklick 1983, 291, summarizing an unpublished paper by Rueschemeyer.

16 Maus wrote on the history of sociology (1956, 1962), but in an unsociological way that revealed the cost of sidelining *Wissenssoziologie*. In his writing while a student, Maus rejected Mannheim and defended applied sociology (Maus 1939–40), aligning himself with other *Reichssoziologen* (sociologists of the Third Reich; Klingemann 1996, 2009). After 1945, Maus continued to advocate a break with Weimar traditions via "empirical sociology" (Maus 1951; König and Maus 1962).

17 Parsons, who had studied with Alfred Weber in Germany before 1933, publically informed Alfred Weber after 1945 that the latter's work was "not sociology" (von Beyme 2000, 219).

18 While the Cambridge School approach is referred to as "contextual," it is important to emphasize the difference between this use of "context" and the broader *contextual* approaches encompassing social, political, economic, and intellectual factors in explaining scientific change.

19 The *Nestbeschmutzung* (nest-fouling) charge is from a comment on my own work on the historical sociology of US sociology; the "me-search" phrase is from a notorious memo by the graduate director in a top US sociology department that counseled students to avoid entering the professional "circle of doom" by writing on such topics; the final phrase illustrates the high emotional pitch that sometimes accompanies such discussions, from Eschmann 1934, 955.

20 Examples of former Nazis in the postwar West German social sciences include Gunther Ipsen, who retired from Munich University in 1965; Wilhelm Mühlmann, who retired from Heidelberg in 1970, Helmut Schelsky, who left Bielefeld in 1973 and retired from Münster in 1978; and the sociologist-cum-historian Werner Conze, who retired in 1979.

21 Francophone journals dedicated exclusively to the history of the social sciences include *Anamnèse, Bérose, Gradhiva, Revue d'histoire des sciences humaines*, and *Revue d'histoire et d'archives de l'anthropologie*. Journals that publish extensively in this domain include *Actes de la recherche en sciences sociales, Les études sociales, Genèses, La revue pour l'histoire du CNRS*, and *Zilsel*.

22 Raphael's (1994) magisterial study of the French *Annales* school is organized around Bourdieu's categories.

23 See Pestre 2004 for a summary of the first thirty years of SST; and Rohracher 2015 for a recent overview; for critique, see Camic 2011; and Albert and Kleinman 2011.

24 For a compelling effort to blend STS and Bourdieusian field theory for explicitly, in a historical case study of competition between Western medicine and traditional Chinese medicine, see Lei 2014. Some of the authors in Camic, Gross, and Lamont 2011 set out to apply STS ideas to the social sciences, with mixed results.

25 Latour claims to be engaging in a "radical realism" and to reject empiricism (1999, 4–5), but these objections are philosophically incoherent and at odds with his other writing.

26 A number of ambitious studies of social science have been inspired by and contributed to the ongoing development of this approach. These diverse Bourdieu-inspired and neo-Bourdieusian studies of the historical sociology of the human and social sciences include Blondiaux 1998; Breslau 1998; Fabiani 1988; Fourcade 2009; Hauchecorne 2011; Henry 2012; Heilbron 1991, 1995, 2015; Heilbron, Lenoir, and Sapiro 2004; Karady 1972; Joly 2012, 2017; Kauppi 1996; Kropp 2015; Lei 2014; Moreno Pestaña 2006; Pérez 2015, 2022; Pinto 2009; Pollak 1978, 1979; Raphael 1994; Ringer 2004; Steinmetz 2005, 2017a, 2017c.

27 Following scientific objectification, a third epistemic break may return the analyst to the level of actors' subjectivity, whose meaning can now be better understood (Pels 2014). Bourdieu insisted that "there are extraordinary advantages in the fact of being native, on condition one knows what this implies, that is, everything it hides" (Bourdieu 2013, 207).

28 *Thorstein Veblen* by Camic (2020) is a brilliant example of the biographical approach to the historical sociology of social science; see also Gross 2008, a biography of Richard Rorty.

29 On historical forgetting, see Hölscher 1990; Ricoeur 2004; Weinrich 2004; the entire oeuvre of Sigmund Freud; and the entire field of psychoanalysis since Freud. Stoler (2011) rejects the terminology or forgetting, amnesia, and repression in this context in favor of "aphasia." Yet aphasia is just as problematic as any conceptual language in the human sciences that imports terms from the natural and medical sciences. Aphasia does not capture the key psychic and collective process of burying memory, and elides the key *moral* dimension in discussions of forgetting (Ricoeur 2004, 412–56). Finally, aphasia has a *linguistic* emphasis, whereas repressed material, including repressed social science, takes embodied, emotional, visual, and material forms, in addition to linguistic ones.

30 This is not the same as arguments about "information" or "knowledge society"—terms that suggest that we have entered a revolutionarily new, "purified and sanitized version of free-market capitalism" (Fuller 2007, 84).

References

Acham, Karl. 1995. *Geschichte und Sozialtheorie: Zur Komplementarität kulturwissen-schaftlicher Erkenntnisorientierungen*. Freiburg: Karl Alber Verlag.

Agblémagnon, F. N'Sougan. 1965. "La différence de psychologie et de sensibilité provoque-t-elle une différence de comportement entre occidentaux d'une part, africaines de l'autre, quant aux méthodes de la recherche et quant à l'interprétation des résultats? (pour l'Afrique)." In *État et perspectives des études africaines et orientales*, edited by the Association des universités partiellement ou entièrement de langue française, 128–44. Montreal: Therien freres.

Albert, Mathieu, and Daniel Lee Kleinman. 2011. "Bringing Pierre Bourdieu to Science and Technology Studies." *Minerva* 49: 263–73.

Asad, Talal, ed. 1973. *Anthropology and the Colonial Encounter*. London: Ithaca Press.

Bachelard, Gaston. (1938) 2002. *The Formation of the Scientific Mind*. Manchester: Clinamen.

Baehr, Peter. 2019. *The Unmasking Style in Social Theory*. London: Routledge.

Baker, Keith Michael. 1975. *Condorcet: From Natural Philosophy to Social Mathematics*. Chicago: University of Chicago Press.

Balibar, Étienne. 1978. "From Bachelard to Althusser: The Concept of 'Epistemological Break.'" *Economy and Society* 7, no. 3: 207–37.

Barber, Bernard. 1990. *Social Studies of Science*. New Brunswick, NJ: Transaction.

Bastide, Roger, ed. 1967. *Contributions à la sociologie de la connaissance*. Paris: Éditions Anthropos.

Beiser, Frederick C. 1995. "Introduction to the Bison Book Edition." In Georg Wilhelm Friedrich Hegel, *Lectures on the History of Philosophy*, vol. 1, ix–xi. Lincoln: University of Nebraska Press.

Bendix, Reinhard. 1943. "The Rise and Acceptance of German Sociology." MA thesis, University of Chicago.

Berger, Peter, and Thomas Luckmann. 1967. *The Social Construction of Reality: A Treatise in the Sociology of Knowledge*. London: Penguin Books.

Bernal, J. D. 1939. *The Social Function of Science*. New York: The Macmillan Company.

Bernal, J. D. 1954. *Science in History*. 4 vols. London: Watts.

Berque, Jacques. (1947) 2001. "Pour une nouvelle méthode politique de la France au Maroc." In *Opera minora*, vol. 3, edited by François Pouillon, 45–80. Paris: Éditions Bouchène.

Berque, Jacques. 2001. *Opera minora*. Vol. 2, *Histoire et anthropologie du Maghreb*, edited by Gianni Albergoni. Paris: Éditions Bouchène.

Beyme, Klaus von. 2000. "Interview am 5.5.1993 in Heidelberg." In *Alfred Weber zum Gedächtnis: Selbstzeugnisse und Erinnerungen von Zeitgenossen*, edited by Eberhard Demm, 219–21. Frankfurt am Main: Peter Lang.

Bhaskar, Roy, and Alex Callinicos. 2003. "Marxism and Critical Realism." *Journal of Critical Realism* 1, no. 2: 89–114.

Bitbol, Michel, and Jean Gayon, eds. 2015. *L'épistémologie française, 1830–1970*. Paris: Presses Universitaires de France.

Blondiaux, Loïc. 1998. *La fabrique de l'opinion: Une histoire sociale des sondages*. Paris: Éditions du Seuil.

Blue, Gregory. 1998. "Joseph Needham, Heterodox Marxism and the Social Background to Chinese Science." *Science and Society* 62, no. 2: 195–217.

Bluntschli, Johann Caspar. 1864. *Geschichte des allgemeinen Statsrechts und der Politik, seit dem sechzehnten Jahrhundert bis zur Gegenwart*. Munich: J. G. Cotta.

Bodin, Jean. (1576) 1969. *Method for the Easy Comprehension of History*. New York: Norton.

Boltanski, Luc. 2012. *Enigmes et complots: Une enquête à propos d'enquêtes*. Paris: Gallimard.

Bourdieu, Pierre. 1977. *Outline of a Theory of Practice*. Cambridge: Cambridge University Press.

Bourdieu, Pierre. 1984. *Distinction: A Social Critique of the Judgement of Taste*. Cambridge, MA: Harvard University Press.

Bourdieu, Pierre. 1990. "A Lecture on the Lecture." In *In Other Words: Essays towards a Reflexive Sociology*, translated by Matthew Adamson, 177–98. Stanford, CA: Stanford University Press; Cambridge: Polity.

Bourdieu, Pierre. 1996. *The Rules of Art*. Cambridge: Polity.

Bourdieu, Pierre. 1999. "The Social Conditions of the International Circulation of Ideas." In *Bourdieu: A Critical Reader*, edited by Richard Shusterman, 220–28. Oxford: Blackwell.

Bourdieu, Pierre. 2004. *Science of Science and Reflexivity*. Chicago: University of Chicago Press.

Bourdieu, Pierre. 2007. *Sketch for a Self-Analysis*. Cambridge: Polity.

Bourdieu, Pierre. 2013. "The Right Use of Ethnology, Interview with Mahmoud Mammeri." In *Algerian Sketches*, edited by Tassadit Yacine, 203–23. Cambridge: Polity.

Bourdieu, Pierre. 2017. *Manet: A Symbolic Revolution*. Cambridge: Polity.

Bourdieu, Pierre. 2022. *Retour sur la réflexivité*. Paris: EHESS.

Bourdieu, Pierre, Jean-Claude Chamboredon, and Jean-Claude Passeron. (1968) 1991. *The Craft of Sociology: Epistemological Preliminaries*. New York: de Gruyter.

Breslau, Daniel. 1998. *In Search of the Unequivocal: The Political Economy of Measurement in U.S. Labor Market Policy*. Westport, CT: Praeger.

Breuer, Stefan. 2012. "Soziologie." In *Stefan George und sein Kreis: Ein Handbuch*, edited by Achim Aurnhammer, Wolfgang Braungart, Stefan Breuer, and Ute Oelmann, 1158–68. Berlin: De Gruyter.

Brown, Andrew, Steve Fleetwood, and John Michael Roberts, eds. 2002. *Critical Realism and Marxism*. London: Routledge.

Brückner, Johann Jakob, and William Enfield. 1791. *The History of Philosophy: From the Earliest Times to the Beginnings of the Present Century*. Vol. 1. London: Printed for J. Johnson.

Bruun, Hans Henrik. 2007. *Science, Values and Politics in Max Weber's Methodology*. New expanded ed. London: Routledge.

Bukharin, N. I. 1931. "Theory and Practice from the Standpoint of Dialectical Materialism." In *Science at the Cross Roads: Papers Presented to the International Congress of the History of Science and Technology, held in London from June 29th to July 3rd, 1931*, 1–23. London: Kniga.

Camic, Charles. 1997. "Uneven Development in the History of Sociology." *Schweizerische Zeitschrift für Soziologie/Revue Suisse de sociologie* 23: 227–33.

Camic, Charles. 2011. "Bourdieu's Cleft Sociology of Science." *Minerva* 49 (September): 275–93.

Camic, Charles. 2020. *Veblen*. Cambridge, MA: Harvard University Press.

Camic, Charles, Neil Gross, and Michèle Lamont, eds. 2011. *Social Knowledge in the Making*. Chicago: University of Chicago Press.

Canguilhem, Georges. 1943. *Essai sur quelques problèmes concernant le normal et le pathologique*. Clermont-Ferrand: Impr. La Montagne.

Canguilhem, Georges. 1958. "Qu'est-ce que la psychologie?" *Revue de Métaphysique et de Morale* 63, no. 1: 12–25.

Canguilhem, Georges. 1968. "L'histoire des sciences dans l'oeuvre épistemologique de Gaston Bachelard." In *Études d'histoire et de philosophie des sciences*, 173–86. Paris: Vrin.

Chall, Leo P. 1958. "The Sociology of Knowledge." In *Contemporary Sociology*, edited by Joseph S. Roucek, 286–303. New York: Philosophical Library.

Cohen, G. A. 2001. *Karl Marx's Theory of History: A Defence*. Princeton, NJ: Princeton University Press.

Cohen, I. Bernard, ed. 1994. *The Natural Sciences and the Social Sciences: Some Critical and Historical Perspectives*. Dordrecht: Kluwer Academic.

Collyer, Fran. 2011. "Reflexivity and the Sociology of Science and Technology: The Invention of 'Eryc' the Antibiotic." *Qualitative Report* 16, no. 2: 316–40.

Comte, Auguste. 1852. *Cours de philosophie positive*. Vol. 1. Paris: Bachelier.

Comte, Auguste. 1855. *The Positive Philosophy of Auguste Comte*. London: J. Chapman.

Conant, James Bryant. 1947. *On Understanding Science: An Historical Approach*. New Haven, CT: Yale University Press; London: G. Cumberlege.

Condorcet, Marie Jean-Antoine-Nicolas de Caritat, marquis de. 1795. *Esquisse d'un tableau historique des progrès de l'esprit humain*. Paris: Agasse.

Coser, Lewis A. 1965. *Men of Ideas: A Sociologist's View*. New York: Free Press.

Coser, Lewis A., and B. Rosenberg. 1957. *Sociological Theory*. New York: Macmillan.

Crane, Diana. 1972. *Invisible Colleges: Diffusion of Knowledge in Scientific Communities*. Chicago: University of Chicago Press.

Crombie, A. C. 1963. *Scientific Change: Historical Studies in the Intellectual, Social, and Technical Conditions for Scientific Discovery and Technical Invention, from Antiquity to the Present*. New York: Basic Books.

Cullather, Nick. 2002. "Damming Afghanistan: Modernization in a Buffer State." *Journal of American History* 89, no. 2: 512–37.

Curtius, Ernst Robert. 1932. *Deutscher Geist in Gefahr*. Stuttgart: Deutsche Verlags-Anstalt.

Dahlke, Otto. 1940. "The Sociology of Knowledge." In *Contemporary Social Theory*, edited by Harry Elmer Barnes, Howard P. Becker, and Frances Becker, 64–89. New York: Appleton-Century.

Das, Robin R. 1981. "The Place of Werner Stark in American Sociology: A Study in Marginality." PhD diss., Fordham University.

Daston, Lorraine. 2001. "The History of Science." In *International Encyclopedia of the Social and Behavioral Sciences*, edited by N. J. Smelser and P. B. Baltes, 6842–48. Oxford: Pergamon.

Daston, Lorraine. 2016. "History of Science without *Structure*." In *Kuhn's "Structure of Scientific Revolutions" at Fifty: Reflections on a Science Classic*, edited by Robert J. Richards and Lorraine Daston, 115–32. Chicago: University of Chicago Press.

Daston, Lorraine, and Peter Galison. 2007. *Objectivity*. New York: Zone Books.

Daston, Lorraine, and Elizabeth Lunbeck, eds. 2011. *Histories of Scientific Observation*. Chicago: University of Chicago Press.

David-Fox, Michael. 2016. *Revolution of the Mind: Higher Learning among the Bolsheviks, 1918–1929*. Ithaca, NY: Cornell University Press.

Dayé, Christian. 2020. *Experts, Social Scientists, and Techniques of Prognosis in Cold War America*. Cham, Switzerland: Palgrave Macmillan.

Dayé, Christian, and Stephan Moebius, eds. 2015. *Soziologiegeschichte: Wege und Ziele*. Berlin: Suhrkamp.

Dear, Peter. 2012. "Historiography of Not-So-Recent Science." *History of Science* 50, no. 2: 197–211.

De Gré, Gerard. 1941. "The Sociology of Knowledge and the Problem of Truth." *Journal of the History of Ideas* 2, no. 1: 110–15.

Diemer, Alwin. 1968. "Die Differenzierung der Wissenschaften in die Natur- und die Geisteswissenschaften und die Begründung der Geisteswissenschaften als Wissenschaft." In *Beiträge zur Entwicklung der Wissenschaftstheorie im 19. Jahrhundert*, edited by A. Diemer, 174–223. Meisenheim am Gian: Verlag Anton Hain.

Dosse, François. 1997. *History of Structuralism*, vol. 2: *The Sign Sets, 1967–Present*. Minneapolis: University of Minnesota Press.

Durkheim, Émile. 1910. "Review of Wilhelm Jerusalem." *Soziologie des Erkennens: Année sociologique* 11, 1906–9: 42–44.

Durkheim, Émile. (1912) 1915. *The Elementary Forms of the Religious Life*. New York: Macmillan.

Endreß, Martin. 2001. "Zur Historizität soziologischer Gegenstände und ihre Implikationen für eine wissenssoziologisch Konzeptualisierung von Soziologiegeschichte." In *Jahrbuch für Soziologiegeschichte 1997/1998*, 65–89. Opladen: Leske und Budrich.

Engels, Friedrich. 1910. *Socialism, Utopian and Scientific*. Chicago: C. H. Kerr.

Erickson, Paul, Judy L. Klein, Lorraine Daston, Rebecca Lemov, Thomas Sturm, and Michael D. Gordin. 2013. *How Reason Almost Lost Its Mind: The Strange Career of Cold War Rationality*. Chicago: University of Chicago Press.

Eschmann, Ernst Wilhelm. 1934. "Die Stunde der Soziologie." *Die Tat* 25, no. 12: 953–66.

Fabiani, Jean-Louis. 1988. *Les philosophes de la République*. Paris: Éditions de Minuit.

Fabiani, Jean-Louis. 1989. "Sociologie et histoire des idees: L'epistemologie et les sciences sociales." In *Enjeux philosophiques des années 50*, 115–30. Paris: Éditions du Centre Georges Pompidou.

Fassin, Didier. 2017. "The Endurance of Critique." *Anthropological Theory* 17, no. 1: 4–29.

Feuerhahn, Wolf. 2020. "Moral sciences, Geisteswissenschaften (1795–1900): Parcours transnationaux d'étiquetages savants." *Revue d'histoire des sciences humaines* 37: 121–41.

Finlay, Robert. 2000. "China, the West, and World History in Joseph Needham's *Science and Civilisation in China*." *Journal of World History* 11 (Fall): 265–303.

Fleck, Christian. 2011. *A Transatlantic History of the Social Sciences: Robber Barons, the Third Reich and the Invention of Empirical Social Research*. London: Bloomsbury Academic.

Fleck, Christian. 2013. "Lewis A. Coser: A Stranger within More Than One Gate." *Czech Sociological Review* 49: 951–68.

Fleck, Ludwik. (1935) 1979. *Genesis and Development of a Scientific Fact.* Chicago: University of Chicago Press.

Fontenelle, M. de. 1790. "Préface des éléments de la géométrie de l'infini." In *Oeuvres de Fontenelle*, vol. 6, 35–56. Paris: Jean-François Bastien.

Forman, Paul. 1971. "Weimar Culture, Causality, and Quantum Theory, 1918–1927: Adaptation by German Physicists and Mathematicians to a Hostile Intellectual Environment." *Historical Studies in the Physical Sciences* 3: 1–115.

Foucault, Michel. 1954. *Maladie mentale et personnalité.* Paris: Presses Universitaires de France.

Foucault, Michel. 1966. *Les mots et les choses: Une archéologie des sciences humaines.* Paris: Gallimard.

Fourcade, Marion. 2009. *Economists and Societies: Discipline and Profession in the United States, Britain, and France, 1890s to 1990s.* Princeton, NJ: Princeton University Press.

Frängsmyr, Tore. 1973. "Science or History: George Sarton and the Positivist Tradition in the History of Science." *Lychnos* 74: 104–44.

Franklin, Jonathan S. 2016. *A History of Professional Economists and Policymaking in the United States: Irrelevant Genius.* London: Routledge.

Freudenthal, Gideon, and Peter McLaughlin, eds. 2009. *The Social and Economic Roots of the Scientific Revolution: Texts by Boris Hessen and Henryk Grossmann.* Dordrecht: Springer.

Frisby, David. (1983) 1992. *The Alienated Mind: The Sociology of Knowledge in Germany, 1918–33.* 2nd ed. London: Heineman Educational Books.

Fuller, Steve. 1994. "Teaching Thomas Kuhn to Teach the Cold War Vision of Science." *Contention* 4, no. 1: 81–106.

Fuller, Steve. 1995. "On the Motives for the New Sociology of Science." *History of the Human Sciences* 8, no. 2: 117–24.

Fuller, Steve. 2000. *Thomas Kuhn: A Philosophical History for Our Times.* Chicago: University of Chicago Press.

Fuller, Steve. 2007. *The Knowledge Book: Key Concepts in Philosophy, Science and Culture.* Stocksfield: Acumen.

Gabel, Joseph. 1991. *Mannheim and Hungarian Marxism.* New Brunswick, NJ: Transaction.

Gayon, Jean. 2016. "L'institut d'histoire des sciences." *Cahiers Gaston Bachelard* 14: 15–63.

Gerhardt, Uta. 2007. *Denken der Demokratie: Die Soziologie im atlantischen Transfer des Besatzungsregimes.* Stuttgart: Franz Steiner Verlag.

Giddens, Anthony. 1991. *Modernity and Self-Identity: Self and Society in the Late Modern Age.* Stanford, CA: Stanford University Press.

Giddens, Anthony. 1989. "A Reply to My Critics." In *Social Theory of Modern Societies: Anthony Giddens and His Critics*, edited by David Held and John B. Thompson, 249–301. Cambridge: Cambridge University Press.

Gieryn, Thomas F. 2018. *Truth-Spots: How Places Make People Believe.* Chicago: University of Chicago Press.

Gillispie, Charles C. 1957. "Perspectives." *American Scientist* 45, no. 2: 169–76.

Gilman, Nils. 2003. *Mandarins of the Future: Modernization Theory in Cold War America.* Baltimore, MD: Johns Hopkins University Press.

Gluck, Mary. 1985. *Georg Lukács and His Generation, 1900–1918.* Cambridge, MA: Harvard University Press.

Goldmann, Lucien. (1955) 2016. *The Hidden God: A Study of Tragic Vision in the Pensées of Pascal and the Tragedies of Racine.* London: Verso.

Gouldner, Alvin. 1965. *Enter Plato: Classical Greece and the Origins of Social Theory.* New York: Basic Books.

Gouldner, Alvin. 1970. *The Coming Crisis of Western Sociology.* New York: Basic Books.

Gouldner, Alvin. 1980. *The Two Marxisms.* New York: Oxford University Press.

Graham, Loren R. 1985. "The Socio-political Roots of Boris Hessen: Soviet Marxism and the History of Science." *Social Studies of Science* 15, no. 4: 705–22.

Graham, Loren R. 1993. *Science in Russia and the Soviet Union: A Short History.* Cambridge: Cambridge University Press.

Grimoult, Cédric. 2003. *Histoire de l'histoire des sciences: Historiographie de l'évolutionnisme dans le monde francophone.* Geneve: Librairie Droz.

Gross, Neil. 2008. *Richard Rorty: The Making of an American Philosopher.* Chicago: University of Chicago Press.

Grünwald, Ernst. 1934. *Das Problem der Soziologie des Wissens: Versuch einer kritischen Darstellung der wissenssoziologischen Theorien.* Vienna: Wilhelm Braumüller.

Hacking, Ian. 1999. *The Social Construction of What?* Cambridge, MA: Harvard University Press.

Harding, Sandra. 2003. *The Feminist Standpoint Theory Reader: Intellectual and Political Controversies.* New York: Routledge

Hauchecorne, Mathieu. 2011. "La fabrication transnationale des idées politiques. Sociologie de la réception de John Rawls et des 'théories de la justice' en France (1971–2011)." PhD diss., University of Lille.

Hegel, Georg Wilhelm Friedrich. 1995. *Lectures on the History of Philosophy: Greek Philosophy to Plato.* 3 vols. Lincoln: University of Nebraska Press.

Heilbron, Johan. 1991. "Pionniers par défaut? Les débuts de la recherche au Centre d'études sociologiques (1946–1960)." *Revue française de sociologie*, 27, no. 3: 365–79.

Heilbron, Johan. 1995. *The Rise of Social Theory.* Minneapolis: University of Minnesota Press.

Heilbron, Johan. 2011. "Practical Foundations of Theorizing in Sociology: The Case of Pierre Bourdieu." In *Social Knowledge in the Making,* edited by Charles Camic, Neil Gross, and Michèle Lamont, 181–208. Chicago: University of Chicago Press.

Heilbron, Johan. 2015. *French Sociology.* Ithaca, NY: Cornell University Press.

Heilbron, Johan, Rémi Lenoir, and Gisèle Sapiro, eds. 2004. *Pour une histoire des sciences sociales: Hommage à Pierre Bourideu.* Paris: Fayard.

Heilbron, Johan, and George Steinmetz. 2018. "A Defense of Bourdieu: Professional Sociology and the American Left." *Catalyst* 5: 35–49.

Henry, Odile. 2012. *Les guérisseurs de l'économie: Sociogenèse du métier de consultant, 1900–1944*. Paris: CNRS.

Hessen, Boris. (1931) 2009. "The Social and Economic Roots of Newton's *Principia*." In *The Social and Economic Roots of the Scientific Revolution: Texts by Boris Hessen and Henryk Grossmann*, edited by Gideon Freudenthal and Peter McLaughlin, 41–101. Dordrecht: Springer.

Hirschhorn, Monique. 1997. "The Place of the History of Sociology in French Sociology." *Schweizerische Zeitschrift fur Soziologie* 23, no. 1: 3–7.

Hollinger, David A. 1996. *Science, Jews, and Secular Culture: Studies in Mid-Twentieth-Century American Intellectual History*. Princeton, NJ: Princeton University Press.

Hölscher, Lucian. 1990. "Geschichte und Vergessen." *Historische Zeitschrift* 249: 1–17.

Hülsdunker, Josef, and Rolf Schellhase, eds. 1986a. *Soziologiegeschichte: Identität und Krisen einer "engagierten" Disziplin*. Berlin: Duncker and Humblot.

Hülsdunker, Josef, and Rolf Schellhase. 1986b. "Zur Aktualität der Soziologiegeschichte." In *Soziologiegeschichte: Identität und Krisen einer "engagierten" Disziplin*, edited by Josef Hülsdunker and Rolf Schellhase, 9–12. Berlin: Duncker and Humblot.

Jaeschke, Walter. 1993. "Einleitung." In G. W. F. Hegel, *Vorlesungen über die Geschichte der Philosophie*, vii–xl. Hamburg: F. Meiner Verlag.

Joly, Marc. 2012. *Devenir Norbert Elias: Histoire croisée d'un processus de reconnaissance scientifique. La réception française*. Paris: Fayard.

Joly, Marc. 2017. *La révolution sociologique: De la naissance d'un régime de pensée scientifique à la crise de la philosophie (XIXe–XXe siècle)*. Paris: La Découverte.

Kaiser, David. 1998. "A Mannheim for All Seasons: Bloor, Merton, and the Roots of the Sociology of Scientific Knowledge." *Science in Context* 11, no. 1: 51–87.

Karádi, Éva, and Erzsébet Vezér, eds. 1985. *Georg Lukács, Karl Mannheim und der Sonntagskreis*. Frankfurt am Main: Sendler.

Karady, Victor. 1972. "Naissance de l'ethnologie universitaire." *L'Arc* 48: 33–44.

Käsler, Dirk. 1984. *Die frühe deutsche Soziologie 1900 bis 1934 und ihre Entstehungs-Milieus: Eine wissenschaftssoziologische Untersuchung*. Opladen: Westdeutscher Verlag.

Käsler, Dirk. 2002. "From Republic of Scholars to Jamboree of Academic Sociologists: The German Sociological Society, 1909–1999." *International Sociology* 17, no. 2: 159–77.

Kauppi, Niilo. 1996. *French Intellectual Nobility: Institutional and Symbolic Transformations in the Post-Sartrian Era*. Albany: State University of New York Press.

Keller, A. C. 1950. "Zilsel, the Artisans, and the Idea of Progress in the Renaissance." *Journal of the History of Ideas* 11, no. 2: 235–40.

Kettler, David. 1971. "Culture and Revolution: Lukács in the Hungarian Revolution of 1918/19." *Telos*, no. 10: 35–92.

Klingemann, Carsten. 1996. *Soziologie im Dritten Reich*. Baden-Baden: Nomos Verlagsgesellschaft.

Klingemann, Carsten. 2000. "Zur Rezeption von Karl Mannheim im Kontext der Debatte um Soziologie und Nationalsozialismus." *Jahrbuch für Soziologiegeschichte 1996*, 213–37.

Klingemann, Carsten. 2009. *Soziologie und Politik: Sozialwissenschaftliches Expertenwissen im Dritten Reich und in der frühen westdeutschen Nachkriegszeit*. Wiesbaden: VS Verlag für Sozialwissenschaften.

Knöbl, Wolfgang. 2001. *Spielräume der Modernisierung: Das Ende der Eindeutigkeit*. Weilerswist: Velbrück.

Köhnke, Klaus Christian. 1991. *The Rise of Neo-Kantianism: German Academic Philosophy between Idealism and Positivism*. Cambridge: Cambridge University Press.

König, René, and Heinz Maus, eds. 1962. *Handbuch der empirischen Sozialforschung*. Stuttgart: F. Enke.

Kragh, Helge. 1987. *An Introduction to the Historiography of Science*. Cambridge: Cambridge University Press.

Kropp, Kristoffer. 2015. *A Historical Account of Danish Sociology: A Troubled Sociology*. London: Palgrave.

Kruse, Volker. 1998. "Historische Soziologie als 'Geschichts- und Sozialphilosophie'—zur Rezeption der Weimarer Soziologie in den fünfziger Jahren." In *Erkenntnisgewinne, Erkenntnisverluste. Kontinuitaten und Diskontinuitäten in den Wirtschafts-, Rechts- und Sozialwissenschaften zwischen den 20er und 50er Jahren*, edited by Karl Acham, 76–106. Stuttgart: F. Steiner.

Kuhn, Rick. 2009. "Henryk Grossman: A Biographical Sketch." In *The Social and Economic Roots of the Scientific Revolution: Texts by Boris Hessen and Henryk Grossmann*, edited by Gideon Freudenthal and Peter McLaughlin, 253–56. Dordrecht: Springer.

Kuhn, Thomas S. 1957. *The Copernican Revolution: Planetary Astronomy in the Development of Western Thought*. Cambridge, MA: Harvard University Press.

Kuhn, Thomas S. (1962) 1970. *The Structure of Scientific Revolutions*. 2nd ed. Chicago: University of Chicago Press.

Kuklick, Henrika. 1983. "The Sociology of Knowledge: Retrospect and Prospect." *Annual Review of Sociology* 9: 287–310.

Lamy, Jérôme, and Arnaud Saint-Martin. 2015. "La sociologie historique des sciences et techniques: Essai de généalogie conceptuelle et d'histoire configurationnelle." *Revue d'histoire des sciences* 1, no. 1: 175–214.

Latour, Bruno. 1999. *Pandora's Hope: Essays on the Reality of Science Studies*. Cambridge, MA: Harvard University Press.

Latour, Bruno. 2005. *Reassembling the Social: An Introduction to Actor-Network Theory*. Oxford: Oxford University Press.

Latour, Bruno, and Steve Woolgar. 1979. *Laboratory Life: The Social Construction of Scientific Facts*. Beverly Hills, CA: Sage.

Laudan, Larry. 1977. *Progress and Its Problems: Toward a Theory of Scientific Growth*. Berkeley: University of California Press.

Laudan, Rachel. 1993. "Histories of the Sciences and Their Uses: A Review to 1913." *History of Science* 31: 1–33.

Lei, Xianglin. 2014. *Neither Donkey nor Horse: Medicine in the Struggle over China's Modernity*. Chicago: University of Chicago Press.

Lepenies, Wolf. 1988. *Between Literature and Science: The Rise of Sociology*. Cambridge: Cambridge University Press.

Lerner, Daniel. 1959. "Social Science: Whence and Whither." In *The Human Meaning of the Social Sciences*, edited by Daniel Lerner, 13–39. New York: Meridian Books.

Lindenfeld, David F. 1997. *The Practical Imagination: The German Sciences of State in the Nineteenth Century*. Chicago: University of Chicago Press.

Ludz, Peter Christian, ed. 1972. "Soziologie und Sozialgeschichte." Special issue, *Kölner Zeitschrift für Soziologie und Sozialpsychologie* 16.

Lukács, György. 1923. *Geschichte und Klassenbewusstsein: Studien über marxistische Dialektik*. Berlin: Malik-Verlag.

Lukács, György. 1954. *Die Zerstörung der Vernunft*. Berlin: Aufbau-Verlag.

Lüschen, Günther, ed. 1979. *Deutsche Soziologie seit 1945: Entwicklungsrichtungen und Praxisbezug*. Opladen: Westdeutscher Verlag.

Mandler, Peter. 2019. "The Language of Social Science in Everyday Life." *History of the Human Sciences* 32, no. 1: 66–82.

Mannheim, Karl. 1926. "Das konservative Denken." *Archiv für Sozialwissenschaft und Sozialpolitik* 57: 68–142, 470–95.

Mannheim, Karl. (1929) 1959. *Ideology and Utopia: An Introduction to the Sociology of Knowledge*. New York: Harcourt, Brace.

Mannheim, Karl. (1935) 1951. *Man and Society in an Age of Reconstruction*. 2nd ed. New York: Harcourt, Brace.

Maquet, Jacques J. 1951. *The Sociology of Knowledge: Its Structure and Its Relation to the Philosophy of Knowledge; A Critical Analysis of the Systems of Karl Mannheim and Pitirim A. Sorokin*. Boston: Beacon.

Marx, Karl. 1975. *Collected Works*. 50 vols. New York: International Publishers.

Marx, Karl. 1976. *Capital: A Critique of Political Economy*. New York: Vintage Books.

Marx, Karl, and Friedrich Engels. 1978. *Marx-Engels Reader*. 2nd ed. Edited by Robert C. Tucker. New York: Norton.

Maurel, Chloé. 2010. "L'histoire de l'humanité de l'UNESCO (1945–2000)." *Revue d'histoire des sciences humaines* 22: 161–98.

Maus, Heinz. 1939–40. "Zur gesellschaftliche Funktion der Soziologie." *Archiv für Rechts- und Sozialphilosophie* 33: 149–86.

Maus, Heinz. 1951. "Empirische Sozialforschung." *Aufklärung* 1: 233–34.

Maus, Heinz. 1956. "Geschichte der Soziologie." In *Handbuch der Soziologie*, edited by Werner Ziegenfuss, 1–120. Stuttgart: F. Enke.

Maus, Heinz. 1962. *A Short History of Sociology*. London: Routledge and K. Paul.

McEvoy, John G. 1997. "Positivism, Whiggism, and the Chemical Revolution: A Study in the Historiography of Chemistry." *History of Science* 35: 1–33.

Meja, Volker, and Nico Stehr. 1982. *Der Streit um die Wissenssoziologie*. Vol. 1. Frankfurt am Main: Suhrkamp.

Merton, Robert K. 1935. "Science and Military Technique." *Scientific Monthly* 41, no. 6: 524–45.

Merton, Robert K. 1937. "The Sociology of Knowledge." *Isis* 27, no. 3: 493–503.

Merton, Robert K. 1938. "Science, Technology and Society in Seventeenth Century England." *Osiris* 4: 360–632.

Merton, Robert K. 1949a. "Karl Mannheim and the Sociology of Knowledge." In *Social Theory and Social Structure*, edited by Robert K. Merton, 247–64. Glencoe, IL: Free Press.

Merton, Robert K. 1949b. "The Sociology of Knowledge." In *Social Theory and Social Structure*, edited by Robert K. Merton, 456–88. Glencoe, IL: Free Press.

Merton, Robert K. 1952. "Foreword." In *Science and the Social Order*, edited by Bernard Barber, 7–20. Glencoe, IL: Free Press.

Merton, Robert K. 1959. "Social Conflict over Styles of Sociological Work." In *Transactions of the 4th World Congress of Sociology*, 21–46. Also in Merton (1970) 1973, 47–69.

Merton, Robert K. (1970) 1973. "Social and Cultural Contexts of Science." In *The Sociology of Science: Theoretical and Empirical Investigations*, edited by Robert K. Merton, 173–90. Chicago: University of Chicago Press.

Merton, Robert K. 1977. "The Sociology of Science: An Episodic Memoir." In *The Sociology of Science in Europe*, edited by Robert K. Merton and J. Gaston, 3–144. Carbondale: Southern Illinois University Press.

Merton, Robert K., and Daniel Lerner. 1951. "Social Scientists and Research Policy." In *The Policy Sciences: Recent Developments in Scope and Method*, edited by Daniel Lerner and H. D. Lasswell, 282–307. Stanford, CA: Stanford University Press.

Mills, C. Wright. 1958. *The Causes of World War III*. New York: Ballantine Books.

Mills, C. Wright. 1959. *The Sociological Imagination*. New York: Oxford University Press.

Moebius, Stephan. 2006. *Die Zauberlehrlinge: Soziologiegeschichte des Collège de Sociologie (1937–1939)*. Konstanz: UVK Verlagsgesellschaft.

Moebius, Stephan, and Andrea Ploder, eds. 2017–19. *Handbuch Geschichte der deutschsprachigen Soziologie*. 3 vols. Wiesbaden: Springer VS.

Moore, F. J. 1918. *A History of Chemistry*. New York: McGraw-Hill.

Moreno Pestaña, Jose Luis. 2006. *En devenant Foucault: Sociogenèse d'un grand philosophe*. Bellecombe-en-Bauges: Éditions du Croquant.

Mulkay, M. J. 1979. *Science and the Sociology of Knowledge*. London: G. Allen and Unwin.

Nichols, Lawrence T. 2010. "Merton as Harvard Sociologist: Engagement, Thematic Continuities, and Institutional Linkages." *Journal of the History of the Behavioral Sciences* 46, no. 1: 72–95.

Nietzsche, Friedrich. 1874. *Vom Nutzen und Nachtheil der Historie für das Leben: Unzeitgemässe Betrachtungen* [part 2]. Leipzig: Fritzsch.

Noble, David F. 2011. *Forces of Production: A Social History of Industrial Automation*. 2nd ed. New Brunswick, NJ: Transaction.

Northrop, F. S. C. 1951. "Preface." In Jacques J. Maquet, *The Sociology of Knowledge: Its Structure and Its Relation to the Philosophy of Knowledge. A Critical Analysis of the Systems of Karl Mannheim and Pitirim A. Sorokin*, xi–xix. Boston: Beacon.

Oakes, Guy. 1987. "Weber and the Southwest German School: The Genesis of the Concept of the Historical Individual." In *Max Weber and His Contemporaries*, edited by Theodor Mommsen and Jürgen Osterhammel, 434–46. London: Unwin Hyman.

Paltrinieri, Luca. 2016. "Philosophie, psychologie, histoire dans les années 1950: Maladie mentale et personnalité comme analyseur." In *L'angle mort des années 1950: Philosophie et sciences humaines en France*, edited by Giuseppe Bianco and Frédéric Fruteau de Laclos. Paris: Publications de la Sorbonne.

Payne, Christine A. 2019. "The Question of Ideology in Light of Perspectival Knowledge: The Truths of Marx and Nietzsche." *Critical Sociology* 45, no. 2: 199–212.

Pels, Dick. 2014. "After Objectivity: An Historical Approach to the Intersubjective in Ethnography." *Hau: Journal of Ethnographic Theory* 4, no. 1: 211–36.

Pérez, Amín. 2015. "Rendre le social plus politique: Guerre coloniale, immigration et pratiques sociologiques d'Abdelmalek Sayad et de Pierre Bourdieu." PhD diss., EHESS.

Pérez, Amín. 2022. *Combattre en sociologues: Pierre Bourdieu et Abdelmalek Sayad dans une guerre de libération (Algérie, 1958-1964)*. Paris: Agone.

Pestre, Dominique. 1995. "Pour une histoire sociale et culturelle des sciences: Nouvelles définitions, nouveaux objets, nouvelles pratiques." *Annales: Histoire, Sciences Sociales* 50, no. 3: 487–522.

Pestre, Dominique. 2004. "Thirty Years of Science Studies: Knowledge, Society and the Political." *History and Technology* 20, no. 4: 351–69.

Peter, Lothar. 1991. *Dogma oder Wissenschaft? Marxistisch-leninistische Soziologie und staatssozialistisches System in der DDR*. Frankfurt am Main: IMSF.

Peter, Lothar. 2001. "Warum und wie betreibt man Soziologiegeschichte?" *Jahrbuch für Soziologiegeschichte 1997/1998*: 9–64.

Pickering, Mary. 2009. *Auguste Comte: An Intellectual Biography*. Vol. 2. Cambridge: Cambridge University Press.

Pinto, Louis. 2009. *La théorie souveraine: Les philosophes français et la sociologie au XXe siècle*. Paris: Éditions du Cerf.

Pollak, Michael. 1978. *Gesellschaft und Soziologie in Frankreich: Tradition und Wandel in der neueren französische Soziologie*. Königstein: Hain.

Pollak, Michael. 1979. "Paul F. Lazarsfeld, fondateur d'une multinationale scientifique." *Actes de la recherche en sciences sociales* 25, no. 1: 45–59.

Porter, Theodore M. 1986. *The Rise of Statistical Thinking, 1820-1900*. Princeton, NJ: Princeton University Press.

Priestley, Joseph. 1775. *The History and Present State of Electricity, with Original Experiments*. London: C. Bathurst.

Raphael, Lutz. 1994. *Die Erben von Bloch und Febvre: Annales-Geschichtsschreibung und nouvelle histoire in Frankreich 1945-1980*. Stuttgart: Klett-Cotta.

Raphael, Lutz. 2012. "Embedding the Human and Social Sciences in Western Societies, 1880–1980: Reflections on Trends and Methods of Current Research." In *Engineering Society: The Role of the Human and Social Sciences in Modern Societies, 1880–1980*, edited by Kerstin Brückweh, 41–56. New York: Palgrave Macmillan.

Restivo, Sal, and Rachel Dowty. 2008. "Obituary: Bernard Barber and Mary Douglas." *Social Studies of Science* 38, no. 4: 635–40.

Ricoeur, Paul. 2004. *Memory, History, Forgetting*. Chicago: University of Chicago Press.

Ringer, Fritz K. 2004. *Max Weber: An Intellectual Biography*. Chicago: University of Chicago Press.

Robin, Ron. 2001. *The Making of the Cold War Enemy: Culture and Politics in the Military-Intellectual Complex*. Princeton, NJ: Princeton University Press.

Rohracher, Harald. 2015. "Science and Technology Studies, History of." *International Encyclopedia of the Social and Behavioral Sciences*, 2nd ed., 21: 200–205. Oxford: Elsevier.

Roscher, Wilhelm. 1874. *Geschichte der National-Oekonomik in Deutschland*. Munich: R. Oldenbourg.

Rueschemeyer, Dietrich. 1958. "Probleme der Wissenssoziologie: Eine Kritik der Arbeiten Karl Mannheims und Max Schelers und eine Erweiterung der wissenssoziologischen Fragestellung, durchgeführt am Beispiel der Kleingruppenforschung." PhD diss., University of Cologne.

Salin, Edgar. 1948. *Um Stefan George*. Godesberg: H. Küpper.

Savérien, M. 1766. *Histoire des progrès de l'esprit humain dans les sciences exactes, et dans les arts qui en dependent*. Paris: Lacombe.

Schauer, Alexandra. 2017. "Soziologie in Deutschland zur Zeit des Nationalsozialismus." In *Handbuch Geschichte der deutschsprachigen Soziologie*, vol. 1, edited by Stephan Moebius and Andrea Ploder, 117–48. Wiesbaden: Springer VS.

Scheler, Max. (1912) 1972. *Ressentiment*. New York: Schocken.

Scheler, Max. 1925. "Wissenschaft und soziale Struktur." In *Verhandlungen des vierten Deutschen Soziologentages am 29. u. 30. Sept. 1924 in Heidelberg*, 118–80. Tübingen: Mohr.

Scheler, Max. 1926. *Die Wissensformen und die Gesellschaft*. Leipzig: Der Neue-Geist Verlag.

Schumaker, Lyn. 2001. *Africanizing Anthropology: Fieldwork, Networks, and the Making of Cultural Knowledge in Central Africa*. Durham, NC: Duke University Press.

Shapin, Steven. 1995. "Here and Everywhere: Sociology of Scientific Knowledge." *Annual Review of Sociology* 21: 289–321.

Shryock, Richard Harrison. 1956. "The History and Sociology of Science." *Items* (Social Science Research Council) 10, no. 2: 13–16.

Sica, Alan. 2010. "Merton, Mannheim, and the Sociology of Knowledge." In *Robert K. Merton: Sociology of Science and Sociology as Science*, edited by Craig Calhoun, 164–81. New York: Columbia University Press.

Singaravélou, Pierre. 2011. *Professer l'Empire: Les sciences coloniales en France sous la IIIe République*. Paris: Publications de la Sorbonne.

Singh, Sourabh. 2019. "Science, Common Sense and Sociological Analysis: A Critical Appreciation of the Epistemological Foundation of Field Theory." *Philosophy of the Social Sciences* 49, no. 2: 87–107.

Sivin, N. 1982. "Why the Scientific Revolution Did Not Take Place in China—or Didn't It?" *Chinese Science* 5 (June): 45–66.

Skinner, Quentin. 1969. "Meaning and Understanding in the History of Ideas." *History and Theory* 8, no. 1: 3–53.

Solovey, Mark. 2020. *Social Science for What? Battles over Public Funding for the "Other Sciences" at the National Science Foundation*. Cambridge, MA: MIT Press.

Sorokin, Pitirim Aleksandrovich. 1937–41. *Social and Cultural Dynamics*. 4 vols. New York: American Book Company.

Speier, Hans. 1938. "The Social Determination of Ideas." *Social Research* 2: 182–205.

Stanley, Thomas. 1656. *The History of Philosophy*. Vol. 1. London: Printed for Humphrey Moseley and Thomas Dring.

Stehr, Nico, and Volker Meja, eds. 2005. *Society and Knowledge: Contemporary Perspectives in the Sociology of Knowledge and Science*. New Brunswick, NJ: Transaction.

Steinmetz, George. 1997. "German Exceptionalism and the Origins of Nazism: The Career of a Concept." In *Stalinism and Nazism: Dictatorships in Comparison*, edited by Ian Kershaw and Moshe Lewin, 251–84. Cambridge: Cambridge University Press.

Steinmetz, George. 1998. "Critical Realism and Historical Sociology." *Comparative Studies in Society and History* 40, no. 1: 170–86.

Steinmetz, George. 2004. "The Uncontrollable Afterlives of Ethnography: Lessons from German 'Salvage Colonialism' for a New Age of Empire." *Ethnography* 5, no. 3: 251–88.

Steinmetz, George. 2005. "Positivism and Its Others in the Social Sciences." In *The Politics of Method in the Human Sciences: Positivism and Its Epistemological Others*, edited by George Steinmetz, 1–56. Durham, NC: Duke University Press.

Steinmetz, George. 2007. *The Devil's Handwriting: Precoloniality and the German Colonial State in Qingdao, Samoa, and Southwest Africa*. Chicago: University of Chicago Press.

Steinmetz, George. 2010. "Ideas in Exile: Refugees from Nazi Germany and the Failure to Transplant Historical Sociology into the United States." *International Journal of Politics, Culture, and Society* 23, no. 1: 1–27.

Steinmetz, George. 2011. "Bourdieu, Historicity, and Historical Sociology." *Cultural Sociology* 5, no. 1: 45–66.

Steinmetz, George. 2017a. "Field Theory and Interdisciplinary: Relations between History and Sociology in Germany and France during the Twentieth Century." *Comparative Studies in Society and History* 59, no. 2: 477–514.

Steinmetz, George. 2017b. "Field Theory in Bourdieusian Sociology." Invited paper, plenary session on field theory, American Sociological Association, Montréal, August 17.

Steinmetz, George. 2017c. "Sociology and Colonialism in the British and French Empires, 1940s-1960s." *Journal of Modern History* 89, no. 3: 601-48.

Steinmetz, George. 2018. "Scientific Autonomy, Academic Freedom, and Social Research in the United States." *Critical Historical Studies* (Fall): 281-309.

Steinmetz, George. 2020. "Soziologie und Kolonialismus: Die Beziehung zwischen Wissen und Politik." *Mittelweg 36* 29, no. 3 (June-July): 17-36.

Steinmetz, George. 2021. "Komparative Soziologie, kritischer Realismus und Reflexivität." Special issue, *Kölner Zeitschrift für Soziologie und Sozialpsychologie.*

Steinmetz, George. 2023. *The Colonial Origins of Modern Social Thought: French Sociology and the Overseas Empire.* Princeton, NJ: Princeton University Press.

Steinmetz, George, and Ou-Byung Chae. 2002. "Sociology in an Era of Fragmentation: Alvin Gouldner's *Coming Crisis of Western Sociology* after 30 Years." *Sociological Quarterly* 43, no. 1: 111-37.

Stintzing, Roderich von. 1880-1910. *Geschichte der deutschen Rechtswissenschaft.* 3 vols. Munich: R. Oldenbourg.

Stocking, G. W., Jr. 1965. "On the Limits of 'Presentism' and 'Historicism' in the Historiography of the Behavioral Sciences." *Journal of the History of the Behavioral Sciences* 1: 211-18.

Stocking, George W., Jr. 1968. *Race, Culture, and Evolution: Essays in the History of Anthropology.* New York: Free Press.

Stoler, Ann Laura. 2011. "Colonial Aphasia: Race and Disabled Histories in France." *Public Culture* 23, no. 1: 121-56.

Struik, D. J. 1942. "On the Sociology of Mathematics." *Science and Society* 6, no. 1: 58-70.

Tenbruck, Friedrich H. 1979. "Deutsche Soziologie im internationalen Kontext: Ihre Ideengeschichte und ihr Gesellschaftsbezug." In "Deutsche Soziologie seit 1945: Entwicklungsrichtungen und Praxisbezug," edited by Gunther Luschen. Special issue, *Kölner Zeitschrift für Soziologie und Sozialpsychologie* 21: 71-107.

Tenbruck, Friedrich H. 1992. "Was war der Kulturvergleich, ehe es den Kulturvergleich gab?" In *Zwischen den Kulturen? Die Sozialwissenschaften vor dem Problem des Kulturvergleichs,* edited by Joachim Matthes, 13-36. Göttingen: O. Schwartz.

Tennemann, Wilhelm Gottlieb. (1816) 1832. *A Manual of the History of Philosophy.* Oxford: D. A. Talboys.

Therborn, Göran. 1976. *Science, Class and Society: On the Formation of Sociology and Historical Materialism.* London: NLB.

Tiedemann, Dietrich. 1794. *Geist der spekulativen Philosophie.* 6 vols. Marburg: Neuen Akademischen Buchhandlung.

Tilley, Helen. 2011. *Africa as a Living Laboratory: Empire, Development, and the Problem of Scientific Knowledge, 1870-1950.* Chicago: University of Chicago Press.

Trenn, Thaddeus J. 1979. "Preface." In *Genesis and Development of a Scientific Fact,* edited by Ludwik Fleck, viii-xix. Chicago: University of Chicago Press.

von Schelting, Alexander. 1936. Review of *Ideologie und Utopie* by Karl Mannheim. *American Sociological Review* 1, no. 4: 664-74.

Wagner, Peter. 1990. *Sozialwissenschaften und Staat: Frankreich, Italien, Deutschland 1870-1980*. New York: Campus Verlag.

Wagner, Peter. 2001. *A History and Theory of the Social Sciences: Not All That Is Solid Melts into Air*. London: Sage.

Wagner, Peter, Carol H. Weiss, Björn Wittrock, and Hellmut Wellmann. 1991. "Social Science and the Modern State." In *Social Sciences and Modern States: National Experiences and Theoretical Crossroads*, edited by Peter Wagner, Carol H. Weiss, Björn Wittrock, and Hellmut Wellmann, 28-85. Cambridge: Cambridge University Press.

Wagner, Peter, and Björn Wittrock. 1991. "States, Institutions, and Discourses: A Comparative Perspective on the Structuration of the Social Sciences." In *Discourses on Society: The Shaping of the Social Science Disciplines*, edited by Peter B. Wagner, Björn Wittrock, and Richard Whitley, 331-58. Dordrecht: Kluwer Academic.

Weinrich, Harald. 2004. *Lethe: The Art and Critique of Forgetting*. Ithaca, NY: Cornell University Press.

Weiß, Johannes. 1995. "Negative Soziologie." *Ethik und Sozialwissenschaften* 6: 241-46.

Weyer, Johannes. 1986. "Soziologie—ein Phantomfach? Einige Konsequenzen der 1945 erfolgten Weichenstellungen für die Identität der heutigen Soziologie." In *Soziologiegeschichte: Identität und Krisen einer "engagierten" Disziplin*, edited by Josef Hülsdünker and Rolf Schellhase, 87-103. Berlin: Duncker and Humblot.

Whatmore, Richard. 2016. "Quentin Skinner and the Relevance of Intellectual History." In *A Companion to Intellectual History*, edited by Richard Whatmore and Brian Young, 97-112. Chichester, UK: John Wiley and Sons.

Whitehead, Alfred North. 1917. *The Organisation of Thought, Educational and Scientific*. London: Williams and Norgate.

Wilson, Edward O. 1998. *Consilience: The Unity of Knowledge*. New York: Knopf.

Wittrock, Björn, Johan Heilbron, and Lars Magnusson. 1998. "The Rise of the Social Sciences and the Formation of Modernity." In *The Rise of the Social Sciences and the Formation of Modernity*, edited by Johann Heilbron, Lars Magnusson, and Bjorn Wittrock, 1-35. Dordrecht: Kluwer.

Woolgar, Steve. 1991. "The Turn to Technology in Social Studies of Science." *Science, Technology and Human Values* 16: 20-50.

Woolgar, Steve, and M. Ashmore. 1988. "The Next Step: An Introduction to the Reflexive Project." In *Knowledge and Reflexivity*, edited by Steve Woolgar, 1-13. London: Sage.

Yeo, Richard. 1991. "Reading Encyclopedias: Science and the Organization of Knowledge in British Dictionaries of Arts and Sciences, 1730-1850." *Isis* 82: 24-49.

Yeo, Richard. 1993. *Defining Science: William Whewell, Natural Knowledge, and Public Debate in Early Victorian Britain*. Cambridge: Cambridge University Press.

Zhmud, Leonid. 2006. *The Origin of the History of Science in Classical Antiquity*. Berlin: Walter de Gruyter.

Zilsel, Edgar. 1942. "The Sociological Roots of Science." *American Journal of Sociology* 47, no. 4: 544–62.

Znaniecki, Florian. 1940. *The Social Role of the Man of Knowledge*. New York: Columbia University Press.

Zuboff, Shoshana. 2019. *The Age of Surveillance Capitalism: The Fight for a Human Future at the New Frontier of Power*. New York: PublicAffairs.

spaces of real possibilities

Counterfactuals &
the Impact of Donors
on the Social Sciences

ÁLVARO MORCILLO LAIZ

IN *AN INVITATION TO REFLEXIVE SOCIOLOGY*, Pierre Bourdieu noted that "the more brutal form of censorship" is to distort "competition by preventing people who want to enter into the game from doing so—by turning down meritorious applications for fellowships" (1992, 190). My goal in this chapter is to bring some light on how the denial of support and its opposite, the awarding of grants and fellowships, gradually, but inexorably alter the history of social sciences. More specifically, and more modestly, I explore two typical and crucial questions encountered by scholars interested in the effects of grant making: whether donors' policies alter the research agendas of prospective recipients and what would have happened to a research program, department, or research center if a certain grant had not been awarded. To shed some light on these questions, I resort to counterfactuals, which are essential to establishing *causality* and, in addition, a useful tool to make explicit actual *possibilities* that are not realized.

Whether donors brutally or gently impose their agendas on recipients is obviously relevant for the sociology and history of science, but it also resembles other questions important for sociologists and political scientists.

From the perspectives of the sociology and history of science, the questions this chapter examines connect to a number of important debates, such as whether factors internal or external to the scientific enterprise drive its progress (Shapin 1992). The externalist perspective was epitomized in David Bloor's "Strong Program," which aspired to illuminate how social life shapes our idea of truth. Historians and sociologists of science from this persuasion are interested in the problem of science funding. Conversely, internalists emphasize logic and methods as the drivers of a Popperian scientific enterprise. Robert Merton's sociology of science as a "sociology of scientists" (1973), broadly isolated from social and political influence, nicely complements Popper's views. Without aspiring to settle this issue, the arguments advanced here should be understood within this debate and its implications for the history of social sciences. These questions are most obviously relevant for sociology and political science if we consider the local adoption of donors' policies as an instance of "norm diffusion" (Dobbin, Simmons, and Garrett 2007; Finnemore 1996). Donors' clout is a common topos in the literature on development (Ketola 2016; Krause 2014), but scholars are only beginning to understand donors' centrality in the worldwide spread of human rights activism since the 1970s (Wong, Levi, and Deutsch 2017). Inasmuch as the question of adoption is dependent not only on the resources granted by the donor but also on its expertise, the questions raised here impinge on the problem of the international expertise (Sending 2015).

Questions about the impact of awards can be explored by using counterfactuals. These are *modus ponens* logical arguments, if A, then B, but with the peculiarity that A, the antecedent, never occurred. Counterfactuals are, therefore, thought experiments that are used to ask questions about what the consequences of an imagined, but not necessarily unlikely event would have been. Even if social scientists pay scarce attention to counterfactuals, they are routinely, often implicitly, used in many logical operations, most prominently in identifying the causes of events (Weber [1906] 2012). Counterfactuals are also necessary to study unique or rare events, like revolutions, for which it is difficult or even impossible to find an ideal term of comparison, that is, one in which all relevant traits except the one we want to study remain constant (Fearon 1991; Kiser and Levi 1996). Beyond its use as a methodological tool, counterfactuals can also be further exploited to explore *possibilities* that were not realized. Such explorations draw the attention of social researchers toward the importance of contingency. Here I will use counterfactuals in both ways.

Taking the relation between the Rockefeller Foundation (RF) and a recipient, El Colegio de México, as a case study, this chapter asks whether the support of the RF accounts for the Colegio's incursion into the social sciences in 1960 and its emphasis on international relations (IR), understood mainly as area studies. The chapter further asks whether in Mexico RF support explains the separation of IR from the rest of political science, of which IR is usually understood to be a subfield.

Between the 1940s and the 1960s, the relation between the RF and the Colegio linked actors who played distinct parts in the global history of the social sciences. Since the 1920s, the RF was involved in any major development in US sociology, political science, and economics, a topic to which I return later. Having been a crucial actor for decades makes the RF particularly relevant to the study of the impact of funding. It was only during the years analyzed here, the late 1950s, that the RF lost its position as the world's most influential private donor in the social sciences to the Ford Foundation (Latham 2000; Berman 1983).

As for the Colegio, it is an academic organization that readers unfamiliar with Latin American social sciences will not know, but its past is significant not only for Mexico but also for Latin America as a whole. The Colegio was arguably the first research center in the region where the norm was that faculty and students worked full time on their academic duties. A further peculiarity of the Colegio was that it was conceived originally, and as a result of earlier RF support it succeeded, as an academic organization to train students not only from Mexico but also from other parts of Latin America.

The chapter first discusses the basics of science patronage and of philanthropic foundations. Then it explains in some detail what counterfactuals are and how they have been used in the past. After presenting in the third section the organizations and individuals relevant for the study of IR in Mexico around 1960, the fourth section uses counterfactuals to shed light on the possibilities implicit in the negotiations that preceded an RF decision to grant an award to the Colegio.

Science Patronage and Philanthropic Foundations

Patronage is almost inseparable from social science. The reason is that, in general, academic sociology, political sciences, and even economics are incapable of financing themselves through the market. Admittedly, students' fees provide some social science disciplines with a more or less regular source of income, but this pays mainly for teaching-related operations and is insufficient for ambitious research (Turner and Turner 1990; Turner 2014). To finance salaries, library collections, research trips, surveys, databases, and all other means necessary to conduct research, scholarship is dependent on patrons, who expect rewards in the form of prestige and potential uses of knowledge and inventions. In principle, scholarship could be financed through awards granted to conduct research, a form of patronage widespread until the nineteenth century, but awards like the Nobel Prize are nowadays a form of recognition rather than a way to finance sustained research efforts. In view of the needs intrinsic to modern inquiry, and the scarcity of donors, it becomes more than plausible that philanthropic foundations can have determinant leeway in a field where research funding satisfies a fraction of the needs.

Rather than focusing on the state, I look at philanthropic foundations, the actor that can be assumed to be the major science patron everywhere at any time (Ezrahi 2001). When the state wages a war, including a "cold" one, this bears on science (Solovey 2013; Rohde 2013), as well as *contemporary* social science (see, for instance, McFate and Laurence 2015). However, a number of reasons account for my stressing philanthropic foundations, whose past influence has arguably been overproportional to the share of funding they have contributed (Geiger 2018, 94–110). One reason is that philanthropic foundations pioneered some of the forms of patronage, including transnational science patronage, which were subsequently practiced by states (Ninkovich 2010). This is the case for IR (Guilhot 2011a; Berman 1983, chap. 4) and for the social sciences as a whole (Fisher 1993). A second reason to focus on philanthropic foundations is that their patronage is more selective than that granted by the state; one of the origins of the clout of philanthropic foundations is that they grant the requests of *some* academic organizations and scholars while denying support to others. In short, philanthropic foundations are much smaller patrons of the social sciences than the state, but their influence has been significant because of their innovative and selective character.

Since philanthropic foundations are at the center of the case analyzed here, it is necessary to provide readers with basic information on what they are, how they operate, and their link to science. To be more precise, this chapter is concerned with a special type of foundation, *the US general-purpose foundation*, which did not exist until the early twentieth century (Andrews 1963). Only during the Progressive Era were such large fortunes amassed that it became necessary to create a new, more complex, versatile, and long-lasting vehicle for the amounts that donors assigned to philanthropy (Zunz 2014). Just like the size of the philanthropists' fortunes, it was also exceptional that by the second decade of the twentieth century, large donors managed for the first time to overcome the reservations that Anglo-Saxon law cherished against immobilizing large numbers of assets for no specific purpose (Karl and Katz 1981, 245). In the past, various motives had led donors like Andrew Carnegie and John D. Rockefeller to give. For this chapter, their importance is limited because in their lifetimes donors like Carnegie and Rockefeller were allowed for the first time to define the purview of the activities of their respective general-purpose foundations in such broad terms as to make irrelevant the philanthropists' original reasons for the giving. Actually, this indifference was legally sanctioned: the act that incorporated the Rockefeller Foundation in 1917 set as its goal no less than "to promote the well-being of mankind throughout the world." Since the goal of the general-purpose foundation was usually stated in such general terms, its administrators obtained a free hand to define policies.

In very broad strokes, these were the peculiarities of the general-purpose, philanthropic foundations, but what are they and what do they do? What US general-purpose foundations have in common is that they are endowed organizations that, without needing to either sell services or goods (as a commercial enterprise would) or to extract levies (as states do), are capable of financing both their own administrative costs and grant-making activities. According to US law, the RF and similar organizations are private foundations: charities of this type are compelled to distribute yearly a share of their income to help accomplish public purposes. At the helm of a foundation are a president and a board of trustees, who, according to their respective charters, are entitled to establish the purposes for which the interest, and even the capital, could be spent (Andrews 1963, chap. 3). This autonomy, combined with the power resulting from their large endowments and the self-reproducing character of the boards—trustees freely choose who replaces those who die or retire—has attracted criticism (Fleishman 2009). Censure was not news to the general-purpose foundations, which were disliked and feared since their beginnings and for the following fifty years the object of several inquiries by the US Congress (Karl and Karl 2001; Zunz 2014, chap. 6). In short, philanthropic foundations are vehicles for charitable purposes, defined almost without restrictions by a self-reproducing board.

The answer to the question of *how* foundations operate is that their founders "made" them after their business corporations. Rockefeller and Carnegie amassed their fortunes by building large, highly rationalized, and highly profitable corporations. The lessons that this experience provided them became an intrinsic part of the practices according to which philanthropies operated (Jordan 1994). Among those practices were the accumulation and processing of information, the use of secrecy, the control of timing in their relations to potential grantees, and the "advice" given to them, long before a submission.

As they monitored potential and actual grantees, officers executed these practices with virtuosism and according to handbooks in which senior officers tried to codify their *metis*; these (mostly) men were highly qualified professionals with PhDs and above-average salaries, but until the 1990s foundations did not trim their relatively high overhead costs, which they saw as the price to pay for contributing to change, in our case in the social sciences (Freund 1996; Morcillo Laiz 2022).

Arguably, one main reason why foundations turned out to be so successful, particularly in their public *health* campaigns (Brown 1979; Cueto 1994), was that the newest methods of rational administration, which the tycoons-turned-donors had previously tested in their companies, were combined with the financial autonomy derived from a sizable endowment. Furthermore, the most rational form of knowledge, science, gained very early a place of pride in foundation programs; in the case of the RF, science became the center of its philanthropic activities for several decades. Foundations seem to have an elective affinity for science and an even stronger one for medical science (see Morcillo Laiz 2020). These donors, exposed as they are to a critical scrutiny that could jeopardize their sweet deal with the American fiscus, feel at ease working on relatively uncontroversial issues in which the claim that "foundations do good deeds" enjoy credibility. There are only a few such issues (i.e., humanitarian aid, education, science, and health). Arguably, such an elective affinity goes a long way toward explaining the RF's decades of involvement in what we call today global health—a field the RF shaped more than any other during the decades in which it was among the largest foundations worldwide. Today's largest philanthropy, the Bill and Melinda Gates Foundation, spends more on health than on any other policy. Here the affinity between philanthropy, health, and science comes to its zenith in Seattle's Institute for Health Metrics and Evaluation. Funded by the Gates Foundation, this Institute reflects the aforementioned philanthropies and rational domination utmost expression in quantitative indicators (Birn 2014; Youde 2013). Science patronage was not among the foundations' initials goals, but it nonetheless preceded that by the US government by decades. The act that incorporated the RF did mention "research" among its means, but it was only a 1928 reform that placed "the advancement of knowledge" at the core of its aid program (Rockefeller Foundation 1929, 3, 27, 175, 213). A few years earlier, the Carnegie Corporation, at that time the largest endowment, had set in its charter its goal "to promote the advancement and diffusion of knowledge and understanding among the people of the United States" (Carnegie Corporation of New York 1911). As they ventured into *science* patronage, foundations turned out to be particularly effective and transformative whenever they managed to identify cutting-edge projects whose impact eventually diffused well beyond specialisms; a comparable effectiveness characterized their attempts to redraw disciplinary boundaries (Kohler 1991; Fisher 1993). Failures also abound, though, such as the RF's University Development Program in the 1960s (see, generally, Fleishman 2009, chap. 12). As the involvement of the US state in funding all disciplines began to grow in the 1950s, the involvement of foundations diminished, but they remained a significant source of support, particularly in medical research (Callahan 2018, 244–56).

The RF became involved in the *social* sciences comparatively late. The origin of such concern was social work, a topic close to the beginnings of philanthropy as a rationally organized, incorporated form of charity. In reality, it was not the RF but another Rockefeller philanthropy, the Laura Spelman Rockefeller Memorial, that specialized in social issues and awarded the first grants and fellowships to social scientists in the 1920s (Bulmer and Bulmer 1981). Once the memorial was dissolved, the RF added a new Division of Social Sciences (DSS), whose first three directors were economists. For decades, they funded organizations like the Brookings Institution and the National Bureau of Economic Research or research on "social problems," such as Simon Kuznets's measurement of national income, social security, and population as well as sampling for public opinion research and race relations.

The consequences of the RF's involvement in the social sciences are at the center of a hitherto unresolved debate on the importance of foundations for the history of sociology and its methods. After researchers obtained access to the plentiful records of the Rockefeller philanthropies in the late 1970s, a debate pitted Marxist authors like Robert Arnove (1980) and Donald Fisher (1984) against two scholars closer to the establishment, Martin Bulmer (1984) and later Jennifer Platt (1998; for a summary of the polemic, see Ahmad 1991). Simply put, the first group of authors held that philanthropies like the RF thwarted the critical potentialities of social science, boosted quantitative sociology, and preempted other possible developments within the discipline, thanks to their policy of selective and, in the case of some recipients, massive and continuous grant making (Fisher 1983, 1993). By contrast, Bulmer and Platt argued that foundations simply financed new lines of inquiry favored by scholars as well as the new methods that they practiced, including those contributing to the quantification of the discipline. This and other internal preferences of scholars, not those of the foundations, transformed social sciences during the interwar and early postwar years (Platt 1998; Bulmer and Bulmer 1981). Platt's argument encountered skepticism (Turner 1998). Despite the simplifications of my account, it should be enough to make plausible that we can advance to the debate about whether philanthropic foundations changed sociology and its methods by using counterfactuals.

Methodology: Counterfactuals, Process Tracing

As a matter of fact, Platt's contribution to the debate is based on a counterfactual: she argues that even if the foundation money had been absent, the history of sociological research methods would remain unchanged (but foundations offered money, and scholars, including pioneer methodologists, took it). This has prompted one of Platt's reviewers to warn us that when studying science, the problems characteristic of counterfactuals come up "in a particularly difficult form" (Turner 1999, 214). Such a warning makes clear why it is convenient to offer here sound definitions of counterfactuals and some notes about their current status in the social sciences.

As mentioned in the introduction, counterfactuals possess the simple and definite structure of *modus ponens* logical arguments, if A, then B, but with the peculiarity that A, the antecedent, never occurred. Arguments like this have been called *restrained counterfactuals*. Scholars use them when they depart from an *actual* event to define the range of possibilities that could also have come to happen, and use counterfactuals to explain the event that actually occurred (Megill 2007, 151, 153). To put it differently, a restrained counterfactual is a thought experiment in which the author mentally suppresses a real antecedent to imagine whether this or other events would have occurred in the absence of the antecedent. This exercise yields valuable information about the actual event.

Restrained counterfactuals are the type of counterfactuals on which Max Weber dwells in his essay on "Critical studies in the logic of the cultural sciences" and more specifically in the essay's section on "objective possibility and adequate causality" ([1906] 2012, 169–84). According to Weber, scholars routinely and implicitly use counterfactuals to identify sufficient and necessary causes, but in controversial cases Weber recommends making their counterfactual arguments explicit. The obvious reason these thought experiments are essential is that social scientists almost never have the opportunity to compare two events that are identical but for one characteristic (Kiser and Levi 1996). The rarer the occurrences of an event are, the more important it is to entertain these thought experiments. The limited availability of cases makes it necessary to ponder, for instance, what would have been different in the history of the French Revolution if there had been no assembly of the estates. However, before introducing imaginary antecedents like this, certain rules should be followed, the most important of which is *cotenability* (Fearon 1991, 193; Goodman 1983, 15). Cotenability comes close to Weber's idea of objective possibility—one that according to logic could have happened; it means that the imagined antecedent of a counterfactual must be compatible—or at least as much compatible as possible—with all else we know about the actual case at the branching point where the imagined world separates from the actual one.

Counterfactuals of a different kind—*exuberant* ones (Megill 2007, 151, 153)—have been used to think and write about society since antiquity, as when Livy wondered, *What if* Cleopatra's nose had been smaller?[1] A few early modern and nineteenth-century examples also exist, dealing with possible worlds such as in Charles Gibbon's musing about a Muslim victory at Tours in AD 732, which would have led to an Oxford University in which the Koran is taught (Evans 2014, 2–9; Gibbon [1776–88] 1910, 5, 399). Counterfactual writing permits the description of an imagined world and has often been used to this goal. Authors have fancied worlds without World War I, without Lenin's early death, without Hitler, or without whatever else they disliked. This is why counterfactual writing in an extreme form is called, among other things, *alternative history* and has frequently been a strategy for conservative *political* writing, outright wishful thinking, or even Holocaust denial (Evans 2014, 32–33, 83, 86, 124). Such a partisan use of counterfactuals is one reason that the disciplines with positivist mainstreams have long questioned whether counterfactuals are appropriate tools for scholarship, as suggested by the title of a book on the subject, *Forbidden Fruit* (Lebow 2010).

In fact, during the twentieth century, the mistrust toward counterfactuals in political science and sociology has been so widespread that the significant engagements with counterfactuals can be broadly, and quickly, summarized as follows: Weber's treatment of the subject was ignored for decades. His positive appraisal of counterfactuals could have granted them some currency, particularly because postwar US social science relied on Weber so heavily to argue certain methodological points of view (some of which were not Weberian at all; Factor and Turner 1984, chap. 8). Regarding counterfactuals, Weber's merits and shortcomings were recognized only many decades later by two political scientists influential in methodological questions (Elster 1978; Fearon 1991); soon thereafter counterfactuals were also discussed in an influential book on methods by a trio of Harvard professors (King, Keohane, and Verba 1994). As the Cold War was coming to an end, sociologists and political scientists caught up with philosophers, who had studied the logic of counterfactuals since the early postwar years (Goodman 1983). In economics, a career based on counterfactuals such as Robert Fogel's could culminate in a Nobel Prize (Evans 2014, 26–27).

By the mid-1990s, the genre experienced a renaissance into enhanced scholarly dignity and productivity throughout the social sciences. Among historical works, the most famous example is possibly a volume edited by Niall Ferguson (1996), while in political science another one was published with contributions by famous and methodologically conscious political scientists like Fearon, Lars-Erik Cederman, and Margaret Levi (Tetlock and Belkin 1996). Interdisciplinary joint ventures even exist between psychology, political science, and history (Tetlock, Lebow, and Parker 2006). Counterfactuals, and those using them, have in the meantime become so prominent that a major British historian has written a small book to demonstrate that they are largely useless (Evans 2014).

To calm the anxiety of the most positivist readers: the present chapter makes no major rewrites of human history; it only extends a gentle invitation to ruminate about one exuberant counterfactual. In fact, it does not use counterfactuals to study major political or military crises, as the bulk of alternative history does, but it resorts to restrained counterfactuals to better understand the consequences of science patronage—and its denial.

At this point, at least two of the three connections between the topic of this chapter—social science patronage—and the method employed—counterfactuals—should be evident. First, counterfactuals allow us to explore the consequences of grants to a recipient by asking what characteristics of the recipient would be different *if the grant had not been awarded*. Second, further possible worlds and the contingency of the historical one can be detected by using counterfactual thinking, for instance, by asking what would have happened if a different applicant among all who had an *objective possibility* had obtained the grant.

Third, and less evident for readers unfamiliar with foundations, a particularity intrinsic to science patronage is that not everybody obtains it. The connection between science patronage and denial, which could be easily dismissed as a nonevent (no grant awarded), is that patrons reckon with the effect of not giving to some (not promoting certain things, not letting them happen). Indeed, they are conscious of the fact that their power also resides in not giving if they do not want to, and with the consequences of giving to some in a milieu where rivals lack the resources and prestige donors grant.

In the following section, I use counterfactuals in a technical sense to show that certain episodes in the history of social sciences were directly linked to science patronage granted by foundations. If patrons had not given support, certain research centers, research projects, and scholarly careers would not have existed or would have been completely different. But in the conclusion, I also invite the reader to use exuberant counterfactuals to imagine what would have happened if an award had been given to a different recipient or if no award at all had been granted.

The Study of International Relations in Mexico around 1960

Among Latin American academic organizations, the Colegio was arguably the first that hired full-time faculty and enrolled full-time students; from the beginning, the ambitions of its founders and funders involved the whole of Latin America; the Colegio also pioneered graduate training in the social sciences, preceded only by the Escola de Sociologia e Política de São Paulo. One of the reasons why the Colegio succeeded is that it managed to integrate some of the talented scholars who fled the Spanish Civil War. For three years in the 1940s, the Colegio hosted an innovative Centro de Estudios Sociales (CES), which failed to attract RF support and closed, but its Centro de Estudios Históricos (CEH) and its Centro de Estudios Lingüísticos y Literarios (CELL), both still existing, received several multiyear RF grants between 1942 and 1948 (Morcillo Laiz 2019). In the early 1970s, the Colegio turned into a model for two academic organizations that tried to accommodate more refugee scholars, but this time from South America: the Facultad Latinoamericana de Ciencias Sociales (FLACSO), which opened a new seat in Mexico City, and the Centro de Investigaciones y Docencia Económicas (CIDE). The Colegio still exists today. Its peculiar character within Latin America can be appreciated in the proportion of students per professor: although the Colegio is a public academic organization, its annual report indicates that it employs around 180 researchers, who train around 460 students.

Back in the late 1950s, the Colegio was a fledgling research center that had seen better days. Since the RF support to the CEH and the CELL was phased out in the early 1950s, the Colegio had stagnated and diminished in size. Its seat was a completely inadequate villa from the prerevolutionary times of Porfirio Díaz; every center occupied a former bedroom, and the library was in the villa's living room (González 1976, 547).[2] To make matters worse, the more prominent of the two Colegio founders, Alfonso Reyes, was ailing and would die soon thereafter. The other founder, Daniel Cosío Villegas, was committed to a multiplicity of undertakings, including representing Mexico at the United Nations Social and Economic Council (ECOSOC).

In the late 1950s, Mexico lacked a good IR program. Since the CES closed in 1946, the Colegio did not have a program in the social sciences, let alone in IR, but deficiencies characterized the situation elsewhere in Mexico. In theory, sociological research was conducted at the Instituto de Investigaciones Sociales (IIS) at the Universidad Nacional Autónoma de México (UNAM). The IIS, however, employed very few people as full-time scholars; it is debatable whether the label *sociologists* would have been appropriate for them (Morcillo Laiz 2008). The IIS director, Lucio Mendieta y Núñez, was trained in law and was mainly interested in the assimilation of indigenous populations, which he saw as the essential requisite if they were to contribute to the Mexican state's drive toward progress. In any case, the Mexican-centeredness of the IIS made it unlikely that someone would pursue an interest in IR. Since the early 1940s Mendieta had been in occasional contact with the RF, but its officers deeply disliked Mendieta's project of sociology in the service of the state as well as his personality. These sentiments were probably mutual. With Mendieta at the helm, IIS remained a sociology backwater, remarkable only by the continuity of its journal and the occasional publication of a significant book (Germani 1956; Medina Echavarría 1953).

From an IR perspective, IIS was less important than some of the UNAM schools. Degrees in social sciences, political sciences, and diplomatic sciences were offered at the Escuela Nacional de Ciencias Políticas y Sociales (ENCPyS), which was the product of a compromise between the interests of several schools within UNAM, most prominently the law school (Morcillo Laiz 2008, 162–69). Thus, law became the discipline that occupied most of the curriculum for the degree in *ciencias diplomáticas*, as the IR degree was originally called; less than 10 percent of the time was assigned to courses specifically related to this degree, such as diplomatic history.[3] Foreign visitors like the RF officers would not necessarily have recognized the curriculum as being in the social sciences, let alone IR. In addition to the ENCPyS, the UNAM law school, the Facultad de Derecho, also offered political science courses and, more importantly for this chapter, international law courses. From the law school, rather than from the ENCPyS, came the rivals who competed with the Colegio for RF support for an IR program. No rival to the Colegio was the UNAM School of Economics, the Escuela Nacional de Economía, where numerous Marxists and even Comintern members taught; it was therefore an absolute taboo for the RF. Finally, the Mexico City College offered an IR degree but was not perceived as a competitor (Ochoa Bilbao 2011, chap. 3).

When the RF resumed its contacts with the Colegio in the late 1950s, both the relations between the United States and Latin America and between the RF and its Division of Social Science (DSS) were undergoing a transformation. After the end of World War II, Latin American governments were disappointed because of the lack of a Marshall Plan comparable to the one Europe benefited from. By the late 1950s, this discontent and bad relations with the rest of the hemisphere were becoming increasingly difficult for the US government to ignore, among other reasons because, as former colonies became independent states, their governments were increasingly a factor to reckon with in international politics (Rabe 1988). Indeed, improving the poor relations with Latin America became a US foreign policy priority after the Cuban Revolution in 1959 and the rapprochement between Cuba and the Soviet Union. The most visible result of the new policy was John F. Kennedy's Alliance for Progress, a US$20 billion program of economic assistance for Latin America that was part of the US anticommunist crusade. After Dean Rusk became its president in 1952, the RF had accorded increasingly more attention and resources to developing countries (Rusk left in 1961 to become Kennedy's secretary of state). During Rusk's tenure at the RF, the DSS director, Joseph Willits, was replaced by Kenneth W. Thompson, who was much more willing to promote the social sciences—or, to be more precise, the study of international relations—throughout the world (Guilhot 2011b). As US foreign policy and the interests of a reorganized RF aligned, new opportunities opened for Latin American scholars.

Within this changing international context, it seems logical that the RF intensified its contacts with its former partner, the fledging Colegio. The school's leaders were indubitably liberal—in the European sense of the word—and it had been a bulwark against communism in Mexican academia (Ortoll and Piccato 2011). While the Colegio's Centro de Estudios Internacionales (CEI) will be our focus here, it is useful to succinctly report about other developments at the Colegio in the 1960s. At the time, the RF did not only contribute half of CEI's budget, but it also helped relaunch the two preexisting centers, CEH and CELL. In these efforts, the RF was not alone; in 1962 the Colegio also obtained support from the Ford Foundation (FF), which most notably financed a Centro de Estudios Económicos y Demográficos, from which centers for sociology and for demography and urban studies were later born (Lida, Matesanz, and Zoraida Vázquez 2000, 126, 334-44, 387, 410). A center of regional studies was established in collaboration with UNESCO, the Centro de Estudios de Asia y África (CEAA). The pattern was always similar: Cosío attracted third-party funding to inaugurate the new centers. As this support was phased out, the Mexican government assumed most of their costs. One main reason this approach worked was that the availability of external funding coincided with a period of fiscal buoyancy in Mexico, with average yearly GDP increases of almost 5 percent during the 1960s and 1970s.[4]

My concern in this chapter is with the decision to establish the CEI in 1960. Shortly after its inauguration, the CEI offered a five-year IR degree. About twenty students from Mexico and other Latin American countries were admitted to this graduate program; several of them were diplomats. A few of them eventually became CEI faculty. Despite its name, only about a fifth of the courses included in the curriculum were from this discipline; another half were in area studies on the world's cultures and their politics. The remaining courses were either methodological or introductions to economics law, and so on. As far as IR theory is concerned, the CEI was decidedly realist, which was the paradigm preferred by Thompson, the DSS director and a student of Hans J. Morgenthau, the most prominent realist IR scholar (Guilhot 2011b). The curriculum was oriented toward the training of diplomats, not only from Mexico but also from other Latin American countries. Indeed, diplomats and teachers of international law were deeply involved from early on; one of them, Francisco Cuevas Cancino, became the first CEI director. The teaching staff came from law but also economics and history, from both the Colegio and outside. Indeed, one of the major challenges for CEI was to find teachers capable of offering area studies courses. As long as the young graduate students affiliated with CEI were abroad for training in their respective world areas and in IR theory, foreign scholars with the necessary qualifications had to be invited from foreign countries to teach the courses. In this effort, CEI also benefited from the help of UNESCO and the Organization of American States; a section within CEI on "Estudios Orientales" was soon established, encompassing faculty and visitors working on Asia and Africa; this section is the origin of the CEAA.

The CEI occupied a peculiar disciplinary space that overlapped with the one defined by the source of its foreign funding, the RF's DSS. The CEI was situated between political science, IR, and area studies. From this perspective, its name, Centro de Estudios Internacionales, is most informative. The use of "Estudios" rather than "Relaciones" corresponds to the actual content of the curriculum, since international studies is a broader category than IR; it is composed not only of IR theory and a few problems considered as intrinsic parts of IR like security and the study of international organizations. In addition, international studies includes the study of non-US "cultural" areas like Latin America and the Middle East (Schmidt 2010). In other words, the CEI's name corresponds with our current usage of the term (but not necessarily the usage back then). Apart from its stated goal of offering training to diplomats from the newly independent states, this RF program was also an attempt by the DSS director to introduce a boundary between IR and political science, which Thompson, Morgenthau, and other realist IR scholars perceived as dominated by behaviorism (Guilhot 2011a). Their attempt to sever IR from the rest of political science widely failed in the United States; since then, a separation has prevailed in countries like Mexico, where almost all BA degrees are either in political science or in IR (rather than in both); IR departments are separated from political science departments (or do not exist officially, as at the Colegio); and professional associations are not only independent but also antagonistic. The separation also exists in some foreign academic organizations, many of them having been deeply involved with the RF, most prominently at the London School of Economics. By contrast, in the United States and most of Europe, IR is a subfield within political science. In Mexico IR came to occupy a peculiar disciplinary space may be related to the agenda of the CEI funders. This is a hypothesis that counterfactuals can help us to explore.

Two Counterfactuals to Study the CEI Negotiation

To better understand the relation between the CEI and the RF, I raise two counterfactual questions: First, if the RF had not granted support from its DSS budget to CEI, would CEI have ever been established? Second, if the RF had not favored the study of IR as severed from political science, would the Colegio have established a center whose purported remit was exclusively studying and training in IR? To answer these questions, it is necessary to examine the negotiations that preceded the award of the CEI grant. Of particular importance are the encounters and the letters exchanged between the RF officers, Reyes, and Cosío.

To accomplish this goal, I draw mainly on documents from the archives of the Rockefeller Foundation. More specifically, I use the files on the CEI, which include the grant actions, correspondence, diary entries recording visits to Mexico from RF officers' interviews, and draft curricula and other information on the CEI. Admittedly, the Colegio archives as well as those of Reyes and Cosío could also contain relevant evidence about how they defined the disciplinary space that CEI should occupy. This is true, but it is highly unlikely that these Mexican collections would contain direct proof of the impact of the RF agenda on the CEI. The reason is that the common administrative practice at the Colegio at the time was that Reyes and Cosío would meet, frequently informally and often in their homes, discuss issues, and take a stance that would then be communicated to the RF, leaving no trace of their reasoning or of discrepancies on any major issue. Reyes's diaries occasionally mention the meetings with RF officers, but nothing of substance is included about the conversations. As for Cosío, his memoires are misleading about his contacts with the RF on the CEI (1977). His personal papers are inaccessible, and his biographer has preferred to focus on Cosío's accomplishments (Krauze 2001). In the archive of the Colegio, the collection on the RF appears to be incomplete for the 1950s, and no specific series on the early CEI exists. In any case, it is highly unlikely that Reyes and Cosío, together or separately, had left an explicit testimony of their adapting to the policies of any foreign donor, much less a US one.

Despite these silences, the preserved record shows that between 1956 and 1959, Reyes and Cosío debated with RF officers about the future CEI. In personal encounters and letters, the exchanges on the Colegio meandered from vague ideas to an increasing level of specificity. Initially, Cosío and Reyes expressed ideas, although perhaps it would be better to say mere wishes, about studying IR and training members of the Mexican foreign service at the Colegio. Although since the beginning the conversation was about "developing at the Colegio work on international relations," on a number of occasion Reyes and even Cosío mentioned the social sciences.[5] To wit, in 1957 Reyes described the Colegio plans as including "courses in the Social Sciences and the Humanities,"[6] while Cosío spoke of "courses on modern civilization: economics, history, philosophy, political science, sociology, and literature. The Mexican Foreign Office, he [Cosío] said, was willing to make graduation from such a school mandatory for acceptance into the Foreign Service, and that Alfonso Reyes was ready to support the venture."[7]

As late as May 1959, Cosío described "a proposed center for international relations" as consisting "of a series of courses for three groups of fifteen students for three years each, i.e. forty-five students over nine years. They would be drawn from all over Latin American, and would be given full-time teaching on International Law, Political Science, International Organisations and international Economics"; the main targeted public would be Mexican and other Latin American diplomats. It is revealing that in this same conversation, Cosío mentioned Medina's short-lived CES as a predecessor of the planned center.[8] After this conversation, IR is the only discipline mentioned in the record, although the precise focus continued to be unclear. Five months later, the preliminary version of the curriculum emphasized "fundamental knowledge on economics, law, history and international relations proper."[9] Between 1956 and 1959, Cosío and the RF had made some progress on defining how Colegio would go into the social sciences and the preferred types of students.

The two main partners in this negotiation were the Colegio and the RF, but other individuals and organizations were also involved. Inside these two organizations, individuals disagreed time and again: on one occasion Cosío claimed, "The Rector [sic] of the Colegio de Mexico [Reyes] refused to permit the group to be attached to the Colegio."[10] The goodwill of some officers within the DSS and the Division of Humanities benefited the Colegio, but during the negotiation with Cosío both the DSS director, Thompson, and the foundation's president, Rusk, showed repeated skepticism about the Colegio as the best host institution for the future IR center as well as about the intensity and pace of RF support.

In the case of Thompson, such skepticism increased after talks with two Mexicans, César Sepúlveda and Francisco Cuevas, who started two separate efforts to convince the RF that rather than at the Colegio, the new center should be established at the UNAM. Ironically, Cosío had established the contact between them and the RF. Sepúlveda, whom he called a "friend," was a practicing lawyer who taught a course on state theory at the UNAM, which he presented as a "world affairs" module.[11] Sepúlveda's alternative proposal was to establish a center within the UNAM, similar to IIS and isolated from the bureaucracy and politicking inherent to ENCPyS. While Sepúlveda enjoyed a good relationship with the influential law school at the UNAM and would eventually receive RF support for his international law seminar there, his proposal would not come to fruition, and he would only be allowed to teach at the CEI (Morcillo Laiz 2016, 596).

Sepúlveda was intellectually no rival to Cosío's real competitor, Cuevas. He was the other Mexican who almost successfully tried to dissuade the RF from establishing the new center at the Colegio. Cuevas was a former Guggenheim Fellow and the author of several books on international law and IR. In front of RF officers, he argued that the new center could be associated with ENCPyS, which was experiencing an overhaul under its new director, Pablo González Casanova. Cuevas must have made his point forcefully: after listening to him, Thompson wrote to Cosío that Cuevas "makes an extremely favorable impression"[12] and to the RF officers that "this conversation [with Cuevas] is one which might well suggest a reopening of basic RF thinking about opportunities in Mexico."[13] Eventually, and paradoxically, Cuevas would end up being the first CEI director, thanks to RF's backing.

The answer to the question of which Mexican academic organization should host the new center came from the minister of foreign affairs, Manuel

Tello, another of Cosío's acquaintances. In early 1959, Tello received a memorandum from Cosío that contained a description of a center for the training of Mexican and Latin American diplomats,[14] which Tello discussed with an RF officer in June. In October, Cosío claimed that support from Tello and the Mexican president was forthcoming: up to US$200,000 for five years (which now would be $1.7 million).[15] RF immediately granted US$10,000 (which now would be $85,000) to the Colegio for the library. Officially, the CEI opened in January 1960, but teaching began one year later.

The limited amount of the RF grant made Cosío furious. As he explained to Thompson, the decision of the Mexican government in favor of the Colegio was reached because Cosío had assured the minister that support from abroad would be forthcoming once foreign donors received an indication that the CEI was actually going to be established at the Colegio.[16] Rusk, the RF president, was unimpressed. While he realized that from the perspective of the Mexican government, Cosío was "the chosen instrument," Rusk indicated that in addition to awarding the library grant, the RF should "keep our eyes on it a bit further."[17] In the following months, Cosío let them know about all the preparatory work he was doing: selecting faculty and students, editing a new IR journal, spending the library grants on IR books and journals, and building a new seat for the Colegio. Almost a year later, further support was approved: a second US$15,000 grant for the library (which now would be $127,000) and US$60,000 (which now would be $510,000) for visiting professors' "salaries, research and travel expenses" plus three Rockefeller fellowships for Colegio members and the promise of granting a few more in the coming years.[18] Afterward the CEI received no more funding from the RF, but it was replaced by even larger grants from the Ford Foundation (Lida, Matesanz, and Zoraida Vázquez 2000, 340–43, 355, 390).

Conclusion

Taking the RF and the Colegio's CEI as an example and counterfactuals as a method, the goal of this chapter was to show the centrality of the patronage granted—or denied—by donors in order to give a full account of the history of the social sciences. More specifically, the ambition was to demonstrate that counterfactuals are an appropriate method to answer the type of questions that scholars interested in the history and sociology of science *must* raise: What would have happened to an intellectual project or to a discipline if a patron had not given support to a certain research center, research projects, or scholarly career?

If the RF had not granted support to the CEI, it seems extremely unlikely that the CEI would have ever been established. Simply put, without RF support Tello and the Mexican government would not have granted money to CEI. Even if the government had conferred support without the RF having previously signaled strong interest in the CEI, which the record suggests was a highly unlikely possibility, the public resources available to the CEI would have been substantially smaller. This is the first counterfactual, but we can add further, nested ones: if deprived of what RF granted—library funds, visiting professors, and Rockefeller fellowships—the CEI's attraction for prospective students in Mexico and abroad would have decreased notably; it would have also been unable to provide its future faculty with fellowships to obtain training abroad. In short, if the CEI had lacked RF support, the most likely consequence is that it would never have been founded; if it had been established, it would have become a smaller, weaker academic unit, which the Colegio might have closed down a few years later, as happened to CES in the 1940s.

If the RF had not favored the separation between IR and political science, the Colegio would probably not have established a center dedicated exclusively to IR. Without the RF's policy of separation, the Colegio and its CEI, possibly under a different name, would have occupied a different disciplinary space within the social sciences. (This is the second counterfactual.) The impact of the donor on the disciplinary agenda of the recipient can be easily appreciated in the gap between Reyes's and Cosío's initial ambition of opening an interdisciplinary center for the social sciences, including sociology and political science, and the actual CEI, which combined area studies with some IR theory and the study of international organizations.

The two preceding counterfactuals fulfill the requisite of cotenability, but some readers may still be skeptical. First let's consider cotenability: at the point of branching, it was possible that the RF would not grant the second, major award, and if Thompson had not been the DSS director, the policy of promoting IR as an alternative to political science might easily not have been in place. Skeptical readers may nonetheless object to the first counterfactual, that to open an international studies program like the CEI was a most reasonable choice for Cosío because in the late 1950s he was collaborating with the Mexican foreign ministry. While this is true, the evidence presented here shows that Reyes and Cosío originally had a vague but different and clearly more interdisciplinary idea of which social sciences should be represented in the new center. Readers who are still skeptical should also consider the following, additional aspects. First, even Reyes's and Cosío's early references to international studies in their conversations with RF representatives may have been in response to the growing interest of the RF in the training of diplomats. This RF interest initiated in 1956 as a response to the increasing international presence of the newly independent countries and particularly to the Bandung Conference. Cosío may well have been informed about this RF interest through his contacts with other members of the ECOSOC. Second, at the time of his first conversations with the RF on the CEI, Cosío was involved in diplomacy, but he also had links to other social sciences: he initiated his career in Mexico's public sector as an economist; in the late 1950s, he was still in touch with the main Mexican economic institutions, like the finance ministry and Mexico's central bank. To open a program to train economists at the Colegio would have been an equally reasonable choice for Cosío. Third, in the 1960s the Colegio expanded in ways that seem to confirm that Cosío restricted the new center to international studies because this was what the RF was ready to pay for. In 1961, as the CEI had just started to operate, Cosío began to negotiate with the Ford Foundation for the establishment of a Centro de Estudios Económicos y Demográficos, which was inaugurated in 1963.[19] Since its beginning, this center employed sociologists alongside economists, the two social sciences, apart from political science, mentioned in the conversation between Cosío and an RF officer in 1957.[20] The sociologists obtained their own Ford-funded center in 1968. In view of my replies, even readers who reject the counterfactual claim that without the RF the CEI would not have been inaugurated will surely accept that the RF's interest in diplomats set the sequence according to which the Colegio became active in different disciplines and subfields within the social sciences, setting IR and political science in Mexico onto the separate paths that they are still following.

In sum, the history of Mexican—and Latin American—social sciences cannot be severed from the science patronage granted by US philanthropic foundations and other foreign donors. In sociology, political science, and economics, many academic organizations in Latin America have received awards from external donors, leading to periods of more intense activity and impact within the respective disciplines. Among the most famous recipients of awards are the Escola de Sociologia and the Centro Brasileiro de Análise e Planejamento (CEBRAP), both in São Paulo (Miceli and Smith 1993); the Chilean economists at two major universities (Valdés 1995); and both sociology and then political science in Buenos Aires (Pereyra 2006; Morales Martín and Algañaraz 2016). It would be difficult, not to say extremely bold, to argue that contemporary Latin American social sciences would be exactly as we know them if the RF, Ford, and other external patrons had not been involved in the field. A counterfactual brings us this far. It is another, much larger question to pinpoint the extent of their impact and to decide whether it has been for better or worse.

Notes

1 Livy, *Ad urbe condita*, book 9, sections 17–19.
2 For the perspective of an RF officer, see Rockefeller Archive Center/RF/ RG1.2/323S/Box 62/Folder 485 (hereafter F485), February 25, 1959.
3 See a description of the curriculum in the UNAM journal, *Ciencias Políticas y Sociales* 13, no. 47 (1967): 61.
4 "GDP Growth (Annual %)—Mexico," World Bank, accessed June 19, 2022, https://data.worldbank.org/indicator/NY.GDP.MKTP.KD.ZG?locations=MX.
5 Charles B. Fahs, January 17, 1956, F485.
6 Alfonso Reyes, May 17, 1957, F485.
7 Daniel Cosío Villegas, May 18, 1957, F485.
8 Daniel Cosío Villegas in Montague Yudelman's diary, February 25, 1959, F485.
9 Daniel Cosío Villegas in Kenneth W. Thompson's diary, October 29, 1959, F485.
10 Daniel Cosío Villegas in Montague Yudelman's diary, May 15, 1956, F485.
11 Daniel Cosío Villegas to Kenneth W. Thompson, May 13, 1959; César Sepúlveda in Kenneth W. Thompson's diary, May 13 and 28, 1959, F485.
12 Kenneth W. Thompson to Daniel Cosío Villegas, May 28, 1959, F485.
13 Kenneth W. Thompson, diary entry, May 15, 1959, F485.
14 Archivo de la Secretaría de Relaciones Exteriores, III/380 (72)/29053, Centro de Estudios Internacionales.
15 Daniel Cosío Villegas in Kenneth W. Thompson's diary, October 29, 1959, F485.
16 Daniel Cosío Villegas to Kenneth W. Thompson, November 23, 1959, F485.
17 Dean Rusk diary entry, November 16, 1959, F485.
18 Thompson to Cosío, September 8 and October 7, 1960, Rockefeller Archive Center/RF/RG 1.2/323S/Box 62/Folder 486.
19 Rockefeller Archive Center, Ford Foundation Records, Log File 61-1407.
20 Daniel Cosío Villegas in John P. Harrison's diary, May 18, 1957, F485.

References

Ahmad, Salma. 1991. "American Foundations and the Development of the Social Sciences between the Wars: Comment on the Debate between Martin Bulmer and Donald Fisher." *Sociology* 25, no. 3: 511–20.
Andrews, F. Emerson. 1963. *Philanthropic Foundations*. New York: Russell Sage Foundation.
Arnove, Robert F., ed. 1980. *Philanthropy and Cultural Imperialism: The Foundations at Home and Abroad*. Bloomington: Indiana University Press.

Berkovitch, Nitza, and Neve Gordon. 2008. "The Political Economy of Transnational Regimes: The Case of Human Rights." *International Studies Quarterly* 52, no. 4: 881–904.

Berman, Edward H. 1983. *The Influence of the Carnegie, Ford, and Rockefeller Foundations on American Foreign Policy: The Ideology of Philanthropy*. Albany: State University of New York Press.

Birn, Anne-Emanuelle. 2014. "Philanthrocapitalism, Past and Present: The Rockefeller Foundation, the Gates Foundation, and the Setting(s) of the International/Global Health Agenda." *Hypothesis* 12, no. 1: 1–27, e6.

Bourdieu, Pierre, and Loïc Wacquant. 1992. *An Invitation to Reflexive Sociology*. Chicago: University of Chicago Press.

Brown, E. Richard. 1979. *Rockefeller Medicine Men: Medicine and Capitalism in America*. Berkeley: University of California Press.

Bulmer, Martin. 1984. "Philanthropic Foundations and the Development of the Social Sciences in the Early Twentieth Century: A Reply to Donald Fisher." *Sociology* 18, no. 4: 572–79.

Bulmer, Martin, and Joan Bulmer. 1981. "Philanthropy and Social Science in the 1920s: Beardsley Ruml and the Laura Spelman Rockefeller Memorial, 1922–29." *Minerva* 19, no. 3: 347–407.

Callahan, David. 2018. *The Givers: Wealth, Power, and Philanthropy in a New Gilded Age*. New York: Knopf.

Carnegie Corporation of New York. 1911. "Charter: Act of Incorporation." New York.

Colegio de México. 2018. "Informe de Actividades 2017." Mexico City: Colegio de México.

Cosío Villegas, Daniel. 1977. *Memorias*. Mexico City: Mortiz.

Cueto, Marcos, ed. 1994. *Missionaries of Science: The Rockefeller Foundation and Latin America*. Bloomington: Indiana University Press.

Dobbin, Frank, Beth Simmons, and Geoffrey Garrett. 2007. "The Global Diffusion of Public Policies: Social Construction, Coercion, Competition, or Learning?" *Annual Review of Sociology* 33, no. 1: 449–72.

Elster, Jon. 1978. *Logic and Society: Contradictioned and Possible Worlds*. Chichester: John Wiley and Sons.

Evans, Richard J. 2014. *Altered Pasts: Counterfactuals in History*. Waltham, MA: Brandeis University Press.

Ezrahi, Y. 2001. "Science and the State." In *International Encyclopedia of the Social and Behavioral Sciences*, edited by Neil J. Smelser and Paul B. Baltes, 13657–64. Oxford: Pergamon.

Factor, Regis A., and Stephen P. Turner. 1984. *Max Weber and the Dispute over Reason and Value*. London: Routledge.

Fearon, James D. 1991. "Counterfactuals and Hypothesis Testing in Political Science." *World Politics* 43, no. 2: 169–95.

Ferguson, Niall. 1996. *Virtual History*. New York: Macmillan.

Finnemore, Martha. 1996. "Norms, Culture, and World Politics: Insights from Sociology's Institutionalism." *International Organization* 50, no. 2: 325–47.

Fisher, Donald. 1983. "The Role of Philanthropic Foundations in the Reproduction and Production of Hegemony: Rockefeller Foundations and the Social Sciences." *Sociology* 17, no. 2: 206–33.

Fisher, Donald. 1984. "Philanthropic Foundations and the Social Sciences: A Response to Martin Bulmer." *Sociology* 18, no. 4: 580–87.

Fisher, Donald. 1993. *Fundamental Development of the Social Sciences: Rockefeller Philanthropy and the United States Social Science Research Council.* Ann Arbor: University of Michigan Press.

Fleishman, Joel L. 2009. *The Foundation: A Great American Secret; How Private Wealth Is Changing the World.* New York: PublicAffairs.

Freund, Gerald. 1996. *Narcissism and Philanthropy: Ideas and Talent Denied.* New York: Viking.

Geiger, Roger L. 2018. *Research and Relevant Knowledge: American Research Universities since World War II.* New York: Oxford University Press, 1993. London: Routledge.

Germani, Gino. 1956. *La sociología científica: Apuntes para su fundamentación.* Mexico City: Instituto de Investigaciones Sociales, Universidad Nacional.

Gibbon, Edward. (1776–88) 1910. *Decline and Fall of the Roman Empire.* Vol. 5. Edited by Christopher Dawson. London: Everyman's Library.

González, Luis. 1976. "La pasión del nido." *Historia Mexicana* 25, no. 4: 530–98.

Goodman, Nelson. 1983. *Fact, Fiction, and Forecast.* Cambridge, MA: Harvard University Press.

Guilhot, Nicolas, ed. 2011a. *The Invention of International Relations Theory: Realism, the Rockefeller Foundation, and the 1954 Conference on Theory.* New York: Columbia University Press.

Guilhot, Nicolas. 2011b. "The Realist Gambit: Postwar American Political Science and the Birth of IR Theory." In *The Invention of International Relations Theory: Realism, the Rockefeller Foundation, and the 1954 Conference on Theory*, edited by Nicolas Guilhot, 128–61. New York: Columbia University Press.

Jordan, John M. 1994. *Machine-Age Ideology: Social Engineering and American Liberalism, 1911–1939.* Chapel Hill: University of North Carolina Press.

Karl, Barry D., and Alice Karl. 2001. "Foundations and the Government: A Tale of Conflict and Consensus." In *Philanthropy and the Nonprofit Sector in a Changing America*, edited by Charles T. Clotfelter and Thomas Ehrlich, 52–72. Bloomington: Indiana University Press.

Karl, Barry D., and Stanley N. Katz. 1981. "The American Private Philanthropic Foundation and the Public Sphere 1890–1930." *Minerva* 19, no. 2: 236–70.

Ketola, Markus. 2016. "Understanding NGO Strategies to Engage with Donor-Funded Development Projects: Reconciling and Differentiating Objectives." *European Journal of Development Research* 28, no. 3: 479–94.

King, Gary, Robert O. Keohane, and Sidney Verba. 1994. *Designing Social Inquiry: Scientific Inference in Qualitative Research.* Princeton, NJ: Princeton University Press.

Kiser, Edgar, and Margaret Levi. 1996. "Using Counterfactuals in Historical Analysis: Theories of Revolution." In *Counterfactual Thought Experiments in World Politics: Logical, Methodological, and Psychological Perspectives*, edited by Philip E. Tetlock and Aaron Belkin, 187–207. Princeton, NJ: Princeton University Press.

Kohler, Robert E. 1991. *Partners in Science: Foundations Managers and Natural Scientists, 1900–1945*. Chicago: University of Chicago Press.

Krause, Monika. 2014. *The Good Project: Humanitarian Relief NGOs and the Fragmentation of Reason*. Chicago: University of Chicago Press.

Krauze, Enrique. 2001. *Daniel Cosío Villegas: Una biografía intelectual*. 2nd ed. Mexico City: Tusquets Editores.

Latham, Michael E. 2000. *Modernization as Ideology: American Social Science and "Nation Building" in the Kennedy Era*. Chapel Hill: University of North Carolina Press.

Lebow, Richard Ned. 2010. *Forbidden Fruit: Counterfactuals and International Relations*. Princeton, NJ: Princeton University Press.

Lida, Clara E., José Antonio Matesanz, and Josefina Zoraida Vázquez. 2000. *La Casa de España y El Colegio de México: Memoria 1938–2000*. Mexico City: El Colegio de México.

McFate, Montgomery, and Janice H. Laurence. 2015. *Social Science Goes to War: The Human Terrain System in Iraq and Afghanistan*. New York: Oxford University Press.

Medina Echavarría, José. 1953. *Presentaciones y planteos: Papeles de sociología*. Mexico City: Instituto de Investigaciones Sociales, Universidad Nacional.

Megill, Allan. 2007. *Historical Knowledge, Historical Error: A Contemporary Guide to Practice*. Chicago: University of Chicago Press.

Merton, Robert K. 1973. *The Sociology of Science: Theoretical and Empirical Investigations*. Chicago: University of Chicago Press.

Miceli, Sergio, and Bradford Smith, eds. 1993. *A Fundação Ford no Brasil*. São Paulo: FAPESP, Editora Sumaré.

Morales Martín, Juan Jesús, and Víctor Hugo Algañaraz. 2016. "Ciencias sociales, políticas de autonomía académica y estrategias de internacionalización en la última dictadura militar argentina (1974–1983): Un análisis de los casos de la Facultad Latinoamericana de Ciencias Sociales y el Centro de Estudios de Estado y Sociedad." *Revista mexicana de ciencias políticas y sociales* 61, no. 227: 223–45.

Morcillo Laiz, Álvaro. 2008. "Historia de un fracaso: Intermediarios, organizaciones y la institucionalización de Weber en México (1937–1957)." *Sociológica* 23, no. 67: 149–92.

Morcillo Laiz, Álvaro. 2016. "La Rockefeller Foundation, el Colegio de México, el Instituto di Tella y las Ciencias Sociales en Español (1938–1973)." In *Max Weber en Iberoamérica: Nuevas interpretaciones, relevancia para el estudio de la región y recepción*, edited by Álvaro Morcillo Laiz and Eduardo Weisz, 573–606. Mexico City: Fondo de Cultura Económica.

Morcillo Laiz, Álvaro. 2019. "*La gran dama*: Science Patronage, the Rockefeller Foundation and the Mexican Social Sciences in the 1940s." *Journal of Latin American Studies* 51, no. 4: 829–54.

Morcillo Laiz, Álvaro. 2020. "New Viruses, Old Foundations: COVID-19, Global Health, and the Bill and Melinda Gates Foundation." *Orders beyond Borders*, May 28, 2020. https://ordersbeyondborders.blog.wzb.eu/2020/05/28/new -viruses-old-foundations-covid-19-global-health-and-the-bill-and-melinda -gates-foundation/.

Morcillo Laiz, Álvaro. 2022. "The Cold War Origins of Global IR. The Rockefeller Foundation and Realism in Latin America." *International Studies* Review 24, no. 1, 1-26.

Ninkovich, Frank A. 2010. *The Diplomacy of Ideas: U.S. Foreign Policy and Cultural Relations, 1938-1950*. Cambridge: Cambridge University Press.

Ochoa Bilbao, Luis. 2011. *La carrera de relaciones internacionales en México: Orígenes y situación actual*. Mexico City: El Colegio de México; Benemérita Universidad Autónoma de Puebla.

Ortoll, Servando, and Pablo Piccato. 2011. "A Brief History of the Historia Moderna de México." In *A Companion to Mexican History and Culture*, edited by William H. Beezley, 339-60. Chichester, MA: John Wiley and Sons.

Pereyra, Diego Ezequiel. 2006. "International Networks and the Institutionalisation of Sociology in Argentina (1940-1963)." PhD diss., University of Sussex.

Platt, Jennifer. 1998. *A History of Sociological Research Methods in America: 1920-1960*. Cambridge: Cambridge University Press.

Rabe, Stephen G. 1988. *Eisenhower and Latin America: The Foreign Policy of Anticommunism*. Chapel Hill: University of North Carolina Press.

Rockefeller Foundation, 1929. *Annual Report.* New York: Rockefeller Foundation.

Rohde, Joy. 2013. *Armed with Expertise: The Militarization of American Social Research during the Cold War*. Ithaca, NY: Cornell University Press.

Schmidt, Brian C. 2010. "The History of International Studies." In *The International Studies Encyclopedia*, edited by Robert Allen Denemark, 12: 3418-38. Chichester: Wiley-Blackwell.

Sending, Ole Jacob. 2015. *The Politics of Expertise: Competing for Authority in Global Governance*. Ann Arbor: University of Michigan Press.

Shapin, Steven. 1992. "Discipline and Bounding: The History and Sociology of Science as Seen through the Externalism–Internalism Debate." *History of Science* 30, no. 4: 333-69.

Solovey, Mark. 2013. *Shaky Foundations: The Politics-Patronage-Social Science Nexus in Cold War America*. New Brunswick, NJ: Rutgers University Press.

Tetlock, Philip E., and Aaron Belkin, eds. 1996. *Counterfactual Thought Experiments in World Politics: Logical, Methodological, and Psychological Perspectives*. Princeton, NJ: Princeton University Press.

Tetlock, Philip E., Richard Ned Lebow, and Geoffrey Parker, eds. 2006. *Unmaking the West: "What-If?" Scenarios That Rewrite World History*. Ann Arbor: University of Michigan Press.

Turner, Stephen P. 1998. "Did Funding Matter to the Development of Research Methods in Sociology?" *Minerva* 36, no. 1: 69-79.

Turner, Stephen P. 1999. "Does Funding Product Its Effects? The Rockefeller Case." In *The Development of the Social Sciences in the United States and Canada: The Role of Philanthropy*, edited by Theresa R. Richardson and Donald Fisher, 213–26. Stamford, CT: Ablex.

Turner, Stephen P. 2014. *American Sociology: From Pre-disciplinary to Post-normal.* New York: Palgrave Macmillan.

Turner, Stephen P., and Jonathan Turner. 1990. *The Impossible Science: An Institutional Analysis of American Sociology*. Newbury Park: Sage.

Valdés, Juan Gabriel. 1995. *Pinochet's Economists: The Chicago School in Chile*. Cambridge: Cambridge University Press.

Weber, Max. (1906) 2012. "Critical Studies in the Logic of the Cultural Sciences." In *Max Weber: Collected Methodological Writings*, edited by Sam Whimster and Hans H. Bruun, translated by Hans H. Bruun, 139–84. New York: Routledge.

Wong, Wendy H., Ron Levi, and Julia Deutsch. 2017. "Domesticating the Field: The Ford Foundation and the Development of International Human Rights." In *Professional Networks in Transnational Governance*, edited by Leonard Seabrooke and Lasse Folke Henriksen, 82–100. Cambridge: Cambridge University Press.

Youde, Jeremy. 2013. "The Rockefeller and Gates Foundations in Global Health Governance." *Global Society* 27, no. 2: 139–58.

Zunz, Olivier. 2014. *Philanthropy in America: A History*. 2nd ed. Princeton, NJ: Princeton University Press.

the social life of concepts

or, How to Study the Idea of Creativity?

BREGJE F. VAN EEKELEN

[Language is a set of] signs which take on the changeable and often reversed
social relations of a given society, so that what enters into them is the contradictory
and conflict-ridden social history of the people who speak the language.
—RAYMOND WILLIAMS, *POLITICS AND LETTERS*

IN 2022, more than 500,000 high school students from over seventy countries will be subjected to a test to assess their "creative abilities."[1] This assessment is tagged onto the Programme for International Student Assessment
(PISA) test, which examines and ranks the skills of fifteen-year-old teenagers
in mathematics, science, and literacy worldwide. PISA's effort in commensu-
ration of high school students' abilities was started in 2000 and was initiated
and facilitated by the Organisation for Economic Co-operation and Development (OECD 2014, 2019, 2021). Concepts such as "creativity," "quality,"
"human factors," and "excellence" have histories that are entangled with the
social sciences, and they circulate ubiquitously in the present.[2] The word
creativity is often summoned as a positive term—increased creativity usually
suggests progress one way or another. However, as with other seemingly
superficial and ubiquitous terms—I call them *Teflon concepts*—it can be hard

to find a productive angle to study their presence. For anthropologists who encounter these concepts in their fieldwork, neither ignoring nor dismissing a social science concept is very fruitful however. For these concepts, whatever we think of them analytically, can influence everyday understandings people have of themselves and the worlds they inhabit. As Anthony Giddens phrased it, social science's findings "very often enter constitutively into the world they describe" (1984, 20). Their mobilizations likely matter, and they warrant both social scientific and historical scrutiny. The relevant question is: How?

The employment and social life of concepts is an understudied aspect in the field of the history of social science, and can be a baffling sight for any sociologist or anthropologist who encounters them in their fieldwork—it is as if we step through Alice's mirror into our fieldsites only to see social science's concepts come alive (Ferguson 1999; Martin 1994; Tsing 2000). What to make of these familiar terms? What makes encounters with these concepts methodologically complicated is that it is at first blush unclear whether one should bring out the theoretical toolbox (the usual "kit" one brings along when discussing social science in the making), or whether another analytical frame is desirable to analyze the reflexive uses of a term. But if concepts are an effective force in the social world—if they not only emerge in particular conjunctures but create new ones as well (Strathern 1995; see also Haraway 1989; Riles 2000)—it is all the more urgent to figure out what they do. Hence, while I too can be exasperated by yet another moment in which creativity is conjured in what seems like an unreflective, shallow, or depoliticizing way— for example, swamped in policy discourse, misrepresenting social processes— the real problem is not the blatant (ab)use of the concept, but the fact that I don't have an apposite toolkit at the ready to study these particular conjurings of the term. In this chapter, I draw on the twentieth-century history of social scientific investments into the concept of creativity, not for history's sake—intriguing though it may be—but to discuss how histories of concepts can be usefully employed to generate questions that capture the life of these ubiquitous concepts in their worldly setting.[3]

Studies of "social etymologies" of traveling concepts form a productive starting point in my attempt to combine history and cultural anthropology to study the past and present lives of social science concepts, their production and circulation, in academia and the worlds beyond. Social etymologies detail the framing of a concept as it is appropriated, translated, and developed in the social settings of its emergence, including but not limited to "expert" settings. Following studies by Crouch (1998), and Fraser and Gordon (1994), social etymologies tend to the "critical political semantics" that underpin the shifts in meaning of social concepts. Their studies of social etymologies are elaborations of Raymond Williams's seminal work on the historical trajectories of a series of contested keywords that together form a vocabulary for the study of society and culture (1985).[4] The point of writing the social history of a traveling concept is thus not to write an analysis that seeks to get at the "core" of the meaning of a concept (e.g., through a search for origins, or through a hermeneutic reading of deeper meaning).[5] Rather, it seeks to detail the framing of the concept as it is mobilized, translated, and developed in the particular settings of its travel and appropriation—and how that concept, in return, might coshape its new setting.

In what follows, I take my research on the concept of creative thinking and its social life as a case to investigate what the study of concepts can contribute to histories of social science, on the one hand, and to contemporary sciences of social worlds, on the other. A brief excursion into the mid-twentieth-century life of creativity will be followed by an exploration of what the heterogeneous field of histories of social science stands to gain from diachronic studies of its concepts, and what cultural anthropologists could contribute to these studies. This is followed by a discussion of what studies of concepts, particularly their historical entanglements, could contribute to anthropological encounters with social science concepts in the present. By foregrounding the histories and lives of social science concepts, my hope is ultimately that we can find ways to detect the politics and public issues that are at play in the uptake and appropriations of these Teflon terms.

Creativity, Inc.

In 1955, the *Wall Street Journal* reported on the rise of creativity in business, noting that brainstorming "represents another mating of the Age of Freud with the Century of the Salesman." Brainstorming and other creative thinking techniques were developed in the 1940s and 1950s within manufacturing industries in the United States such as Motorola (with an idea clinic), US Steel, Reynolds Metals, General Electric, Ethyl Corp, New York Telephone Corporation, and Boeing Airplane Co. By 1960, courses in creative thinking had been offered to fifteen hundred employees at US Steel and to one thousand employees of the AC Spark Plug Division of General Motors Corporation, as well as at a Ford Motor plant in Mexico (Osborn 1962, 24–26). Most creative thinking sessions in corporate locations specifically included rank-and-file workers—even "hen-raisers and miners of marble were offered creativity clinics at their respective conventions" (Osborn 1962, 26). As I will elaborate below, while creative thinking was developed squarely at the heart of industrial (and military) settings, the process itself was often pitted *against* predominant utilitarian rationalities championed by management, the military, and bureaucracies. As the *Wall Street Journal* recounted, in brainstorm conferences, "recourse is had in the subconsciousness of the brainstormers in an atmosphere of anything goes: the participants throw out whatever ideas come in their heads" (1955). The rationality that was spurned in these sessions was a managerial rationality. Brainstorming was, for instance, explicitly antihierarchical. It often bypassed management altogether. Focusing instead on the self-expression of lower-level employees, it was geared at the democratic expertise of "no expertise"—where "everybody can have ideas." Moreover, creative thinking was separated from other forms of thinking practices, such as hierarchical structuring and practical matters. The very technique of brainstorming was based on the development of "creative potential," which was seen as antithetical to the critical, evaluative mind (Osborn 1948). An "explosion of ideas" could become a tool to increase productivity only if the judicial mind—in widespread use in these settings one may presume—was temporarily kept in check.

However, even in their embrace of irrationality—"the crazier an idea, the better"—the early days of creative ideation were rather organized affairs. They indexed a managed kind of intensity, or an institutionalized form of freedom. A brainstorming session was, for example, ideally conducted by a chairman, an idea collector, five guests, and five employees known for their creative ability, all seated in a yellow-painted room (yellow was deemed conducive for thought) (*Wall Street Journal* 1955; see also *Time* 1957). The desired creativity was labeled work, and achieving it entailed effort—uninhibited thinking could become a habit if trained: "Imagination, like muscle, can be built up by exercise" (Osborn 1953, 92). Moreover, the two minds or rationales were usually reincorporated, when, after a brainstorm, ideas were not seldom sorted out by an executive using his judicial mind. This hierarchical reintegration suggests that brainstorms were a controlled explosion—perhaps in a carnivalesque sense. They were in essence a transient phenomenon: after the brainstorms—which were often finished by filling out a form signing over the rights to any and all ideas to the corporation, military unit, or nation—the participants were to return to their conveyor belts, offices, or military rituals.

Besides hands-on training in thinking outside the box, articles on ideation and creativity documented and sustained the life of the concept. They blossomed in publications written in the 1950s and 1960s for the manufacturing industry (e.g., *Popular Mechanics, Mechanical Engineering, G.E. Review*), the military (*Army-Navy Journal, Military Review*), advertising (*Printers' Ink, Advertising Agency*), and management (*Advanced Management*). These articles and the practices they debated drew on a variety of disciplinary insights. The social sciences (sociology, anthropology, psychology) figured prominently among them, but they were seemingly effortlessly paired with engineering, chemistry, military R&D, industrial research, philosophy, literary studies, and (art) education.

One way in which their disparate insights were drawn together was through the production of bibliographies. The Industrial Research Institute issued one of the first bibliographies on creativity in 1955, followed by a bibliography on "creativity in science, engineering, business, and the arts" from Industrial Relations News (Deutsch and Shea 1958). In 1960, the Graduate School of Business at the University of Chicago crafted a bibliography on psychological and psychiatric approaches to creativity (and here it is easy not to notice the oddity: How do business and psychiatry usually interface, if at all? [Stein and Heinze 1960]). While the manufacturing industries were important in the production and circulation of creative thinking techniques, the military played a key role in the history of the traveling concept as well.[6] One of the first bibliographies on creativity was funded by the US Navy and issued by the Psychological Lab of the University of Southern California Los Angeles (Guilford, Christensen, and Wilson 1953). Other bibliographies were compiled by the US Naval Research Laboratory (on creativity in the physical sciences [Benton 1961]), the Armed Services Technical Information Agency (1963), and Lockheed Martin Missiles and Space Company (Evans and Stromer 1964).

In 1954, members of the US Air Force were first offered creative problem-solving courses, and by 1960, thirty-seven thousand members had been trained in creative thinking techniques (Osborn 1962, 24). Here too, in addition to training their mental muscles, the participants were encouraged to combine the irrationality of thinking freely and wildly, with the managerial discipline of "making notes and using check lists" and "setting deadlines and quotas" (Osborn 1948, 78–87). Brainstorming's oft-forgotten military idiom of "using the brain to storm a problem in commando fashion" itself indexes the tension between rationality and irrationality (Osborn 1948, 52). But while creativity's disciplining practices can be read as extensions of scientific and managerial logics into the realm of "free thinking," the emergence of brainstorming also marks a critique of those very rationalities. For while creative thinking developed as a value-generating practice squarely at the heart of military-industrial settings, it was pitted *against* predominant utilitarian rationalities of, for example, management, the military, and bureaucracies (Iverson 1962; Moses 1956; Rand 1960; Whyte 1952, 1956). I have hypothesized that in order to overcome the boundaries imposed by these modern rationalities, creative ideation promised a form of *counter-knowledge*: an understanding that comes about by not following the rules of thought (van Eekelen 2017).

The military invested enthusiastically in research into these modes of thinking otherwise. Most postwar funding of academic inquiries into creativity was supplied by the Office of Naval Research (ONR), which, following the war, had effectively become the peacetime institution for the distribution of federal funds for fundamental research.[7] Cold War challenges that tested the limits of military rationality and protocols proved to be fertile ground for the uses of free flows of ideas. Creativity, it turned out, was essential for thinking through—not to mention acting in—yet-to-be-experienced scenarios. For instance, in 1951, the US Air Force appointed the psychologist Paul Torrance as its new "director of survival research." The air force's Survival Training Program taught "men to think creatively about surviving in emergency and extreme conditions." Torrance, who later made a name for himself in the field of creativity studies, most notably through the Torrance Tests of Creative Thinking, traced his interest in the concept to the conundrum of survival: in "actual emergency and extreme conditions, the air-crewman was facing a new situation for which he had no learned and practiced solution" (Shaughnessy 1998, 443). This unprecedented situation required creative behavior. A similarly extreme condition that couldn't draw on previous experience was an unexampled nuclear war. "Thinking the unthinkable," as Herman Kahn called the pondering of the many outcomes of a nuclear war, required knowledge production strategies that could probe the unknown (Sharon Ghamari-Tabrizi 2005). Finally, creativity garnered urgency in the context of the space age as well: knowledge based on past experience wouldn't generate the intelligence required to shuttle an American to the moon. The investments in education through the National Defense Education Act (1958) solidified the existing strands of creativity research into what one stakeholder called the "Sputnik inspired era of creativity" (Lowenfeld 1960, 22; see also Mendelsohn and Griswold 1964, 431). One of its manifestations was the widespread testing of military personnel and school-age children, not just in terms of intelligence but also for their creative ability, a move echoed in PISA's creativity-adjusted aptitude test for fifteen-year-olds.

At this intersection of military and industrial interests in thinking outside the box, a field of "creativity studies" came into its own, which also facilitated the anchoring of academic parties in the contact zone. The field was institutionalized through a foundation (the Creative Education Foundation, founded in 1954), courses, publications, symposia, and annual problem-solving institutes.[8] Perhaps a sign of its emergence, the field vigorously tracked its own existence—through bibliographies, timelines, tallies, handbooks. This is why we know that by 1958, universities, corporations, and governmental agencies had organized over two thousand courses in creative thinking in the United States (Guilford 1958, 16). The field of creativity studies attracted engineers, psychologists, anthropologists, and philosophers, as well as numerous experts from the military and industry. It was not unusual for creativity experts themselves to embody the intersection of sectors—for instance, the consultant Harold F. Harding, who organized the first creativity seminar at Batelle Memorial Institute was a major general in the US Army Reserve who had consulted for the US Army Command and General Staff College. He was also a professor of rhetoric at Ohio State University (see Parnes and Harding 1962, 3). This is not to say that insights moved effortlessly between these spheres. When psychologist Abraham Maslow (better-known for his "hierarchy of needs" pyramid) was invited to give a lecture to military officers at the US Army Engineer School in Fort Belvoir, Virginia, in April 1957. In his talk, titled "Emotional Blocks to Creativity," he explicitly addressed the potential incommensurability of knowledge spheres. Reflecting on his position, he shared:

> I am a little startled to find myself in this situation. . . . I have been amazed to be plucked at in the last couple of years by big industries of which I know nothing, or organizations like yourself whose work I don't really know at all, and I find myself a little uneasy, like many of my colleagues, on this score, because I am not sure what I can deliver exactly. (Maslow [1957] 1962, 94)

Maslow nonetheless proceeded, urging the officers in the army's Creative Engineering Seminar to get in touch with their "deeper self." If they let go of their inclinations to control their unconscious—"this portion of ourselves of which we generally are afraid" (96)—they would find their "ability to play—to enjoy, to fantasy, to laugh, to loaf, to be spontaneous" (96). Ultimately, they were to be able to "regress in the service of ego" (99).

In its beginnings, the field yoked together a seemingly disparate set of theories—perhaps in line with the mid-twentieth-century interdisciplinary zeitgeist.[9] Besides methods for how the subconscious mind can be put to use, they included industrial research; studies of whether inventive and creative ability can be created in engineering students; anthropological studies of national differences in creativity; and studies of inventions, hunches, poetry, projective tests such as the Thematic Apperception Test, and other forms of measurement of understanding, imagination, intelligence, and aptitudes (what was notably absent are any economic studies of the value of creativity) (van Eekelen 2017). One way this interdisciplinary field was made palatable for different audiences was the production of the aforementioned bibliographies. These bibliographies were documents in which a rather varied set of knowledges (philosophy, sociology, anthropology, psychology, engineering, military R&D, industrial research, literary studies, and [art] education) were sorted and metabolized for different publics, and in which the category of creativity was legitimated as a concept worthy of study and practice in different contexts and fields. As can be gleaned from the institutions that produced these bibliographies, when creativity studies sought to establish itself as a more academic field of study in the late 1950s, both industry and the military were already prime sites for the adoption, study, and development of this concept. And the material that was channeled and generated in these settings was to a large extent the material that was being drawn together in the field of creativity studies. So while the 1965 bibliography of the Creative Education Foundation (Razik 1965) might be considered the "founding" bibliography for the field, it followed in the footsteps of about ten other institutions that had compiled their own lists of sanctioned references.

When looking at processes that contribute to the life of a social science concept, "scientization" is obviously a vital element in a chain of events that foster the life of a concept. Thanks to social science's investments in creativity research, the concept has been anchored into nature/nurture debates, and infused with psychoanalytic overtones. It has been operationalized, made testable (through, e.g., Rorschach tests, drawing completion tests, figure preference tests, symbol-equivalence tests, anagram tests, and mosaic construction tests), and measurable (e.g., Torrance Tests of Creative Thinking, and soon the PISA test). Likewise, a variety of creative thinking techniques became an object of unrelenting scientific scrutiny (e.g., Are engineers creative? Does brainstorming work? Should it be carried out in groups or individually?). However, it is important to note that the concept's scientization mattered, not only for science itself *but also for its invested parties*, and perhaps more so (e.g., military, industry, government). Scientization, in other words, had a blossoming life outside academia. Or, as was the case with creativity, the academy was folded into these extra-academic settings, this contact zone, which had funded, encouraged, generated, and facilitated creativity research all along.

However, the institutionalization of creativity studies came at a time when the concept was far from common sense. In 1948, for instance, the *New York Times* called brainstorming a "bizarre" method (Littledale 1948). Resistance to creative thinking techniques was also reported in *Imagination: Underdeveloped Resource*, a research report written by a group of Harvard students who took a course on manufacturing in 1955 (Student Research Group). Starting from the premise that creativity can be acquired, and with the aim to stimulate "creative thinking in business," they had documented and assessed a variety of idea-generating techniques, as well as the opposition they encountered. Because organized ideation was such a new terrain, they wrote, those who introduced this unorthodox technique to their own company were "liable to abuse and ridicule" (1955, 54). They continued: "Some people may even question his sanity. Conceivably, it may cost him his job" (54). At both MIT and Boston University, courses in creative thinking and engineering were thwarted (54). While one reason for its shady image was that it was reportedly hard to prove that ideas have actual dollar value (54), the concept of creativity itself also created very particular anxieties. Echoing the political zeitgeist, some worries concerned the communal aspects of joint ideation and collective deliberation. The students reported for instance on a letter they received from a large US corporation stating that "creative thinking sounds like just the kind of thing to make Senator McCarthy take off into the stratosphere" (Student Research Group 1955, 53). Similarly, in a critical note, *Time* had reported that some observers, while sympathetic to brainstorming, were worried about the "gobbledygook about 'creative ideation,' 'buzz sessions,' 'idearamas,' 'imagineering,' etcetera," most especially its communal aspects. Alluding to the paradox of brainstorming "in commando fashion," the magazine worried that "the emphasis on group thinking may produce the very regimentation it seeks to avoid" (*Time* 1957). Indeed, while early creativity manuals stipulated the collective nature of creative thinking exercises—storming a problem together—later manuals were adapted to include more individualistic approaches, such as "solo brainstorming" (e.g., Osborn 1962, 22).

The fearsome attributes of creativity were an effect, paradoxically, of both its known and unknown qualities. On the one hand, "creative thinking" sounded all too familiar—and thus seemingly nonscientific. And on the other hand these processes were not familiar enough. "Creative thinking," "ideation," "buzz sessions," and "brainstorming" sounded nonsensical—"as if they had been taken from a science fiction magazine" (Osborn 1962, 22)—which made it an uncanny practice with *no place* in business, the military, or the university.

Multisited Histories of Social Science

If we look at the history of creativity through the looking glass, what does the heterogeneous field of histories of social science gain from studies of its concepts, a concept like creativity, and what, if anything, might cultural anthropologists contribute to these studies? A straightforward contribution is methodological: a historical study of social science concepts complements studies of the more "usual suspects" in histories of social science (often modeled as histories of existing disciplines, theoretical developments, key institutions, or notable authors). The methodological primacy of concepts does not mean that institutional histories, intellectual biographies, and disciplinary histories do not have their merit. But in the social life of concepts, as with creativity, these histories are reshuffled and not so discrete.

Moreover, while the production of a social science concept—and social science more broadly—is often retrospectively imagined to have taken place in academia, the social life of creativity—and doubtlessly other concepts—illuminates the interrelations between industry, the military, and the social sciences not centrally discussed in history of social science literature.[10] Moreover, in addition to detailing their sites of production, studies of the life of social science concepts require investigations in how they circulate, are taken up, and are mobilized for particular purposes. As is clear in the case of creativity, a concept's production continues in its circulation, its appropriation, its social and public life. Its historical trajectory suggests that this life is not an afterthought; in fact, the circulation and popular use *preceded*, affected, and facilitated its social scientific objectification. That travel has been constitutive of the concept of creativity can be gleaned from the fact that without its mobilization in military and industrial settings, it is unlikely that the same investments would have been made to objectivize the term.[11]

These multisited histories also add a historical dimension to sometimes one-dimensional debates on relations between the private sector and (social) science funding. Rather than uncovering dark histories of influence, or holding on to some timeless ideal of autonomy, we might have to (a) historicize and situate invocations and imaginations of autonomy itself, and (b) to find ways to engage the worldly histories within which social science emerges. Whereas the history of creative thinking provides an example of the entanglement of the sociocultural sciences in universities with extra-academic settings, the story of their interrelations is not automatically included in social science histories. The contact zone of military social sciences or corporate social sciences is eyed and entered wearily by many, or regarded as a one-way relation where sociocultural methods have been brought in and applied (see van Eekelen 2017). Extra-academic settings aren't generally framed as generative of methodological or conceptual innovation for sociocultural sciences. Yet there is a long history to the imbrications of scientists of culture, values, and the social and the worlds beyond academia (how could there not be?). That is, however understandably—and justifiably—wary sociocultural scientists may be when invited to think about public–private knowledge exchanges, there is a longer history of traffic between the academy and military-industrial contexts. Moreover, the history of creativity suggests that these encounters have not simply "limited" the scientific status of the knowledge involved. Some of this traffic has bolstered the production and circulation of academic insights. To sum up, I posit here that histories of social science concepts do not only rethink and refract the concept under scrutiny, in this case the concept of creativity. They also invite us to rethink the way we imagine current social science, and social science history.

Histories and the Present

Conceptual shifts have cultural consequences, recoverable at the level of social practice.—SARAH FRANKLIN, "Science as Culture, Cultures of Science"

If social science objectifications do not always precede the life/circulation of the term, and if they come about in extra-academic settings, the challenge is to formulate questions that speak to the life of social science concepts in their worldly settings. Here anthropologists may fruitfully collaborate with (or complement) historians of concepts (see also Gluck and Tsing 2009; Stade 2014). Cultural anthropologists are attuned to the constitutive and reiterative processes that a trajectory of a concept depends on rather than the content of the concept (the thing stripped away from these processes). Cultural anthropologists, moreover, often track a concept in its travels from one sphere to another, and trace how they distribute and produce differences. In their peripheral visions of concepts as objects of ethnographic enquiry, anthropologists thus bring into view the relationships within which concepts occur and the thought (and ultimately, practice) they make (im)possible (Strathern 1995). These differentiated uses, moreover, can be studied in the past and in the present. Unlike most historians, who are trained to wait patiently until the dust settles, anthropologists can study histories of the present *and* the present.

In my experience, ethnographic studies of concepts such as creativity are nevertheless in danger of compounding the interest in a concept. Paradoxically, one may need to take a step back to get a more in-depth view of contemporary mobilizations of a social science concept. With a Teflon concept in particular, it is hard to detect the difference that makes a difference—it all sounds too familiar, and the words are nearly the same. Interestingly, histories of concepts are unusually productive in creating that distance when faced with a Teflon concept like creativity, quality, or excellence in ethnographic proximity. On the one hand, historical distance can generate forms of ethnographic intimacy in present conjunctures that may otherwise elide us—by highlighting a concept's historical instability, the present can emerge as the unruly object it is, waiting for more granular ethnographic analysis. On the other hand, histories of concepts offer a toolkit for engagement: they provide anthropologists with nonscalable tools tailored to each and every concept, which can be used to probe the articulations in the present. To be specific, their particular trajectories provide relevant questions that can put the contemporary uses of the concept (including depoliticizing ones) in perspective. Historical research may showcase for instance that concepts that may seem to have no political connotations turn out to have political histories and footprints too, which may generate questions that will scratch the concept's apolitical surface and provide analytical entry points. I will use the remainder of this chapter to illustrate this point: that social histories offer us concept-specific toolkits—in this case related to administration, work, and geopolitics—that can be critical for studying the use of concepts and the ways they are "reflexively implicated" (Giddens 1984, 20).

THE HISTORY OF CREATIVITY is shot through with questions of nature/ nurture: Is it something everyone is born with, or is it something that can be taught, if approached in the right way? Tangerman (1963)—and many colleagues—made the case that while we are born with creative abilities, and while we flourish "naturally" at an early age, formal education "smothers" creativity, sending the natural ability into a tailspin. Once working in industry, and with "negative" creative ability (whatever that means—but it was due to education), corporations took it upon themselves to retrain employees in their creative abilities. If creativity is innate, there is not much anyone can or should do about it. But if creativity can be cultivated, it can become an object of government. (Creative) education, as a site for scientific study and intervention became caught up in this process. For instance, in the wake of the Cold War, educational settings—both civilian and military—

became prime sites to measure creativity, to stimulate creative ability, and to evaluate techniques to stimulate creative thinking (van Eekelen 2017; see also Bennett 2015; Cohen-Cole 2014). If we take these historical entanglements with us into the present, for instance with the PISA test, we take along queries such as the following: To what extent is creativity nowadays subject to study and disciplinary action? Who administers creativity? What are the stakes? Where tests, creative practices, scientific studies, bibliographies, graphs, accounting categories all proffer material transformations that have made "creativity"—seemingly irreversibly—real, what technologies are nowadays used to naturalize creativity?

In addition to tests of people's creative ability—innate or trained—the history of creativity is also rife with efforts to measure its outcomes— contributing to debates over whether ideas and knowledge are measurable. Whether or not ideas are measurable depends on the technologies used for collecting them. The history of creative thinking showcases, for instance, how during World War II, ideas were measurable: they were collected in idea drives, and their quantitative results were published in newspapers (van Eekelen 2018b). In the 1950s and 1960s, creativity itself was subject to efforts to make it measurable (van Eekelen 2017). Nowadays, while the PISA test suggest that creative abilities are measurable, the products of our imagination such as knowledge, creativity, and ideas are often presumed unmeasurable *and therefore valuable*—or measurable as derivative, as in intangible assets in accounting (van Eekelen 2015a, 2015b).[12] It is important to note that both with categories of nature and nurture, or with measurable or immeasurable qualities, I do not suggest an irreversible movement in one direction—for example, from nature to nurture or from measurable to immeasurable. Rather, through the looking glass, these categories actually appear rather unstable—and this instability makes them good to think with.

THE ADMINISTRATION AND MEASUREMENT of creativity also tie it to work—notwithstanding the ways in which creativity is currently perceived as lopped off from "work." Creativity is rarely dubbed work itself as it was in the 1950s, and nowadays creative thinking or loose thought is often severed from economic, material, and military spheres and definitely from manufacturing spheres—it is all too often considered a departure from manufacturing economies. What the history of the concept suggests, however, is that an appreciation for creative thinking may spring forth from highly rationalized military industrial settings, at least in the particular period from 1935 to 1970. Rather than signaling a succession of industrial societies—as is often suggested in invocations of, for instance, a creative economy—I read the history of a rising interest in creativity as an *effect* of industrial modes of production. To be sure, a technique like brainstorming resists the very logics of the military and the manufacturing industries. And it foreshadows the rise of post-Fordist inspirational discourse—Boltanski and Chiapello's "new spirit of capitalism" (1999)—and the simultaneous falling out of fashion of disciplining productivity terms. But rather than an appropriation and concurrent depoliticization of countercultural sensibilities by post-Fordist managers, as Boltanski and Chiapello have it, what I have underscored above is that it was *within* the military, and *within* the manufacturing industry, that an appreciation for creative practices had come into its own. If anything—and strangely—in the case of creative ideation, a spirit roamed around in military and industrial contexts in the 1950s–60s, well before hippies picked it up, and long before it would be picked up again as capitalism's countercultural "new" spirit of management. Given these complex entanglements, it also remains relevant and interesting to inquire what present invocations of creativity have to do with industry and industrial work. Is it mostly indexing a naturalization of anxiety related to the outsourcing of production? And who is imagined to be part of a transformation toward creativity in Reagan's "creative society" (1966) or Europe's "creative economy" (Schlezinger 2017), and who becomes completely invisible?

If creativity is invoked in particular workplaces and not others, it remains to be seen how creativity is imagined to be related to work. Is creative ideation framed as antithetical to work or as intertwined with work? A poster titled "imagineering" from World War II (Office of Emergency Management 1942–43) generates several lines of inquiry for the present (for more analysis see van Eekelen 2015b). It depicts an office worker and a worker on the shop floor—they are both imagineering. In terms of workspaces, can we envision "Imagination in the office" *and* "Imagination on the shopfloor," as suggested by the poster, or can we only think in places considered at a remove from "work"—ironically exemplified by converted factory spaces—and why (van Eekelen 2015a; Designboom 2019)? Moreover, what is the role of the body and the mind in ideation, and how are both conceptualized? With respect to the mind, what model of the brain is for instance espoused—is it conceived of as two hemispheres (a judicial and a creative one—where one exercises one's mental muscle), a nervous system, or a cybernetic information machine, a computer (see Modern, this volume)? With respect to the body, the poster depicting workers ideating in their workspaces also raises the question of whether and how ideation or creativity is related to practice; and, if so, what type of practice—manual/intellectual, embodied/disembodied? And of course the query looms: Who gets to do the thinking—manual workers, engineers, miners of marble, entrepreneurs? And who owns the fruits of ideation—do we still sign over all and every right to the corporation as participants in early brainstorming sessions would? Finally, the social life of creativity queries the temporalities of thinking that are at stake. Does creativity harness fifteen minutes of free thought that needs to be administered by a creativity expert or fostered through self-discipline (copious note-taking as mentioned before), or does it index an unlimited search for fundamental knowledge that may be harnessed through the institutionalization of freedom (e.g., through freedom from administrative labor, or from the short-term temporal discipline of grant proposals [see van Eekelen 2018a])?

WHETHER ANTITHETICAL TO WORK, or interwoven with labor processes, creativity is often imagined to change both the person who is creative and her relations with others. In the 1950s, the notion of the "idea man" gave workers a new way to think of themselves. As the *Wall Street Journal* put it: "One by-product of this atomic and space age is the new play on brainpower and leadership. The uncommon man, not the common man, the leader, not the follower; the thinker, not the non-thinker, are the ones in demand" (1955). Creativity was invoked, for example, to take the edge off of standardized, routinized, mind-numbing work. In a context in which mass production and mass consumption emerged, with concomitant labor situations and gray flannel suits, creativity was dangled as a means to stand out (even if everybody did it). This generates a wide range of questions: How and why is creativity imagined to change a person, and his or her relations with others? How does creativity discourse (re)frame relations with management? Creativity also raises interesting questions related to expertise and nonexpertise—it often proffers, as I discussed earlier, the expertise of "no expertise"—where "everybody can have ideas." Really?

As can be surmised from countless postwar articles that detail blocks to creativity (e.g. Kubie 1965; Maslow 1957; Mears 1961), some forms of knowledge and expertise were framed as stifling creativity, including those banking on experience and tradition. This marks an interesting shift. During World War II embodied experience was highly rated as a source of creative thinking—"Men and women who work with machines have good ideas," the War Production Board suggested, intimating that it was worker's embodied experience with machines that guaranteed good ideas (1942; van Eekelen 2018b). In the aftermath of World War II we see a decline in the value of past experience. The Cold War garnered a world of unknowns, a new world at the cusp of unexampled futures (atomic, but also carving a path to the moon). Experience—and the hierarchies that are often harnessed by experience—came to be framed as something that hampered creative thinking and the production of new knowledge (Ghamari-Tabrizi 2005; van Eekelen 2017). These shifts suggest, I posit, that it is still relevant to query how current calls on creativity reframe the value attributed to expertise, experience, and tradition.

AND FINALLY, what is creativity imagined to contribute or overcome (e.g., to push the frontiers of military knowledge production; to train soldiers to survive behind enemy lines)? What knowledge is it supposed to yield? What types of unthinkables is it supposed to render thinkable—for example, unexampled infrastructures of a post–atomic, bombed-out landscape (Ghamari-Tabrizi 2005) or tabletop exercises on a fictional coronavirus pandemic (Johns Hopkins Center for Health Security 2019)? And, not unrelated, what are the geopolitical stakes of a call for creativity? For instance, in a response to Russian inventiveness during the Cold War, symbolized by *Sputnik*, the concept of creativity was employed to rally Americans to rethink their education system and the ways in which knowledge production and innovation could be improved (van Eekelen 2017). In the 1990s, while calls for creativity, knowledge, and ideas were reliably cast in a positive spirit (progress), they simultaneously indexed anxieties about the inability of postindustrial countries to compete in the realm of standardized labor. As *Businessweek* fused the optimism and pessimism in one sentence, "Globalization, outsourcing, and the emphasis on innovation and creativity are forcing businesses to shift at a dramatic rate from tangible to intangible investments" (Mandel, Hamm, and Farrel 2006; van Eekelen 2015b). A creative economy was thus invoked to contend with global reorganizations of production. In each case, it is worth asking what (if any) political challenge is being addressed or elided by the invitation to think in terms of creativity.

To sum up, tracing the social life of concepts helps us to think through what may potentially be at play in the uptake/uses of a term, both in the past and in the present. As I said in the introduction, by foregrounding the histories of social science concepts, my goal is ultimately to find ways to detect the politics and public issues that are at play in contemporary uptakes and uses of these terms—especially when it is at first blush hard to detect any issues. The study of social life of concepts provides a tool to illuminate their historical particularity and instability, and to generate vantage points from which to think through the present.

Conclusion

The study of the social life of concepts seeks to combine history and anthropology to study the past and present lives of social science concepts, their production and circulation, in academia and the worlds beyond. By way of conclusion, I would like to raise one more question. How do we write about the social life of a concept? What form of writing is apposite for a life that intensifies at times, consolidates in certain areas, and fizzles in others? The vitalism implied in a "life" seems to suggest continuity, stability, essence, identity (and perhaps growth and refinement). In tracking the life of social science concepts one finds rather discontinuity, appropriation, mutation—concepts can take on reversed meanings, they can nest in unforeseen contexts. Can I call it a social life when I write about the tentative and fragmented nature of appropriations, push-back, professionalization, implementation, application, scientization, and popularization of a concept? Two points are important to remember. First, that "social life" refers to the worlds within which a concept is called on—as its worldly entanglements shift, so does the concept, even as it sounds the same. The point is exactly to get a feel for the potential instability of a concept when it is conjured in a next setting. And second, "social life" is ultimately a metaphor; it should not be taken too literally. What I seek to describe is in some sense an afterlife—with a temporality so shot through that fragments may be the most appropriate form.

Notes

1   This test was originally planned for 2021 and was then delayed by a year because of the pandemic. This is not the first time that the planned incorporation of creativity misfires. The year 2009 was hailed as the "European year of creativity"—but it is better known as the Great Recession.
2   This is obviously not an exhaustive list; think also of globalization, human capital, and culture.
3   For more detailed histories of this term, see van Eekelen 2015a, 2015b, 2017, 2018a, 2018b.
4   Like Williams, Reinhart Koselleck has also argued that language, society, and history are inextricably entwined and that this nexus is usefully entered through histories of concepts, which fuse the history of ideas with social history (1989).

5　An intellectual history that establishes the progeny of concepts, for instance, is of limited use when part of the challenge is that the same concept is made to work slightly differently as it is mobilized in new contexts.

6　As two reviewers remarked, a parallel history is to be written about the social life of "operations research"; but see Mirowski 2001.

7　E.g., ONR Contract No. N6onr-23810 between the Office of Naval Research and the University of Southern California; ONR Contract No. N6ori-20 between Psychometric Laboratory of the University of Chicago and the Office of Naval Research. ONR was established in 1946 and followed in the footsteps of the Office of Coordinator of Research and Inventions (1941–45) and the Office of Research and Inventions (1945) (see Darley 1957, 319; see also Sapolsky 1990; Mirowski 2001).

8　The *Journal of Creative Behavior*, for instance, was founded in 1967.

9　Hunter Crowther-Heyck (2006) has written an excellent study of the history of this interdisciplinary moment.

10　Philip Mirowski's (e.g., 2002) and David Price's (2008) works are interesting studies of exactly this contact zone, but their work is not often taken up as standard reading for the history of economics and cultural anthropology, respectively. Kristoffer Kropp, John Modern, Amín Pérez, and George Steinmetz (this volume) also show us that there are other sites of encounter where social science came about.

11　According to Giddens (1984, 18–20), the traffic from public "lay" knowledge to science is more often studied than the reflexive implication of science in that which it seeks to describe. A good example of the former is Emily Martin's work, which has shown how science of the immune system was deeply influenced by folk notions of the body, rather than the other way around (Martin 1994). My sense is that for social science studies, even this traffic, which differs from the travel of social science concepts after its academic conception, is still sparsely taken into account.

12　I have written elsewhere about how the contemporary idea that "ideas have value" has become common sense through its adoption in bureaucratic machineries. It is expressed as "intangible assets" in Financial Accounting Standards, as the category "information economy" in the Standard Industrial Classification Model, and as knowledge in knowledge-adjusted GDPs (van Eekelen 2015a).

References

Armed Services Technical Information Agency. 1963. "Creativity." In *Research and Development Management: A Report Bibliography 1959-62*. US. Arlington, VA. https://archive.org/details/DTIC_AD0400611/mode/2up.

Bennett, Eric. 2015. *Workshops of Empire: Stegner, Engle, and American Creative Writing during the Cold War*. Iowa City: University of Iowa Press.

Benton, Mildred Catherine. 1961. *Creativity in Research and Invention in the Physical Sciences: An Annotated Bibliography* [*sic*]. Washington: U.S. Naval Research Laboratory.

Boltanski, Luc, and Eve Chiapello. 1999. *The New Spirit of Capitalism*. Translated by Gregory Elliott. London: Verso.

Cohen-Cole, Jamie. 2014. *The Open Mind: Cold War Politics and the Sciences of Human Nature*. Chicago: University of Chicago Press.

Crouch, Margaret A. 1998. "The 'Social Etymology' of 'Sexual Harassment.'" *Journal of Social Philosophy* 29, no. 3: 19–40.

Crowther-Heyck, Hunter. 2006. "Patrons of the Revolution: Ideals and Institutions in Postwar Behavioral Science." *Isis* 97, no. 3: 420–46.

Darley, John G. 1957. "Psychology and the Office of Naval Research: A Decade of Development." *American Psychologist* 12, no. 6: 305–23.

Designboom. 2019. "Old Garment Factory Is Converted into Bali's Newest Creative Studio." *Designboom*, April 15, 2019. https://www.designboom.com /architecture/jasmine-mariani-kinship-factory-conversion-bali-indonesia-04 -15-2019/, accessed June 2021.

Deutsch and Shea, Inc. 1958. *Creativity: A Comprehensive Bibliography on Creativity in Science, Engineering, Business, and the Arts*. New York: Industrial Relations News.

European Commission. 2008. "Decision No 1350/2008/Ec of the European Parliament and of the Council of 16 December 2008 concerning the European Year of Creativity and Innovation (2009)." December 16, 2008. https://eur -lex.europa.eu/legal-content/EN/TXT/?uri=celex:32008D1350.

Evans, George R., and Peter R. Stromer. 1964. *Creativity, Innovation, and Invention: An Annotated Bibliography*. Sunnyvale, CA: Lockheed Martin Missiles and Space Company.

Ferguson, James. 1999. *Expectations of Modernity: Myths and Meanings of Urban Life on the Zambian Copperbelt*. Berkeley: University of California Press.

Franklin, Sarah. 1995. "Science as Culture, Cultures of Science." *Annual Review of Anthropology* 24: 163–84.

Fraser, Nancy, and Linda Gordon. 1994. "A Genealogy of Dependency: Tracing a Keyword of the U.S. Welfare State." *Signs: Journal of Women in Culture and Society* 19, no. 2: 309–36.

Ghamari-Tabrizi, Sharon. 2005. *The Worlds of Herman Kahn: The Intuitive Science of Thermonuclear War*. Cambridge, MA: Harvard University Press.

Giddens, Anthony. 1984. *The Constitution of Society*. Cambridge, UK: Polity Press.

Gluck, Carol, and Anna Tsing, eds. 2009. *Words in Motion: Toward a Global Lexicon*. Durham, NC: Duke University Press.

Guilford, J. P. 1958. "Can Creativity Be Developed?" *Art Education* 11, no. 6: 3–18.

Guilford, J. P., Paul R. Christensen, and Robert C. Wilson. 1953. *A Bibliography of Thinking, Including Creative Thinking, Reasoning, Evaluation, and Planning*. Los Angeles: University of Southern California, Psychological Lab.

Haraway, Donna Jeanne. 1989. *Primate Visions: Gender, Race, and Nature in the World of Modern Science*. New York: Routledge.

Iverson, Robert G. 1962. *Rational Management of Creativity*. Washington, DC: George Washington University Press.

Johns Hopkins Center for Health Security. 2019. "About the Event 201 Exercise." Accessed July 8, 2022. https://www.centerforhealthsecurity.org/our-work /exercises/event201/about.

Koselleck, Reinhart. 1989. "Social History and Conceptual History." *International Journal of Politics, Culture, and Society* 2, no. 3: 308–25.

Kubie, Lawrence. 1965 (June). Blocks to Creativity. *International Science and Technology*, no. 42: 69–78, 85–86.

Littledale, Harold A. 1948. "Imagination Yea—Shyness Nay." *New York Times* November 7, 1948.

Lowenfeld, Viktor. 1960. "Creative Intelligence." *Studies in Art Education* 1, no. 2: 22–25.

Mandel, M., S. Hamm, and C. Farrel. 2006. "Why the Economy Is a Lot Stronger Than You Think." *BusinessWeek*, February 13, 62–70.

Martin, Emily. 1994. *Flexible Bodies: Tracking Immunity in American Culture from the Days of Polio to the Age of AIDS*. Boston: Beacon.

Martin, Emily. 2007. *Bipolar Expeditions: Mania and Depression in American Culture*. Princeton, NJ: Princeton University Press.

Maslow, Abraham Harold. (1957) 1962. "Emotional Blocks to Creativity." In *A Source Book for Creative Thinking*, edited by Sidney Jay Parnes and Harold Friend Harding, 93–104. New York: Charles Scribner's Sons.

Mears, Roberet. B. 1961. "Stimulating Creativity in Research and Development." *Research Management* 4, no. 4: 147–52.

Mendelsohn, G. A., and B. B. Griswold. 1964. "Differential Use of Incidental Stimuli in Problem Solving as a Function of Creativity." *Journal of Abnormal and Social Psychology* 68, no. 4: 431–36.

Mirowski, Philip. 2001. *Machine Dreams: Economics Becomes a Cyborg Science*. Cambridge: Cambridge University Press.

Moses, George. 1956. "Do You Dare to Be Different." *Advertising Agency Magazine* 49, no. 10: 65–68.

New York Times. 1966. "Alex F. Osborn, 77, a Founder and Officer of B.B.D.&O., Dies." May 6, 1966.

OECD. 2014. "Are 15-Year-Olds Creative Problem-Solvers?" *PISA in Focus* 38, no. 4: 1–4.

OECD. 2019. "Innovation Strategy for Education and Training." Accessed February 20, 2019. http://www.oecd.org/education/ceri/IS%20Project _Conference%20Brochure_FINAL.pdf.

OECD. 2021. "PISA 2021 Creative Thinking Framework (Third Draft)." Accessed June 1, 2021. https://www.oecd.org/pisa/publications/pisa-2021-creative -thinking-framework.pdf.

Office of Emergency Management, War Production Board. 1942–43. *Imagineering: Imagination in the Office. Imagination on the Shopfloor*. National Archives

Identifier: 534198. Local Identifier: 179-WP-349. https://catalog.archives.gov
/id/534198.

Osborn, Alex F. 1948. *Your Creative Power: How to Use Imagination*. New York:
Charles Scribner's Sons.

Osborn, Alex F. 1953. *Applied Imagination: Principles and Procedures of Creative Thinking*. New York: Charles Scribner's Sons.

Osborn, Alex F. 1962. "Developments in Creative Education." In *A Source Book for
Creative Thinking*, edited by Sidney Jay Parnes and Harold Friend Harding,
19–30. New York: Charles Scribner's Sons.

Parnes, Sidney Jay, and Harold Friend Harding. 1962. *A Source Book for Creative
Thinking*. New York: Charles Scribner's Sons.

Price, David H. 2008. *Anthropological Intelligence: The Deployment and Neglect of
American Anthropology in the Second World War*. Durham, NC: Duke University Press.

Rand, Paul. 1960. "Our Biggest Threat Is Conformity." *Printer's Ink* 273, no. 9:
50–55.

Razik, Taher A. 1965. *Bibliography of Creativity Studies and Related Areas*. Buffalo:
State University of New York.

Reagan, Ronald. 1966. *The Creative Society*. University of Southern California,
April 19, 1966.

Riles, Annelise. 2000. *The Network Inside Out*. Ann Arbor: University of Michigan
Press.

Sapolsky, Harvey M. 1990. *Science and the Navy: The History of the Office of Naval
Research*. Princeton, NJ: Princeton University Press.

Schlesinger, Philip. 2017. "The Creative Economy: Invention of a Global Orthodoxy." *Innovation: The European Journal of Social Science Research* 30, no. 1:
73–90.

Shaughnessy, Michael. 1998. "An Interview with E. Paul Torrance: About Creativity." *Educational Psychology Review* 10, no. 4: 441–52.

Stade, Ronald. 2014. "Emergent Concept Chains and Scenarios of Depoliticization: The Case of Global Governance as a Future Past." In *Anthropology Now
and Next: Essays in Honor of Ulf Hannerz*, edited by T. H. Eriksen, C. Garsten,
S. Randeria, and U. Hannerz, 205–40. New York: Berghahn Books.

Stein, Morris Isaac, and Heinze, Shirley. J. 1960. *Creativity and the Individual: Summaries of Selected Literature in Psychology and Psychiatry*. Chicago: Free Press,
University of Chicago, Graduate School of Business.

Strathern, Marilyn. 1995. *Shifting Contexts: Transformations in Anthropological Knowledge*. London: Routledge.

Student Research Group. 1955. *Imagination: Underdeveloped Resource; A Critical Study
of Techniques and Programs for Stimulating Creative Thinking in Business*. Cambridge, MA: Harvard Graduate School of Business Administration.

Tangerman, E. J. 1963. "Some Thoughts about Today's Creativity." *Product Engineering* 34: 105–7.

Time. 1957. "New Ways to Find New Ideas." February 18, 1957. http://www.time
.com/time/magazine/article/0,9171,809155,00.html.

Torrance, E. Paul. 1967. "The Minnesota Studies of Creative Behavior: National and International Extensions." *Journal of Creative Behavior* 1, no. 2: 137–54.

Tsing, A. 2000. "The Global Situation." *Cultural Anthropology* 15, no. 3: 327–60.

van Eekelen, Bregje F. 2015a. "Accounting for Ideas: Bringing a Knowledge Economy into the Picture." *Economy and Society* 44, no. 3: 445–79.

van Eekelen, Bregje F. 2015b. "Knowledge for the West, Production for the Rest? Narratives of Progress and Decline in Knowledge Economies." *Journal of Cultural Economy* 8, no. 4: 479–500.

van Eekelen, Bregje F. 2017. "Creative Intelligence and the Cold War: US Military Investment in Undisciplined Thought 1945–1965." *Conflict and Society* 4: 92–107.

van Eekelen, Bregje F. 2018a. "Discipline and Creativity: Anti-conformity, Questions of Usefulness, and Free Thinking in Military and Industrial Settings." *IAS Newsletter*. https://www.ias.edu/ideas/van-eekelen-discipline-creativity.

van Eekelen, Bregje F. 2018b. "Uncle Sam Wants Your Ideas: A Brief History of Embodied Knowledge in American World War II Posters." *Public Culture* 30, no. 1: 113–42.

Wall Street Journal. 1955. "Brainstorming: More Concerns Set Up Free-Wheeling 'Think' Panels to Mine Ideas." December 5, 1955.

Wall Street Journal. 1958. "Reading for Business." March 19, 1958.

War Production Board. 1942. *War Production Drive: Official Plan Book*. Washington, DC: Government Printing Office.

Whyte, William Hollingsworth. 1952. "Groupthink." *Fortune*, March, 114–17, 142, 146.

Whyte, William Hollingsworth. 1956. *The Organization Man*. New York: Doubleday and Company.

Williams, Raymond. 1979. *Politics and Letters: Interviews with "New Left Review."* London: Verso.

Williams, Raymond. 1985. *Keywords: A Vocabulary of Culture and Society*. New York: Oxford University Press.

epistemological crises in legal theory

The (Ir)Rationality
of Balancing

CAREL SMITH

Jurisprudence was the first of the social sciences to be born.—KARL GEORG WURZEL,
"METHODS OF JURIDICAL THINKING"

IN HER CONTRIBUTION TO *Kuhn's Structure of Scientific Revolutions at Fifty*
(2016), Lorraine Daston argues that Thomas Kuhn's most lasting contribution to the philosophy of science is probably his revolutionary idea that scientific learning and research is driven by perceived similarity to a paradigm
rather than by following rules. Not deduction, but a variety of reasoning
methods such as analogy, exemplary reasoning, and balancing, the use of
which require "trained judgment," is characteristic of scientific reasoning.
This idea, says Daston, is still a controversial one, since it conflicts with the
dominant view that knowledge that cannot be expressed in *rules* is denied
the status of genuine knowledge. The very word *rationality*, in fact, has been
narrowed down to rules since the mid-nineteenth century (Daston 2016,
128). Where rules fall short, one speaks of tacit knowledge (Polanyi), practices (Wittgenstein), pattern recognition (cognitive scientists), or judgments
(lawyers). That is for many a sure sign "that we have left the crystalline realm
of the rational" (Daston 2016, 126). Yet, "the stubborn resistance of phenomena

as diverse as legal judgments, language acquisition, pattern recognition, and scientific training . . . suggests that the phenomenon of learning and reasoning from exemplars . . . is both real and encompasses far more than just science" (Daston 2016, 128).

Daston's paradoxical observation is confirmed by the academic discipline of law. Solid methodological research on the production of knowledge in legal practice and legal science affirms that legal reasoning includes types of reasoning such as comparison of cases, analogy and balancing to such extent that legal reasoning can better be characterized by exemplary reasoning than by rule-following. This characterization, however, is invariably rejected by legal scholars and practitioners of considerable size and varying impact. For them, exemplary reasoning is subjective and irrational. In this contribution I will elaborate on the thesis that most lawyers and legal scholars, at present as well as in the past, perceive the law as a rule-governed activity, except for one glorious moment, when legal scholars and judges sought affiliation with the social sciences to determine the law. I will investigate the implications of this connection for the study of law, and particularly focus on the method of "balancing of interests." The acceptance and dismissal of this method turns out to be exemplary of the shifting appreciation of the use of the social sciences for the study of law.

Before I defend the thesis, some context is required. The next section explicates the reciprocal relation between legal practice and legal scholarship. The following three sections discuss the pendulum of views about legal methodology, from the rule-based models of the nineteenth century, to the models that favor balancing and comparison, back to the current appreciation for deduction and categorization. In the last two sections, I will address the paradox that balancing as a method of judicial decision was considered rational from a social science perspective, whereas balancing came to be rejected as irrational from a perspective that regards law as a self-sufficient discipline that favors rule-based reasoning.

Legal Scholarship and Legal Practice: A Continuum

From a layman's perspective, it seems straightforward: legal practitioners create and apply the law, whereas legal scholars study the phenomenon of the law as it manifests itself through legislation, precedents, and the operations and conduct of its practitioners; legal practitioners are thus part of the law and take an internal perspective, whereas legal scholars are outside the law and regard the law from an external perspective. The truth is that traditional legal scholarship and legal practice form a continuum. The questions that legal scholars ask and seek to answer are not unlike the questions that judges, representatives, and administrators are forced to answer, such as questions about how legal doctrines should be interpreted, what implications a Supreme Court ruling has, and what rules should be created.

The scholarly orientation toward the legal profession can be explained by the demand to adjust the law to the continuous flow of new phenomena and changing conditions that are characteristic of modern society. Sometimes the adjustments are the result of explicit legislation, but more often the necessary changes are incorporated into existing law—for example, by extending the scope of a regulation or applying a precedent analogically. The implications of these alterations and additions should then be examined, an investigation that includes an assessment of the desirability of the adjustment or addition. This is done foremost by legal academics who have the means (especially time) to examine such issues more systematically than legal practitioners do. The normative position is characteristic for traditional legal scholarship, and it is called "prescriptivism": "the demand that each piece of scholarship offer some account, however nebulous, of the stakes for how the law should be modified or interpreted or how legal decisionmakers should do their jobs" (Balkin and Levinson 2006, 175). The result is a continuous exchange of opinions and insights between legal science and legal practice on how the law should be interpreted and applied. Since beliefs on the functioning of language or the role of moral principles in legal adjudication affect the decisions or conclusions considerably, methodological reflection on legal adjudication is a topic that is relevant for both scholars and practitioners. It explains why not only the ethical standards and behavior of candidate justices but also their "legal philosophy" are the topics of intense scrutiny. The upshot is that, when legal scholars discuss the merits and demerits of deduction and exemplary reasoning, it concerns the production not only of knowledge of legal doctrine but also of legal practice.

Legalism and the "Case Law Method" versus *Freirechtsbewegung* and Legal Realism

Two nineteenth-century movements, or schools, epitomize the view that the law is a rule-governed activity. In Europe, the codifications led to what is called legalism, the view that all law can be found in written law, such as statutes, so that the task of the judge is principally limited to mere application, and the task of legal doctrine to infer from the body of existing law the proper meaning.[1] For the United States (with its common law system), it was Christopher Columbus Langdell, dean of Harvard Law School, who invented the "case law method," whereby the student learns to infer from a relatively closed set of legal cases (particularly the decisions of appellate courts) the entire implicit rational system of law (Langdell 1871; Forrester 1996). In both approaches, the lawyer is a neutral and impartial arbitrator who only establishes what is in the law. Both legalism and the Langdellian "case law method" resulted in a formalist or "internalist approach" of the law: to resolve legal issues, judge or legal scholar should focus exclusively on the current system of rules (laws, treaties, directives) and precedents.

Both variants of the internalist approach were strongly criticized at the end of the nineteenth century. In Europe, legal scholars as diverse as François Gény (1917), Eugen Ehrlich (1903), Hermann Kantorowicz (1906), and Karl Georg Wurzel (1917) formed the movement of the *Freirechtsbewegung* (Free Law Movement), although this movement never attained the status of a "school." In the United States, it is the movement of Legal Realism, preceded by the towering figure of Oliver Wendell Holmes and inspired by the Freirechtsbewegung, that campaigned against the formalistic approach of legal scholarship and legal adjudication (Herget and Wallace 1987). Both the Freirechtsbewegung and Legal Realism rejected the claim that legal adjudication is a rule-governed activity to the extent that the proper use of these standards unequivocally leads to the correct or most reasonable answer (Gmelin 1917). According to Ehrlich (1917, 73), all declaration of law is by its very nature creative. What in the legal judgment surfaces as the decision's ground—the rule—is actually the result of decisions. That is true even for decisions in the "clear cases," where the decision, so to speak, is the result of straightforward rule application (such as the minimum age of eighteen years in order to vote in US elections). These cases are "simple," because neither judge nor legal doctrine see any sensible reason (viewpoints, factors, interests) to deviate from the standard meaning of the rule. Although the clear cases make up the absolute majority of cases (think of default judgments), in the more complex cases neither facts nor law can be ascertained as effortlessly as in the clear cases. If legal adjudication is a rule-governed activity at all, those rules can better be characterized as rules of thumb, none of which have absolute priority. In one case, linguistic interpretation prevails, in others systematic or teleological interpretation. The rulings of the judges are explained not by adherence to a strict methodology but by the fact that the judges are men "nourished on the same thoughts and other lifegiving forces as the rest of us" (Green 1928, 1020). This includes, of course, prejudice and ideology (for the origins of the role of ideology in scientific research in general, see Steinmetz, this volume).

An illuminating example of the role of ideology, under the veil of logic, is the (in)famous case *Lochner v. New York* (1905).[2] In this case, the majority of the Supreme Court decided that the due process clause (Fourteenth Amendment)[3] implied a freedom of contract to such an extent that it renders unconstitutional a New York law requiring that bakery employee hours should be not more than ten hours a day and sixty hours a week. In his dissent, Holmes stated that this decision exposes the prejudices of the Court, since the Court had authorized other interferences with the liberty of contracts, such as Sunday laws, usury laws, and the prohibition of lotteries. This shows, says Holmes, that this case is decided on a particular economic theory, one that opposes state intervention and favors Mr. Herbert Spencer's *Social Statics*.

All judging is thus part of the process of governing; therefore, judging involves politics (Frank 1932; Gény 1917). To make a justified use of prejudice and ideology in judicial decision, both movements strongly support the use of the social sciences by judges and legal scholars (Oliphant 1928). Judicial decision, says Gény (1917, 15), requires "free investigation" of all the circumstances, including "scientific data as far as possible based on statistics and every other means of learning social facts, as well as ethical, political, and economic considerations." Gmelin (1917, 87) gives an extensive list of the knowledge that judges and legal scholars should possess, a list that seems to express a highly ambitious research agenda of the social sciences rather than the training program of jurists:

> A reasonable administration of justice depends on paying due regard to actual life and its circumstances. It requires a knowledge of the ideas present in the minds of the litigants, presupposes a deep study of the practical ends pursued by individuals in their struggle for existence. It demands the knowledge of the manner of expression and the educational status of the average person, as well as of the manner in which he is likely to conceive right and wrong. Finally, it requires some knowledge of the standard by which individuals measure themselves and others in their business and legal relations.

Despite these ambitious objectives, the role of the social sciences had been not as grandiose as in Gmelin's vision, but a rather limited one, something that Balkin and Levinson (2006, 170) ascribe to a combination of factors, such as the difficulty getting funding for social science studies, the rather rudimentary nature of the social sciences at that time, and the fact that the Realists had only a limited training in doing social research. In one respect, however, the influence of both movements had been profound and lasting. Since they considered the law not an end in itself, but a means toward the administration of justice, they promoted the "method of free decision," or the "sociological method" (Gmelin 1917). This method prioritizes the socially desirable consequences of the decision, rather than consistency or logical inference.

The Quintessence of the Sociological Method: Balancing of Interests

For the advocates of the sociological method, deciding is an act of will (Gmelin 1917, 130). And because it is an act of will, judicial decision is guided, not only by considerations internal to the law (such as consistency or principles as the separation of powers), but also by ideological considerations that are external to the law, as asserted by Holmes in *Lochner*. The problem with cases such as *Lochner* is that the ideological elements were concealed, or even denied. Once we explicitly recognize the constitutive role of ideology, we may use it in a more justified manner. Gény (1917, 16), for example, states that the purpose of legal science is to find the necessary rules for the government of human relations. The two guideposts of our judicial investigation are justice and general utility, "meaning by the latter expression that which by common opinion is considered as promoting the welfare of the greater number" (Gény 1917, 43). The law should reconcile conflicts of interests (Gmelin 1917, 102; Gény 1917, 36); judges and scholars should thereby always be guided by the socially desirable consequences (Gény 1917, 16; Kohler 1917, 193; Pound 1917, 210). The sociological method, in sum, focuses on the "real" interests, both of the contending parties and society, and seeks to arrive at the correct decision by balancing them against each other. The metaphor of "balancing" seems indeed inevitable, since judging, according to both movements, involves the consideration of the relative importance of conflicting viewpoints, factors, or interests in all stages of the decision.

The characterization of the judicial decision as a balancing judgment has ancient roots. When Aristotle defines justice as the mean, lying between two extremes (Aristotle 1953, 1129a3), he uses a spatial metaphor. That mean, according to Aristotle, is not the exact midpoint between two extremes, for justice is not simple reciprocity, but reciprocity based on proportion: "If an official strikes someone," he says, "it is wrong for him to be struck in return; and if someone strikes an official it is right for him not only to be struck in return but to be punished as well" (1133b28). Justice, for Aristotle, is thus a sort of proportion (1131a). To find out what is proportionate in reward or punishment, one has to assess the particularities of the case—merit, position, voluntariness or involuntariness of action, and so on. Doing justice is thus intimately connected to the assessment of factors whose import is relative to the case and to those of the other party. Here the spatial metaphor makes way for the metaphor of weighing and balancing, as the import of these factors cannot be measured in isolation. It is this metaphor that is most often connected to justice, as is revealed by the omnipresence, both in space and time, of the balance as the symbol for justice.

It is remarkable that those early twentieth-century movements, which are so much associated with modernity—with science, progress, utilitarianism, and instrumentalism—adopted this classic picture of the balance to circumscribe the office of the judge, since balancing seems hardly a scientific method. When Gény (1917, 36) contends that the sociological method "weighs" all the conflicting interests "in the scales of justice" and gives the preponderance to the "most important" of them tested by "some social standard," one wonders how the weight of each interest is determined, whether balancing of incommensurable interests is possible, and how disagreements on the proper social standard can be settled. This is indeed part of the critique of the sociological method. But the Freirechtsbewegung and Legal Realism considered balancing of interests for a combination of reasons far more rational a method than the formalist's approach, according to which conceptual analysis and logical inference suffice as methods of legal adjudication. One of these reasons has been touched on above and is epistemological in character. Since the judge and legal scholar are confronted with conflicting viewpoints, factors, or interests in all stages of the process of legal decision-making, the decision is the result of choices based on the relative weight of each of these interests or viewpoints. The role of balancing in legal decision-making is thus an epistemological fact. To deny that role in the administration of justice would be irrational (for the role of underlying values in scientific research, see Kingsberg Kadia, this volume).

If balancing is inevitable, as both movements claim, it is better to critically examine the normative standards that determine the preponderance of one factor over others and to employ only those standards that are deemed appropriate. Standards such as the guideline that the decisions should promote the welfare for the greater number (Gény 1917, 43), or that the unmistakable wish of the majority of the population should be leading (e.g., Holmes's criterion in *Lochner*) reveal that both movements had a pragmatic, instrumental view of law. Although the instrumental view did not compel a balancing approach, writes American legal scholar Alexander Aleikinoff (1987, 960), it was certainly a logical application of the advocated sociological method, as it openly embraced a view of the law as purposeful and demanded a particularized, contextual scrutiny of the social interests at stake. Aleikinoff mentions other factors that enhanced the Realist's acceptance of balancing as a rational mode of deciding. It was a way to adjust the law to the rapid social developments in a more flexible and less time-consuming way than would have been possible through legislation. It was, furthermore, in tune with the broader intellectual movement of the first half of the twentieth century that favored empirical observation over logical deduction from fixed categories. Finally, it was directly linked up with substantive developments in the social sciences: "In political science, pluralist theory taught that law and policy were the outcome of competition among interests. In economics, theoretical advances sparked the development of cost-benefit analysis" (1987, 961).

Just as the social sciences demand empirical observation of the ways in which societies actually function, so could the balancing judge assume the role of a social scientist, "trading deductive logic for inductive investigation of interests in a social context" (Aleikinoff 1987, 961). The appreciation of balancing as a reasonable and rational tool of decision-making in law was thus directly linked up with the view of legal scholarship and jurisprudence as scientific activities, intimately connected with the methods of the social sciences. Exemplary for this view was the integration of international law and international relations theory under a "common agenda," a merging which, according to international law scholar Martti Koskenniemi, is characterized by a pervasive rule-skepticism and an emphasis on flexible, policy-dependent instruments (Koskenniemi 2001, 483).

Balancing, in sum, was considered a rational mode of settling legal disputes, given the fact that all dispute resolution takes place within a normative framework and requires a normative standpoint of the judge or legal scholar. As a method to decide constitutional disputes, balancing was dominant in the United States between the 1940s and 1980s, so much so that this period is called "the age of balancing" (Aleikinoff 1987). In Europe and other parts of the world, balancing, in the form of the so-called proportionality test, is still considered the prevalent method to decide constitutional disputes.[4]

Balancing and the Turn toward Formalism

With hindsight, Alexander Aleikinoff's seminal article "Constitutional Law in the Age of Balancing," published in 1987, may be regarded as the beginning of the growing criticism of the method of weighing and balancing. He raises two related objections to the use of balancing as a method of settling constitutional disputes. First, balancing transforms constitutional discourse from an interpretive enterprise into a general discussion of the reasonableness of governmental conduct (1987, 987). That is problematic, because it is not the court's job to speak out on the reasonableness or acceptability of the law and draw up new rules based on that judgment. The principle of the separation of powers, one of the cornerstones of the Western legal order, relegates the judge to the mere application of existing law rather than creating law through a balancing of interests. The second objection concerns the method itself. According to Aleikinoff, balancing is an empty methodology (1987, 983). Analyzing the case law of the Supreme Court, he concludes that there is no system of identification, evaluation, and comparison of interests: "Weights are asserted, not argued for" (1987, 982). If it is to be considered a method at all, it can better be characterized as a form of exemplary reasoning, based on comparison of similarities and differences. In what seems a remarkable return to the formalist's approach of the study of law, Aleikinoff asserts that not a method as irrational as balancing, but the method of categorization is the proper judicial tool, that is, the method of determining whether a particular conduct falls within the scope of an existing right. Although Aleikinoff admits that categorization requires interpretation, the judge can resort to the traditional interpretive techniques, such as text, structure, precedent, consequences, history, intent, ethical tradition, and notions of fundamental rights (Aleikinoff 1987, 1002). The combined use of these perspectives, Aleikinoff affirms, usually conjures up the rule that governs the case at issue: categorization is reasoning according to the rules of legal adjudication, leading to a legal rule according to which the case at issue has to be settled.

Aleikinoff's criticism turns out to be programmatic for the controversy over balancing as a method of adjudication in constitutional law. The debate focuses on the nature of legal adjudication, on the one hand, and on the rationality of the method of balancing on the other. Against Aleikinoff and company, who consider the approach of balancing as a rhetorical device rather than as a genuine method, balancing is defended as a regulated, and thus rational, form of legal reasoning. Among its advocates are many from the jurisdictions that use the proportionality test (especially Europe). They contend that the proportionality test is a highly structured way of reasoning that puts the actual balancing of interests, what is called "proportionality in strict sense," at the end of the chain of reasoning. It therefore reduces the act of the actual balancing to a limited number of cases and with regard to a limited number of factors and interests (Panaccio 2011).[5] According to the German legal theorist Robert Alexy, a leading legal theorist and tireless advocate of balancing, actual balancing proceeds according to a scheme (the Weight Formula)[6] that works according to the rules of arithmetic (Alexy 2003). The formal structure of balancing, he contends, resembles the general scheme of subsumption:[7] "In both cases a set of premises can be identified from which the result can be inferred. The Subsumption Formula represents a scheme which works according to the rules of logic; the Weight Formula represents a scheme which works according to the rules of arithmetic" (Alexy 2003, 448).

In presenting the proportionality test as rational (in contrast to Aleinikoff's second objection against balancing), Alexy and company seek to redress the criticism that balancing is incompatible with the judge's office (Aleinikoff's first objection). Judicial balancing, they hold, is not subjectively assigning values to identified interests. It is a rule-governed activity, which restricts the creativity of judges and scholars in difficult legal cases to the extent that the rule that results can better be characterized as a *discovery* than a creation or invention of the judge (Dworkin 1977).

In an article about the historical origins of American balancing and German proportionality, Cohen-Eliya and Porat (2010) seek to explain the paradox that in the United States balancing is under attack, whereas the proportionality test is blossoming elsewhere. Proportionality, they write, has become the postwar paradigm in constitutional law, offering a two-stage system of protecting rights.[8] The United States, although the driving force behind the global success of constitutionalism, by contrast moves away from this development, and increasingly defends a rights-based approach in constitutional law, adhering to a categorical approach (e.g., Schauer 2005).

The paradox can be explained as follows. Although the United States diverges from the other countries with respect to the appreciation of the method of balancing, it seems that this variance is due to a similar concern for the protection of individual rights. Whereas the proportionality test was created (initially in Prussia and Imperial Germany) as part of an attempt to protect individual rights against a background of little textual support for such protection, balancing was the US answer "to check the overzealous (libertarian) protection of rights by the U.S. Supreme Court based on an excessively literal reading of the constitutional text" (Cohen-Eliya and Porat 2010, 266). As a method of constitutional dispute resolution, US balancing views rights not as trumps but as particular social interests that can and should be balanced against other interests. This explains the current critique of balancing. It is motivated by an anxiety that an instrumental use of the method of balancing by the Supreme Court leads to an erosion of individual rights in favor of social interests.[9] The same concern urges international law scholars such as Koskenniemi to criticize the flexible concept of international law with its deformalized concept of law, and to espouse the culture of formalism, "the culture of resistance to power, a social practice of accountability, openness, and equality whose status cannot be reduced to the political positions of any of the parties whose claims are treated within it" (Koskenniemi 2001, 500). The contradiction between the flourishing proportionality test and the urge for categorization is thus merely apparent: they both aim to protect "rights" against "policies."

Critique of Balancing: Paradox and Problem

Although the scholarly debate between the opponents and advocates of the method of balancing still exists, the gap between the two positions is less insoluble than it was thirty years ago. The advocates of balancing have moved in the direction of categorization, by picturing balancing as a rule-governed process, whereas the opponents favor categorization, discarding the method of balancing altogether. The turn to categorization is remarkable, especially since it is based primarily on a critique of the instrumental use that had been made of balancing, favoring policies above the protection of individual rights against the government. But this particular use is due not to the method of balancing as such, which can be used either way, but to ideological considerations—to the belief that the fundamental rights are nothing but social interests that have to compete with other social interests. And one wonders why the method of balancing is the target of critique, rather than the utilitarian or instrumental beliefs about justice.

The weakness of the critique of balancing as a method manifests itself when we consider their remedy for balancing: categorization. Categorization is the technique by which the applicability of a provision is determined on the basis of definition. If, for example, a municipal ordinance prohibits the entrance of vehicles in the park, and different persons enter the park with a bicycle, on roller skates, and on a Segway, the method of categorization seeks to answer the question whether each of these acts should be considered as violations of the ordinance by determining whether the particular means of transport can be classified as a vehicle within the meaning of the provision.[10] But how does the judge or scholar manage to decide this issue of categorization? Aleinikoff (1987, 1002) is definitely right when he states that one may resort to the traditional interpretive techniques, such as text, structure, precedent, consequences, history, intent, ethical tradition, and notions of fundamental rights, but this validates once more the claim of the Freirechtsbewegung and the Legal Realists that there is no such thing as "mechanical jurisprudence,"[11] since judicial decision requires choices, that is, judgment, between legitimate points of view. This is true for the procedure of the proportionality test as well. Alexy (2003, 448) emphasizes the striking similarities between deduction and balancing. Both the operation of deduction and balancing, he contends, are completely formal, contributing nothing to the decision itself. Everything depends on the premises, and in this respect both deduction and balancing are on the same footing, "as *judgments* remain in both cases the basis."[12]

The recent call for categorization, says legal scholar Stephen Gottlieb, is due to the misunderstanding or simplification that, unlike balancing, rules do constrain judicial discretion. The truth is that categorization masks balancing: "Rules incorporate balancing a step deeper in the analytical regression. . . . Categorization is often balancing; it requires deciding which category to put things in, and that is often done by noticing the consequences and deciding (often subconsciously) if they are tolerable, better, or worse than certain alternatives" (Gottlieb 1994, 845–46).

This is also the gist of Justice Benjamin Cardozo's exposition (1921, 9) of the dilemmas of his office:

> What is it that I do when I decide a case? To what sources of information do I appeal for guidance? In what proportions do I permit them to contribute to the result? In what proportions ought they to contribute? If a precedent is applicable, when do I refuse to follow it? If no precedent is applicable, how do I reach the rule that will make a precedent for the future? If I am seeking logical consistency, the symmetry of the legal structure, how far shall I seek it? At what point shall the quest be halted by some discrepant custom, by some consideration of the social welfare, by my own or the common standards of justice and morals? Into that strange compound which is brewed daily in the caldron of the courts, all these ingredients enter in varying proportions.

These characterizations of the craft of legal scholarship reverberate in the definition of the Roman jurist and praetor Celsus: law is the art of the good and the equitable (*Ius est ars boni et aequi*). Factors such as "the good" and "the equitable," or "consistency" and "symmetry," have to be balanced, since they enter each case, as Cardozo states, in varying proportions. This is not only the general experience of the practitioners of law but the result of meticulous epistemological research as well: not deduction, but exemplary reasoning, such as analogy, weighing and balancing, and comparison of cases, are characteristic for legal reasoning.

Conclusion: Deduction versus "Trained Judgment"

This is the paradox: balancing as a method of judicial decision is considered reasonable and rational from the perspective of socio-legal scholarship, whereas balancing is rejected as irrational from a formalist point of view, that is, from a perspective that regards law as an autonomous and self-sufficient discipline. And this is the problem: by declaring the method of balancing irrational, legal adjudication as such is in fact declared irrational, since balancing is at the core of legal adjudication, even when the judge or scholar limits herself to the approach of categorization. And one wonders what induced Aleinikoff and company to deny the credibility of balancing categorically rather than criticizing the excessive and opportunistic use of this tool.

The paradox might be explained by Daston's point (referred to in the first section) that knowledge that cannot be expressed in rules is denied the status of genuine knowledge (Daston 2016, 126). In the same volume, Ian Hacking (2016, 101) argues that we owe this view to the success of deduction. Deduction (*syllogismos*) was invented (or discovered) by Aristotle. Due to the aspect of logical consequence and validity that fits the view of knowledge as universally valid knowledge, deduction acquired the status of the "gold standard" of rationality, whereas other types of reasoning that, to a greater or lesser degree, are context-sensitive, such as analogy or argument by example, resemblance, or model, were discarded, to the extent that the concept of rationality is confined to reasoning according to rules (Daston 2016, 128; regarding the theoretical rift between universalism and particularism in science, see Langlitz, this volume).

We owe to Kuhn the idea that scientific learning and research is driven by perceived similarity to a paradigm rather than by following rules. The core idea of the paradigm is not the paradigm as "disciplinary matrix" but the paradigm as exemplar (Bird 2005, 101)—that is, as an accepted example of actual scientific practice. Daston's comment (2016, 126) that "neither Kuhn, nor anyone else had succeeded in hammering out a systematic, analytical language for talking about knowledge without rules" seems redundant, since Kuhn's point is that any explicit methodology that aims to cover the scientific practices in a particular field offers, by definition, an incomplete set of the assumptions, methodological rules, and criteria of the discipline. What is missing is what turns this set of methodological rules into a living instrument. It requires education, practice, and experience to handle the combined methods and valuation criteria of the discipline in a sensible way. It requires, in sum, trained judgment.

The role of paradigm as exemplar is not limited to the sciences. Candidate judges, for example, describe their training as a process of being initiated and disciplined in a culture rather than as a training in methodology:

> During the training, not a set of methodological rules and instructions when and how to apply them are central, but the practices of senior judges. The judges serve as role model, that is, as exemplar, for the novices. The training has been completed successfully only after the novice has internalized the behavioral norms of the seniors, first through copying, then by internalizing the behavior of the judges. (Smith 2012, 3)

And graduate students in law, although receiving a formal training in legal methodology, consider the so-called jurisprudence meetings—weekly gatherings of the research staff, where recent court rulings are discussed and colleagues present their papers—as their true exposure to legal scholarship. That does not mean that the explicit methodological rules are useless, but their role is generally limited to guidelines to be recalled as to suggest improvements or clarify critique. And the problem with guidelines—if it is a problem—is that they cannot be applied "mechanically" but require judgment.

With the focus set slightly differently, the role of paradigms in science exhibits the social embeddedness or collective aspect of what might be called expertise. For how do we recognize a skilled scientist, scholar, or lawyer? Recognition is a reciprocal relation. We have to be versed in a craft or field to recognize the skills in others. Skilled lawyers, even if they take opposite positions, have no difficulty in recognizing each other's qualities. That is due to their similar training, to the fact that they consult the same articles and precedents and draft comparable pleading notes. It results not only in a common grammar or language in which any legal problem can be discussed[13] but also in a fund of common values and goals[14] that directs the substantive choices to be made. Due to these shared standards of both form and substance, even a balancing judgment with which one dissents can be accepted as a valid and reasoned one: one would have weighed the interests differently, but the valuation still fits the standards of the profession.

Contrary to logic, then, reasoning methods such as balancing, analogy, similarity, and exemplar are context sensitive. They resist a clear and precise analysis and explication not because they are obscure, but because they are *relational* (Hacking 2016, 109). What is reasonable to one audience is not necessarily reasonable to another audience. This substantiates the view that "rationality" is not an intrinsic, timeless quality; it has a history, something that is connected to the conjunctures of social, political, and economic life. This might explain the shifts in appreciation of balancing. It seems to me that the epistemological crisis in legal theory, exemplified by the critique of balancing of interests, indicates a more serious problem: a declining trust in institutions such as law and science. A satisfactory explanation for this development, though, requires an interdisciplinary approach, combining the social sciences and law, not unlike the kind of approach that the Freirechtsbewegung and the Legal Realists envisioned a century ago.

Notes

1 Compare Montesquieu's characterization of the judge in the republic as *la bouche de la loi* (mouth of the law) (Montesquieu 1949).
2 *Lochner v. New York*, 198 U.S. 45 (1905).
3 The due process clause holds that no state shall deprive any person of life, liberty, or property without due process of law.
4 It should be noted that this development is not confined to constitutional law but also applies to other parts of the law, particularly tort and contract law, where the legitimate interests of others are explicitly part of the assessment of the dispute. A clear example of this development offers article 6:248, 2 of the Dutch Civil Code (1992), which states: "A rule, to be observed by parties as a result of their agreement, is not applicable insofar this, given the circumstances, would be unacceptable to standards of reasonableness and fairness."
5 For the difference in character between balancing and the proportionality test, see also Bomhoff 2008, who argues that continental balancing is connected to a formal concept of rationality, operating according to an inferential system, whereas the rationality of American balancing is connected to ethical imperatives and utilitarian and other expediential rules.
6 The Weight Formula, $W_{i,j} = I_i/I_j$, is based on Alexy's "Law of Balancing": "The greater the degree of non-satisfaction of, or detriment to, one right or principle, the greater must be the importance of satisfying the other" (Alexy 2003, 436, 444).
7 The Subsumption Formula is connected with the syllogism and can be written, in barest form, thus: "If P than Q; P; therefore Q."
8 Compare also Jackson 2015.
9 See, highly influential, Dworkin 1977.
10 This example of H. L. A. Hart's ([1961] 1994, 126) has spawned a flood of comments. Hart used this example to showcase that the meaning of the law is not determinate and fixed.

11　The term is from Roscoe Pound (1908, 605).
12　Emphasis mine.
13　For the term *grammar* in this respect, see Koskenniemi 2005, 571.
14　Or the "structural bias" of a legal system, to emphasize that each system de facto prefers some outcome or distributive choices to other outcomes or choices. See Koskenniemi 2005, 606–7.

References

Aleinikoff, T. Alexander. 1987. "Constitutional Law in the Age of Balancing." *Yale Law Journal* 96: 943–1005.

Alexy, Robert. 2003. "On Balancing and Subsumption: A Structural Comparison." *Ratio Iuris* 16, no. 4: 433–49.

Aristotle. 1953. *Nicomachean Ethics*. Translated by J. A. K. Thompson. Harmondsworth, UK: Penguin.

Balkin, Jack M. and Sanford Levinson. 2006. "Law and the Humanities: An Uneasy Relationship." *Yale Journal of Law and the Humanities* 18: 155–86.

Bird, Alexander 2005. "Naturalizing Kuhn." *Proceedings of the Aristotelian Society* 105, no. 1: 99–117.

Bomhoff, Jacco. 2008. "Balancing, the Global and the Local: Judicial Balancing as a Problematic Topic in Comparative (Constitutional) Law." *Hastings International and Comparative Law Review* 31: 555–86.

Cardozo, Benjamin N. 1921. *The Nature of the Judicial Process*. New Haven, CT: Yale University Press.

Cohen-Eliya, Moshe, and Porat, Iddo. 2010. "American Balancing and German Proportionality: The Historical Origins." *International Journal of Constitutional Law* 8: 263–86.

Daston, Lorraine. 2016. "History of Science without Structure." In *Kuhn's Structure of Scientific Revolutions at Fifty: Reflections on a Science Classic*, edited by Robert J. Richards and Lorraine Daston, 115–32. Chicago: University of Chicago Press.

Dworkin, Ronald. 1977. *Taking Rights Seriously*. Cambridge, MA: Harvard University Press.

Ehrlich, Eugen. 1903. *Freie Rechtsfindung und freie Rechtswissenschaft*. Leipzig: C. L. Hirschfeld.

Ehrlich, Eugen. 1917. "Judicial Freedom of Decision: Its Principles and Objects." Translated by Ernest Bruncken. In *Science of Legal Method: Selected Essays*, 48–84. Boston: Boston Book Company.

Forrester, John. 1996. "'If P, Then What?': Thinking in Cases." *History of the Human Sciences* 9, no. 1: 1–25.

Frank, Jerome. 1932. "What Courts Do in Fact." *University of Illinois Law Review* 26: 761–72.

Gény, François. 1917. "Judicial Freedom of Decision: Its Necessity and Method." Translated by Ernest Bruncken. In *Science of Legal Method: Selected Essays by Various Authors*, 2–46. Boston: Boston Book Company.

Gmelin, Johann G. 1917. "Dialecticism and Technicality." Translated by Ernest Bruncken. In *Science of Legal Method: Selected Essays by Various Authors*, 86–145. Boston: Boston Book Company.

Gottlieb, Stephen E. 1994. "The Paradox of Balancing Significant Interests." *Hastings Law Journal* 48: 825–66.

Green, Leon. 1928. "The Duty Problem in Negligence Cases." *Columbia Law Review* 28: 1014–45.

Habermas, Jürgen. 1996. *Between Facts and Norms*. Translated by William Rehg. Cambridge: Polity.

Hacking, Ian. 2016. "Paradigms." In *Kuhn's Structure of Scientific Revolutions at Fifty: Reflections on a Science Classic*, edited by Robert J. Richards and Lorraine Daston, 96–112. Chicago: University of Chicago Press.

Hart, Herbert L. A. (1961) 1994. *The Concept of Law*. Oxford: Oxford University Press.

Herget, James E., and Wallace, Stephen. 1987. "The German Free Law Movement as the Source of American Legal Realism." *Virginia Law Review* 73, no. 2: 399–455.

Jackson, Vicky C. "Constitutional Law in the Age of Proportionality." *Yale Law Journal* 124: 3094–196.

Kantorowicz, Hermann (under the pseudonym Gnaeus Flavius). 1906. *Der Kampf um die Rechtswissenschaft*. Heidelberg: Carl Winter.

Kohler, Josef. 1917. "Judicial Interpretation of Enacted Law." In *Science of Legal Method: Selected Essays by Various Authors*, 187–201. Boston: Boston Book Company

Koskenniemi, Martti. (1989) 2005. *From Apology to Utopia: The Structure of International Legal Argument*. Cambridge: Cambridge University Press.

Koskenniemi, Martí. 2001. *The Gentle Civilizer of Nations: The Rise and Fall of International Law 1870–1960*. Cambridge: Cambridge University Press.

Kuhn, Thomas S. (1962) 1996. *The Structure of Scientific Revolutions*. 3rd ed. Chicago: University of Chicago Press.

Langdell, Christopher C. 1871. *A Selection on the Law of Contracts*. Boston: Little, Brown and Co.

Montesquieu. 1949. *The Spirit of the Law*. Translated by Thomas Nugent. New York: Hafner.

Oliphant, Hermann. 1928. "A Return to Stare Decision." *American Bar Association Journal* 14: 71–162.

Panaccio, Charles-Maxim. 2011. "In Defence of Two-Step Balancing and Proportionality in Rights Adjudication." *Canadian Journal of Law and Jurisprudence* 24: 109–28.

Pound, Roscoe. 1908. "Mechanical Jurisprudence." *Columbia Law Review* 8: 605–23.

Pound, Roscoe. 1917. "Courts of Legislation." In *Science of Legal Method: Selected Essays*, 202–28. Boston: Boston Book Company.

Schauer, Frederick. 2005. "Freedom of Expression Adjudication in Europe and the United States: A Case Study in Comparative Constitutional Architecture."

In *European and US Constitutionalism*, edited by Georg Nolte, 49–68. Cambridge: Cambridge University Press.

Smith, Carel E. 2012. "Revitalizing Paradigms: Exemplars in Legal Research and Education." *Law and Method* 2, no. 1: 3-6.

Wurzel, Karl-Georg. 1917. "Methods of Juridical Thinking." Translated by Ernest Bruncken. In *Science of Legal Method: Selected Essays by Various Authors*, 286–428. Boston: Boston Book Company.

the reinvention of sociology

Into the Trenches
of Fieldwork at the
Time of the Algerian
Liberation War

AMÍN PÉREZ

The word "conversion" is surely not too strong to describe the transformation, both
intellectual and emotional, which led me from phenomenology of emotional life . . .
to a vision of the social world and of practice that is both more distant and more
realistic, with the aid of an experimental apparatus designed to favor the transformation of *Erlebnis* into *Erfahrung.*—PIERRE BOURDIEU, *THE BACHELORS' BALL*

WHAT HAPPENS WHEN A social scientist is transformed by his or her field?
When his or her initial academic profession is disrupted by a war, and this
situation reorients his or her vocation? When his or her scholastic resources
get reshaped by an affective encounter and an improbable collaboration
challenges the way of scientifically framing the world by thinking about
politics without thinking politically? And when, trapped on this moving
train, they take the objective chances offered to them to challenge the course
and practice of their science? Only exceptional conditions create symbolic
revolutions. This study proposes to uncover one of those creative projects
grounded on improbable circumstances and collaborations that have renewed the practices and epistemological frameworks of social sciences: Pierre

Bourdieu's experience in the midst of the Algerian War of Independence from the French Empire.

Bourdieu's ethnographical research in Algeria was a particular determinant in his sociological work (Lane 2000; Yacine et Adnani 2003; Wacquant 2004; Martin-Criado 2008; Yacine 2013; Heilbron 2011; Steinmetz 2017; Pérez 2017). Several works have emphasized how this specific moment gave light to a series of concepts that grounded his *theory of practice* (e.g., Hammoudi 2007; Steinmetz 2018) and were at the source of his usage of photography as a research instrument (Schultheis 2014), and of his research on economy (Boyer 2003; Duval 2017), kinship (Bensa 2004), the state (Poupeau 2018), and postcolonial studies (Go 2016). However, we have hardly interrogated how this fieldwork brought into being a sociological imagination that concocted a new practice of social sciences. Bourdieu's first published studies show how he is observing the situation of crisis of peasants in Algeria and in Béarn at the same time as he points out the significance of the meaning, principles, and methods of sociology. This shows how the sense and practice of this discipline was not completely evident or did not correspond to how it was then practiced in the academic field. How did he come to reshape a conception of social sciences? On the one hand, the practice of fieldwork was not entirely original. An empire's colonies were the ideal place where ethnographical work was conducted by administrators, the army, ethnologists and sociologists (Steinmetz 2013, 1–50). On the other hand, Bourdieu, who previously had never stepped foot into the field, read ethnographical manuals while in the field. How, then, was his fieldwork so innovative? I will contend that his unorthodox way of practicing fieldwork can only be understood as the product of an unexpected encounter and collaboration with a native schoolteacher and anticolonial activist Abdelmalek Sayad. Further, I will restore the social conditions of their innovative fieldwork, at a time when it was rare to find European sociologists who did fieldwork and coauthored books alongside the colonized, when the ethnologists who carried out research in the context of colonial liberation wars were few and far between, when simultaneous fieldwork in the metropolis and its colony was unusual, and when few were combining scientific rigor with political concerns.

This study offers a reappraisal of this pathbreaking ethnographic moment, located in Bourdieu's first ethnographic immersion in Algeria ([1958] 1962, [1964] 2020, [1963] 2021) and in France (1962). Combining his published work with unpublished material from his personal papers, including correspondences, manuscripts, and field notebooks, my aim is to reestablish how this ethnographical experience shaped a reflexive and committed sociology based on revealing the social dynamics governing the privileges and injustices of our world. In tracking Bourdieu into the field, I propose to restore the sociological circumstances that provided him with a creative project for the social sciences. To do so, I will show three steps of this symbolic revolution: when he makes his first forays into sociology, though ethnography is still unthinkable; when he doesn't know how to practice fieldwork and learns by doing it; when fieldwork becomes the practice from which an alternative social science is constituted.

Becoming a Sociologist during Decolonization

Bourdieu was conscripted for his military service in Algeria at the age of twenty-five. Not a single sign would have predicted that this promising young philosopher was going to switch to sociology during his time in this colony. The dual experiences of growing up in a modest family with a strong social sensitivity toward the working classes and attending the highly prestigious École Normale Supérieure (ENS) of Paris (1951–54) explain his tendency to play the game of the academy while being an outsider to academism and its distance from social reality. It was precisely this displaced position of being *in* while being *out* that oriented his path to a more empirically grounded science, the history and epistemology of science, rather than to the ontological and existentialist philosophical approaches that then prevailed at ENS (Honneth, Kocyba, and Schwibs 1986).

At ENS, becoming a sociologist is not even thinkable. Sociology is a marginal discipline, without any autonomy in the curriculum. It is taught as a certificate of the major in philosophy titled "Morals and Sociology." At that time, neither the theorist's sociology of Georges Gurvitch nor the empiricist sociology à la Jean Stoetzel represented a solid work for the *normalien* milieu (Heilbron 2015). Following his schooling, Bourdieu started to work on a doctoral dissertation on "the temporal structures of affective life," under the supervision of Georges Canguilhem (Bourdieu [2004] 2008). But the experience of the war in Algeria would profoundly reorient his way of thinking about and practicing science.

When Bourdieu arrived in Algeria in 1956, two years had passed since the formal beginning of one of the most violent national liberation wars in history (1954–62). The Algerian masses decided to end the colonial system that had legally denied their political rights, had expropriated the Indigenous from their lands, and had established a system of social injustices since 1830 (Thénault 2005).

Bourdieu was profoundly shocked by the circumstances of the war and deeply troubled by the distorted rhetoric dominating the intellectual debate at that time: between those close to power who legitimized "French Algeria," those who proposed reforms without fundamentally affecting the colonial order, and those revolutionary intellectuals close to the National Liberation Front (FLN) who argued for independence by any means necessary. No philosophical or political approaches were able to help him understand the impasse and the disarray the Algerian masses were experiencing and the possible path to change. It was in this context that Bourdieu took his first steps toward sociology.

But what did sociology mean to Bourdieu at this particular time? He gathered substantial secondhand documentation on Algerian society to uncover the mechanisms of domination that structured the colonial order. Bourdieu compiled abundant ethnological work from the colonial period (e.g., work by Honoteau and Letourneux, and by Masqueary); he conversed with various historians and sociologist specialists on North Africa, such as Émile Dermenghem, André Nouschi, and Jacques Berque; and he read native literature, particularly books by Mouloud Feraoun. The latter was a well-known Algerian writer who met Bourdieu, reviewed his work, and discussed the war with him. His ethnographic literature from his natal village, Tizi Hibel in Kabyle (1954), provided Bourdieu with a luminous account from an Indigenous point of view on the peasant conditions and the principles that regulated their economy, such as trust, honor, and reciprocity. Feraoun's semi-autobiographical works not only provided Bourdieu with an ethnographical perspective at a time when he was not an ethnographer; this native framework, lacking in most of the literature at that time, also guided him to other research objects of study, besides magic, religion, and myths, that prevailed in colonial ethnology as a tautological approach to explain the underdevelopment and "primitive logic" of Algerian culture. The result of this research was Bourdieu's first book, *Sociologie de l'Algérie* (1958), published in English as *The Algerians* ([1958] 1962).

Inspired by a Durkheimian analysis of the functioning of primitive societies and the American culture-and-personality school, Bourdieu showed how Algerian groups (the Kabyles, Shawia, Mozabites, Arabic-speaking people) incorporated cultural patterns that constituted their social community of beliefs and practices, before they were distorted by the intervention of an external agent: the French Empire. His aim was not only to bring new light to the relations of power, diverging from the usual lens of acculturation and deculturation from which the clash of civilizations was analyzed (Herskovits, Linton, and Redfield 1936), but also to reveal the deliberate colonial policies that accelerated the total disintegration of traditional Algerian society.

Before this book came out, he was already thinking of writing two more articles and another book ([2008] 2013, 39–51, 72–82). His close colleague Nouschi, a historian of Algerian rural society and communist partisan, suggested that Bourdieu break with the usual ahistorical portrayal of Algerian society and oriented him in the direction of fieldwork. In a letter sent to Nouschi in 1958, Bourdieu expressed reluctance about the overly descriptive dimension of some ethnographic works, which diluted the analytical scope of the study of a social fact. Though Bourdieu was aware of the weakness of his approach, fieldwork did not yet represent for him a capital research element of sociology: "I leave out completely the ethnographic details which, I must admit, often weighed heavily on me, and I take up the questions in a more overall fashion. I think that in this way I'll leave myself less exposed to the acid criticisms of these sly 'specialists' who, in parentheses, understand nothing about sociological analysis" (Bourdieu [2008] 2013, 319).

At this stage, Bourdieu conceived of sociology as a critical instrument. This scientifically informed political position allowed him to break with the frameworks of intellectuals close to power who disregarded the colonial (and therefore political) situation that generated this precarious situation (Balandier 1951), and to break with those reformist intellectuals who minimized the effects of colonization and merely proposed its reform. In the introductory note to his new chapter, "The Internal Logic of the Original Algerian Society" ([2008] 2013, 72–82), published only in the first edition, Bourdieu writes: "The sociologist's purpose is not to judge but to understand. Now the understanding of a civilization, different from our tradition supposes that putting in suspense all normative ideals, we cease to hold our 'culture' as the absolute center of reference, and we understand that 'culture' according to their logic, their norms and their own values" (Bourdieu 1959, 41).

This first moment of sociology was characterized by an informed critical perspective of reality, breaking with the ethnocentrism through which Algerian society was represented and its misery legitimized. However, the shift to doing fieldwork was soon to come because of the need to understand the possible conditions of decolonizing the Algerian masses. Bourdieu's encounter with his student Abdelmalek Sayad in 1958 at the University of Algiers would be crucial in renewing the very way he conceived of and practiced social sciences (Pérez 2022).

Sayad, a schoolteacher and anticolonial activist, discussed with Bourdieu the main theories illustrating the end of colonization. The closeness between teacher and student owed much to their common trajectories: both of them were descendants of a small rural family, both attended the highest scholarly institution in their country, and both rejected the appeal of academic consecration in order to feel useful in the political landscape of the war they experienced (Pérez 2017). The combination of Bourdieu's scholarly disposition and Sayad's intimate knowledge of Algeria, in addition to his political resources in the anticolonialism movements, were vital in allowing them to transcend both the political position of many "Orientalist" scholars who defended a French Algeria and the general statements made by anticolonists who denounced the system and called for its end. If Bourdieu and Sayad had aligned with the latter group, this position would not have provided the means to truly end colonial domination. In these circumstances, the matter was not only to be against colonialism but also to know how to transcend it. The move to fieldwork came from this need to build a deep analysis of the effects of domination that would survive decolonization and the ways of thinking about a possible emancipation.

The Revelations of Fieldwork

The difficulties of the conditions of war and being confronted for the first time with ethnography, without any a priori knowledge of the methods and frameworks used at that time, was undoubtedly a decisive factor in orienting Bourdieu and Sayad toward practicing a rigorous methodology where everything was questioned. Four elements characterize their practice of fieldwork: the making of the turbulent present as an object of study, going into the field to understand the forms of violence the colonized were subjected to and making this suffering publicly known, the simultaneous analysis of both Sayad and Bourdieu's native peasant villages, and the combination of posing political and scientific questions to find out how to transcend domination.

HOW AND WHAT TO OBSERVE?

Bourdieu and Sayad conducted fieldwork for the first time at the very moment when the war was claiming the most victims (1959–62). This was also the time when the French Empire had implemented a series of political reforms aimed at reducing the inequality that was socially ravaging this colony. The Association for Economic, Demographic and Social Research (ARDES) was created to produce knowledge that would support those policies. A group of statisticians from France carried out censuses and polls. Bourdieu was asked to join it to conduct sociological research.

This institution was seeking out predefined objects of study, such as the living conditions in forced resettlements centers created by the army—and, widely criticized by the international community, the consumption and standard of living of Algerian families, or a census of employment in the colony. Bourdieu and Sayad were given the autonomy to carry out and redefine their works based on the questions that arose during fieldwork. This is how two of their major books were conceived: *Travail et travailleurs en Algérie* (*Work and Workers in Algeria*; Bourdieu [1963] 2021), on the changes in the relationship to labor within the working classes and the experience of unemployment due to the rise of the monetary economy; and *Uprooting* (Bourdieu and Sayad [1964] 2020), on the effects of the displacement of rural populations.

The very practice of fieldwork at the heart of decolonization would reveal to them another dynamic of society. This dynamic differed from Orientalism's study target, which completely neglected this present circumstance of war: colonial ethnology, which focused on collecting the folkloric details of so-called archaic societies. It also diverged from French structural anthropology, which centered on the search for structural invariants in human societies. The challenge for Bourdieu and Sayad was to understand how to scientifically grasp "turbulent political issues" in order to constitute a useful sociology. To accomplish this goal, they called on other young Algerian and French students to join them. Bourdieu and Sayad conducted fieldwork together in different regions of Algeria that they discovered while studying it. As Bourdieu pointed out, they "had visited together the most remote corners of Algeria: the resettlement centers of the Collo peninsular and the Orléansville plain, the forbidden roads of the Ouarsenis amid bomb warnings and alerts, Great and Little Kabylia, the shantytowns and the housing estates of Algiers and Constantine, and so many other places" ([2008] 2013, 295), to observe the profound changes within a society that would not emerge unscathed from the fight for independence. Their collaboration was based on Sayad's intimate knowledge of Algeria and Bourdieu's outsider view.

Nothing was defined in advance. The practice and reflection were done in practice. To capture a society in turmoil, Bourdieu and Sayad did not dismiss any potential tools: observations, interviews, questionnaires, statistical censuses, photography,[1] the psychoanalytic technique Rorschach used to assess the personality of people, or the combination of ethnographical and statistical research. Everything was also conceivably an object of study. In the following excerpt from a letter Bourdieu sent to Sayad as he left for Christmas in France, one could observe his interest in empirically grounding their work with a rigorous observation of the changes this society was experiencing:

My dear friend,

... I believe, now more than ever, that you can do crucial research both from a linguistic and a sociological standpoint. I think you would have to buy a tape recorder to record entire conversations that you could then transcribe. In the first phase, you must accumulate raw material, without worrying too much about analysis. I think that the frameworks we have established are sufficient for the moment. . . .

For the research on housing, if you have a team, give a little speech, have them see the errors (you attended, I believe, the rundown I had given to Hélie and Nechem), give them instructions (writing on the sheets attached the insignificant answers obtained from the questionnaire and general observations, digressions, etc.), indicate the plan for the preliminary observations: 1) clothing 2) attitudes 3) linguistic system: elegance or a search for the expression, etc. Perhaps you could attend (as a spectator) one of the surveys and then afterwards do the critique. (Pierre Bourdieu, Lasseube, Winter 1959)[2]

The statement "to accumulate raw material, without worrying too much about analysis" reveals their interest in capturing social reality in an inductive way rather than imposing their questions onto fieldwork. Indeed, the object of study would be constructed progressively. Bourdieu and Sayad kept field diaries in which they noted their questions, the themes, and their reflections on their place as ethnographers. According to Sayad, the two sociologists spent "whole evenings, during which the information collected and the observations recorded, were minutely debated and dissected, all this was a true laboratory . . . where hypotheses were forged, where interpretations were tested, where theories were experimented with" (Sayad 2002, 65–66).

The results of their ethnographies were constantly confronted with censuses and polls recorded by the statisticians of ARDES. The practice of fieldwork allowed them to see that the questionnaires made within the empire's framework and for the metropole held no meaning for the traditional society of the colony. For instance, they observed how some peasants who were familiar with a monetary economy categorized themselves as unemployed, while others continued to frame their care for a farm in the nonproductive seasons as part of their work and social life. The very practice of fieldwork revealed to them the strength of ethnography in deeply understanding Algerian society:

To study such a complex and wide-ranging phenomenon, one could not content oneself with a statistical study, inevitably superficial, focused on the entire population under consideration (supposing that it had been possible), nor on a single monograph. A set of monographs rather quickly realized, that aim to grasp the local variants in particular, upon establishing the fundamental data, seemed to us to constitute the best use of the means and the time available (that is to say three months, from June to September 1960). (Bourdieu and Sayad 1964, 41)

Bourdieu and Sayad learned how to conduct fieldwork in situ. Their passion for ethnography increased when the practice revealed to them how powerful this tool could be in terms of grasping the dynamics of a society.

Most of their ethnographic fieldwork was collectively conducted between 1959 and 1961. However, Bourdieu and Sayad continued on until 1963. The stakes were considerable for both young scholars, who had only recently begun practicing ethnography. The conviction of the social utility of this work was consolidated during their work on the transformations happening in colonial Algeria.

FOR WHOM AND FOR WHAT?

Carrying out fieldwork in the midst of war was very difficult. The collective ethnography even stopped momentarily, when the right-wing Secret Army Organization (OAS) arose and deployed the most violent actions in a last-ditch attempt to save "French Algeria." In the draft of a research program on Algeria written just after its independence, Bourdieu specifies that "the increases of war clashes in 1961 and the actions of the OAS prevented the completion of the research expected to provide information on the particularly precious demographic and social structures."[3]

Such a violent context has irremediable effects on the experience of the ethnographer. Bourdieu and Sayad's field diaries and their writings of that time reveal the difficulties of fieldwork in wartime. Despite the dramatic and demoralizing situation they faced, they were able to overcome these obstacles due to their "passionate interest" in fieldwork and their belief in the political usefulness of this practice during the war. Though the colonial administration commissioned the study on the resettlements, its goals were entirely bypassed by the pair, who instead focused their attention on the most brutal suffering caused by the war. Their objective: to understand, rather than just observe things from afar while remaining neutral. In one of his fieldwork notebooks, Sayad recounts the overall feeling of tension during the incessant bombings while they were conducting research in the concentration camps of the Algerian Northeast. While some of the students from the research team deserted because of this, others continued, convinced of the usefulness of the research: "A dramatic situation. Do not believe that it is exaggerated, the interviewers are demoralized; there are a lot of [military] operations underway.... I believe it is necessary to be in support of the demonstration, not what is convenient" (Collo, September 1960).[4]

The usefulness of this work in Algeria was constantly discussed between the young ethnographers despite the highly dangerous conditions of conducting research there (Bourdieu [1963] 2021, 31–47). As Bourdieu pointed out in the foreword of his second book, *Work and Workers in Algeria*:

> From the first day, the problem had been explicitly stated and all had understood that having chosen to do this study rather than not to do it,—the only real choice—we could, with the necessary concessions to its realization, carry it out with all the desirable objectivity. If despite the difficult circumstances in which they were to work, they were able to collect documents as lively and as accurate as those which one will be able to read, it is above all because they brought to the research a passionate interest and that they felt a tender sympathy towards their interlocutors. Having chosen to conduct, in a difficult and, if you will, "impure" situation, a search in which they expected anything other than the confirmation of naive ideologies, they simply fulfilled their task as public writers, without giving themselves the illusion of accomplishing a historic mission or a moral duty. (Bourdieu [1963] 2021, 26–27)

The challenge was to be in the field, to record and grasp the social reality reporters were not uncovering and denunciations of colonialism were not considering. They had no pretentions about "fulfilling a responsibility to history"; rather, they intended to restore the meaning that the population gave to the transformations they were living through. Bourdieu and Sayad acknowledged the courage involved in the denunciation of torture and crimes against Algerians, as well as the demand for the right to insubordination. However, for them the issues faced in colonial Algeria could not only be limited to moral critique or political indignation expressed through manifestos. Bourdieu and Sayad proposed to continue their silent work in the shantytowns and rural areas of Algeria, to understand the profound tragedies of the war and the social misery affecting Algerians' lives.

The findings in the fieldwork in the Algerian countryside constantly reminded Bourdieu of those of the Southwest of his childhood. Intrigued by these similarities, Bourdieu undertook informal fieldwork in his native village during one of his short trips home during the summer of 1959. In the winter, Bourdieu wrote his first sketches on honor in the Kabyle society (Bourdieu [1977] 1979, 95–132). The analogies he had found in Béarn had left him more than astonished. He rapidly shared this with Sayad, and they started to put together different aspects of their findings with the aim of understanding the social dynamics in these two rural worlds.

Their fieldwork now extended past the initial innovation of comparing insider–outsider views on a social phenomenon in Algeria. The challenge became to interrogate Bourdieu's and Sayad's native worlds to question the evidence available there, even though they had grown up without really understanding it. This scientific gesture was not easy. To do so, Bourdieu would draw inspiration from a new generation of French ethnologists eager to break with the museum and folklorist conception of ethnology, which focused on the search for cultural objects and reconstruction of popular practices and beliefs. Marcel Maget was one of the leading representatives of this new wave of ethnographers. The challenge was to establish localized ethnographic studies, using a field diary such as that of British social anthropology, questionnaires, and village monographic surveys and statistics (Laferté and Renahy 2006). Bourdieu met Maget between his first fieldwork in Algeria and his first ethnographic attempt in his native village during the summer of 1959. He was inspired by Maget's ethnographic guide and fieldwork on the rural world (1953, 1955) and informed him of the challenges of distancing himself from the familiar terrain: "I have other problems as well, that I will reiterate: I know too much, and it's boring for me, originating from here, to write about it. It is better that I tell you, and you will surely suggest a tip. In any case, I'll be very entertained."[5]

To neutralize this bias of a known fieldwork site, Sayad and Bourdieu simultaneously thought about the same questions for both societies. Their families and their close friends quickly became privileged informants. The analysis of the analogies between their hometowns of Aghbala and Lasseube was not limited to letters between Bourdieu and Sayad from north and south of the Mediterranean Sea; Sayad also came to Béarn to do fieldwork with Bourdieu. Aligning with Maget's ethnographical perspective, Bourdieu and

Sayad rejected any division of the labor of compilation, description, and analysis of the facts observed, as stated at that time by Claude Lévi-Strauss (1958), between ethnographer, ethnologist, and anthropologist. For them, the circulation of knowledge and know-how was at the heart of their work.

Bourdieu and Sayad seek to understand the experiences of a peasantry in a crisis of reproduction, by observing jointly the contradictions engendered by the social and economic dispossession of a way of life (the peasant condition) and the difficulties of adapting to the new laws of the market. As Loïc Wacquant pointed out,

> In Bearn as in Algeria, Bourdieu articulates the same problematic of the clash of civilizations and its multisided impacts on social structure and subjectivity, including the "dedoubling of consciousness and conduct" according to the conflictive principles of sentiment and interest, the erosion of traditional hierarchies and authorities (based on lineage, age, and gender), and the recursive relationship between the devolution of customary social units, the unleashing of individual competition, and the skewing of social strategies. (2004, 393)

The strength of thinking together about peasant conditions in both places has also contributed to universalizing what used to be framed as singular, different, or even from another time in history. By universalizing the social condition, it has allowed them to dispel myths and stereotypes through which these societies were represented between modern and primitive standpoints. Nevertheless, Bourdieu insisted on the need to discipline this universalization of analysis. Drawing on his simultaneous observations between Kabylia (Aghbala) and Béarn (Lasseube), Bourdieu explained to Maget the importance of considering the specificities of the social history of each community. In addition to the potential of these simultaneous observations, Bourdieu also shared with Maget the analogies he saw between Kabylia and Corsica.

Ethnography became a means of restoring a social meaning of behaviors and giving humanity back to the populations studied. Talking about this work with Sayad, Bourdieu later underlined: "The ethnosociologist is a kind of organic intellectual of humanity, and as a collective agent can contribute to denaturalizing and de-fatalizing human existence by placing his skill at the service of a universalism rooted in the comprehension of different particularisms" (Bourdieu [2008] 2013, 294).

Thinking about the fieldwork in both places together "provides a way out of the national framework in which researchers, be they ethnologists or sociologists, tend to become ensnared" (Poupeau 2018, 426). This transnational fieldwork was not only the determinant in breaking with the disciplinary boundaries of ethnology and sociology or dichotomies between modern or primitive worlds. This fieldwork and the other ethnographic research conducted at that time (e.g., *Work and Workers in Algeria*) was decisive in renewing Bourdieu's first sociological moment, as outlined in *Sociologie de l'Algérie* (1958). This ethnographical work contributed to moving from a general description of homogenous cultural groups to a detailed social stratification framework and developing a situated approach to the practices and representations of individuals in time and space (Martin-Criado 2008).[6] This work was also innovative at a time when ethnology in France and more broadly in European societies (Maget 1968) was just starting to be compared to the interests of exotic fieldwork (Lévi-Strauss [1955] 1973), and at a time when rural sociology was rarely grounded by fieldwork (Bourdieu [2002] 2007). Finally, this ethnography carried out simultaneously on both processes of crisis in Kabylia and Béarn, observing how people were experiencing these contradictions of seeing a way of life disappearing while they did not have the means to adapt to a new one, was also decisive in grasping the social conditions necessary to transcend this situation.

IN SEARCH OF SOCIAL TRANSFORMATION

Bourdieu and Sayad's scientific project of understanding the mechanisms that were both accelerating the Algerian masses' pauperization and determining the margins of freedom from which they could benefit became more precise as their fieldwork progressed. They took advantage of the autonomy ARDES gave them to reshape their questions. They observe economic practices, the process of industrialization, and the conversion of peasants who had become agricultural workers in large colonial farms while working on their land through seasonal rites; they also observed the changes caused by displacement and its effects on populations settled in shantytowns.

These different fieldworks enriched one another. Thus, the employment research provided them with information about the attitude toward work in the urban areas that they then could relate to the experiences of peasants turned farm laborers on large colonial farms. Similarly, the analysis of honor undertaken by Bourdieu during this period helped to clarify some new economic conduct, such as credit and savings; research on resettlement camps and modern housing were cross-referenced with analyses of consumer practices and the domestic economy. Finally, all of this fieldwork into the living conditions of proletarians, subproletarians, and Algerian peasants was constantly cross-referenced and profoundly grounded by the general question of the capacities necessary to these populations to carry out the revolution.

As they carried out the fieldwork, the young ethnographers concluded that independence would not necessarily imply emancipation. This was confirmed during their post-decolonization fieldwork in 1962. Their apprehensions of seeing the elite reproduce the colonial system without the colony were becoming a reality. In these circumstances, the objective was not to liberate the peasants and workers from the situation in which they lived in a subjective key, but to constitute a knowledge that could provide the means to change the background of their objective conditions.

It is no accident that during the war Bourdieu and Sayad attempted to understand the resources each social agent needed to function within their respective situations. They confronted the conditions of life and the aspirations of the peasants and workers in order to restore the rationality of those agents' actions both in the economic field and in the political one. For Bourdieu and Sayad, the practice of fieldwork could not only play a key role in transcending the unacceptable reality of war. It could also provide people with an understanding of the social conditions that would enable them to emancipate themselves long-term from the contradictions engendered by colonial policy, the war, and the eruption of capitalism. This is very clear in Bourdieu's article on the social conditions allowing subproletarians to change their precarity and consider starting a political revolution: "Asking what are the conditions under which individuals can cease simply to experience their suffering, and move on to considering and understanding it, means questioning the conditions of possibility for the positing of the possible" (Bourdieu [2008] 2013, 160).

Bourdieu and Sayad do not limit their analysis to the turbulent daily life of the situation of war and economic precaritization: the high value of this fieldwork also contributes to an understanding of the possible conditions necessary for the social transformation of the Algerian people during the war of liberation and after independence.

The historical context of decolonization and Bourdieu and Sayad's political concerns that brought them into the fieldwork, the conjunction of the native knowledge and the European view, their cumulative political and scholastic dispositions, and the circumstances of thinking simultaneously about the condition of peasants in Algeria and in France were the key factors that allowed them to uncover the unthinkable reality about this colony and its destiny.

Shaping the Meaning and Practice of Social Sciences

Bourdieu and Sayad's ethnographic experience helped them to renew the conceptions and practices of sociology. This conception of science took three forms: a science of social practices aiming at uncovering the mechanism of domination; a combination of scholarship and commitment shaping a specific way of publicly intervening; and a reflexive view of the very practice of science. These three elements are at the heart of what is known today as "critical sociology," or what Bourdieu called "reflexive sociology" (Bourdieu and Wacquant 1992). Bourdieu would come back to these dimensions at several stages of his later work in France. It would be more implicit in Sayad's scientific and political work in postcolonial France (Sayad [1998] 2004; Pérez 2020).

A Critique of Domination

In his first ethnography on the crisis of the peasantry in the matrimonial exchanges, Bourdieu writes:

> The primary task of sociology is perhaps to reconstitute the totality from which one can discover the unity of the subjective awareness that the individual has of the social system and of the objective structure of that system. . . . Sociology would perhaps not be worth an hour of effort if its sole aim were to discover the strings that move the actors it observes, if it were to forget that it is dealing with people, even when those very people, like puppets play a game where they do not know the rules, in short, if it did not assign itself the task of restoring to those people the meaning of their actions. (Bourdieu [2002] 2007, 94–95)

These words reflect Bourdieu's aim of building a scientific knowledge that is able to piece together from people's own logics how their condition and contradictory practices are socially and historically organized.

The practice of fieldwork enabled Bourdieu and Sayad to break with an outsider view of social reality and to build a sociology that was empirically grounded yet maintained some distance from the empiricism and theoreticism that then dominated the field. Through their study of the practical and urgent questions posed by these peasants and subproletarians in a world where their social logic and ties were increasingly losing value, a new scientific conceptualization of sociology emerged. The *theory of practice* that arose at that time was not guided by a theoretical positioning between objectivist or subjectivist approaches describing how people perceive, judge, and act in the world. Bourdieu came to think about how our social and mental structures are interlinked through the understanding of a context of social hysteresis where the discrepancies between objective chances and subjective aspirations resulted in an unbearable present for people.[7]

The political force of sociology was discussed during his fieldwork and with Algerian intellectuals, including Mouloud Feraoun and Himoud Brahimi, the Poet of the Casbah. In one of the letters Brahimi wrote to Bourdieu while he was conducting fieldwork, he encouraged Bourdieu to build up a knowledge that could go beyond what the present situation of the war made them think:

> And here sociology has its role to maintain, not for the benefit of one side or the detriment of the other, that which brought about the political revolution, but for the advantage of both. Because, it is not said that after the political revolution there is a revolution of the sociological order.... This science that explains, not only what God expects from man, but what man must give of himself in order for his cause to live beyond all the ideological fabrications and be materialized by the work of the people. For this revolution here, my dear Pierre, I invite you to come to Algeria. Amongst all the Frenchmen I know, you are the best positioned to appreciate this transformation. (Pérez 2022, 170)

Basing sociology on ethnographic work allowed them to understand the modes of domination that would survive a political change of regime. As Bourdieu and Sayad stated in *Uprooting*, "The colonial system survives as long as the contradictions it has left behind are not effectively overcome—an overcoming which would presuppose that they be apprehended and confronted as such" (Bourdieu and Sayad [1964] 2020, 122). The conception of sociology as a critique of domination was far from the normative character of political thought and allowed them to understand the material and symbolic modes of domination that conditioned the lives of the Algerian people. Rather than advocate for a new policy or system, it allowed them to reveal the invisible forces that shape our relationship to the world. The intention: to shape a sociology of social practices able to reveal the mechanisms that perpetuate the privileges and most intolerable conditions so easily, as a precondition of understanding what resources are necessary to challenge our participation in the domination process.

This experience of fieldwork was also fundamental in giving a new meaning to intellectual activity. The challenge was to establish a knowledge capable of creating instruments to understand the possible methods of achieving social emancipation after anticolonial liberation. The need for and political strength of this ethnographical work is discussed in the fieldwork and with Algerian intellectuals. Bourdieu especially criticizes ethnologist Michel Leiris, who emphasized the impurity of the research conducted in colonial situations because it was commissioned by the colonial administration (1950). Bourdieu states that this membership in no way precludes an affinity for the dominated society: "If class barriers separate individuals within the same society, does class solidarity not bring individuals from different societies closer to one another across the colonial barrier?" (Bourdieu [1963] 2021, 32–33). For Bourdieu, the ethnologist must be there and contend with the history in which he or she is situated, considering the stakes of these circumstances and the relations of domination they engender. Bourdieu also rejects the posture of scientific "purity" claimed by Leiris, a purity that would provide the ethnographer with a moral duty in the face of the atrocities of colonialism—as if only our intentions and moral duties free us from scientific and political constraints. For Bourdieu, the real responsibility or requirement of the ethnologist is to "restore to other men the meaning of their behaviors, of which the colonial system, among other things, dispossessed them" (Bourdieu [1963] 2021, 35–36).

The fieldwork allowed Bourdieu and Sayad to see how essential it was to craft a political position informed by sociological research. The matter was to break with the main ideological approaches that then prevailed in the academy: academism and revolutionarism (and their scientific companions, objectivism and subjectivism). "As remote from pure science as from exemplary prophecy" (Bourdieu [1980] 1990, 1), the experience of fieldwork was excellent in molding a kind of "militant craftsmanship." This was none other than the specific intellectual mode of intervention—that is, as intellectuals who intervene based on their knowledge in a precise field in which they specialize (Foucault 2001). At that time, Bourdieu defined the role of sociologists as *écrivains publics* (public writers). Drawing on empirical research, Bourdieu conceived of sociology as an instrument for restoring the meaning of social actors' actions and perceptions and the conditions that could lead them to hope for other futures. At stake was breaking with those intellectuals close to power and their imperial gaze, which legitimized (and contributed to the perpetuation of) the colonial order, as well as with those "universal" or "total" intellectuals who stand as master figures of truth without a clear understanding of the complexities lived in this war. The matter was to respond to the urgent stakes posed in the present through the precise knowledge of research.

Sociology was gradually becoming a critical instrument for better understanding society and doing politics differently. For Bourdieu and Sayad, the matter was not to just "be there," in the field, where the action was happening. It was also a matter of strengthening this science of a rigorous method and plurality of views and making it public. It is not coincidental that the idea of the "collective intellectual" arose during the decolonization era and reappeared when the most brutal effects of neoliberalism regularized precarity in Europe (Bourdieu [2003] 2012). It could not be at any other time than at that precise moment of the struggle against colonialism. This collective intellectual was shaped in two ways: first, by bringing together a cumulative approach from historians, poets, literature-ethnographers, psychologists, philosophers, economist, writers, and activists (e.g., the conjunction of Bourdieu's scholarly disposition and Sayad's anticolonial activism); and second, by constructing and proposing to the masses a politics of education, which allowed Bourdieu and Sayad to provide them with resources to better adapt to their economic and political situation (Bourdieu [1963] 2021; Bourdieu and Sayad [1964] 2020).

REFLEXIVITY

Finally, doing first-time fieldwork in the dangerous conditions of war helped keep Bourdieu and Sayad from taking everything for granted and reminded them of the need to be particularly vigilant about their own scientific practice. Thinking reflexively about their role while conducting research, their values, and the particular conditions of their fieldwork became a precondition of their practice.

Everything was noted: from the best method of starting an interview with a peasant to the best way of confronting their hypothesis in the fieldwork. The methods were also constantly renewed in the context of war: discussions on the best methodological approach, the testing of theories, the best way to start an interview with the peasants, and the strategies to evade army surveillance were simultaneously part of their reflexive moment. Indeed, doing fieldwork under the protection of the army (the only way of doing their first fieldwork with ARDES in the forced resettlements) meant finding strategies to thwart military surveillance. More generally, it was necessary to be able to investigate without being perceived as the type of "journalists, civil and military social assistants" who questioned the Algerians only to hear the answers they expected: "Are you doing very well here? But still, you are better here than up there with the goats, with the jackals!"[8] The summaries made by the different duos of ethnographers after each day of fieldwork show the many suspicions that the institutional framework aroused among their respondents, who mainly feared that the army sent "informants" predisposed to play the game.

Different strategies, including a "rational division of labor" of young ethnographers, were then deployed to better objectify the experiences of the populations studied. Bourdieu reports that researchers who had gone as a duo (a Frenchman and an Algerian) had managed to neutralize the "conformist" trend that the respondents would have in front of two Frenchmen and to break with the "evidence" against the natives (Bourdieu [1963] 2021, 40). This strategy would subsequently be used in France, by forming pairs with Centre de Sociologie Européenne (CSE) researchers from different social backgrounds to control the biases induced by the survey situation.

The account of the fieldwork conditions and methods is one of the most crucial aspects revealed in this ethnographical experience—at a time when anthropology still had a strong tendency to hide the conditions that makes ethnography possible. This reflexive ethnography aligns with the British fieldwork tradition, or the work developed by Ernesto De Martino in the Italian South restoring the obstacles of the fieldwork (e.g., Malinowski [1922] 1984; Evans-Pritchard 1940; De Martino 2015). The foreword of *Work and Workers in Algeria* and some reflexive notes on the situations of the studies integrated into *Uprooting* are also illustrative of the break with the literature of the time, where the relationship of the researcher to fieldwork was limited to autobiographical narratives or preliminary notes placed at the periphery of the analysis.

Both young ethnographers learned, in the fields of Algeria and Béarn, the strength and the obstacles of scientific work in wartime. It also provided them with the means to control the sociological practice while being vigilant of the low autonomy vis-à-vis the external forces, the effects induced by the situations of research, the categories of thought that the researcher mobilizes in fieldwork, and of his or her position as actor of the struggles he or she describes. Reflexivity as the necessary instrument to objectivize the specificities and difficulties of the social sciences (Bourdieu [2001] 2004) was undoubtedly grounded in this transnational experience of fieldwork between Algeria and France.[9]

Conclusion

Improbable social conditions brought Bourdieu and Sayad to collaborate together in a sociological project where the very practice of fieldwork enabled them to renew the conception of this science.

Bourdieu's conversion to sociology, a field situated at the bottom of the disciplinary hierarchy, was not a scholastic choice. His disciplinary reorientation was molded by the desire to understand the struggles of war and conditions of misery experienced by the colonized. He defined his intellectual work as a political pedagogy that used a secondhand documented critique to break with the main theories that legitimized colonialism. As the most brutal forms of domination were transforming the living conditions of Algerians, there was also a need to explain social change—a need neglected by the theoreticist and empiricist way of doing sociology at that time.

In a context where colonialism represented the very negation of history, where colonial ethnology was depoliticized and focused on mechanical situations distant from the agent's actors and their real life, and where the liberation war was the means to break with the ancien régime, a rigorous social science able to grasp this turbulent present needed to be crafted. But this very project was unthinkable. Only atypical conditions could enable the reinvention of sociology. The factor most significant to this project was without doubt the encounter and collaboration in the field between Bourdieu and Sayad. The revelations of their fieldwork, the combination of their political and scholastic inquiries (posed simultaneously in Algeria and France), and the very interrogation of their research conditions, methods, and findings led to their scientific innovations and to rebuilding a reflexive and committed social science.

These objective conditions provided them with scientific tools able to transcend the unacceptable reality of war and the general theories imposed by this conjuncture, to counter the prefabricated theoretical schemes that drew a simplistic portrait of Algerian reality, and to craft an anticolonial position that pictured, in a realistic way, a postcolonial society. These conditions also allowed them to craft an empirically grounded sociology concerned with restoring the mechanisms of domination, with the intention of public intervention, and based on a reflexive analysis. The objective: to constitute a rigorous social science able to reveal false changes or the visualization of true continuities. On the one hand, the ruse of modernity brought other types of domination to traditional society, and colonialism has left and will continue to leave its legacy within capitalism. On the other hand, this study of domination within the colony became the paradigm from which Bourdieu and Sayad would analyze domination during the postcolonial period.

Notes

I am very grateful to the scientific community of the School of Social Science at the Institute for Advanced Study in Princeton, where I prepared this study. I am also thankful to the Fox Center for Humanistic Inquiry (Emory University), where this chapter was for the most part written while I was a Fellow (2018–19). Finally, I want to thank Munirah Bishop for her careful revision of the English in this chapter.

1   Margaret Mead's fieldwork research was no doubt one of the most important inspirations for Bourdieu. This is evident, for instance, on the topic of the use of photography. Franz Boas and Claude Lévi-Strauss had used photography for aesthetic purposes. But Bourdieu, following the example of Mead and Gregory Bateson, used it as a scientific instrument to better capture the details of a culture (Bateson and Mead 1942).

2   Abdelmalek Sayad Archives, Letter from Bourdieu to Sayad, Winter 1959, 20150645/50, National Archives, France.

3   Manuscript of a Research Program on Algeria, Pierre Bourdieu Archives, Grand équipement documentaire—Campus Condorcet, Aubervilliers, France.

4   Abdelmalek Sayad Archives, Notebooks, 20150645/15, National Archives, France.

5   Letter from Pierre Bourdieu, Summer 1959, Marcel Maget Archives, 20130452/2, National Archives, France. I thank Pernelle Issenhuth for this information.

6   Some studies insist on the bias of these works in Algeria and in Béarn, arguing that Bourdieu's ethnographies in both contexts of crises led him to idealize and portray an ahistorical society and to diminish the creative or reaction capacities of the rural population (Goodman 2009; Reed-Danahay 2009; Silverstein 2009).

7   Bourdieu uses the term *hysteresis* to define that process where habitus does not entirely adapt to the transformation of the social structures. The study of the devolution of the Algerian's and Béarnais's traditional way of life, without dispositions and resources necessary to cope with the new situations, allowed Bourdieu to uncover the impasses and the contradictions of the peasant's representations and behaviors.

8   Abdelmalek Sayad Archives, Interview with Abdelmalek Sayad by Federico Neiburg, José Sergio Leite Lopes et Afrânio Garcia Jr., Rio de Janeiro, November 1994, 20150645/65, National Archives, France.

9   Bourdieu would extend this reflexive ethnographic fieldwork to a historical analysis of the social sciences. See, for instance, his article "For a Sociology of Sociologists," initially titled "The Social Conditions of the Sociological Production: Colonial Sociology and Decolonization of Sociology" (Bourdieu [2008] 2013, 283–87). For an overview of Bourdieu's historical sociology of social science, see George Steinmetz's chapter in this volume.

References

Balandier, Georges. 1951. "La situation coloniale: Approche théorique." *Cahiers internationaux de sociologie* 11: 44–79.

Bateson, Gregory, and Margaret Mead. 1942. *Balinese Character: A Photographic Analysis*. New York: New York Academy of Sciences.

Bensa, Alban. 2004. "Pierre Bourdieu et l'anthropologie." In *La liberté par la connaissance*, edited by Jacques Bouveresse and Daniel Roche. Paris: Odile Jacob.

Bourdieu, Pierre. (1958) 1962. *The Algerians*. Boston: Beacon.

Bourdieu, Pierre. 1959. "La logique interne de la civilisation algérienne traditionnelle"; "Le choc des civilisations." In *Le sous-développement en Algérie*, 40–64. Alger: Secrétariat Social.

Bourdieu, Pierre. 1962. "Célibat et condition paysanne." *Etudes Rurales* 5/6: 32–136.

Bourdieu, Pierre. (1963) 2021. *Travail et travailleurs en Algérie*. Paris: Éditions Raisons d'agir.

Bourdieu, Pierre. (1972) 1977. *Outline of a Theory of Practice*. Translated by R. Nice. Cambridge: Cambridge University Press.

Bourdieu, Pierre. (1977) 1979. *Algeria 1960*. Translated by R. Nice. Cambridge: Cambridge University Press.

Bourdieu, Pierre. (1980) 1990. *The Logic of Practice*. Translated by R. Nice. Stanford, CA: Stanford University Press.

Bourdieu, Pierre. (2001) 2004. *Science of Science and Reflexivity*. Translated by R. Nice. Chicago: University of Chicago Press.

Bourdieu, Pierre. (2001) 2003. *Firing Back: Against the Tyranny of the Market 2*. Translated by Loïc Wacquant. New York: Verso Books.

Bourdieu, Pierre. (2002) 2007. *The Bachelors' Ball: The Crisis of Peasant Society in Béarn*. Translated by R. Nice. Chicago: University of Chicago Press.

Bourdieu, Pierre. (2002) 2008. *Political Interventions: Social Science and Political Action*. Translated by D. Fernbach. New York: Verso Books.

Bourdieu, Pierre. (2003) 2012. *Picturing Algeria*. New York: Columbia University Press.

Bourdieu, Pierre. (2004) 2008. *Sketch for a Self-Analysis*. Translated by R. Nice. Chicago: University of Chicago Press.

Bourdieu, Pierre. (2008) 2013. *Algerian Sketches*. Cambridge: Polity.

Bourdieu, Pierre, and Abdelmalek Sayad. (1964) 2020. *Uprooting: The Crisis of Traditional Agriculture in Algeria*. Cambridge: Polity.

Bourdieu, Pierre, and Loïc Wacquant. 1992. *An Invitation to Reflexive Sociology*. Chicago: University of Chicago Press.

Boyer, Robert. 2017. "Économie et sciences sociales. Une alternative. L'impuissance des théories économiques ?" In Pierre Bourdieu, *Anthropologie économique. Cours au Collège de France (1992–1993)*, 293–323. Paris: Seuil-Éditions Raisons d'agir.

De Martino, Ernesto. 2015. *Magic: A Theory from the South*. Translated by Dorothy Louise Zinn. Chicago: University of Chicago Press.

Duval, Julien. 2017. "Situation du cours sur 'Les fondements sociaux de l'action économique' dans l'oeuvre de Pierre Bourdieu." In Pierre Bourdieu, *Anthropologie économique: Cours au Collège de France (1992-1993)*, 265-292. Paris: Seuil-Éditions Raisons d'agir.

Evans-Pritchard, E. E. 1940. *The Nuer: A Description of the Modes of Livelihood and Political Institutions of a Nilotic People*. Oxford: Clarendon.

Fassin, Didier, and Alban Bensa. 2008. *Les politiques de l'enquête: Épreuves ethnographiques*. Paris: La Découverte.

Feraoun, Mouloud. (1950) 1954. *Le fils du pauvre*. Paris: Éditions du Seuil.

Foucault, Michel. 2001. *Dits et écrits II*. Paris: Gallimard.

Go, Julian. 2016. *Postcolonial Thought and Social Theory*. Oxford: Oxford University Press.

Goodman, Jane E. 2009. "The Proverbial Bourdieu: Habitus and the Politics of Representation in the Ethnography of Kabylia." In *Bourdieu in Algeria: Colonial Politics, Ethnographic Practices, Theoretical Developments*, edited by Jane E. Goodman and Paul A. Silverstein, 94-132. Lincoln: University of Nebraska Press.

Goodman, Jane E., and Paul A. Silverstein, eds. 2009. *Bourdieu in Algeria: Colonial Politics, Ethnographic Practices, Theoretical Developments*. Lincoln: University of Nebraska Press.

Hammoudi, Abdellah. 2007. "Phénoménologie et ethnographie: À propos de l'habitus kabyle chez Pierre Bourdieu." *L'Homme* 184, no. 4: 47-83.

Heilbron, Johan. 2011. "Practical Foundations of Theorizing in Sociology: The Case of Pierre Bourdieu." In *Social Knowledge in the Making*, edited by C. Camic, N. Gross, and M. Lamont, 181-505. Chicago: University of Chicago Press.

Heilbron, Johan. 2015. *French Sociology*. Ithaca, NY: Cornell University Press.

Herskovits, Melville J., Ralph Linton, and Robert Redfield. 1936. "Memorandum for the Study of Acculturation." *American Anthropologist* 38: 149-52.

Honneth, Axel, Hermann Kocyba, and Bernd Schwibs. 1986. "The Struggle for Symbolic Order: An Interview with Pierre Bourdieu." *Theory, Culture and Society* 3, no. 3: 35-51.

Laferté, Gilles, and Nicolas Renahy. 2006. "Tradition, Modernization, and Domination: Three Perspectives of French Rural Studies Crystallized around a Single Survey (RCP Châtillonnais, 1966-1975)." Centre d'Économie et Sociologie appliquées à l'Agriculture et aux Espaces Ruraux, Working Paper presented at the Social Science History Association, Minneapolis, MN, November 2-5. https://hal.inrae.fr/hal-02815421/file/11122_2007042311064 6188 _2.pdf.

Lane, Jeremy F. 2000. *Pierre Bourdieu. A Critical Introduction*. London: Pluto Press.

Leiris, Michel. 1950. "L'ethnographe devant le colonialism." *Temps Modernes* (August): 357-74.

Lévi-Strauss, Claude. (1955) 1973. *Tristes tropiques*. Translated by J. Weightman and D. Weightman. New York: Atheneum.

Lévi-Strauss, Claude. 1958. *Anthropologie structurale*. Paris: Plon.

Maget, Marcel. 1953. *Ethnographie métropolitaine: Guide d'enquête directe des comportements culturels*. Paris: Civilisations du Sud.

Maget, Marcel. 1955. "Remarques sur le village comme cadre de recherches anthropologiques." *Bulletin de Psychologie* 7–8: 375–82.

Maget, Marcel. 1968. "Problèmes d'ethnographie européenne." In *Ethnologie générale*, edited by Jean Poirier, 1247–1338. Paris: Gallimard.

Malinowski, Bronislaw. (1922) 1984. *Argonauts of the Western Pacific*. Prospect Heights, IL: Waveland Press.

Martin-Criado, Enrique. 2008. *Les deux Algéries de Pierre Bourdieu*. Bellecombe-en-Bauges: Éditions du Croquant.

Medvetz, Thomas, and Jeffrey J. Sallaz, eds. 2018. *The Oxford Handbook of Pierre Bourdieu*. New York: Oxford University Press.

Pérez, Amín. 2017. "La liberación del conocimiento: Bourdieu y Sayad frente al colonialismo." Foreword to Pierre Bourdieu and Abdelmalek Sayad, *El Desarraigo: La violencia del capitalismo en una sociedad rural*. Buenos Aires: Siglo XXI Editores.

Pérez, Amín. 2020. "Doing Politics by Other Means: Abdelmalek Sayad and the Political Sociology of a Collective Intellectual." *Sociological Review* 68, no. 5: 999–1014.

Pérez, Amín. 2022. *Combattre en sociologues: Pierre Bourdieu et Abdelmalek Sayad dans une guerre de libération (Algérie, 1958-1964)*. Marseille-France: Éditions Agone.

Poupeau, Franck. 2018. "Pierre Bourdieu and the Unthought Colonial State." In *The Oxford Handbook of Pierre Bourdieu*, edited by Thomas Medvetz and Jeffrey J. Sallaz, 421–36. New York: Oxford University Press.

Reed-Danahay, Deborah. 2009. "Bourdieu's Ethnography in Bearn and Kabylia: The Peasant Habitus." In *Bourdieu in Algeria: Colonial Politics, Ethnographic Practices, Theoretical Developments*, edited by Jane Goodman and Paul A. Silverstein, 133–63. Lincoln: University of Nebraska Press.

Robben, Antonius C. G. M., and Jeffrey A. Sluka. 2007. *Ethnographic Fieldwork: An Anthropological Reader*. Malden, UK: Blackwell.

Sallaz, Jeffrey J. 2018. "Is a Bourdieusian Ethnography Possible?" In *The Oxford Handbook of Pierre Bourdieu*, edited by Thomas Medvetz and Jeffrey Sallaz, 481–502. New York: Oxford University Press.

Sayad, Abdelmalek. (1998) 2004. *The Suffering of the Immigrant*. Translated by D. Macey. Cambridge: Polity.

Sayad, Abdelmalek. 2002. *Histoire et recherche identitaire: Suivi d'un entretien avec Hassan Arfaoui*. Saint-Denis: Bouchène.

Schultheis, Franz. 2014. "Pierre Bourdieu and Algeria: An Elective Affinity, by Franz Schultheis." In Pierre Bourdieu, *Picturing Algeria*. New York: Columbia University Press.

Silverstein, Paul A. 2009. "Of Rooting and Uprooting: Kabyle Habitus, Domesticity, and Structural Nostalgia." In *Bourdieu in Algeria: Colonial Politics, Ethnographic Practices, Theoretical Developments*, edited by Jane Goodman and Paul A. Silverstein, 164–98. Lincoln: University of Nebraska Press.

Steinmetz, George. 2013. "Major Contributions to Sociological Theory and Research on Empire, 1830s–Present." In *Sociology and Empire: The Imperial Entanglements of a Discipline*, edited by George Steinmetz. Durham, NC: Duke University Press.

Steinmetz, George. 2017. "Sociology and Colonialism in the British and French Empires, 1945–1965." *Journal of Modern History* 89, no. 3: 601–48.

Steinmetz, George. 2018. "Bourdieusian Field Theory and the Reorientation of Historical Sociology." In *The Oxford Handbook of Pierre Bourdieu*, edited by Thomas Medvetz and Jeffrey Sallaz, 601–28. New York: Oxford University Press.

Thénault, Sylvie. 2005. *Histoire de la guerre d'indépendance algérienne*. Paris: Flammarion.

Wacquant, Loïc. 2004. "Following Pierre Bourdieu into the Field." *Ethnography* 5, no. 4: 387–414.

Yacine, Tassadit and Hafid Adnani. 2003. "L'autre Bourdieu: Celui qui ne disait pas ce qu'il avait envie de cacher." *Awal* 27/28: 229–47.

Yacine, Tassadit. 2013. "At the Origins of a Singular Ethnosociology." In Pierre Bourdieu, *Algerian Sketches*, 13–34. Cambridge: Polity.

from the
national to
the global

PART TWO

how sociology shaped postwar Poland & how Stalinization shaped sociology

AGATA ZYSIAK

Sociology in the current era of globalization is very much part of this geopolitical divide of ignorance and knowledge, where Russian [and Polish] sociologists read and cite western European and North American colleagues frequently, while few Westerners know about the former. And even fewer read them.
—GÖRAN THERBORN, FOREWORD, *SOCIOLOGY IN RUSSIA*

"FOR US, sociology's task is to know what forms and institutions are the best, and what political system makes all us, mortals, happy," announced progressive journal *Przegląd* in 1883 (Chałasiński 1948, 12).[1] At that time, although Poland did not exist on a world map,[2] vivid discussions among Polish intellectuals concerning such novelties as sociology were already taking place. Outside academia, in opposition to conservative circles, a new discipline was born beginning in the nineteenth century, when the liberal intelligentsia,[3] often educated at European universities and focusing on social reform, and other thinkers started to consider themselves sociologists. In this essay, I trace the development of the discipline from its positivist beginning through its interwar institutionalization, and finally focus on the public engagement of sociologists in reconstruction after the Second World War. I trace how sociology shaped postwar reality and adapted during the Stalinization period. I use the case of the industrial city of Łódź, where a vivid sociological community gathered and a new university was established in 1945. The project of an egalitarian and democratic institution was mainly conceptualized, discussed, and put into action by sociologists themselves, who eventually became researchers who could and did diagnose its successes and failures.

The case of Polish sociology offers a story of the constitution and transformation of academic fields in the so-called Second World, or the global East (Waldstein 2010; Trubina et al. 2020). Along with the other chapters in this part, it brings insights into lesser-known academic fields and widens topography of this volume, which also includes India, Mexico, Algeria, and Japan. At the same time, it puts a chapter from Polish social sciences on equal footing with the worldwide hegemons in knowledge production discussed herein.

Inevitably, "Polish sociology" is limited to the usage of national languages and institutional boundaries defined by the national state. On the one hand, it reflects all regional specificity and the interwar independence period, postwar Soviet reforms, sociology's exile from universities as the "bourgeois discipline," and its triumphant return. On the other, it presents an exceptional example of a highly autonomous field, dominated by the intelligentsia ethos but engaged in a postwar project of a new social order. The case of sociology in postwar Łódź not only addresses how we think about a particular university or even academia in general in state-socialist Poland within their historical and sociological contexts; it also contributes to our broader sense of the place of social sciences in social change—especially in the twentieth century—and how we understand intellectuals and academics in their fields of power and competition.

Any strict definition of a "sociologist" is problematic, and indeed, scholars answer this question differently. Classics of sociological thought are mainly selected arbitrarily and retroactively by other scholars writing on the discipline's history. Belonging to sociology's history is defined by an impact and reception (citation index, reprints, establishing schools); an author's focus on sociological issues as we understood them contemporarily; self-definitions or basic usage of the word *sociology*; and finally by a difficult-to-measure esprit de corps of the scientific community—a sense of belonging among sociologists rather than among academics of any other discipline (Sztompka 1984; Szacki 1995; Mucha and Wincławski 2006; Wincławski 2011; Bucholc 2016). With the discipline's institutionalization in the interwar period, definitions come easier. One can follow academic affiliations at sociological departments (or the engagement in efforts to establish them), faculties or research institutes, participation in sociological congresses and associations, and publications in scientific journals. Moreover, doing all the latter, the esprit de corps seems to be particularly strong among Polish scholars and evident in private journals, academic texts, and public speeches. That esprit de corps involves the undeniable and undiscussable conviction among "sociologists" about their community and its boundaries—or, even going further, confidence in Polish sociology's specificity or even exceptionalism; it takes the form of an almost unbearable certainty that only cultural hegemons can uphold.

To what extent has a narrative of being progressive and in opposition played a crucial role in the emergence of this sense of certainty?[4] In the Stalinization period self-descriptions and a sense of belonging became central in defining sociology. I propose this thesis: the period of Stalinization, when sociology was officially banned as a "bourgeois discipline," actually consolidated and strengthened its disciplinary boundaries and identity. That period of identity construction defined an otherwise blurred and fluid discipline's divisions. Finally, a narrative about oppression and captivity was petrified by autoreflexive sociological writings that established the discipline's martyrology.

Interwar Institutionalization

From sociology's beginning, its advocates focused on social reform, secularism, class inequalities, and, before 1918, national independence (in various orders of importance). The first wave of positivist proto-sociologists in 1880s were close to liberal circles inspired by positivism.[5] They referred to Comte or even Darwin and proposed the rule of reason and organic work to educate society. At that time Spencer was also much closer to Marx than today, thus a category of "class" was almost synonymous with "nation" in partitioned Poland. Later on, however, it was Marxism that became the most influential inspiration for those who defined themselves as sociologists and shaped institutional sociology. Soon antipositivism too spread among advocates of sociology and the Chicago school who had overthrown European masters.[6] What needs to be underlined is that sociology developed as part of the social and political reforms movement, in which both leftists (socialist, communist, agrarian) and liberals (positivists) were engaged. Furthermore, first attempts to establish sociology as a university discipline revealed conflicts with the Catholic Church, national democracy, and already established academic fields—and at the same time, those conflicts strengthened sociology's "progressive" and critical identity.

Establishing new independent states in Eastern Europe from 1918 meant building national academic circulations almost from scratch. New Polish sociological institutions built in the interwar period were not shaped by homemade Polish original proto-sociologists but rather by scholars educated and active abroad, experienced in opinion journalism. The generation of the founders brought not only academic culture from three different partitions of Poland, but also intellectual formations from Geneva, Zurich, Paris, or Chicago. A general acknowledgment of sociology as a promising discipline was widespread; many not only attended sociological lectures but also contributed to the rising discipline abroad.

The first attempt to create a chair in sociology took place in 1910 in Cracow, which at that time was a provincial academic center in Austro-Hungary. It was unsuccessful, and sociological chairs would be created only after regaining independence in the 1920s (Poznan in 1920, Warsaw in 1923, and finally Cracow too, in 1930). Because of peculiar institutional trajectories, the leading and most influential figure at that time became Florian Znaniecki, who was already an internationally recognizable scholar thanks to his Chicago experiences and collaboration with William I. Thomas (Thomas and Znaniecki 1996). At that time, his work and approach became a cornerstone for biographical and qualitative sociology worldwide; not surprisingly, his influence in the Polish context was even more fundamental. Znaniecki, a careful reader of Simmel and member of the Chicago school, not only took a leading position as institutional manager but also defined borders of the new discipline and intellectually formed a new generation of sociologists. Znaniecki's *Introduction to Sociology* (1922) promoted culturalism and a "humanistic coefficient" and criticized abstract rationality, naturalism, and ahistoricism; it also criticized methodological positivism for naive scientism and the notion of social progress.[7] Therefore, sociology was defined mainly by an antipositivist approach.

In 1921 Znaniecki had founded the Polish Institute of Sociology, the fifth-oldest sociological institute in Europe, and he inspired the foundation of the Polish Sociological Association in 1931. Znaniecki focused on theory and methodology, but empirical research as well as the diagnosis of society and its problems stood in the center of the developing discipline. Other efficient organizers of sociological institutionalized life, like agrarian politician Władysław Grabski or Ludwik Krzywicki shared a preference for empirical research, analytical induction, and interest in biographical materials (soon competition memoir* came to be recognized as the "Polish method") (Jakubczak 1989; Lebow 2012, 2014).[8] Krzywicki initiated the establishment of the Central Statistical Office and Socio-Economic Institute in Warsaw, an independent think tank associated with the Warsaw School of Economics, a vivid center for competition memoir. And this was happening despite a general opposition in Polish academia toward any "utilitarian uses" of knowledge. Another nonuniversity research center, the National Institute for Rural Culture, employed sociologists and two future rectors of the University of Łódź: Józef Chałasiński and another protégé of Znaniecki, Jan Szczepański.[9] However, these types of initiatives remained on the margins of academic life, whose imagined ideal was "pure science" and the university as an ivory tower. And the latter was actually becoming increasingly detached from the actual situation of the country. By contrast, sociology was strongly politicized and antagonized by older disciplines like philosophy, law, and history. It was seen as a modern, progressive, and practical discipline.

The prevailing conditions of interwar academia were far from satisfactory. One of the main obstacles was the lack of funding, which blocked the academic careers of many young scholars. On the eve of World War II, three thousand faculty, including one thousand academic professors, worked in Poland. Most of them (60–80 percent) were of intelligentsia origins, and only a few (4–8 percent) came from the working classes (Mycielska 1981; Jaczewski 1982). The universities had a rather conservative profile with respect to both their methodological and political aspects. Antisemitism at universities was just one element of increasingly dangerously ethnic tensions throughout the entire country, reflected in the higher education reform of 1933 and the strengthening of the authoritarian regime. Many leftist intellectuals could not find a place for themselves, and some got involved in more progressive projects like an independent Free Polish University in Warsaw (with a small branch in Łódź), while others—more radical and politically active—ended up in political prison. By the late 1930s, a quarter of society was still illiterate, an educational selection system was in place even before the elementary school level, and the social composition of students was very elitist: only 13.7 percent of fifty thousand students—80 percent of Poland's multicultural populace of 35 million—came from peasant or working-class families.

A rising star of the 1930s was Józef Chałasiński. His academic career began in Poznań in the 1920s under Znaniecki's supervision. Because he came from a small town and was fascinated with peasant culture, Chałasiński did not fit comfortably into interwar academia, which was dominated by urban intelligentsia. He became widely known after publishing a four-volume work titled *The Young Peasant Generation* (Chałasiński 1938). The Polish authoritarian government classified the latter as a subversive book which posed a danger to state order not long after its publication. There were even plans to confiscate all printed editions of the work (Gryko 2007, 70). Personal attacks followed: he was called a "sociologist from a barn" and was threatened with hell (Siekierski 1986, 22–23). In the late 1930s he, along with other progressive social scientists such as Krzywicki and Jan Bystroń,[10] protested against antisemitic regulations and atrocities in universities. As a result of this activism, these prominent intellectuals were called "alias-Poles, shabbos goys" in *Alma Mater*, the official journal of the University of Warsaw (Jakubczak 1996, 70).

In addition to the peasantry, Chałasiński was also interested in the intelligentsia and its role in society. His egalitarian views concerning social inequality were widely known before World War II. During the war he wrote a book titled *Chłopi i Panowie* (*Peasants and Masters*), which, unlike his previous works, was a critique of interwar Poland and its social structure. The manuscript was lost, but in a book based on the lost manuscript published in late 1940s, he used even sharper language to describe the prewar intelligentsia than in the original text, writing: "The intelligentsia ghetto was a huge force, reactionary, social, parasite upon Polish cultural life" (Chałasiński 1947, 88), and the "Polish intelligentsia in its structure is related to the underdevelopment of Polish civilization in technical and economic terms" (54).

The interwar years were a time of sociology's institutionalization and rapid development, first research projects, and methodological and theoretical choices. This generation of the founders became inevitable reference points for future scholars. At the same time, the first debates and conflicts fed the discipline's development. The authoritarian and anti-Semitic turn in the 1930s consolidated progressive scholars, especially sociologists—mostly leftist or liberal, sensitive to human suffering and social inequalities and disappointed in the political reality of interwar Poland. Furthermore, those elements of interwar sociology were later propagated as crucial parts of the discipline's identity: its leftist and oppositional origins, a preference for qualitative methods like biography and the humanistic approach were underlined in the decades to come.

Agenda of Tomorrow

Further consolidation of the discipline followed during the dramatic events of World War II. The very first generation of institutionalized sociologists was largely gone. Wartime losses among university professors are estimated to have been 38 percent, and among sociologists even as high as 50 percent (Szacki 1995, 110). It was not only the core group of prewar sociologists that had disappeared; another large group, including Florian Znaniecki, remained abroad (Gryko 2007, 23). Because of their absence, a younger generation took over leadership positions in the discipline. This group, including Chałasiński and Stanisław Ossowski, headed to Lublin in 1944, during the establishment of the Provisional Government of the Republic of Poland, to lobby for sociology's reconstruction (Kraśko 1996, 88).[11] Later on, with the new government and university administration, they traveled to the working-class city of Łódź.

Only five public universities and over thirty institutions of higher education were in operation before World War II, and there were none in Poland's second-largest city, Łódź. Because of Warsaw's destruction, and because Łódź was the largest and least-destroyed city in the (new) territory of Poland, it temporarily became the country's informal capital, and many sociologists and others headed there. Even if this group of sociologists hadn't ended up in the proletarian city partly by chance, it was not coincidental that the City of Chimneys became the most prominent center of sociological experimentation in the early postwar years. Because of its identity as the cradle of the 1905 revolution and the labor movement, the textile hub was labeled a "red" city, and it had historically represented the figure of the "other" in Polish culture. Those who returned from Lublin were not only prominent sociologists from the younger generation; they were also leftist and liberal intellectuals. Even if their party affiliations were different, they shared the common heritage of the interwar coalition against antisemitism, rising nationalism, and the authoritarian regime. After the war, the members of this disparate group moved relatively closer to each other, and they hoped to build new institutions for the new times. As Jan Szczepański, who also ended up in Łódź, noted in his diary: "One cannot deny how primitive Lublin government is, however their agenda is the agenda of tomorrow!" (Szczepański 2013). Consequently, it was in Łódź that the strongest postwar sociological center was built.

A large, diverse, and politically progressive academic environment flourished. It is worth recalling that, following the tumult of the interwar period and buoyed by postwar hopes, the leftist viewpoint as an authentic choice and not political opportunism was widespread. "[After the war] one became a Marxist as easily as in the recent century one became a positivist.... It was about taking advantage of historical circumstances and about doing the most fundamental work for Poland" (Mencwel 1997, 488). Now, instead of Poznań, Łódź was a center of sociology and the Znaniecki school. However, the postwar period did not entail a paradigmatic revolution. Marxism, already widespread among sociologists, simply remained an important philosophical orientation. Political changes proposed by the new government answered postulates proposed by Krzywicki, Chałasiński, or Stanisław Ossowski, who advocated for sociology's usefulness in a "great laboratory"—the postwar Poland. Support for a new political project was highest among sociologists compared with other academic faculty (Szacki 1995, 111).

A Marxist academic press was established and began publishing the influential journal *Kuźnica* (*Forge*), which boasted leftist radicals, mostly communists, on its editorial board.[12] It also published the pro-agrarian *Wieś* (*Country*) and the progressive journal *Myśl Współczesna* (*Contemporary Thought*), among numerous other periodicals.[13] The vice minister of education was promoting the concept of the so-called representative Polish university in a working-class city, announcing that it "symbolizes an act of historical justice, and the desire of Polish Democracy to open its doors wide to higher education for the working masses; it symbolizes the convergence of knowledge and work, and the cooperation between workers and scholars" (Bieńkowski 1946). All of this made Polish academia seem like a great construction site, which stimulated the imagination of the leftist intellectuals. One could hope that the revolution knocking at the gates of the university could radically erase all the weaknesses of the conservative and elitist interwar academia. The incredible speed of the postwar reconstruction could already be felt a year after the war. In the academic year 1937–38, 782 chairs hired 1,064 professors (along with their deputies); by 1946–47, there were already 1,229 chairs with 1,462 professors (Kersten 1993, 11). Sociology was also a popular choice among students, especially in Łódź, where it was the second most popular major in 1947–48; 218 students enrolled for sociology classes in 1948–49 (compared to only 123 in Poznań, sociology's cradle; see Kraśko 1996, 99).

In Łódź social scientists began many bottom-up initiatives, and sociologists were the most actively engaged in establishing new projects. Sociologists there conducted research focused on social stratification, the conditions of the working classes, internal mobility, urbanization, national consciousness, and identity (Bucholc 2016, 24). The "primary year" and "preparatory course" were new institutional tools designed to widen universities' enrollment of people whose lives were affected by the war and/or who were from a working-class background. Among them, the strongest voice belonged to university's second rector, Józef Chałasiński. He was a prominent figure among the traveling sociologists and would develop considerable agency in the postwar decades. His radical notions about intelligentsia were by no means a postwar adaptation to political climate; they are easily traced in his writings from 1930s. Therefore, he was not keen to support any projects that sought only to reform the interwar model, as it would merely reproduce its pathologies. His main conclusion was that the ivory tower of academia was both detached from social reality and indifferent to the needs of the population. Chałasiński advocated a radical change and a break from interwar academia. He wanted a university open to the needs of society and accessible to all social strata, especially to the working class and peasantry.

In 1948 Chałasiński also published an article that aimed to rewrite sociology's history and underscored its progressive—even radical—origins (Chałasiński 1948). According to Chałasiński, Polish sociology developed close ties with various social issues, and from its very beginning, it was designed to shape, reform, and ultimately change the established social order. He argued for the socialistic roots of sociology, in opposition to conservative institutionalized academia, which treated sociology as a noxious novelty.[14] To further highlight its progressive roots, he reminded readers that the interwar journal *Przegląd Socjologiczny* (*Sociological Review*) was accused of being a tool of communist propaganda. He also promoted sociology as an internationally recognized discipline, a dimension of advocacy that was obviously related to his own vision of the university. He made fun of its beginnings in the nineteenth century, diminishing the first wave of intellectual fascination of Comte as just the Warsaw elites' toy. Finally, he underlined the cooperation between and unity of postwar sociologists and stressed their leftist perspective.

Bourgeoisie Out

But the best time for Łódź as well as the "gentle revolution" was coming to an end.[15] The academic year of 1949–50 was crucial for Polish academia as the central reform of higher education was implemented in a name of scientific socialism (David-Fox and Péteri 2000). Academia was "parametrized" in the Soviet/Fordist style, which meant that all activities were measurable and countable by the Ministry of Higher Education: for example, universities were obliged to respect the assigned quotas of students and graduates. Courses became obligatory, and in opposition to the so-called "aristocratic manner of studying," students were supposed to work similar to workers in a factory: with almost eight hours per day of classes, roll call, and supervision of their efficiency. The first three years of study were designed to prepare students for practical tasks, and the additional final two years to give them more advanced skills and the "magister" (master's) degree. They were expected to contact a future workplace during their studies to obtain work experience. Universities were thus to become part of a production process aimed at training skilled specialists (including humanities training future teachers and office workers). Censorship was strengthened, and international cooperation was strictly controlled—which to some extent led Polish sociology to a further focus on internal affairs of regional knowledge circulation. Knowing what changes would be implemented during the next decades in the United States and Western Europe, however, one cannot deny the transnational aspects of the Stalinization of higher education. Universities were transformed into institutions crucial to the emerging state socialism. Institutions of higher learning became sites where national history and ideology would be delivered and where the future elite would be shaped and produced.

The period of the "gentle revolution" was conducive to the formation of a wide coalition of support for a number of top-down reforms. Academic faculty members, however—even those who were left-leaning—continued to view the changes with skepticism (Connelly 2000). The party started to create separate channels of educational advancement, which were supervised only by the "progressive" intelligentsia, which this time meant officially approved as politically correct.[16] The so-called active members of the professoriate moved from Łódź to Warsaw in the late 1940s. There they created parallel structures subjected directly to the Ministry of Education.

Paradoxically, sociology was characterized as a "bourgeois science" and gradually banned at universities. When Julian Hochfeld and Adam Schaff famously attacked sociology, they precisely named Znaniecki and his pupils, along with Krzywicki, and criticized them for improper interpretations of Marxism (Hochfeld 1951, 119–20).[17] This attack, among others, defined sociology as clearly as ever before. A visible label and a clear distinction marked all faculty: affiliations, definitions, and even the presupposition of intellectual circles became clear-cut. This situation was challenging for sociologists themselves, because in most cases sociologists "actively supported at least some transformations occurring in the country" (Lutyński 1987, 127). The theory of the "separate nature" of the bourgeois and socialist science was promoted. Naturally, the "bourgeois" science ought to be liquidated.

An important shift was also visible in Chałasiński's attitude toward the democratization of science—he stressed that such a process could not take the form of popularizing the culture of higher classes but should instead be focused on creating a completely new type of culture, responding to the aims and experiences of the working masses. Earlier he had been rather interested in the creation of new types of institutions, supporting the democratization of culture, which seemed to be—along with pluralism and democracy—universal. An even more ideological tone was visible in Chałasiński's speech a few months later, at the inauguration of the academic year of 1950–51. In the newspeak, he underlined the special role of science in the Six-Year Plan and its strict and close relationship on the path to industrialization and a socialist society. At the same time, in the second part of the speech, he tried to argue for the humanities as also indispensable in these processes (irreplaceable for promoting Marxism and Leninism). This was one of many attempts to restore sociology to its place at the university. But all of them failed.

Chałasiński, a committed idealist, took on the role of rector at the worst moment, just before the reform's implementation. And he was a truly horrible diplomat: quarrelsome, stubborn, and fierce. His overzealous implementation of the ministry's instructions only made his efforts and his person seem preposterous (Baranowski 1980). Finally, to demonstrate his disappointment, Chałasiński pleaded with the minister of higher education and science for permission to resign from the rector chair, but his request was rejected (Chałasiński 1950).

Referring to the well-known sarcastic remark made by Lenin, "How will proletarians know how to build locomotives?," one might ask, How was it possible to diagnose, research, and create knowledge about the new socialist society when sociology was no longer recognized as a branch of legitimate scientific inquiry (Graham 1993, 89)? In general, from the beginning of sociology's institutional history in Poland, it was considered a progressive and practical discipline. Theoretically, it also should have been useful for the new government and easily could have been applied to new professional training. In the early postwar period, sociology as a field of study bloomed. Research on stratification, demography, upward mobility, often undertaken from a leftist perspective, seemed to fit perfectly with the meritocratic vision of socialist modernization. This seemingly blind implementation of Soviet solutions has another possible interpretation: precisely because of its left-oriented engagement, sociology was dangerous to proposing a closed and therefore competitive vision of social order, additionally legitimized by expertise and research. Banning it opened up possibilities of monopoly for social reform. In addition, academia served as an exile for degraded socialist politicians like Hochfeld.

Moreover, individual people were moved between institutions in order to weaken prewar relations. Most of the pre-Stalinist faculty continued to work, although some, for example Stanisław Ossowski, were banned from teaching. Ossowski was a pre-war colleague of Chałasiński's, and during the war the two had fled together when the rightist underground accused them of spreading dangerous left-wing views. Owing to his publications, his support for the conception of "socialist humanism" and his "excessively liberal" attitude, he fell into disfavor with the authorities and was dismissed during higher education reform. Ossowski figures as an imitable model of uncompromisingness, presented as a counter to the more pragmatic approach of the academic community.

Sociology was not the only field to be degraded. The University of Łódź had been demoted to a provincial university by the reform. The further consequences were even more catastrophic than the outflow of professors or institutional mimicry that had been carried out in previous months. Between 1948 and 1955, the number of students decreased by 46 percent (partly because of the secession of medical universities); and only three out of fourteen humanities programs were preserved, and then only after the protests of well-known professors. History was kept, but sociology—most important for Chałasiński—was closed (Baranowski and Baranowski 1990, 133). Although departments were still operating, didactics and recruitment were stopped. During the last months of 1948, both the rebuilding of Warsaw and a general emigration of intellectuals to the "real capital" began. Many who during years of chaos had stayed "in transit" were returning home.

The University of Warsaw was now fighting vigorously for its proud title of "the most politically active university" in the People's Republic. Most of the leftist intellectuals began to leave Łódź beginning in 1948, and even the vivid circle's Marxists fled to Warsaw, criticizing Łódź intellectuals for their dogmatism. Chałasiński, who was always impulsive and stubborn, fiercely attacked the people who were leaving (Baranowski 1985, 44), accusing them of a lack of responsibility, a sense of common good, or careerism. He appealed to the ministry, lamenting that "the needs of Łódź were ignored" (Chałasiński 1964, 63). He emphasized the achievements of the University of Łódź and the excellent results of democratization. He illustrated how close the University of Łódź was to implementing the model of the socialist university.

He demanded more resources and support for the growth of the University of Łódź, which was, as he argued, at the heart of the greatest working-class center and one of the largest national universities in Poland.

Stalinist Consolidation?

On the ground level, the institutional structure of universities was almost unchanged. Departments and research projects simply changed names. Chałasiński was still the head of the Sociology Department at the University of Łódź, although it was renamed the Department of Historical Thought. He created a special unit officially devoted to research on the nineteenth-century press at the newly established Polish Academy of Science in Warsaw. His prominent student, future sociologist of culture—Antonina Kłoskowska,[18] who defended her doctoral thesis in 1950, was hired there. While the last issue of *Przegląd Socjologiczny* (*Sociological Review*) was published in 1950, a new periodical was established soon after—the *Przegląd Nauk Historyczno-Społecznych* (*Social-Historical Sciences Review*), which provided a platform for stable and durable sociological exchange.

Sociology adapted to the new conditions of the Stalinist years in its own way. While it was difficult to maintain the status quo, and even more difficult to cultivate institutional sociology without a dedicated teaching cadre, it is worth recalling that students who enrolled in 1948, graduated in 1953 (the year of Stalin's death), and that sociology as a separate discipline was reintroduced into the curricula of universities just four years later, in 1957. Actually, the first signs of the Thaw had appeared in 1954,[19] initially at the University of Warsaw, where sociological lectures were first reinstated (Bucholc 2016, 31). Following the Thaw of 1956, sociology was no longer considered a "bourgeois relic." Moreover, sociologists did not disappear; they could continue teaching courses on a variety of subjects in different degree programs, and those banned from teaching were still hired as faculty. According to Connelly, of the eleven assistants dismissed as a result of the Stalinist reform, nine of them continued their academic careers. Furthermore, in the most frenzied period of Stalinism, 1951–54, the titles of professor and associate professor were awarded to 302 people, only 41 of whom were party members (Connelly 1999, 198; Connelly 2000). In 1953 only 9 percent of students (Szczepański 1959, 477) and 10.7 percent of professors belonged to the party (Fijałkowska 1985, 464; Hübner 1987, 174). In the GDR, Czechoslovakia, and Poland, local parties were adept at constructing the new elites. But whereas in the first two countries they focused on young academics and successive intakes of students, in Poland the process was more complex. Hostility to both communism and Russia was rife among most of the academic community, which is usually explained by historical events and the community's social structure and background. The party initially opted for a conciliatory policy, and the majority of the prewar scholars who survived the war and came back to Poland returned to high positions, regardless of their views. The dominant loyalty was to the academic community, not to the party.

By 1957, most universities opened enrollment for sociology, and larger organizational changes followed. Sociological periodicals experienced a revival with the publication of both new and old titles; the Polish Sociological Association was founded; and many Polish sociologists began to engage in international academic cooperation. The reestablishment of sociology was much more difficult in smaller cities. However, in Łódź, the Department of Sociology, with Chałasiński as its head, was quickly inaugurated, although it is worth noting that by this time he was beginning to lose his status in academia in the eyes of both the government and other sociologists. His term as rector ended in 1952 as a result of his unsuccessful attempts to protect the University of Łódź, and he was marginalized as both a university official and an academic because of several controversial articles he published during the Stalinist period, first because he was considered too pro-government and later because he was too critical of the state. After many career highs and lows, he moved to Warsaw to take a chair at the Polish Academy of Sciences.

In a way, even Marxism itself survived the Stalinization period as theoretical orientation—its Stalinists critics were not treated seriously. Pro-Stalinist scholars who openly supported political reforms instead of hegemonizing academia were rather ghettoized in departments of Marxism-Leninism and had little influence on the academic community and on philosophical Marxism. Officially it was still a dominant paradigm (but with revisionist interpretations), thus a focus on empirical studies or methodology was a safer political choice. This escapism toward empirical research was soon dominated by functional structuralism. Sociologists started to travel abroad, participated in the International Socialist Alternative (ISA) conventions, and gained better access to the international circulation of knowledge. Foreign organizations provided scholarships, funds, and possibilities to travel, but stable funding sources and large investments in research provided by the state were crucial for sociology's revival. At that time, the first wave of serious internal diversification also began as many subdisciplines emerged.

But after 1956 the most important shift was that sociology regained its role in public life. For the first time after Sovietization, scholars were

encouraged to diagnose the results of socialist cultural policies: the democratization of education, the mass culturalization efforts, the management in
factories. Once again, sociologists became desirable experts commissioned by
the government to teach but also, more importantly, to diagnose social ills
and recommend improvements. As early as the mid-1950s, Chałasiński, Jan
Szczepański, and many others, all of whom were educated by the interwar
masters of academic sociology, led various research projects carried out by
the postwar generation of sociologists.

The state introduced new founding schemes and public opinion surveys,
and ordered reports to design new policies. The cultural dissemination policies needed animators, and the rapidly developing sociology of work meant
that thousands of sociologists were hired at large companies. This increasing need for expertise turned scholars into state socialist managers. They
produced considerable databases, numerous reports, analyses, and scientific
monographs. Based on their current assessments, there is no reason to doubt
their reliability, as their authors have had many an opportunity to rectify
the results. Instead, they and the subsequent generations of researchers
continue to make use of these findings and can still be regarded as a "solid
reference point" (Domański 2008, 8). Many authors underscore the role of
pragmatism, ritualistic references to Lenin, and the strong presence of media-
tors between the political establishment and the academic community during the People's Republic of Poland. However, those were apparent actions,
while a core set of research, daily practices, and intellectual circulations was
happening despite or even simply "next to" governmental policies.

Conclusion

What is interesting is how progressive academics like Chałasiński, the most
vicious critics of interwar academia, were pushed by the reform into the position of supporting traditional academia and the intelligentsia. For leftist
and liberal sociologists, the postwar years represented a "gentle revolution"
preceding Stalinization—a truly ambivalent period when "their traditions,
their ethos were at the same time implemented and overwhelmed" (Kersten
1993, 121). In Chałasiński's case, two of his main aims were somehow realized,
but from above and, in the end, almost entirely without his input. The social
revolution of 1939–56 and the socialist modernization project created opportunities for advancement on an unprecedented scale. Only to a limited extent,
however, did it transform the academic field in terms of values, rules of the
field, and the university model. When confronted with overly strong political

pressure, progressive sociologists, even those pushed into a more radical position because of their social origins, supported academia and its inner ethos.

Postwar history of sociology focuses strongly on power relations between academia and politics or captivity under a totalitarian regime, to such an extent that the Stalinization is seen as worse even than the occupation during World War II (Szacki 1995, 114). When one considers that institutional exile of sociology effectively started only in 1951 and that signs of the Thaw had already appeared in 1954, this seems to be an exaggeration. Enrollments were open in 1956; sociology departments regained their names, and usually the same faculty were hired. Sociological journals and association were reestablished. The new generation active after the Thaw were those educated in the late 1940s by interwar scholars who returned to sociology after only a few years away. Sociology reverted to an already established institutional frame divided into universities focused on teaching, research academies of science, and professional research institutes sponsored by government agendas.

The pace of recovery, the fastest in the Soviet bloc, is not surprising when one takes into account that sociologists not only remained at universities but also kept their research projects and networks going. Empirical sociological research was openly conducted. Despite the break in enrollments during the Stalinist years, sociology's limited presence in curricula, and its mimetic adaptation to Stalinist reforms, the discipline seemed to be stronger for having overcome wartime disruption and the rupture that characterized the postwar period. It is often pointed out that continuity within interwar academia revealed itself after 1956. However, this was only possible because of Stalinization's very limited effects on academia in general, and on sociology in particular: the Stalinist period played a role simply as a defining factor for the field. Martyrology of sociologists led to the strengthening not only of the intelligentsia ethos but also of the discipline's identity. Furthermore, the new generation of social researchers educated after the war and during "the worst years of Stalinization" provided an example of the successful reproduction of the traditional university. An indicator of the latter is that even Chałasiński is today presented above all as a doyen of sociology rather than as a radical reformer and pioneer of the idea of the socialist university.

Notes

The research for this article was conducted at University of Łódź, Poland, financed by the Polish National Science Center, research grant Preludium 2 contracted as umo-2011/03/N/HS6/01948.

1 *Przegląd Tygodniowy* was a Warsaw-based weekly, the Polish *encyclopédistes'* and Positivists' platform.

2 Before 1918, the territories of the Second Republic were part of the Kingdom of Prussia, Austro-Hungary, and the Russian/Soviet empires.

3 A silent protagonist of this article is the intelligentsia, a status group characteristic of Eastern Europe and Russia, an educated and professionally active social stratum with the self-inscribed symbolic role of cultural and moral leaders (particularly important during the partition period). Members of the intelligentsia were often criticized by sociologists as cultural hegemons protecting their own status of a moral leader of the nation, but at the same time critics inevitably belonged to this stratum.

4 I often use the adjectives progressive or conservative to describe individuals or intellectual circles. Because of multilayered divisions, Polish political history is defined by shifts and unstable alliances. I allow myself to simplify a narrative by following descriptions proposed by many sociologists themselves. For a relatively brief insight, see Porter-Szücs 2014.

5 In Poland, the term *positivism* is used in at least two contexts: (1) academic, referring to methodological positivism; and (2) sociocultural, inspired by the latter and defined in opposition to Romanticism. Sociocultural positivists believe that Poland's independence can be restored not by uprisings but organic work, education, and rule of reason.

6 To compare situation in other national circulations see Miriam Kingsberg Kadia's chapter in this volume.

7 Despite Znaniecki's *Introduction to Sociology*, only one other sociological textbook was printed—Jan Stanisław Bujak's *Sociology: Informational and Bibliographical Introduction* from 1931, designed for popularization and teaching.

8 Władysław Grabski (1874–1938), an economist, historian, and National Democratic politician, was prime minister of Poland in 1920 and again from 1923 to 1925. He also initiated the Rural Sociology Institute at the Warsaw University of Life Sciences. Ludwik Krzywicki (1859–1941) was an economist, statistician, sociologist, and socialist activist, and one of the early champions of sociology strongly inspired by Marxism. * Competition memoir or memoir-writing competitions (*konkursy pamiętnikarskie*)—a sociological method developed in the 1920s; personal diaries/autobiographies were gathered in publicly announced competitions, with awards for the best submissions. Usually competition focused on a certain social group like the unemployed or young peasants, and later on, also on a proposed subject. Collections of these personal stories would number in the thousands of submissions.

9 Józef Chałasiński (1904–79) was an agrarian and sociologist from Znaniecki's school, an organizer of competitions memoirs, and a furious intelligentsia critic. Jan Szczepański (1913–2004), another student of Znaniecki, was a sociologist who became an important institutional figure in the postwar period.

10 Jan Stanisław Bystroń (1892–1964) was a sociologist and ethnographer who taught sociology in Warsaw beginning in 1934.

11 Stanisław Ossowski (1897–1963) was a sociologist educated in Warsaw, one of the most important figures of the post-1956 sociology in Poland.

12 *Kuźnica* (1945–48) was a Marxist social-literary weekly where major debates between members of the intelligentsia took place. In 1948, it merged with another cultural weekly, *Odrodzenie* (Renaissance/Revival), under the title *Nowa Kultura*.

13 *Wieś* (1944–54) was a social-literary weekly for rural intellectuals that focused on regional culture and education. It moved to Warsaw in 1949. *Myśl Współczesna* (1945–51) was a Marxist philosophical monthly scientific journal edited by Chałasiński until 1948, then by Adam Schaff.

14 Franciszek Bujak (1875–1953) was an economic historian who was also interested in social issues. Thanks to his work on rural areas in Poland, he is often considered a proto-sociologist.

15 The term *gentle revolution* was introduced in 1945 by a prominent intellectual and editor Jerzy Borejsza to describe the early postwar years as time of hope and reconstruction.

16 The unification congress of the Polish Workers' Party and Polish Socialist Party took place in 1948, and the party formed by that unification was the Polish United Workers' Party, the single party that ruled Poland until 1989.

17 Julian Hochfeld (1911–66) was a Marxist, a socialist politician, and a sociologist. In 1948 he was forced to academia from politics and took a Stalinist approach toward his own discipline. Adam Schaff (1913–2006), a philosopher educated in Paris and Moscow, was a Stalinist engaged in higher education reform.

18 Antonina Kłoskowska (1919–2001) was a sociologist educated in 1940s at University of Łódź. She served as Chałasiński's assistant and was well-known for her work on mass culture in 1960s.

19 The 1954 "proto-Thaw" was known as the Gomułka Thaw, or the Polish October. The year 1956 was a crucial period of transition, but changes were seen much earlier, and not only in the field of social sciences.

References

Baranowski, Bohdan. 1980. "Pierwsi rektorzy Uniwersytetu Łódzkiego." *Życie Szkoły Wyższej* 7/8: 87 91.

Baranowski, Bohdan. 1985. *Pierwsze lata Uniwersytetu Łódzkiego, 1945–1949.* Łódź: Uniwersytet Łódzki.

Baranowski, Bohdan, and Krzysztof Baranowski. 1990. *Trudne lata Uniwersytetu Łódzkiego: 1949–1956.* Łódź: Wydawnictwo UŁ.

Bieńkowski, Władysław. 1946. "Przemówienie p. Wiceministra Władysława Bieńkowskiego na uroczystej inauguracji roku akademickiego na Uniwersytecie Łódzkim dnia 13 stycznia 1946r." AUŁ, Biuro Rektora. sygn. 1856.

Bucholc, Marta. 2016. *Sociology in Poland: To Be Continued?* London: Palgrave Macmillan.

Chałasiński, Józef. 1938. *Młode pokolenie chłopów*. Warsaw: Państwowy Instytut Kultury Wsi.

Chałasiński, Józef. 1947. *Społeczna genealogia inteligencji polskiej*. Crakow: Czytelnik.

Chałasiński, Józef. 1948. "Trzydzieści lat socjologii polskiej." *Przegląd Socjologiczny* 50: 1–54.

Chałasiński, Józef. 1950. "Memoriał Rektora ws. warunków pracy i rozwoju UŁ," Archiwum Akt Nowych, Biuro Rektora. sygn. 298.

Chałasiński, Józef. 1964. "Początki uniwersytetu robotniczej Łodzi." In *Tranzytem przez Łódź*, edited by I. Bołtuc-Staszewska, 43–92. Łódź: Wydawnictwo Łódzkie.

Connelly, John. 1999. "The Foundations of Diversity: Communist Higher Education Policies in Eastern Europe 1945–1955." In *Science under Socialism: East Germany in Comparative Perspective*, edited by K. Macrakis and D. Hoffmann, 125–39. Cambridge, MA: Harvard University Press.

Connelly, John. 2000. *Captive University: The Sovietization of East German, Czech, and Polish Higher Education, 1945–1956*. Chapel Hill: University of North Carolina Press.

David-Fox, Michael, and György Péteri, eds. 2000. *Academia in Upheaval: Origins, Transfers, and Transformations of the Communist Academic Regime in Russia and East Central Europe*. Westport, CT: Bergin and Garvey.

Domański, Henryk, ed. 2008. *Zmiany stratyfikacji społecznej w Polsce*. Warsaw: PAN.

Fijałkowska, Barbara. 1985. *Polityka I twórcy 1948–1959*. Warsaw: PWN.

Graham, Loren R. 1993. *Science in Russia and the Soviet Union: A Short History*. Cambridge: Cambridge University Press.

Gryko, Czesław. 2007. *Józef Chałasiński—człowiek i dzieło: Od teorii wychowania do kulturowej wizji narodu*. Poznań WWSPiA.

Hochfeld, Julian. 1951. "O niektórych aspektach przeciwstawności materializmu historycznego i socjologii burżuazyjnej." *Myśl Filozoficzna* 1–2: 106–54.

Hübner, Piotr. 1987. *Nauka polska po II wojnie światowej—idee i instytucje*. Warsaw: COM SNP.

Jaczewski, Bohdan. 1982. "Nauka." In *Polska odrodzona 1918–1939: Państwo, społeczeństwo, kultura*, edited by J. Tomicki, 507–553. Warsaw: Wiedza Powszechna.

Jakubczak, Franciszek. 1989. "Zasoby pamiętników: Zasady i zakres ich użytkowania." *Ruch Prawniczy, Ekonomiczny i Socjologiczny* 2: 259–68.

Jakubczak, Franciszek. 1996. "Józefa Chałasińskiego ethos nieposłuszeństwa w myśleniu." In *Chałasiński dzisiaj: Materiały z konferencji naukowej*, edited by A. Kaleta, 65–74. Toruń: Wydawnictwo UMK.

Kersten, Krystyna. 1993. *Między wyzwoleniem a zniewoleniem: Polska 1944–1956*. London: Aneks.

Kraśko, Nina. 1996. *Instytucjonalizacja socjologii w Polsce 1920–1970*. Warsaw: PWN.

Lebow, Katherine. 2012, "The Conscience of the Skin: Interwar Polish Autobiography and Social Rights," *Humanity: An International Journal of Human*

Rights, Humanitarianism, and Development 3, no. 3: 297–31. https://www.doi.org
/:10.1353/hum.2012.0027.

Lebow, Katherine. 2014. "Autobiography as Complaint: Polish Social Memoir
between the World Wars." *Laboratorium: Russian Review of Social Research* 6,
no. 3: 13–26.

Lutyński, Jan. 1987. "Niektóre uwarunkowania rozwoju socjologii polskiej i ich
konsekwencje." *Studia Socjologiczne* 195, no. 2: 127–141.

Mencwel, Andrzej. 1997. *Przedwiośnie czy Potop: Studium postaw polskich w XX wieku.*
Warsaw: Czytelnik.

Mucha, Janusz, and Włodzimierz Wincławski, eds. 2006. *Klasyczna socjologia
polska i jej współczesna recepcja.* Torun: Wydawnictwo Uniwersytetu Mikołaja
Kopernika.

Mycielska, Dorota. 1981. "Drogi życiowe profesorów przed objęciem katedr aka-
demickich w niepodległej Polsce." In *Inteligencja polska XIX i XX wieku: Studia,*
vol. 2, edited by R. Czepulis-Rastenis, 244–290. Warsaw: PWN.

Porter-Szücs, Brian. 2014. *Poland in the Modern World: Beyond Martyrdom.* Oxford:
Wiley Blackwell.

Siekierski, Stanisław. 1986. "Z dziejów recepcji Młodego pokolenia chłopów."
Przegląd Humanistyczny 1–2: 21–33.

Szacki, Jerzy. 1995. *Sto lat socjologii polskiej: Od Supińskiego do Szczepańskiego.* Warsaw:
PWN.

Szczepański, Jan, ed. 1959. *Wykształcenie a pozycja społeczna inteligencji: Praca
zbiorowa,* vol. 1. Łódź: PWN.

Szczepański, Jan. 2013. *Dzienniki z lat 1945-1968.* Ustron: Galeria Na Gojach.

Sztompka, Piotr, ed. 1984. *Masters of Polish Sociology.* Wrocław: Zakład Narodowy
im. Ossolińskich.

Therborn, Göran. 2017. "Foreword." In *Sociology in Russia,* edited by L. Titarenko
and E. Zdravomyslova. London: Palgrave Macmillan.

Thomas, William Isaac, and Florian Znaniecki. 1996. *The Polish Peasant in Europe
and America: A Classic Work in Immigration History.* Urbana: University of Illinois Press.

Trubina, Elena, David Gogishvili, Nadja Imhof, and Martin Müller. 2020. "A Part
of the World or Apart from the World? The Postsocialist Global East in
the Geopolitics of Knowledge." *Eurasian Geography and Economics* 61, no. 6:
636–62.

Waldstein, Maxim. 2010. "Theorizing the Second World: Challenges and Prospects." *Ab Imperio* 1: 98–117.

Wincławski, Włodzimierz. 2011. "Dorobek twórczy historiografii i polskiej socjologii—cz. I." *Roczniki Historii Socjologii* 1: 27–56.

Znaniecki, Florian. 1922. *Introduction to Sociology,* Poznan: Wydawnictwo Uniwersytetu Poznańskiego.

the public anthropology of violence in India

CHITRALEKHA

THE DISCIPLINARY CONCERNS OF an "anthropology of violence" in India began to be articulated in the late 1980s, a time when contexts of political unrest and violence were also emerging as sites of ethnographic interest in the West. Western anthropology's (continuing) relationships with colonialism had already been made visible (Asad 1973); its ongoing "reflexive turn" rendered fields of violence too as sites of reflexive encounters rather than objects of authorial authority (Taussig 1987; Feldman 1991; Scheper-Hughes 1992). Just a few years ahead, Nancy Scheper-Hughes's impassioned advocacy for a militant anthropology initiated debate on anthropology's public possibilities (Scheper-Hughes 1995). Almost without exception, however, these studies of violence were still in "other" societies[1]—it would be several years (and troubled events) before Western anthropologists would engage with questions of violence amid their own publics (Asad 2007; Fassin 2013b; Gusterson 2016). In India, on the other hand, emerging from the darkest experiences of a newly born nation, anthropology of violence was shaped by those historical particularities and political imaginations tied to social purpose and often activist work.

I cite this difference not to argue for different possibilities when ethnographic research is conducted by those with ascriptive ties to the region under study, or further insider–outsider debates to fieldwork, but to point toward linkages between concerns of the anthropology of violence in India and the shared historical reflexivities of its founders. Scheper-Hughes, whose own work makes a powerful case for critical possibilities of long ethnographic investment (including in "other lands"), in fact, made note of such public/political purpose evinced in anthropological production at the time in India: "The idea of an active, politically committed, morally engaged anthropology strikes many anthropologists as unsavory, tainted, even frightening. This is less so in parts of Latin America, India, and Europe (Italy and France, for example), where the anthropological project is at once ethnographic, epistemologic, and political and where anthropologists do communicate broadly with 'the polis' and 'the public'" (Scheper-Hughes 1995, 415–16).

The figures associated with the project Scheper-Hughes remarks on in India possibly did not (at the time) identify their practice as public anthropology, or public ethnography as Fassin frames it to include critical ethnography in alternate disciplinary domains that bring to publics beyond academia "the findings of an ethnography analyzed in light of critical thinking, so that these findings can be apprehended, appropriated, debated, contested, and used" (Fassin 2013b, 628; see also Fassin 2017). But the political purpose seen as inherent to the work of public anthropology, its concern with the opening of the public sphere to questions with a potential impact on policies, and the crossover of ethnography to arenas of activism and reform (Fassin 2013b, 626), have in fact described anthropology of violence in India.

Early writings in this domain engaged with the historical challenges of a deeply diverse and still very young nation-state—collective violence, social suffering, justice, and the embattled question of secularism, among others. Public circulation of academic engagements with these concerns had relationships with the enabling structures of what was also then an Indian (as opposed to Hindu) nationalist media milieu. If in colonial India, public opinion was channelized by a nationalist press against its colonial rulers, in the first four decades of independent India, the media in fact partnered with the state to spread its message of self-reliance and national development among the people. But barring the dark breach of rights during the emergency (declared by Indira Gandhi in 1975 and enforced for nineteen months), Indian media was at the time (in relative terms) an autonomous and free institutional space (Chaudhuri 2017).[2] These imaginations and discursive circulations of a secular, ethnically, and culturally heterogenous India were by no means pan-

Indian, but originated among and addressed particular members of a "split public"—the urban, English-speaking, intellectual elite (Rajagopal 2001).[3] But within the limitations of this (national, English-speaking) mediated cultural space, a few sociologist-anthropologists (as indeed several political scientists and historians) were public figures in a way that was perhaps not the case in many other national contexts at the time. These scholars took the findings of their research to publics beyond academic circles and contributed to constitutions of popular discourse around the thematic concerns of their work, through their columns in newspapers and, in later decades, participation in discussions on national television. Critically, this work of major figures engaged with anthropology of violence in India, was informed by (and reflected) their engagements with civil society institutions such as the People's Union for Democratic Rights (PUDR) or the People's Union for Civil Liberties (PUCL). These important human rights bodies were also structurally entangled and dependent in many ways for their work of fact-finding and advocacy for justice, with public universities in India. In a period when the epistemological structures of universities still cohered around the originary envisioning of their relationship with nation-building, these alliances were also not as easily seen as conflictual or seditious as they are now.[4]

There have been important efforts to document the disciplinary histories of sociology and anthropology in India as well as the critical concerns that shaped arenas of its endeavor (Das 2003a; Uberoi, Sundar, and Deshpande 2007). Despite the formidable body of anthropological scholarship on collective violence in India, however, there is little documentation of the political and social milieu of the times and locales that contributed to delineate its founding work—an important task of social and intellectual history that remains to be done. This chapter makes a limited effort in this direction, examining the founding engagements of anthropology of violence in India in two major contexts of political unrest that haunted the period: ethnic violence and left radicalism. Reflecting on the historical reflexivities (and agency) that authored particular ways of seeing violence and its afterlife in these contexts, it engages particularly with the work of Veena Das, Dipankar Gupta, and Rabindra Ray, whose work constituted among the earliest significant anthropological engagements with these sites.

Das, an anthropologist of repute in the United States, in the past had a long association with Delhi University, where she was faculty between 1967 and 2000. Drawing from fieldwork in the 1970s among urban Punjabi families who had migrated to India as refugees during the traumatic riots of the Partition in 1947, and later with families of those killed in retaliatory carnage against Sikhs in 1984, her work engaged and intermingled several spaces of theoretical and philosophical seeking. Addressing, among others, questions of speech/voice, subalternity, suffering, time, subjectivity, and attention to the everyday, Das's writings in this period did not just radically redefine existent approaches to understanding of collective violence in anthropology; they constituted among the most significant contributions to public anthropology. Another important strand of work engaged with understanding of contexts to ethnic antagonisms, violence, and militancy in India, emerged in the writings of Dipankar Gupta, an eminent sociologist and anthropologist at Jawaharlal Nehru University, Delhi (1980–2009). Gupta's sociological and anthropological inquiries delved into diverse subjects of public importance in India, addressing questions of stratification, caste, modernity, citizenship, and justice. Das and Gupta traversed diverse spaces of theoretical and empirical, seeking, addressing, and redefining existent approaches to understandings of collective violence in anthropology, but also engaging more broadly with interrelated critical conversations in the historical and social sciences at this time.

Among the most productive of these exchanges included their engagements with the historiographical interventions of the early volumes of the Subaltern Studies Collective in India, which disputed elite, nationalist accounts of the transition from colonialism to nationhood and sought to recover forms of subaltern agency silenced in/by archival histories. Convinced of the emancipatory promise of the project, however, Gupta critiqued Guha's understanding of subaltern resistance—"the politics of the people," which for Guha formed an "autonomous domain [which] neither originated from elite politics nor [whose] existence depended on the latter" (Guha 1983); Gupta pointed toward the epistemological limitations of this approach, which closed off possibilities of relational understandings of how subaltern politics was constituted and manifested in relationship with other forms of social power. Gupta's criticism from a Marxist and materialist perspective emphasized the dangers of ethnicized formulations of autonomous peasant identity, which relied on the "independent organizing principle of the insurgent's mind" as the motor of historical change (Gupta 1985, 9; see Thomas, this volume, for a genealogical consideration of the originary moment of institution of the program, whose critical attention to the theme of subalternity in the *Prison Notebooks* foreclosed as much as it disclosed). Das's long anthropological attention to the domain of the "ordinary" already allied her in many ways with what was at the heart of the subaltern studies project: the displacement of the European (or, as Das would possibly see it, any) anthropologist or historian as the subject of discourse and Indian society as its object; and in relation, the centrality of the historical moment of rebellion in understanding subalterns as subjects of their own histories. For Das, this entailed not a rejection of Western categories but the beginning of a new and autonomous relationship with them. An influential and important contributor to the Subaltern Studies Collective (Das 1989), her engagement was in the nature of a thoughtful interlocutor deeply and intimately acquainted with the revolutionary potential of its work—and, at the same time, of its moments of critical shortfall.

A discussion of the founding strands of (public) anthropology of violence in India can hardly be completed without examination of early anthropological writing on the Naxalite movement. A revolutionary left uprising with its origins in the late 1960s in the Indian state of West Bengal, whose armed struggle for land redistribution, just wages, and human dignity, involved the interest and participation of several academics and students in Bengal, and later other states in India. Rabindra Ray's rich (and complex) work in the late 1980s, which drew from his own past immersion in the field—not as an ethnographer but as a participant in the movement—was the first anthropological examination of the left radical violence of the times. Challenging existent scholarship on Naxalism by influential political theorists (including Sumanta Banerjee, Biplab Dasgupta, and Manoranjan Mohanty), and digressing radically from the directions of Guha's writing on revolution, Ray described instead the compulsions of what he saw both as an analytical and ethical task of his anthropology: to draw attention to the urgent differences between the "literate" (codified, or formalized) ideology of the CPI(M-L) (Communist Party of India [Marxist-Leninist]) and their "existential" ideology.

In a vast field marked by different contexts and approaches, the sections ahead by no means offer a comprehensive review; they leave out eminent figures in the social sciences more broadly, whose work also made significant contributions to anthropology of violence.[5] It is hoped these lapses may be overlooked in a chapter whose limited objective is to point toward the public concerns that marked early trajectories of anthropology of violence in India. In the absence of archival material or published biographies of contexts to the work of its founders, these preliminary linkages I trace are sourced primarily from engagements evidenced in their own writing.

Speech of the Survivor and Anthropological Listening

In the introductory chapter of *Life and Words: Violence and the Descent into the Ordinary* (2007), Veena Das writes that two major events anchored her ethnographic and anthropological reflections: the partition of India in 1947, and the assassination of the then–prime minister Indira Gandhi by her Sikh body-guards in 1984. Das points out that these events spanned a period when the nation-state was established firmly in India as the frame of reference within which forms of community found expression. The story of lives enmeshed in violence, as she sees it, is part of the story of the nation.[6] The historical reflexivities evident in Das's pathbreaking contributions to anthropology of violence also evoked some of its earliest preoccupations with what were seen as its urgent public tasks. The question of the speech of the survivor and, related, the problem of (recovery of) her voice was possibly the most central of these tasks. In this context, I attend particularly to Das's early reflections on speech and voice in the sixth volume of *Subaltern Studies* (1989), and to her writing on social suffering and ethnographic listening in a chapter titled "Our Work to Cry: Your Work to Listen" in her edited volume *Mirrors of Violence: Communities, Riots and Survivors in South Asia* (1990a)—which was also the first comparative examination of anthropology of violence in South Asia. Finally, I briefly discuss Das's reflections on anthropology in public life in the aftermath of violence, in an essay titled "Trauma and Testimony: Implications for Political Community" (2003b).

In a review essay in the late 1980s, Das argued for an anthropology that would address the question of how the worldview of the victim may be made explicit: "But that would require an engagement with our field that re-opens the entire question of ethics. *I tend to think that the speech of the victim must occupy the central place in the narrative of the anthropologist*" (Das 1987, 13; italics mine). This preliminary insistence on the criticality of anthropological attention to the speech of the survivor—and to (re)thinking modes of anthropological "listening"—found complex and nuanced articulation a few years later in her discussion in the sixth volume of *Subaltern Studies* (Guha 1989). For Das, the question was not whether anthropology can obliterate the objectified character of social institutions, but whether it is at all possible to establish a relationship of authenticity toward them. She pointed out that even the work of Goffman and Foucault, who were committed to recovering the knowing subject, showed how the reified and alienating power of society flows through the tiniest capillary branches of society. How, then, can the representational closure with which thought presents itself be shown to be the product of thinking subjects? Are there reflexive devices that act as "corrections" or "interrogations" in relation to a given society? (Das 1989, 312). Das concludes that once we acknowledge that traces of rebellion are embodied in the form of a record produced in the context of the exercise of bureaucratic and legal domination, we also have to accept that the speech of the subaltern, when it becomes available for study, has already been appropriated by forms of authority (Das 1989, 315). Yet, recalling Guha's interest in the relation between everyday life and the historic moment, she adds:

> The attempt to relate this to the everyday life of the subaltern, I hope, will be the next theoretical task of this group of scholars. Subalterns are not in my opinion morphological categories, but represent a perspective in the sense in which Nietzsche used this word. The development of this perspective, I hope, will also mean a new relationship with the chroniclers of the cultures under study.... It is not that non-official sources are not abundant or not easily accessible, but rather that the legitimacy of those who are producing these materials needs to be recognized by official history. (Das 1989, 324)

Das's preoccupation with the speech of the survivor/subaltern is a theme that she grapples with again in "Our Work to Cry: Your Work to Listen," a deeply evocative essay that traverses the harshness and unrequited grief involved in mourning unheroic death, and the abrogation of subjectivities even in such context of deep loss (and often collective activism) to entrenched patriarchies. I address here only one aspect: Das's ethnographic engagement with an eleven-year-old deaf-mute child, Avatar, on a bus journey along with several other children, who, on passing a particular location, drew her attention with agitated gestures to the struggle and death of his father, who had been hanged from a tree at that spot (Das 1990b; cited from Das 2007, 201). Das writes that in the mimed performance, Avatar's hands had become those of the murderers and his face that of the victim. His body was a repository of knowledge and memory that surely must have been beyond him, for what he had been initiated into was a mode of dying. Following Stanley Cavell, Das reflects that if what she was witness to in Avatar's language was his language of initiation, it was initiation into a form of life and not simply into learning which objects which words point to. It was the figure of life that was put into question, and henceforth what politics would mean for him would also be linked to what it is to kill and be killed.

> I am not offering some kind of deterministic picture of what they would become as adults, but simply saying that their vision of the world and their place in it would perhaps always have to include such words as victim, riots, martyrs, terrorists—what these words are and what they can be made to do just as for those who grew up in the Gandhian world, politics were about *satyagraha,* civil disobedience, fasting, nonviolence. Will these

words and these worlds come to cross each other? That would seem to be the challenge of democracy now. (Das 1990b; cited from Das 2007, 203)

Rather than describing moments of horror, Das then attempts to describe what happens to the subject and world when the memory of such events is folded into ongoing relationships, when a shared language has to be (re)built with no assurance that there are conventions on which such a language could in fact be founded. If a possible vicissitude of such fatal moments is that one could become voiceless—not in the sense that one is left without words but in the sense that these words become lifeless—anthropological knowing, for her, also involves understanding of the conditions under which it becomes possible for the subject to share experience. There is no unitary collective subject such as the African self or the Indian self (see Das's engagement with Achille Mbembe on this point in Das 2003b), only forms of inhabiting the world in which one tries to make the world one's own, or to find one's voice both within and outside the genres that become available in the descent to the everyday. Testimony of the survivors as those who spoke because the victims could not was best conceptualized for her not through the Derridean metaphor of writing but through the contrast between saying and showing: "I try to defend a picture of anthropological knowledge in relation to suffering as that which is wakeful to violence wherever it occurs in the weave of life and the body of the anthropological text as that which refuses complicity with violence by opening itself to the pain of the other" (Das 2003b, 297). For Das, the work of anthropology of violence held meaning then in the wakefulness of the forms of her engagement with those such as Avatar, and in her writing, showing not just the pain but also the likely destruction of possible futures of one who, in being both mute and a child, has neither speech nor voice.

The targeted episodes of violence by state-sponsored mobs against the Sikh community in 1984 (sometimes called "riots" in official and academic literature) were not the first episode of ethnic violence in India since the Partition. But it was the first time since then that death and devastation were witnessed across vast tracts of the country, mainly in Delhi and the northern states. But that year also marked the beginnings of a more encouraging turn in the history of communal violence in India: interventions of civil society in gathering and providing a truer picture of the political constitution of such violence—and those culpable for it. Painstaking and detailed reports prepared by the People's Union for Democratic Rights and the People's Union for Civil Liberties (PUDR and PUCL 1984) were particularly important for their impact on popular opinion. India unfortunately saw several episodes of ethnic violence after 1984, including horrifying riots in Mumbai after the destruction of a historic mosque by Hindu nationalists in 1992, and the pogrom against Muslims in 2002 in Gujarat, a significant third event that had critical relationships with trajectories of anthropology of violence in the country.

In "Trauma and Testimony," an article published after the terrible violence of 2002 (this time in Gujarat and against Muslims in retaliation for the death of Hindu *kar sevaks* [religious workers] who died when the railway coach they were traveling in was set on fire, allegedly by a Muslim mob), Das reflects that forms of action developed in 1984 were important for expanding the forms of mobilization in 2002. Asking whether such forms of civil society activism also had import for our understanding of what constitutes ethnography, she recalls that her own understanding at the time of how to do an ethnography of the state evolved in unexpected ways. As members of the Delhi University Relief and Rehabilitation Team, which was supported by a local newspaper, she and her colleagues had to operate within the cracks and schisms found in the state to be able to muster enough resources to work in the affected localities. One important point was established about communal riots in India by the labor of various civil rights groups, lawyer activists, and university teachers in 1984: that far from the state being a neutral actor whose job was to mediate between already constituted social groups and their factional interests, several functionaries of the state were in fact actively involved as perpetrators of violence or, at the very least, complicit in the violence against Sikhs. But Das points out that even as many agents of the state were themselves engaged in breaking the law, it was still possible to use certain resources of the state because norms of secularism and democracy had also been internalized by many actors in the system.

Pondering on what it meant for anthropological knowledge to be responsive to suffering, Das wrote:

> The point was not that one divided one's activities into neat spheres to correspond to a division between academic and activist work. . . . The form of doing anthropology itself was shaped by the needs of immediacy or activism. . . . There is no pretence here at some grand project of recovery but simply the question of how everyday tasks of surviving—having a roof over your head, being able to send your children to school, being able to do the work of the everyday without constant fear of being attacked—can be accomplished. I found that the making of the self was located not in the shadow of some ghostly past but in the context of making the everyday inhabitable. (2003b, 294–95)[7]

Nation-State and Secular Humanism

An important contribution to (public) anthropology of violence at this time was constituted in the diverse writings of Dipankar Gupta. Digressing from Das's concern with anthropological responsiveness to suffering, the everyday of survival, and the continuity of life in the aftermath of violence, Gupta insisted on understanding the critical place of the nation-state in constitutions of both ethnic violence and, often, its aftermath—militancy. I draw attention here particularly to aspects of his early work on the context to the Khalistan movement for a separate homeland for Sikhs (Gupta 1996, 2000; see Gupta 2005a, 2005b, 2011a, 2013, for later critical discussions on these subjects).

Gupta pointed out that despite the growing body of opinion in sociological and anthropological scholarship that identities are not permanently inscribed on our psyches but undergo context-related changes, it was far from universally accepted when sociologists and anthropologists actually studied communal and ethnic movements—mostly in "other cultures." Anthropological study of ethnic movements had been by far the study of "primordial mobilisations," positing irreducible cultural factors, and peculiarities of cultural and historical constitution of (the most) egregious party in dispute. Identities in this case were viewed as stable formations, and communities (Sikhs, Maharashtrians, etc.) were seen as driven to violence by the logics of their respective cultures. Gupta contends in *The Context of Ethnicity*, however, that movements were in fact "ethnic" or "communal" only with reference to a third party—the nation-state. Based on extensive fieldwork in several villages in (then) militancy-ridden Punjab as well as in the old areas of the city of Delhi, his work describes the importance of looking beyond warring dyads to factor in the triadic framework with which they actually work. For a secessionist sentiment to develop out of an ethnic situation, Gupta shows that the nation-state must be perceived by one prong of the dyad as irretrievably partisan toward the others. Sikh secessionists or Kashmiri militants, for instance, who view the Indian state as a "Hindu Sarkar," feel justified in employing violence, as the nation-state itself is illegitimate in their eyes. Using Lacan's ideas of the imago and correlative space, Gupta accounts for self-images in times of ethnic tensions, and the accompanying perceptions of social reality. Not only is the imago prone to change, he argues, but the self is also made up of contrary and "alienating images" (Lacan 1977, 16), with many "imaginary exploits" (70): ethnic and communal identities in moments of quiescence can be quite different from those identities that emerge in moments of conflict.

The conflict situation, is one of *jouissance*, or the endless play of metonymy and endlessly "desiring something else" (Lacan 1977, 167). Gupta argues that the contemporary Sikh identity, the imago, had emerged not in quiescence but in a period of heightened ethnic rivalry, in moments of *jouissance*. It had in fact emerged in reaction to its perceived other, the Hindus, who the votaries of the Sikh imago believed had wronged them deeply, judged them unjustly, and most critically, treated them without respect or recognition (Gupta 1996, 102–8).

Gupta's work, primarily about the Sikh militancy, is informed by thick detailing of historical comparison to ethnic mobilizations in India since 1947, particularly with the post-Partition riots in Delhi, a city famous for its "secular" credentials in pre-Independent India. After the Partition, millions of Punjabis moved to the Indian side of Punjab, to Delhi, and elsewhere in India. Delhi's population had practically doubled, with an extraordinary influx of refugees from Pakistan, and as Gupta's respondents recall, even pre-Partition residents went along with the violence including in working-class areas, where the left was quite strong. Yet Gupta finds out that in election after election, it was the "secular" Congress Party that returned to power. Although communal passions were particularly strong in Delhi, the Hindu nationalist Jana Sangh (whose local leaders were in great part responsible for Delhi's communal sentiments) received between 20–25 percent of the votes, well behind the Congress, which received above 40 percent until 1967. While the complex factors that decide electoral fates possibly included the wariness about Jana Sangha after Gandhi's assassination, Gupta traces Delhi's electoral choices to the national governance of the Congress Party. In a fascinating chapter, "Partition Makes the Nation-State," based on his fieldwork in the old city areas of Delhi, he reconstructs from the memories and empirical records of political choices of its residents in the years following independence, an account of the emotions and imaginings that constructed the idea of the Indian nation-state in the wake of the brutalities of Partition (Gupta 1996). Gupta reflects that by 1967, memories of Partition had possibly dimmed, and the secularism of the Congress Party did not appeal to a large section of refugees in Delhi; but going by historical records of election statistics, most seemed to have still felt that Congress was a better choice at the national level. Comparative historical contexts such as these are often woven together with Gupta's account of the immediate context to the secessionist mobilization in Punjab to strengthen his arguments on the linkages that bind structures of the state, instruments of its governance, and the sentiments of its citizens.

These ideas are developed further in *Culture, Space and the Nation-State* (Gupta 2000), which makes a concerted attempt to "extend the concerns of anthropology to include considerations of the nation-state" (9).

The approach to understanding of ethnic violence for Gupta was then not so much attentive to the subject who lives the consequences of such violence (or enacts it) as to an anthropology of the nation-state: its institutions, citizens, and governance, and their interlinkages with projects of self and sociality. Likewise, a persistent theme in his writing is the idea (and desired prospect) of "secular humanism," the consequence of breakdown of cultural determinism, and acknowledgment of religious and other ascriptive animosities as historically conditioned, not autonomously powered social or cultural forces:

> We now realise that tolerance and bigotry are equally divided between different communities, and their varying manifestations are on account of divergent socio-historical conditions. This realization is a vital precondition for embracing secular humanism, and who knows how far we can go from there in lessening the tragedies of the human condition. As secular humanism is undaunted by cultural logics and by their claims to history, it can assert, with the authority of progressive historical consciousness/s, that religious, communal or even political differences, be guaranteed protection. (Gupta 1996, 168)

Reflecting that democracy without secular humanism is a structure without sentiment, reduced to adult suffrage and periodic elections, he cautions: "Mobocracy, corruption, majoritarian tyranny, and minority persecution, are all well-known consequences of democracy. If one is to protect and consolidate democracy, then one must invest in democratic sentiments—the foremost amongst them being secular humanism" (Gupta 1996, 169).

The preoccupation with secularism we find in Gupta's work was not unusual in a university ethos that was invested in protecting the hard-won, constitutionally determined "national ideology" of secularism, seen as the only just framework to ensure protection of the rights of religious minorities in a diverse nation-state scarred by the communal frenzy and bitterness of Partition. Different from the ideological histories of its constitution and the meanings to its practice in Western democracies, secularism in India was constituted by the originary imperatives of justice in a newly formed democracy, and described by the particular historical urgencies of its becoming. It is not the place here for an exposition into the deeply contested terrain of secularism, which after Talal Asad's "anthropology of secularism" can hardly be viewed in innocence again. For our limited purposes, suffice it to say, as Asad insisted, that secularism is seen best as an ideology or a political identity that shapes public discourse and practice rather than as a matter of divergence from local legal and religious codes. This way of understanding secularism calls for the study of the discursive production of public life (the "political medium" in Asad's words), in order to examine the unique context and the particular conditions within which it operates. It has played out differently within the historical particularities of the constitution of the discourse in India than in many contexts in the West.

As Das pointed out, the violence against Sikhs in 1984 saw the beginnings of civil society efforts to record, and draw public attention to, those actually responsible for the atrocities against the community; but it also became the subject of renewed attention (after the violence of the partition) in academic research and reflections, including in the work of anthropologists discussed in this chapter. Nearly two decades after the violence against Sikhs, which could not have happened without the patronage of members of the Congress Party, India witnessed another brutal pogrom, this time against Muslims in Gujarat. Following the 2002 pogrom, there was a visible turn in his sociological and anthropological writing: from examination of contexts to violence, to thinking about an "intolerant secularism" that insists on the inalienable rights of citizens and on due process of the law (Gupta 2002), and of justice before reconciliation (Gupta 2011b).[8]

Revolution, University, (Existential) Ideology

Left extremism in India had its beginnings in the Naxalbari uprising of May 1967 in West Bengal, a localized struggle, organized by CPI(M-L) revolutionaries against oppressive agrarian relations, that inspired the hopes and imagination of the downtrodden as well as middle-class students and youth across India. Rabindra Ray's monograph *The Naxalites and Their Ideology*, published in 1988 by Oxford University Press, marked the earliest and certainly the most reflexive anthropological writing on the beginnings of what is today often referred to as India's longest-running insurgency.

Ray's concern with the Naxalites dates back to his work with Student-Youth Federation, a pro-Naxalite students' organization that he joined in his final graduate year in Delhi in 1969. Together with some other students from this group, he left Delhi in 1970 to "preach revolution," as he puts it, in the North Bihar countryside. He remained there for a couple of years under the direction of the North Bengal/North Bihar Border Region Committee of the CPI(M-L), returning to his parents' home with the disintegration of the Naxalite organizations and, after a while, to Delhi. There he associated with a Trotskyist nucleus attempting to build up organizations of factory workers in the adjoining industrial areas of Ghaziabad and Faridabad. At the time, still working within a Marxist perspective, he argued that the failure of the movement lay in its disregard of the revolutionary potential of the industrial proletariat and in its Stalinist authoritarian organization. In the course of this association he deepened both his understanding of Marxist theory and his own critique of it.

Once a participant in the movement, Ray was aware that discontents of the abysmal poverty of the Indian dispossessed, while related to Naxalite rebellion against the status quo, did not fully explain their activity, for the Naxalites fought in the cause of a class other than their own. Unwilling to accept documented explanations of the Naxalites as middle-class romantics, or adventurists, or of those he refers to as already "partisan" (Ray 1988, 4), who see nothing problematic about commitment to an armed group and are concerned more with questions of why the Naxalites failed, Ray sees both positions arising out of attention solely to the literature produced by the Naxal revolutionaries, or its formalized documents and disputes. He begins his book with the following mission: "In attempting a sociological interpretation of the ideology and practice of the 'Naxalite' terrorists in West Bengal we must have recourse to the meaning of this practice for the Naxalites themselves. However, their overt ideological statements do not reveal the meaning and significance of their actions. Hence I shall seek to distinguish their 'existential ideology' from their 'literate ideology'" (1).

Doubtless, Ray's project arose from his own location and history of participation in the Naxalite cause; his questioning of and increasing unease with the legitimacy of Naxalite violence—and the validity of the Naxalite worldview—were hardly common or popular among academics at the time. He writes:

> The paradoxes of the history of the CPI(M-L) present themselves, the most striking of which is of course is that of a party committed to agrarian mass revolution being intimately involved in the exercise of urban terror. It is indeed this observation, more than any other, which provokes my principal argument, namely that the meaning that the literature of the CPI(M-L) is apt to convey to an observer (on the purely linguistic level) is very different from the meaning it "contained" (at an existential level) for the participants. Separated in meaning, this literate ideology and existential

ideology are nevertheless related to each other and transformed into each other, if by nothing else than the activity of the Naxalites. (1988, 5)

For Ray, the existential ideology of the Naxalites was a nihilistic one, consisting in immediate experience of the devaluation of the highest values—an "active nihilism" that undertook to destroy the sham of values it had seen through. It defined itself positively only through its oppositional stance—nowhere more explicitly than in its attack on "revisionism." Its underlying and unstated ideology, the existential ideology, was nothing other than the very collapse of ontology, the loss of veritable being, or nihilism. In its political implications this ontology, or collapse of ontology, was in fact *anti*political (1988, 16). For the partisan, as Ray sees it, Naxalism was basically a socioeconomic problem, an expression of economic injustice constituting a political problem, but for Naxalite revolutionaries, it was a question not of disintegration of law and order but of the competing legitimacy of two opposed systems of law and order. Its objective was not social justice but transfer of *power*: "Mazumdar's methods are geared towards precipitating a Revolution. It is not the alleviation of poverty or even the achievement of power that concerns him immediately, but the bringing about of this cataclysmic alteration of the relations of power" (1988, 199). For Ray, the despair with theory that forms a deep undercurrent in the ethos of "Marxist terrorism" and "revolutionism" has a double edge. On the one hand, it springs from the deep-rooted anti-intellectualism of the dominant pragmatism of our times, in the face of which the revolutionist feels himself powerless, from the standpoint of which he or she is condemned to futility; on the other, it is directed as ferocious criticism against those who merely theorize and do not act.

The spirit of Naxalbari, influenced by the Chinese Cultural Revolution, has often been seen as having shared ideological dispositions and motivations with participants in the global youth revolt of the late 1960s extending from Asia to Latin America and from the Continent to the United States (see Kingsberg, this volume, for an examination of student activism in this period in universities in Japan; and Zysiak, this volume, for entanglements between university and social changes some decades prior in postwar Łódź). Although many students in India did in fact align with the Naxalite movement ideologically, Ray points out that it was hardly a universal phenomenon when it came to those who actually joined the armed movement. While it is common to say that the revolutionaries joined from the Bengali *bhadralok* (educated elite), Ray writes that most of those who joined the armed movement—including from Calcutta's Presidency College—were in fact from *madhyabitta* (lower middle-class) backgrounds. Those from *sahebi* (privileged) backgrounds mostly stayed away. Ray delineates a rich anthropological history of the Bengali intelligentsia, divided into the English-speaking intelligentsia and the vernacular intelligentsia. The leadership of the Naxalite movement, according to Ray, belonged to the vernacular intelligentsia; there was also a social divide between them and the English-speaking *bhadralok*.

In a nuanced section called "The Madhyabitta," Ray writes:

> When one speaks of terrorists one is talking of intellectuals largely, for the most part students or ex-students, though of course others, among them industrial workers as well, though not a significant proportion. The organisers of the CPI(M-L) too were, throughout, largely students or ex-students, and mainly from metropolitan centres. . . . The ethos clearly "belongs" to the stratum of the intelligentsia who broke with revisionism. I put the "belongs" in quotes not to show that there is a logical connection between the social circumstances of these revolutionaries and their thought, or even that there is a necessary progression in the evolution of communist culture of which these people, as embodiments, are the natural outcome, or even that by its nature terrorism is an ethos restricted to intellectuals, but because in the circumstances in which this occurred the ethos developed as the specific form of action (of the understanding of action) of this intellectual stratum. Others participated in terrorist acts, but not necessarily with this ethos. Indeed, the ethos made it possible for a large number of criminals to be turned overnight into heroes, who did not by that transformation undertake to share in the ethos itself. (1988, 208–13)

Ray's writing draws out of nihilism its psychological implication, a prognosis of the valuelessness not just of the world but also of the self. Such a nihilism does not preclude a great sense of personal worth, but even where it exists, this worth consists precisely in the insight into the intrinsic worthlessness of the world and the self. In this psychological form, Ray writes that the nihilism of the English-university-educated Naxalites is in fact the despair with an education that makes greatness or even relevance impossible for the Bengali-educated schoolboys also already doomed to mediocrity and the second-rate. Thus, the humanitarian appeal of the Naxalites is, for Ray, at odds not only with their inhuman methods but also with their experience of their own humanity. Both in their awareness of not being part of the crushed, destiny-laden humanity in whose name they exercise the terror, and in their experience of this hatred of themselves as the ground of verity, they contradict the letter and spirit of the humanitarian aspirations to which they claim allegiance. Paradoxically, he points out, they embodied the reinstatement of man as moral agent, if only because they so radically challenged the premises of established morality.

At the time and context within which Ray framed his thesis on Naxalite ideology, pointing out the limited possibilities of knowledge to be accessed from "literate ideology," or from the codified ideas of its leadership, Ray's ideas were perhaps hardly short of revolutionary. His work offered a rich theoretical exposition of (possibilities of) the anthropological task, nudging researchers toward understanding or at least acknowledgment of existential ideology to which access may be, if at all, provided by phenomenology, the "domain of manipulated or manipulable experience in terms of which the self and the world are apprehended" (13). Sadly, Ray's own work gives barely any ethnographic glimpses of the lives, or the lived existence, that may have had relationship with the "existential ideology" that powered the movement, and his own writing. We do not know how the despair with theory that Ray points toward is in fact constituted. What are its remembered experiences? How do "despair with theory" and "nihilism" relate to the lifeworlds of those who were in fact at stake in the movement? The word *revolutionary* is used by Ray with reference to leaders and ideologues—but does Ray not see the peasants of Naxalbari as "revolutionaries" at all? Although these questions are not addressed in Ray's anthropology, they are still reflexive silences that gesture toward the outcomes of a remembered participant observation that did not (and perhaps could not) have bracketed its own subjectivities. While it possibly reiterates the (missed) possibilities of epoch in his ethnography, Ray's despair over the gulf between the literate ideology of the Naxalites and the existential meaning it carried for (at least some categories of) participants in fact emerged from immersion, reflection, and his own persistent struggles with the ethical prospects of theory. Rabindra Ray died early—on January 15, 2019, a few years after his retirement from the Delhi School of Economics. He left bereaved not just his family, colleagues, and students, but also those who knew him through encounters with his anthropological writing, which evidenced the restless integrity but also relentless rigor of his struggles with/ toward truth and justice. For them, many questions will now remain unanswered, but they too can perhaps be content, to quote Ray, that "the questions people choose to ask are themselves more significant pointers to the nature of their involvement with the events, their standpoint and prejudice than the answers that they finally arrive at" (3).

Nearly a decade after the publication in the late 1980s of Ray's brilliant and complex writing of the early stages of the Naxalite movement, Bela

Bhatia conducted ethnographic fieldwork on the Naxalite movement that by then had taken root in central Bihar. Bhatia's work, conducted as part of her doctoral research at the University of Cambridge, drew attention to the need to develop an understanding of the movement by incorporating the "point of view of the participants" (Bhatia 2005, 1536). Based on fieldwork in several villages with members, supporters, and local cadres of different Naxalite groups, Bhatia reflected, "Revolution is not a widely shared goal in the movement, but rather a dream of the leadership. People do aspire to *badal* (change) in their lives and the society at large" (2005, 1547). For many years now, Bhatia, based in the Bastar region of Chhattisgarh (where the locus of the movement has shifted over recent decades), has worked tirelessly with local populations toward realization of peoples' aspirations for change in their everyday lives. The historical leaning of liberal arts universities in India toward understanding of the complex struggles of a revolutionary movement that takes on the might of the state in the name of the poor and the dispossessed, survives, even if precariously so, despite the increasing disenchantment with the methods of the Maoists and the relentless erosion of academic freedom in universities by a right-wing government. There has been much important work on the Maoist movement in recent years by anthropologists (and social scientists more generally) in India, who, while they are not participants as Ray was, also continue to be closely engaged with its mobilizations for justice. This attention, perhaps as a mark of India's recent history, has shifted from matters of mobilization and ideology within the movement to abysmal failures of democracy and justice in addressing its related issues for local populations (Sundar 2016). My own ethnography with the Maoists in the states of Bihar and Jharkhand (then the epicenter of the movement) was an effort to apprehend and document aspects of the existential ideologies of foot soldiers in the armed movement. My work was inspired by Ray's theoretical and philosophical perspective; its findings, though, differed from his.[9]

Conclusion

As may be visible even in the brief glimpses of their work in this discussion, the early writings of anthropologists (all of whom were also sociologists) whose work constituted the formative trajectories of anthropology of violence in India traversed diverse paths of anthropological inquiry. They engaged with paradigmatically different questions: from the epistemological value and ethical urgency to ethnographic immersion in the everyday; from considerations of anthropological address of structures (and sentiments) of the nation-state to explorations of the significance of existential ideology in understanding "revolution." These were projects authored by different ways of seeing the task of an anthropology of violence. Das's body of work, arising from her long engagement with the work of Ludwig Wittgenstein and Stanley Cavell, is uneasy with (if not a critique of) grand projects for building identity and/or self. She engages instead with mindfulness toward experience, and forms of making the experience of violence knowable when saying gives way to showing. Gupta's work, on the other hand, invests in the particularities of local histories but also seeks to make visible their interlinkages with larger structures (and shared sentiments) of nation-states. Ray's intensely philosophical writing, even though it was not based on ethnography in a traditional sense, can be seen as auto-ethnographic in its reflections. In any case, his own past immersion in the "field" of his epistemological examination provided for an extraordinary contribution to anthropological knowledge of the ideology of the Naxalites.

Far from an "Indian anthropology," these early writings of anthropology of violence in India were nevertheless unmistakably informed by a shared history and its reflexive dispositions. The founding figures of the discipline were doing anthropology in a period when independence was still the remembered political consequence of nationalism. Nationalism was still an emancipatory ideology (and sentiment), replete with possibilities for questioning and (re) writing of its forms and limits, and universities were cherished and protected spaces of its critical discursive practices. In a modern India whose distinctive attribute was the emergence (and circulation) of political philosophy in public discourse, their anthropology, with its investment in engaging with the larger public sphere, was in fact a committed public anthropology.

Those were also times in which fieldwork on collective violence could be done, and its findings reflected with integrity in anthropological writing. Ray left the Naxalite movement, went to Oxford, wrote a thesis on a subject as contentious as the Naxalite movement was, and returned to teach at a reputed university in New Delhi. But anthropologists (and social scientists in general) writing on aspects of the Maoist movement contend today with at the least institutional suspicion, and often allegations of being antinational. Bhatia has in recent years faced repeated threats, vandalizing attacks on her home, and harassment by police. Sundar's recent book on the Maoist movement in Bastar faced protest from members of the right-inclined teachers' group National Democratic Teachers' Front, who opposed its contents. Varavara Rao and Anand Teltumbde, scholar-activists and my cocontributors in a recent volume edited by a colleague on the entanglements between Maoist violence and democratic failures in India (Gudavarthy 2017), have been incarcerated for years on charges of being urban Naxalites.

Notes

1 Stoler 1999 and Gusterson 1996 are examples of such early anthropological examinations of questions of violence in one's own society.
2 See Chaudhuri 2017 for the transformation of media and its publics after the liberalization of the Indian economy in the 1990s.
3 Rajagopal traces the historical outcome of a "split public" in India in relationship to different relationships of the local (regional) press and the national (English) media with the Hindu nationalist movement for building a temple at the site of a sixteenth-century mosque, believed by Hindus to be the birthplace of the Hindu deity Ram.
4 See Kidwai 2017 on the political imaginations that constituted the founding structures of public universities in India.
5 For instance, the remarkable oeuvre of the eminent political psychologist and social theorist Ashis Nandy, spanning a vast range of subjects including European colonialism, modernity, and Hindutva, surely had important linkages with the originary work of anthropology of violence in India.
6 These events of unprecedented (and hitherto unimagined) violence, and the long histories of coping with their complex aftermath, were in fact "fields" that generated a significant body of oral history, feminist writing, and social science scholarship in the region. See especially Urvashi Butalia's remarkable work on Partition (Butalia 2000).
7 The everyday is a theme developed further by Das in later works, most compellingly in her essay "Ordinary Ethics" (Das 2012).
8 In the wake of the 2002 riots in Gujarat, and attacks by the United States on Iraq in 2003, Sundar pointed out that by transforming ordinary Muslims into potential terrorists, the right-wing organization Rashtriya Sevak Sangh dehumanized them and made them culpable for their own victimhood; but also, when powerful states use reparations, truth commissions, or war crime tribunals to attribute culpability to others, including their own past selves, they often legitimize ongoing injustices (Sundar 2004). Asking that anthropologists concerned with political violence and justice engage in a comparative examination of culpability for past and ongoing crimes, she makes a compelling case for an "anthropology of culpability" that involves turning on ourselves the same lens through which we examine others.
9 My own writing on the Maoists reflects on the shared, collective compulsions to political mobilization, but also the interpretative meanings to becoming "Maoist." Accounts of guerrillas I lived and traveled with in Jharkhand and Bihar in India, including those from the most oppressed classes, ruminated on the formal struggle for equalization of group identity or resources, but also on what had been a deeply personal quest for recog-

nition and self-cultivation. Engaging with tropes associated for decades with the Maoist movement in India, I explore meanings ascribed by its foot soldiers to their labor and the relationship of the movement with caste and *izzat* (dignity), livelihood, occupational choices and "success," violence, death, and martyrdom (Chitralekha 2017a; see also Chitralekha 2017b, 2010).

References

Asad, Talal, ed. 1973. *Anthropology and the Colonial Encounter*. London: Ithaca Press.

Asad, Talal. 2003. *Formations of the Secular: Christianity, Islam, Modernity.* Stanford, CA: Stanford University Press.

Asad, Talal. 2007. *On Suicide Bombing*. New York: Columbia University Press.

Bhatia, Bela. 2005. "The Naxalite Movement in Central Bihar." *Economic and Political Weekly* 40, no. 15: 1536–49.

Butalia, Urvashi. 2000. *The Other Side of Silence: Voices from the Partition of India.* Durham, NC: Duke University Press.

Chaudhuri, Maitrayee. 2017. *Refashioning India: Gender, Media, and a Transformed Public Discourse*. New Delhi: Orient BlackSwan.

Chitralekha. 2010. "Committed, Opportunists and Drifters: Revisiting the Naxalite Narrative in Jharkhand and Bihar." *Contributions to Indian Sociology* 44: 299–329.

Chitralekha. 2017a. "Coming to Be 'Maoist': Surviving Tropes, Shifting Meanings." In *Revolutionary Violence versus Democracy: Narratives from India*, edited by Ajay Gudavarthy. New Delhi: Sage.

Chitralekha. 2017b. "Why Does the Subject Speak? Prejudgement in Fieldwork with Naxalites and Hindu Rioters." *Journal of Royal Anthropological Institute* 23: 155–74.

Das, Veena. 1987. "The Anthropology of Violence and the Speech of Victims." *Anthropology Today* 3, no. 4 (August): 11–13.

Das, Veena. 1989. "Subaltern as Perspective." In *Subaltern Studies VI: Writings on South Asian History and Society*, edited by Ranajit Guha, 310–25. Delhi: Oxford University Press.

Das, Veena, ed. 1990a. *Mirrors of Violence: Communities, Riots and Survivors in South Asia*. Delhi: Oxford University Press.

Das, Veena. 1990b. "Our Work to Cry: Your Work to Listen." In *Mirrors of Violence: Communities, Riots and Survivors in South Asia*, edited by Veena Das, 345–99. Delhi: Oxford University Press.

Das, Veena, ed. 2003a. *The Oxford India Companion to Sociology and Social Anthropology*. 2 vols. New Delhi: Oxford University Press.

Das, Veena. 2003b. "Trauma and Testimony: Implications for Political Community." *Anthropological Theory* 3, no. 3: 293–307.

Das, Veena. 2007. *Life and Words: Violence and the Descent into the Ordinary*. Berkeley: University of California Press.

Das, Veena. 2012. "Ordinary Ethics." In *A Companion to Moral Anthropology*, edited by Didier Fassin, 133–49. Chichester, UK: Wiley-Blackwell.

Fassin, Didier. 2013a. *Enforcing Order: An Ethnography of Urban Policing*. Cambridge: Polity.

Fassin, Didier. 2013b. "Why Ethnography Matters: On Anthropology and Its Publics." *Cultural Anthropology* 28, no. 4: 621–46.

Fassin, Didier, ed. 2017. *If Truth Be Told: The Politics of Public Ethnography*. Durham, NC: Duke University Press.

Feldman, Allan. 1991. *Formations of Violence: The Narrative of the Body and Political Terror in Northern Ireland*. Chicago: University of Chicago Press.

Gudavarthy, Ajay, ed. 2017. *Revolutionary Violence versus Democracy: Narratives from India*. New Delhi: Sage.

Guha, Ranajit, ed. 1983. *Subaltern Studies II: Writings on South Asian History and Society*. Delhi: Oxford University Press.

Guha, Ranajit, ed. 1989. *Subaltern Studies VI: Writings on South Asian History and Society*. Delhi: Oxford University Press.

Gupta, Dipankar. 1985. "On Altering the Ego in Peasant History: Paradoxes of the Ethnic Option." *Peasant Studies* 13, no. 1: 5–24.

Gupta, Dipankar. 1996. *The Context of Ethnicity: Sikh Identity in a Comparative Perspective*. Delhi: Oxford University Press.

Gupta, Dipankar. 2000. *Culture, Space and the Nation-State: From Sentiment to Structure*. Thousand Oaks, CA: Sage.

Gupta, Dipankar. 2002. "Limits of Tolerance: Prospects of Secularism in India after Gujarat." *Economic and Political Weekly* 37, no. 46: 4615–20.

Gupta, Dipankar. 2005a. "Caste and Politics: Identity over System." *Annual Review of Anthropology* 34: 409–27.

Gupta, Dipankar. 2005b. *Learning to Forget: The Anti-memoirs of Modernity*. New Delhi: Oxford University Press.

Gupta, Dipankar. 2011a. *The Caged Phoenix: Can India Fly?* Stanford, CA: Stanford University Press.

Gupta, Dipankar. 2011b. *Justice before Reconciliation: Negotiating a "New Normal" in Post-riot Mumbai and Ahmedabad*. New York: Routledge.

Gupta, Dipankar. 2013. *Revolution from Above: India's Future and the Citizen Elite*. New Delhi: Rainlight.

Gusterson, Hugh. 1996. *Nuclear Rites: A Weapons Laboratory at the End of the Cold War*. Berkeley: University of California Press.

Gusterson, Hugh. 2016. *Drone: Remote Control Warfare*. Cambridge, MA: MIT Press.

Kidwai, Ayesha. 2017. "University Grants Commission and Jawaharlal Nehru University: A Tale of Exception Told in Two Acts." *Economic and Political Weekly* 52, no. 19: 40–43.

Lacan, Jacques. 1977. *Écrits: A Selection*. London: Tavistock.

PUDR and PUCL. 1984. *Who Are the Guilty? Report of a Joint Inquiry into the Causes and Impact of Riots in Delhi from 31 October to 10 November*. Delhi: PUDR and PUCL.

Rajagopal, Arvind. 2001. *Politics after Television: Hindu Nationalism and the Reshaping of the Public in India*. Cambridge: Cambridge University Press.

Ray, Rabindra. 1988. *The Naxalites and Their Ideology*. Delhi: Oxford University Press.

Scheper-Hughes, Nancy. 1992. *Death without Weeping: The Violence of Everyday Life in Brazil*. Berkeley: University of California Press.

Scheper-Hughes, Nancy. 1995. "The Primacy of the Ethical: Propositions for a Militant Anthropology." *Current Anthropology* 36: 409–40.

Stoler, Ann Laura. 1999. "Racist Visions for the Twenty-First Century: On the Cultural Politics of the French Radical Right." *Journal of the International Institute* 7, no. 1 (Fall). https://hdl.handle.net/2027/spo.4750978.0007.1.02.

Sundar, Nandini. 2004. "Toward an Anthropology of Culpability." *American Ethnologist* 31, no. 2: 145–63.

Taussig, Michael. 1987. *Shamanism, Colonialism, and the Wild Man: A Study in Terror and Healing*. Chicago: University of Chicago Press.

Uberoi, Patricia, Nandini Sundar, and Satish Deshpande. 2007. *Anthropology in the East: Founders of Indian Sociology and Anthropology*. Delhi: Permanent Black.

8

challenging
objectivity
in Japan's
long 1968

MIRIAM KINGSBERG KADIA

THE YEAR 1968 marked a turning point around the world. Near-simultaneous youth radicalism traversed the ideological divisions of the Cold War, engulfing societies in the First World under US domination, the Second World that took its cues from the Soviet Union, and the unaligned Third World. Nonetheless, today, past the fiftieth anniversary of 1968, the academic literature remains dominated by case studies of revolution in Europe and the United States, while events in the non-West have attracted relatively little attention.

The virtual absence of Japan, where up to 20 percent of university students supported the movement in some way, is particularly noteworthy. The 1968 Japanese student protestors are best remembered for attacking the higher education system, yet their actions left scant imprint on either the university as an institution or on their own life trajectories. Accordingly, some works privileging the youth perspective have dismissed the unrest as a passing grievance of elite Japanese college matriculates, lacking the significance of earlier radical episodes in the 1960s (e.g., Wheeler 1974, 259; Kapur 2011, 11).

In these accounts, student activists confront entrenched power holders portrayed as stodgy, uncomprehending bystanders of revolution or even as obstructionists seeking mainly to preserve their own positions. By examining 1968 as a generational struggle from the less commonly adopted vantage point of its older actors, a seismic epistemological shift—or "concept-quake," as George Steinmetz describes it—comes into focus. Far from complacently enjoying the successes of the order they had created, by the 1960s the ostensible targets of student ire were themselves critical of their own long-standing paradigms of knowledge production. Ironically, it was they who inaugurated the changes that ultimately forced them and their ideals from influence.

The Worldview of the Transwar Generation

At the time of the student movement, a cohort of almost exclusively male, middle-aged scholars dominated the ranks of Japanese faculty. Born in the first two decades of the twentieth century or thereabouts, their defining characteristic was their involvement in the academic world throughout the "transwar" years (1930s–60s). During this time, Japanese social scientists cohered around a set of stable assumptions regarding epistemology: how knowledge is created and why that knowledge is valid. Objectivity came to serve as the foundation of their understanding of "truth." In general, they viewed objectivity as the belief in some universally applicable reality, pursued through a scientific research method intended to discipline the individual mind of its perspective and bias.

First articulated as a scholarly value by European philosophers in the early 1800s, within a century, objectivity's credibility was established throughout the disciplines and well beyond the West (Daston and Galison 2007, 30–34). In the heyday of imperialism, the production of authoritative knowledge both signified and supported a Euro-American sense of superiority over colonized and quasi-colonial peoples with their own epistemological traditions. Many non-Western scholars also adopted objectivity to signify their own enlightenment and to seek parity with the great powers. Japan, boasting a long history of empiricist scholarship, was among the first non-Western societies to embrace objectivity. The term *gakujutsu* emerged to denote the quest for universal laws governing the human and natural worlds, the use of a comprehensively delineated method to assure rigor in pursuit of "truth," and impartiality. Beyond these criteria, *gakujutsu* remained a strategically vague concept, its lack of a sophisticated theoretical framing making it accessible beyond the academic world. By the turn of the twentieth century, the term appeared frequently in the mass media, signifying credibility to the public.[1]

Japan's ability to formulate objective knowledge secured its entrance to the Euro-American intellectual community, in turn transforming social science from a Western into a truly transnational enterprise. A shared be-lief in the basis of legitimate research enabled diverse scholars to adjudge, appreciate, and engage with each other's work. To be sure, Japanese schol-ars did not participate on equal terms: then, as now, they remained at the semiperiphery of the global system of knowledge production (described in this volume by Johan Heilbron). But by the 1920s, Japanese researchers were welcome visitors at foreign universities, respected hosts to colleagues from other nations, and routine contributors to international academic journals and conferences (Kingsberg 2012, 327).

Among social scientists in certain disciplines, fieldwork, or intensive em-pirical research among a contained study population, emerged as a method-ological distinction between objective professional scholarship and amateur "armchair" work (Nielsen, Harbsmeier, and Ries 2012, 9–28). In practice, however, the pursuit of universal, scientific, and unbiased "facts" in the field masked the underlying values imputed to them. Objectivity operated less as an actual ideal than as a formula of legitimacy expressing certain truths held to be self-evident. Prior to 1945 the most salient of these truths was the ascendancy of the colonial powers. Unlike Europeans and Americans, who jealously guarded the racial boundary between imperialists and subjects, the Japanese claimed a biological relationship with the populations they ruled or sought to rule. In this way, they naturalized the evolving empire as the outcome of primordial racial confraternity among Asians and Pacific Islanders. In service of this agenda, fieldworkers often gathered "objective" physiological measurements and information on cultural phenomena to confirm similarities between local peoples and their Japanese administrators. Like their Euro-American counterparts, Japanese social scientists committed various abuses in the name of research: raiding graves, purloining artifacts, conducting distressing and intrusive examinations on vulnerable individuals without their consent, and supplying intelligence to the Japanese military (Nakao 2014, 47–69). Creating objective knowledge became tantamount to legitimizing the imperialist polity.

The war also changed the goals of US social science. Following Japan's attack on Pearl Harbor, thousands of American researchers enlisted in the service of the state and armed forces. By some estimates up to three-quarters of professional anthropologists devoted at least part of their time to applied scholarship in the early 1940s (Price 2008, 37). They worked under the banner of democracy, capitalism, and peace—ideals at the moral core of American identity and in antithesis to the fascism, statism, and warmongering of the Axis enemy. The vagueness of each concept facilitated consensus among diverse groups and interests. At its most basic, democracy encompassed just, representative government freely chosen by informed and empowered citizens. Capitalism suggested a free-market economy with few state-imposed barriers to participation or profit. Peace meant secure borders, domestic stability, and (paradoxically) a strong military capable of defending the nation's interests abroad.

The national emergency of World War II and the victory of the United States and its allies in 1945 tightened the linkage between the tenet of objectivity and the advancement of American ideals. US social scientists, shocked and horrified by atrocities and destruction, asserted a new responsibility to create authoritative knowledge in the service of democracy, capitalism, and peace. These values were captured as the goals of modernization, or the ideology that all nations might (with US assistance) achieve its privileged position at the apex of development. The outbreak of the Cold War further solidified modernization as a soft-power strategy in the American rivalry for global dominance with the Soviet Union, correspondingly vilified as authoritarian, communist, and militarist (Gilman 2003, 65–68).

Japan, occupied by the United States from 1945 to 1952, offered both "a test case, and indeed a showcase" of modernization (Conrad 2012, 186). To the American academics accompanying military and bureaucratic personnel, Japanese social scientists promised to be vital partners in the remaking of society in the US image. The Harvard-educated professor of Japanese history Edwin O. Reischauer (1910–90) suggested that scholars had "the great advantage in the war of ideas of being in large part free of the natural suspicion with which any people insulates representatives of a foreign government" (Dower 1975, 49). Yet transwar Japanese social scientists suffered from a potentially more compromising ideological contamination: their wartime support for imperialism, militarism, and fascism.

As articulated by the Allied purge program in early 1946, punishable wartime offenses included "laying down an ideological basis for the policies for the Greater East Asia" and "advocating the supremacy of the Japanese nation to be a leader of other nations"—the very mission of imperial scholarship (Baerwald 1959, 39). Ultimately, however, fewer than one hundred faculty (0.3 percent of the profession) faced even minimal consequences for their academic work in the 1930s and 1940s. Moreover, by the end of the occupation, nearly all had received permission to resume their positions (Conrad 2010, 82). Given the contributions of American scholars to the war effort, many were inclined to see their Japanese counterparts as "no more than normally patriotic for a period of nationalism" (Pelzel 1948, 72).[2]

The case of early postwar Germany, which posed a similar problem of past intellectual complicity with the Nazi state, offered a powerful precedent for the collective pardon of Japanese social scientists. Allied policymakers in occupied Germany scapegoated a few avid supporters of Hitler for developing the racial science that had made horrors such as the Holocaust possible, while endorsing a "conspiracy of silence" among most others regarding their ideological and material support for the Third Reich. Nearly all wartime scholars retained their positions and prominence after 1945 (Moses 2007, 55–69).[3]

Similarly shielding Japanese social scientists from blame for their wartime activities, the occupation nourished their support for American ideals. However, the associations among objective knowledge and democracy, capitalism, and peace were neither made nor forced by the United States. In retrospect, many Japanese intellectuals attributed the loss of the war to the irrationality and unscientific nature of imperial orthodoxy. Defeat did not discredit objectivity; rather, it led to the conclusion that what was needed was more genuinely objective knowledge—now understood as knowledge infused with the ideals of the victorious powers. Nanbara Shigeru (1889–1974), the first postwar president of the University of Tokyo (Tōdai), Japan's oldest and most prestigious institution of higher learning, offered a new vision of research grounded in the "objective" tenets of the American occupiers: "By its very nature, scholarship is . . . based necessarily on objective scientific consciousness and rigorous criteria. In this sense, Japan needs urgently to construct a worldview that rests newly and firmly on a scholarly base. . . . It is the fundamental prerequisite for 'democratic politics,' and it is an extremely important foundation stone for the construction of the new Japan" (Nanbara and Minear 2010, 161). It was this conception of objective knowledge as both the output and the underpinning of democracy, capitalism, and peace that was to inspire transwar scholars for the rest of their careers.

Mutual acceptance of modernization enabled American and Japanese social scientists to establish relations of friendship and sympathy, to rehabilitate Japan's scholarly reputation, to position transwar researchers at the pinnacle of postwar academia, and to integrate them into a new transnational intellectual community that reflected and supported US hegemony. Unwelcome in Japan's former empire in East Asia and Oceania, early postwar Japanese fieldworkers ventured mostly to developing states in South America, Africa, the Middle East, and South Asia (Iida 2007). Gathering information about unfamiliar regions showcased their ability to produce putatively objective knowledge of human diversity, while their assessments of the preconditions and progression of democracy, capitalism, and peace affirmed US power.

Japanese social scientists also cultivated their domestic influence. In an age when few fellow citizens could travel abroad, fieldworkers offered a uniquely "exotic" vantage point on the world through texts, photographs, films, and exhibitions. Skillfully narrated, illustrated, and even televised encounters with foreign cultures proved irresistible to the public, transforming some social scientists into household names. More than ivory-tower academics, these transwar scholars came to function as virtual superstars whose claim to generate objective knowledge validated their authority as spokesmen for modernization.

Rethinking Objectivity

In the late 1960s, as students challenged the validity of objectivity grounded in democracy, capitalism, and peace, transwar scholars did not unite in defense of their long-standing understanding of legitimate knowledge. Rather, many proactively acknowledged the limitations of objectivity and the problems that modernization had created during the preceding quarter-century.

In the United States, the point of reference for early postwar Japanese social scientists, the 1960s witnessed a series of social shocks including the Vietnam War, the civil rights movement, and decolonization and economic breakdown in the developing world. Scholars responded by rethinking their enlistment as producers of knowledge on behalf of US global hegemony. In a speech at the 1966 annual meeting of the American Anthropological Association, Brandeis University professor Kathleen Gough (1925–90) frankly characterized her discipline as the offspring of imperialism and urged her listeners to condemn the misuse of their work in Vietnam and elsewhere (Gough 1968, 403). In a follow-up symposium on the social responsibility of social scientists, published in 1968, a colleague agreed that scholars should hold themselves accountable for the consequences of the "facts" they uncovered:

> The dogma that public issues are beyond the interests or competence of those who study and teach about man is myopic and sterile professionalism and a fear of commitment which is both irresponsible and irrelevant. Its result is to dehumanize the most humanist of sciences.... Our silence permits others in the society less reticent, perhaps less scrupulous, almost certainly less informed, to make their own use of the material presented. (Berreman 1968, 391–92)

Accompanying the questioning of objectivity was a rethinking of fieldwork. For many years, it seemed, absorption with scientific methodology had taken the place of ethical engagement. At the end of the 1960s, some scholars exposed the hidden agendas behind research funding provided by the US government (including the CIA) and private organizations. Others highlighted power dynamics (such as those involving ethnicity and gender) that inevitably informed their work on the ground. They rejected the standard narrative contrivance of a scientific ethnographer capable of normative detachment. Instead, anthropologists acknowledged how their very presence in the field changed that field—often for the worse, as far as research subjects were concerned (Price 2016, 64, 32).

Meanwhile, Japanese social scientists raised similar issues. In a book-length history of academic freedom, cultural historian Ienaga Saburō (1913–2002) criticized his colleagues for avoiding research topics with political relevance and for even taking pride in their own low levels of social consciousness. Rather than objective scholarship, he advocated intellectual contributions that "advance world peace and contribute to human welfare through the pursuit of truth" (Ienaga 1962, 210).[4] Cultural anthropologists Ishida Eiichirō (1903–68) and Kawakita Jirō (1920–2009) debated the long-established relationship between objectivity and fieldwork in the pages of a prominent disciplinary journal. Ishida argued that researchers should familiarize themselves with the theoretical and secondary literature on their topics prior to undertaking fieldwork, as they had traditionally been taught. Kawakita, on the other hand, made the iconoclastic observation that such preparation might lead to excessive commitment to a specific position, thus predetermining conclusions. By suggesting ways in which researchers might be biased, Kawakita challenged the haloed status of the field as the cynosure of objective knowledge production (Ishida 1961; Kawakita 1961).

Concomitant with mounting doubts concerning objectivity were challenges to its attendant ideology of modernization. An especially potent attack appeared in the form of dependency theory, which dismissed the idea that all nations could achieve democracy, capitalism, and peace. The division of states into three "worlds" undercut faith in a universal trajectory of development. Rather than a natural outcome for all societies, "progress" came to seem an illusion enabling wealthy states to exploit the Third World. Dependency theorists regarded modernization not as a doctrine of hope and help but as the self-congratulatory mythology of developed states (Gilman 2003, 65–68; Steinmetz 2005, 31).

The critique of modernization also reflected a rethinking of traditional, positive notions of progress. Scholars argued that, far from categorically improving human welfare, social, political, and economic advances had in fact created new modes of oppression. In 1968, on the eve of the centennial celebration of the establishment of Japan's modern state—a moment for the nation to applaud its accomplishments—archaeologist Egami Namio (1906–2002) filmed a television series that questioned civilization as a desirable goal:

> During the hunter-gatherer stage of human society, there was no war. But agriculture allowed the population to grow, leading to urbanization, new systems of political control, and the possibility of accumulating wealth. Resources became scarce. Wars began with attempts to capture the resources and labor potential of cities. Meanwhile, the development of metalworking techniques allowed for the creation of better weapons. A class of warriors arose to capture the spoils of combat. In this way, the urbanized state became dependent on war. . . . Eventually resources could not keep pace with demand, resulting in military competition that brought humanity to the brink of destruction. (Izumi Seiichi 1966, 160–61)

Critiques of modernization also shaped preparations for the first World Exposition in Japan (and in Asia, for that matter). Like the famed Tokyo Olympics of 1964, Osaka's Expo '70 sought to highlight Japan's status as an exemplary democratic, capitalist, and peaceful member of the global fraternity of states. Reflecting the sense of achievement, event organizers adopted the slogan of "progress and harmony for mankind." Under the leadership of Okamoto Tarō (1911–96), an artist trained in ethnology, a team of eighteen social scientists convened in the late 1960s to gather artifacts for a pavilion devoted to this theme. However, instead of endorsing "progress," they charged:

> The history of World Expositions shows that the concept of progress has always been taken for granted and the expositions have been the places in which big powers demonstrated their scientific and technological abilities. . . . Everyone believed that with the advancement of science comes the world of dreams and the era of happiness. But now the situation has changed. The bitter question of whether "progress" gives us the sense of fullness of life and human and spiritual satisfaction does not cease to trouble us. (Okamoto, Izumi, and Umesao 1970, 39)

For the top floor of the Theme Pavilion, the social scientists planned an exhibit that candidly questioned aspects of modern life, including overpopulation, poverty, pollution, rural flight, racial discrimination, crime, and atomic weapons (Wilson 2012, 168).

Yet if transwar social scientists were willing to acknowledge the problems of the post-1945 order, they remained mute regarding the age of empire. Recognition of the imperialist origins of social science, increasingly routine in the United States and parts of Europe in the late 1960s, found no purchase among transwar Japanese scholars. For the most part, the student movement would follow their script: criticism of the postwar course of modernization, and silence on the prewar past.

The Student Struggle

The generation that matriculated under the occupation was the first to benefit from the democratic reform of Japan's universities, including guarantees of institutional autonomy and freedom of speech. The lowering of the voting age to twenty incorporated students into the electorate and nurtured their interest in governance.[5] By the mid-1950s, Japanese students had established organizations to coordinate political activism across campuses nationwide. In the next few years, these bodies contested the renewal of Japan's military alliance with the United States, denounced the Vietnam War, worked toward communist revolution, and supported a variety of mostly left-wing causes (Koda 2015, 48).

As in the United States, West Germany, France, Italy, Mexico, and other nations, in Japan universities provided a convenient theater for protests. However, to a greater extent than their counterparts elsewhere, Japanese students targeted higher education itself as the object of their reformist energies. Many denounced the steady creep of state encroachment on institutional autonomy. In the early 1960s the government attempted to pass legislation strengthening the control of the Ministry of Education over higher learning. Although the bill failed, universities were forced to accept some measures to increase bureaucratic oversight as well as the removal of students from decision-making organs (Nakazawa 1989, 50).

Many transwar social scientists, like their students, found these state maneuvers alarming. Ienaga Saburō compared prewar and present-day restrictions on university autonomy, concluding, "To say that the situation was better [now] than before 1945 could be difficult" (Ienaga 1962, 255). He argued that capitalism had replaced the divine emperor, imperial Japan's most sacred orthodoxy, as society's new focus of worship. Consequently, university budgets corresponded not to research needs but to the imperative of training workers for the labor force. Under the standard departmental organization, full professors (chairs) maintained control over subordinate ranks of associate and assistant professors as well as graduate and undergraduate students. Denouncing this system as feudalistic and prone to seniority, favoritism, and intellectual stagnation, Ienaga called for greater equality among ranks, increased professor-student cooperation, and unity between academics and administrators (Ienaga 1962, 260).

Concerns regarding intellectual freedom were fueled by a more general sense of crisis in higher education. During the second half of the 1960s, the rate of college attendance in Japan soared to nearly 20 percent. Only the United States, the Soviet Union, and India enrolled a numerically larger student population. Despite the expansion of white-collar employment, the demand for professionals could not keep pace with production; as a result, university graduates struggled to find jobs commensurate with their credentials. The value of a college degree was further undercut by the proliferation of low-quality, tuition-driven two- and four-year colleges. Newly founded and venerable institutions alike suffered from increasing bureaucratization, profit-seeking, and the evaporation of support for the humanities. To many students, the university seemed less a temple of knowledge than a factory conveyor belt shaping graduates into cogs for an industrial capitalist economy (Nagai and Dusenbury 1971, 3, 52).

Perhaps nowhere were students more disappointed by the gap between expectation and reality than at the University of Tokyo. By 1968 Tōdai maintained an enrollment of approximately 13,300 undergraduates and 3,700 graduate students. After gaining admission through a series of highly competitive exams, matriculates were disillusioned by overcrowded classes, low-quality curricula, unattractive campus facilities, and impersonal teaching. Squeezed into dormitories or designated housing, they sought to fill large blocks of unsupervised free time. The ranks of protestors came to include many who were swept along by the enticements of a cheap, lively, mixed-gender social scene, as well as those motivated by a sincere belief in reform (Wheeler 1974, 280–81; Oguma 2018, 7).

The most active phase of the student movement began in the Tōdai Medical College in January 1968, when a group of aspiring doctors objected to a change in internship policy likely to degrade the quality of their training and their postgraduate chances of employment. That spring, as student protests disrupted schools throughout the United States and Europe, the Tōdai movement widened to include students from all university faculties. Many joined together to take over Yasuda Hall, the bureaucratic heart of the campus. When the institutional leadership summoned police to remove the occupiers, the student body united behind them. Within a few days, all departments except law joined the strike. The administration rejected their overtures at collective bargaining, arguing that the status distinctions between students and faculty made negotiations "inappropriate" (Nakazawa 1989, 68).

The movement opened a forum for discussion and critical thinking that many students had not enjoyed in their classes, allowing them to contemplate the aims of their protest. Within "struggle committees," many came to perceive the stalemate at Tōdai as symptomatic of a broader social and intellectual malaise. They rebelled against the transwar generation's association of objectivity with credible knowledge, instead arguing that scholarship could never be impartial. As one student organization declared, "In reality, nothing is neutral. Those who support the position of neutrality are the people who never seriously thought of how and by whom their research results would be used. They deserve the name of 'expert idiots' for they are obsessed with their specialties and incapable of taking social responsibility" (Nakazawa 1989, 184).

Against the transwar generation's faith in objective knowledge as a lever of general social progress, the student movement mounted a Marxist critique of such research as an instrument of power disproportionately benefiting the ruling class. Youth called for subjective scholarship that turned the intellectual weapons of the bourgeoisie against their creators, empowered the disenfranchised, and contributed to self-actualization, popular agency, and the end of social inequality (Yasko 1997, 106–24).

Students also critiqued the "Tōdai within ourselves" (*uchinaru Tōdai*). Matriculates of Japan's leading university had reached the pinnacle of educational attainment, a traditional entry point into the top ranks of the professions, government, and business. They understood, however, that their triumph in the entrance examination system had reinforced a certain intellectual conformity and, due to the tests' emphasis on English language proficiency, subordination to the United States. Moreover, they were conscious of having prioritized individual prestige at the expense of the welfare of the masses. Many had enjoyed the advantages of family wealth and regarded their climb to the top not as evidence of merit but as a troubling perpetuation of social hierarchies. Depicting the university as rotten, the students denounced their own complicity as members of Japan's elite (Tsurumi 1970, 110; Yasko 1997, 140–41).

Activists often couched their aims in language suggesting an anti-imperial agenda. They decried higher learning for "colonizing" individuality in the name of conventionality. They attacked public universities for their association with the national government that had embroiled Japan in the overseas wars of the United States. Students proceeded under the slogan "Dismantle the imperialist university [*Teidai kaitai*]!" (Yasko 1997, 25). This critique remained fixated on the present and did not address the role of the university in creating and legitimizing knowledge that had supported the former empire.

With very few exceptions, Japan's pre-1945 atrocities were conspicuously absent from the litany of youth grievances. In this respect, Japanese activists diverged from their counterparts in West Germany, who denounced the prevailing silence regarding the crimes of the Third Reich and called for the dismissal of former Nazi collaborators from the universities (Steinmetz 2010). Yet another generation would pass before Japanese scholars publicly recognized social science as an imperialist endeavor not only in the nation's present but also in its history.

The Transwar Generation in Crisis

By the end of 1968, 165 Japanese universities had experienced disturbances of some kind, with over sixty compromised by sit-ins and strikes. As at Tōdai, activists made specific demands to improve campus life, including tuition breaks, the democratization of operating procedures, public apologies for administrative violations of student rights, and amnesty for participation in protest activities. Ultimately, over 300,000 students across Japan supported the movement in some capacity. In 1968 alone, over three thousand were arrested (Fuse 1969, 330).[6]

In addition to spreading among universities, the struggle engaged a variety of off-campus left-wing causes such as fomenting Marxist revolution and opposing the Vietnam War. Some students, like their contemporaries in France, Italy, and the United States, attempted to collaborate with labor leaders. Yet however resolutely Japan's college population repudiated its elite status, it was unable to convincingly present itself as an ally of the blue-collar workforce. Activism beyond the university tended to divide the already factionalized students, pitting those drawn to outside causes against others who preferred to focus on internal reform (Fuse 1969, 333).

As the stalemate ground on, on-campus protestors redirected their ire from the university administration to individual faculty members. At Tōdai, they invaded the office and destroyed the papers of Maruyama Masao (1914–96), regarded as the nation's leading mouthpiece of modernization. "Not even the Nazis did anything like this," Maruyama told a leading newspaper (Yasko 1997, 90). Although his renown made him a particular target, Maruyama was far from the only member of his generation to experience such treatment. A biology professor whose research materials were destroyed was so distraught by the loss of years of work that he was unable to continue his academic career. An archaeologist was physically attacked in the classroom, prompting his young daughter to jump out of a window (Kidder 2013, 180).

Student leaders argued that professors "have no right to quietly engage in research while fundamental questions concerning the university system are being raised." They urged faculty to "suspend daily research and reconsider the purposes and impact of your activities! Disclose the evils resident in the system as well as in yourself" (Nakazawa 1989, 109, 141). Even those unmoved by these appeals were inconvenienced by lockouts and inundated by the administrative burdens of extraordinary times. By way of apology for declining to review an article, a prominent Japanese anthropologist wrote to an American journal editor, "As you might be informed, there have occurred big trouble in our University as well as many other universities in Japan. Therefore, almost every day I must attend meetings to settle and find a solution of the trouble. I do not know when the trouble becomes quiet and settled [*sic*]" (Itani 1969). One study estimated that the average productivity of professors of education at all major universities fell by half in 1970 (Shimbori et al. 1980, 148).

In his autobiography, Tōdai professor of cultural anthropology Izumi Seiichi (1915–70) described 1968 as "the worst year" (Izumi Seiichi 1972, 370). Izumi's own students boycotted his classes. Stress compromised his health, and he was hospitalized several times. Most devastatingly, his only son, Izumi Takura (b. 1948), a twenty-year-old aspiring archaeology major at the University of Kyoto, joined the movement. Confronted with his son's radicalism, a furious Izumi Seiichi voiced the perspective of the transwar generation: "Scholarship and politics can absolutely not coexist. The student movement is a political movement completely separate from scholarship. If you want to do real research, you clearly cannot maintain political aims." In response, Izumi Takura reiterated the argument of the student protestors: that scholarship divorced from politics was illusory and meaningless. The argument grew so heated that Izumi Takura left the family home, and a temporary rift developed between father and son (Izumi Kimiko 1972, 291–97).

Although Izumi Seiichi never deviated from the belief in objectivity that defined his generation, in early 1969 he published a more conciliatory piece arguing for a "new image for the contemporary university." He called for the Tōdai administration to address many of the problems cited by students, including bureaucratic interference, the underfinancing of research and teaching, and "guild-style" internal politics. He also acknowledged protestors' disillusionment with modernization. In the past, he wrote, authoritarian regimes had used force to instill unifying symbols such as the emperor. Having rejected such means, however, Japan was left with no way of inculcating rising generations with the ideals of democracy, capitalism, and peace. Lack of individual subjectivity and social disorder, he argued, were the natural results of this failure to inspire present-day youth with the values of the nation (Izumi Seiichi 1970, 248-49).

Although most protestors would likely have disagreed with this narrative, Izumi's words nonetheless suggested his growing appreciation of their position. Many of his colleagues likewise became more supportive of the students as the stalemate ground on, although some hesitated to express sympathy openly due to their investment in their academic careers. Faculty employed by national universities were civil servants, easily threatened with salary reductions when classes were not held. Professors also expressed fears that allying with the student cause would provoke the government to further encroach on academic freedom by empowering the administration at their expense (Nakazawa 1989, 68).

In November 1968, Ōkōchi Kazuo (1905-84), president of Tōdai since 1963, offered his resignation amid rising criticism of his failure to settle the crisis. Ōkōchi belonged to the senior ranks of the transwar generation. His successor, Katō Ichirō (1922-2008), was almost two decades younger. Like the student protestors, he had completed his education in the era of modernization. He had recently returned from a year of research in the United States and was familiar with American traditions of university autonomy. At the same time, the forty-six-year-old Katō had consciously experienced the war and its aftermath and could understand the mentality of the transwar generation. Sympathetic to both the older and younger cohorts, he was an ideal mediator in the conflict between them.

Nonetheless, Katō confronted serious obstacles to restoring normal campus operations. One source of pressure was time. In December 1968 Katō announced the cancellation of entrance examinations for the academic year beginning in 1970. Given the disorder, he believed that Tōdai simply could not accept a new freshman class. Katō hoped that exams might be reinstated if the protests were resolved by mid-January 1969. However, administrative hard-liners continued to refuse key concessions, while students seemed united only in their opposition. In early 1969, a survey of over fifteen hundred students from twenty-one universities found that more than three-quarters were dissatisfied with their education (Tsurumi 1970, 108). Yet they could not agree on the aims of protest. Some wished to see concrete reforms enacted in the universities, whereas others exalted the very struggle as the goal and rejected all attempts at mediation. A few clashes among students turned violent, alienating moderates while encouraging radicals to prolong the dispute for media attention (Wheeler 1974, 271).

Starting in the early 1950s, by convention, police did not enter Japanese university campuses unless invited by the administration. One day after the deadline passed for reinstating entrance exams, however, Katō finally caved to mounting pressure (not least from students eager to graduate) to end the dispute. By this time, police had already removed protestors from universities around the world. On January 18–19, 1969, police attacked student holdouts and their supporters in Yasuda Hall. The clash produced injuries (but no casualties), over a million dollars' worth of damage to physical property and infrastructure, and more than seven hundred arrests.[7] Student resistance at Tōdai was over.

Studying Human Diversity in Japan after 1968

The year 1968 witnessed a concept-quake in Japanese epistemology, heralding the end of several decades of collective faith in objective knowledge and of the intellectual hegemony of the transwar generation. Both during and immediately after the student movement, scholars in Europe and the United States delved into its significance in field and public-facing writings. By contrast, Japanese academia remained mostly silent. The flagship journal of cultural anthropology avoided the very mention of the movement. Weeks after the end of the occupation of Yasuda Hall, the journal published two special issues cataloguing anthropology textbooks, field studies, and university courses, generating a façade of business as usual ("Zenkoku no daigaku ni okeru minzokugaku" 1969). The impulse was not to understand but to elide.

From certain perspectives Japanese society appeared virtually unchanged by the events of 1968. Student participants largely resumed their education, graduated, and joined the ranks of social elites. By 1972, one survey found that over half of college matriculates were satisfied with their school life, while less than 4 percent endorsed violence to change the university as an institution. Economic downturn, the rise of conservative nationalism, and the entrenchment of technocracy further dampened student inclinations toward activism in the early 1970s (Shimbori et al. 1980, 143).

Likewise, universities seemed to emerge from the chaos largely unscathed. After summoning the police to Tōdai, Katō conciliated the campus community by emphasizing his differences with the Ōkōchi regime and by extending new opportunities to participate in various decision-making processes to students. He also offered junior professors a greater role in faculty governance (Nakazawa 1989, 146). Meanwhile, the Japanese government took action to prevent future disturbances. The 1969 Law for Temporary Measures concerning University Management (*Daigaku no un'ei ni kansuru rinji sochi hō*) legalized state intervention and school closures in situations where the administration was deemed to have lost authority.[8] The state also compiled a master plan for higher education, calling for the establishment of up to twenty new universities under strong centralized management (in contrast to the autonomous model implicated in the recent chaos). In 1973, the University of Tsukuba opened in a distant suburb of Tokyo, where the impact of any student disturbances could be minimized (Shimbori et al. 1980, 144).

The seeming return to the status quo obscured larger shifts in the production and personalities of Japanese social science. The student movement catalyzed a wave of relatively early retirements and coincided with a spike in mortality among leading transwar scholars. Ishida Eiichirō succumbed at the height of the cataclysm in 1968. Linguist Asai Erin (b. 1895) followed in 1969; Izumi Seiichi, archaeologist Yamanouchi Sugao (b. 1902), and Kodama Sakuzaemon (b. 1895), a specialist on Japan's Indigenous Ainu population, in 1970. Kodama's colleague Kubodera Itsuhiko (b. 1902), archaeologist and art historian Mizuno Seiichi (b. 1905), and Mishina Shōei (b. 1902), an early enthusiast of Boasian cultural anthropology, died in 1971.

Replacing these doyens were faculty born after 1920. When anthropology classes resumed at Tōdai in the spring of 1969, their instructors included Suzuki Hachishi (1926–2010) and Ikegami Yoshihiko (b. 1934) ("Zenkoku no daigaku ni okeru minzokugaku" 1969, 165). The influx of new scholars gave Japan the world's largest per capita population of academics. Within a decade, even younger faculty, veterans of the student movement, were offering courses at Tōdai. In 1968, one survey had found that academia represented the most popular career aspiration among student activists at the university (Oguma 2015, 8). Passion for reform, it appears, emanated at least partly from a deep commitment to joining the institutions of knowledge production.

In the 1970s this younger cohort completed the epistemological schism with the transwar understanding of objectivity as a necessary and sufficient signifier of credible knowledge. Ironically, many junior academics and former radicals instead embraced the essentially conservative doctrine of Japanese exceptionalism (*Nihonjinron* or *Nihon bunkaron*). Japanese exceptionalism trained an analytical gaze on the self with the goal of understanding and reinforcing Japan's new position as the second-largest economy of the First World. In place of the ideals of modernization, Nihonjinron envisaged Japan as a budding superpower with productive lessons for Europe and the United States. Social scientists depicted the Japanese population as ethnically homogenous and "pure," nurtured and protected by the unique natural environment of the home islands. They further alleged certain positive collective personality traits, including communitarianism, diligence, moderation, modesty, reliability, respectability, self-discipline, seriousness, and studiousness (Aoki 1999; Befu 2001).

In its mission to explain and extoll the particular, Nihonjinron discarded two of the three planks of transwar objectivity: the pursuit of universal laws and (the appearance of) value-free scholarship. The embrace of exceptionalism also impacted the third plank: fieldwork. In the past, transwar social scientists had often studied foreign cultures as a foil for delineating national particularities. After 1968, however, the bulk of academic attention shifted home as scholars attempted to directly define the primordial and unifying forces of national culture. Asia-focused scholarship also thrived as a means of shedding light on the probable origins of the Japanese, and as a source of closely comparative case studies. With the establishment of diplomatic relations with the Republic of Korea (South Korea) in 1965 and with the People's Republic of China in 1972, Japanese scholars were easily able to undertake research in mainland East Asia for the first time since World War II. The study of Southeast Asia also boomed following the end of the Vietnam War (Park 2016, 157–66).

An argument of positive exceptionalism, Nihonjinron discouraged attention to unsavory tendencies and possibilities within the so-called national culture. Perhaps partly as a result, discussions of imperial crimes remained muted. In Europe and the United States, social scientists of the 1970s and 1980s illuminated their disciplines' role in constructing and sustaining colonial regimes (e.g., Asad 1973; Kuper 1973; Stocking 1991). By contrast, in Japan early attempts to narrate the history of anthropology omitted wartime scholarship. A 1975 work obliquely referenced the taboo nature of the topic, declaring, "Only now that three decades have passed is it appropriate to write about prewar anthropology." However, rather than critiquing the legacy of imperialism, the author, a former student of Ishida Eiichirō and Izumi Seiichi, praised prewar fieldwork as the foundation of contemporary research. In describing Japanese knowledge production in the former empire, he eschewed the very use of the word *imperialism* (*teikokushugi*). Instead, he neutralized such scholarship as "overseas research" (*kaigai kenkyū*) (Terada 1975, 256, 252).

In the 1990s, the bursting of Japan's growth bubble heralded a less confident national mood and a rethinking of Nihonjinron. The steadily shrinking ranks of the transwar generation, and the retirements of its immediate students, freed more junior scholars to probe the troubled origins of the social sciences in Japan. Anthropologist Nakao Katsumi (b. 1956) caused a tremendous stir when he presented some initial findings on the "original sins" of his discipline at an annual meeting of Japan's foremost cultural anthropology society (Nakao 2016, 552). Many colleagues soon joined him in exploring the connection between epistemology and power. In 2005, the National Museum for Ethnology (Minzokugaku Hakubutsukan, or Minpaku) established the Ethnology Research Archive to house the personal papers of transwar scholars. Although many damaging documents were privately retained, both Japanese and non-Japanese anthropologists and historians have drawn on these archives to tackle ethnology's pre-1945 past (e.g., Chun 2006; Kreiner 2014; Nakao 2016; Kingsberg Kadia 2020).

The abandonment of Nihonjinron also paved the way for a multicultural (tayōseiteki) understanding of the Japanese. Rather than seeking sources of uniformity, researchers began to emphasize manifestations of difference and diversity. For the first time, they trained a comprehensive analytical gaze on the experiences of disenfranchised domestic groups including descendants of Korean and Chinese settlers, the Indigenous Ainu population, Burakumin (Japan's historical outcastes), and Brazil-born migrant workers of Japanese ancestry (e.g., Fukuoka 1993; Hanasaki 1993; Takayanagi 1993; Maeyama 1996).

Today the term gakujutsu, formerly connoting "objectivity," is taken to mean academic or scientific—a subtle but important shift that suggests the retreat from a notion of unitary universal truth. Many social scientists now view reality as composed of an infinite number of perspectives, not necessarily of equal weight but each nonetheless unique and important in generating accurate and honest representation. Applied to the analysis of 1968 in Japan, such polyvocality directs historians to look beyond student actors. It encourages attention to transwar social scientists who had as much or more at stake in the debate over the basis of legitimate knowledge. More than fifty years later, this way of understanding "truth" allows us to see 1968 for the revolution it truly was.

Notes

1   Between 1890 and 1910, the word gakujutsu appeared over 1,200 times (about five times per month) in the Yomiuri Shinbun, Japan's oldest and most widely circulating newspaper. https://database-yomiuri-co-jp.colorado.idm.oclc.org /rekishikan/. Accessed November 29, 2016.

2   Also facilitating exoneration was the fact that the consequences of social science research in the Japanese empire were borne mostly by Asian subjects—a population that the Allies (excluding China) largely ignored in the postwar pursuit of justice.

3 The transwar continuity of the Japanese and German social scientist communities stands in striking contrast to the wholesale shift of personnel after 1945 in Poland, described by Agata Zysiak in this volume.

4 Today Ienaga is best remembered for his thirty-year legal crusade for responsible representation of Japan's wartime atrocities in national history textbooks.

5 In 2016 the minimum age for voting was lowered to eighteen.

6 This figure represented an approximately fivefold increase over student arrests in 1967.

7 Most arrested individuals were not students, but supporters mobilized for the final showdown.

8 This "temporary" law was finally repealed in 2001.

References

Aoki Tamotsu. 1999. *Nihon bunkaron no hen'yō: Sengo Nihon no bunka to aidentitī*. Tokyo: Chūō Kōron Shinsha.

Asad, Talal, ed. 1973. *Anthropology and the Colonial Encounter*. London: Ithaca Press.

Baerwald, Hans H. 1959. *The Purge of Japanese Leaders under the Occupation*. Berkeley: University of California Press.

Befu, Harumi. 2001. *Hegemony of Homogeneity: An Anthropological Analysis of Nihonjinron*. Melbourne: Trans Pacific Press.

Berreman, Gerald D. 1968. "Is Anthropology Alive? Social Responsibility in Social Anthropology." *Current Anthropology* 9, no. 5: 391–92.

Chun, Kyung-soo. 2006. "Izumi Seiichi no Nyū Ginia hōsa to gunzoku jinruigaku." In *"Teikoku" Nihon no gakuchi: "Teikoku" hensei no keifu*, edited by Sakai Tetsuya, 99–140. Tokyo: Iwanami Shoten.

Conrad, Sebastian. 2010. *The Quest for the Lost Nation: Writing History in Germany and Japan in the American Century*. Translated by Alan Nothnagle. Berkeley: University of California Press.

Conrad, Sebastian. 2012. "'The Colonial Ties Are Liquidated': Modernization Theory, Post-war Japan and the Global Cold War." *Past and Present* 216: 181–214.

Daston, Lorraine, and Peter Galison. 2007. *Objectivity*. New York: Zone.

Dower, John W. 1975. "E. H. Norman, Japan, and the Uses of History." In *Origins of the Modern Japanese State: Selected Writings of E. H. Norman*, edited by E. Herbert Norman and John W. Dower, 3–101. New York: Pantheon.

Fukuoka Yasunori. 1993. *Zainichi Kankoku Chōsenjin: Wakai sedai no aidenteitei*. Tokyo: Chūō Kōronsha.

Fuse, Toyomasa. 1969. "Student Radicalism in Japan: A 'Cultural Revolution'?" *Comparative Education Review* 13, no. 3: 325–42.

Gilman, Nils. 2003. "Modernization: The Highest Stage of American Intellectual History." In *Staging Growth: Modernization, Development, and the Global Cold War*, edited by David C. Engerman, Nils Gilman, Mark H. Haefele, and Michael E. Latham, 47–80. Amherst: University of Massachusetts Press.

Gough, Kathleen. 1968. "New Proposals for Anthropologists." *Current Anthropology* 9, no. 5: 403–35.

Hanasaki Kōhei. 1993. *Shizukana daichi: Matsuura Takeshirō to Ainu minzoku.* Tokyo: Iwanami Shoten.

Ienaga Saburō. 1962. *Daigaku no jiyū no rekishi.* Tokyo: Hanawa Shobō.

Iida Taku. 2007. "Shōwa sanjū nendai no kaigai gakujutsu ekusupedeishon: 'Nihon jinruigaku' no sengo to masu medeiā." *Kokuritsu Minzokugaku Hakubutsukan kenkyū hōkoku* 31, no. 2: 227–85.

Ishida Eiichirō. 1961. "Genchi chōsa to bunken chōsa." *Minzokugaku kenkyū* 25, no. 3: 58–60.

Itani Jun'ichirō. 1969. Letter to Sol Tax, March 12, 1969. *Current Anthropology* Records. File 4, Box 225. Special Collections Research Center, University of Chicago Library.

Izumi Kimiko. 1972. *Izumi Seiichi to tomo ni.* Tokyo: Fuyō Shobō.

Izumi Seiichi. 1966. *Bunmei wo motta seibutsu.* Tokyo: Nihon Hōsō Shuppan Kyōkai.

Izumi Seiichi. 1970. "Bunka to daigaku: Bunka no naka no daigaku zō." Originally published in 1969. In Izumi Seiichi, *Bunka no naka no ningen*, 248–49. Tokyo: Bungei Shunjū.

Izumi Seiichi. 1972. "Yuruyaka na yamayama." In *Izumi Seiichi chosakushū 7: Bunka jinruigaku no me*, edited by Izumi Seiichi, 160–383. Tokyo: Yomiuri Shinbunsha.

Kapur, Nikhil Paul. 2011. "US-Japan Security Treaty Crisis and the Origins of Contemporary Japan." PhD diss., Harvard University.

Kawakita Jirō. 1961. "Ishida kyōju ni ōete." *Minzokugaku kenkyū* 25, no. 3: 62–63.

Kidder, J. Edward, Jr. 2013. *View from the Trenches of Mitaka: Experiences in Japanese Archaeology.* Tokyo: International Christian University Hachirō Yuasa Memorial Museum.

Kingsberg, Miriam. 2012. "Legitimating Empire, Legitimating Nation: The Scientific Study of Opium Addiction in Japanese Manchuria." *Journal of Japanese Studies* 38, no. 2: 325–51.

Kingsberg Kadia, Miriam. 2020. *Into the Field: Human Scientists of Transwar Japan.* Stanford, CA: Stanford University Press.

Koda, Naoko. 2015. "America's Cold War and the Japanese Student Movement, 1948–1973." PhD diss., New York University.

Kreiner, Josef, ed. 2014. *Nihon to wa nani ka: Nihon minzokugaku no nijū seiki.* Tokyo: Tōkyōtō Shuppan.

Kuper, Adam. 1973. *Anthropology and Anthropologists: The Modern British School, 1922–1972.* London: Allan Lane.

Maeyama Takeshi. 1996. *Esunishitei to Burajiru Nikkeijin: Bunka jinruigakuteki kenkyū.* Tokyo: Ochanomizu Shobō.

Moses, A. Dirk. 2007. *German Intellectuals and the Nazi Past.* New York: Cambridge University Press.

Nagai, Michio, and Jerry Dusenbury. 1971. *Higher Education in Japan: Its Take-Off and Crash.* Tokyo: University of Tokyo Press.

Nakao Katsumi. 2014. "Shokuminchi daigaku no jinruigakusha: Izumi Seiichi ron." *Kokusaigaku kenkyū* 5: 47–69.

Nakao Katsumi. 2016. *Kindai Nihon no jinruigakushi: Teikoku to shokuminchi no kioku.* Tokyo: Fūkyōsha.

Nakazawa, Miyori. 1989. "A Rhetorical Analysis of the Japanese Student Movement: University of Tokyo Struggle 1968–69." PhD diss., Northwestern University.

Nanbara Shigeru and Richard H. Minear. 2010. *War and Conscience in Japan: Nanbara Shigeru and the Asia-Pacific War.* Lanham, MD: Rowman and Littlefield.

Nielsen, Kristian H., Michael Harbsmeier, and Christopher J. Ries. 2012. "Studying Scientists and Scholars in the Field: An Introduction." In *Scientists and Scholars in the Field: Studies in the History of Fieldwork and Expeditions*, edited by Kristian H. Nielsen, Michael Harbsmeier, and Christopher J. Ries, 9–28. Aarhus, Denmark: Aarhus University Press.

Oguma Eiji. 2015. "Japan's 1968: A Collective Reaction to Rapid Economic Growth in an Age of Turmoil." Translated by Nikhil Kapur with Samuel Malissa and Stephen Poland. *Asia-Pacific Journal: Japan Focus* 13, no. 12 (1) : 1–27: https://apjjf.org/2015/13/11/Oguma-Eiji/4300.html.

Oguma Eiji. 2018. "What Was and Is '1968'? Japanese Experience in Global Perspective." *Asia-Pacific Journal: Japan Focus* 16, no. 11 (6): 1–18. https://apjjf.org/2018/11/Oguma.html.

Okamoto Tarō and Izumi Seiichi. 1970. *Nihon rettō bunkaron.* Tokyo: Daikōsha.

Okamoto Tarō, Izumi Seiichi, and Umesao Tadao. 1970. *Sekai no kamen to shinzō.* Tokyo: Asahi Shinbunsha.

Park, Dongseong. 2016. "Anthropological Exchanges between Korea and Japan in the Postwar Era." *Japanese Review of Cultural Anthropology* 16: 157–66.

Pelzel, John C. 1948. "Japanese Ethnological and Sociological Research." *American Anthropologist* 50, no. 1: 54–72.

Price, David H. 2008. *Anthropological Intelligence: The Deployment and Neglect of American Anthropology in the Second World War.* Durham, NC: Duke University Press.

Price, David H. 2016. *Cold War Anthropology: The CIA, the Pentagon, and the Growth of Dual Use Anthropology.* Durham, NC: Duke University Press.

Shimbori, Michiya, T. Ban, K. Kono, H. Yamazaki, Y. Kano, M. Murakami, and T. Murakami. 1980. "Japanese Student Activism in the 1970s." *Higher Education* 9, no. 2: 139–54.

Steinmetz, George. 2005. "The Genealogy of a Positivist Haunting: Comparing Prewar and Postwar U.S. Sociology." *boundary 2* 32, no. 2: 109–35.

Steinmetz, George. 2010. "Ideas in Exile: Refugees from Nazi Germany and the Failure to Transplant Historical Sociology into the United States." *International Journal of Politics, Culture, and Society* 23, no. 1: 1–27.

Stocking, George. 1991. *Colonial Situations: Essays on the Contextualization of Ethnographic Knowledge.* Madison: University of Wisconsin Press.

Takayanagi Kaneyoshi. 1993. *Edo jidai Burakumin no seikatsu.* Tokyo: Yūzankaku Shuppan.

Terada Kazuo. 1975. *Nihon no jinruigaku*. Tokyo: Sōsakusha.

Tsurumi, Kazuko. 1970. "Some Comments on the Japanese Student Movement in the Sixties." *Journal of Contemporary History* 5, no. 1: 104–12.

Wheeler, Donald Frederick. 1974. "The Japanese Student Movement: Value Politics, Student Politics and the Tokyo University Struggle." PhD diss., Columbia University.

Wilson, Sandra. 2012. "Exhibiting a New Japan: The Tokyo Olympics of 1964 and Expo '70 in Osaka." *Historical Research* 85, no. 227: 159–78.

Yasko, Guy. 1997. "The Japanese Student Movement, 1968–1970: The Zenkyōtō Uprising." PhD diss., Cornell University.

"Zenkoku no daigaku ni okeru minzokugaku, jinruigaku kankei no kōgi ikkan." 1969. *Minzokugaku kenkyū* 34, no. 2: 159–71.

9

how political commitment delineates social scientific knowledge

KRISTOFFER KROPP

SOCIAL SCIENCE KNOWLEDGE IS produced at the intersection of political, religious, and scientific currents. The European Values Study (EVS), for example, was produced at the intersection of a conservative and Catholic moral and political outlook, opinion polling, and modernization theory. Today the EVS is often presented alongside other transnational social surveys as a "just" source of high-quality data for comparative social science (Bréchon 2012; Heath, Fisher, and Smith 2005). Of course, it is also known for its scientific focus, but it is first and foremost presented as the consecrated source of dispassionate knowledge about European values from the early 1980s to the present. And at first glance this seems to be a fair description. It is directed from a Dutch university department, university professors from all over Europe are involved in its governing bodies, it has close ties to GESIS (the German data archive for the social sciences), and it explores a large range of social phenomena and not only values research in a strict sense. The survey is, in other words, an established, credible source of social science knowledge production, and the survey questions and theoretical framework enjoy considerable standing in social scientific debates about European values and social structures.

However, looking closer we find that the EVS is a product of a very specific set of social conditions and ideas about European values that informed it when it was set up in the early 1980s. What I will show in my analysis of the EVS is that four political and academic currents conjoined to profoundly shape the survey in the late 1970s. More specifically, I show how the agents initiating the EVS brought along a Catholic and politically conservative outlook combined with a commitment to broad conceptions of systems theory–inspired modernization theory and survey practices from the opinion-polling industry. Hence, in the first section of the chapter I analyze a rather different social configuration of interests in social science knowledge production than the dominant, social democratic reform-minded and progressive social science interests linked to the buildup of welfare state institutions in Western societies. Thereafter, I show how this specific configuration shaped the ensuing surveys up to the present time in terms of their organization and production.

Seen from a wider perspective, the chapter is linked to the question of how long-forgotten or hidden historical relations and processes affect concepts, techniques, institutions, and hence the current conditions for social science knowledge production. The underlying goal is thus not just to tell an interesting and unknown history about an important social science project but also to invite critical reflection about the assumptions and social practices involved in social survey research. More specifically, the study raises questions about how the international organization of such projects and the international circulation of techniques and ideas conceal the political origins of knowledge, and about how international academic fields force specific formats on such projects in terms of their organization, production, dissemination, and evaluation.

A Generic Sociological Approach

To understand the connections between religion, politics, and social science, I draw on two notions from Bourdieu. First, the chapter aims to shed historical light on the now hidden or forgotten past of an important social scientific instrument. As Bourdieu argues, "The unconscious is history—the collective history that has produced our categories of thought, and the individual history through which they have been inculcated in us" (2000, 9). Often,

Bourdieu further argues, institutions, scientific categories, and concepts owe a great deal of their perceived neutrality and stability to the fact that their history has been forgotten or hidden, and he posits that in order to grasp contemporary social practices we need to analyze the historical processes through which social scientific institutions, techniques, theories, and problems were produced (Bourdieu 2015). More specifically, I analyze questions about the position and trajectory of the agents involved in setting up the EVS, and the connection between the intellectual work of the agents and their position within specific national social and intellectual spaces.

Just as Bourdieu's sociology is about fields and their properties, the field-theoretical approach has a strong focus on the relations between fields—their homological structures (Bourdieu 1991, 1988). Following Bourdieu, the concept of homological structures captures the idea that we can find similar principles of vision and division across fields, and that these similarities allow and enable agents to form alliances across fields. Using the notion of homological structures, I analyze how ideas, worldviews, and resources move between fields and how they are used. Since the EVS was an international enterprise from the outset, the conjuncture between different national fields and the struggles between different visions of social science knowledge production are important in understanding the development of the EVS (Heilbron, Guilhot, and Jeanpierre 2008; see also Heilbron in this volume).

Statistics, Science, and Social Engagement

Within the social sciences, the social survey is one of the most common forms of empirical material, and in the public space, opinion polls serve as a powerful tool in political struggles and debates. Social statistics in various forms, ranging from censuses to household surveys and social surveys, have been closely entangled with the formation of modern states. Social statistics have enabled state bureaucracies to symbolically unify diverse territories and to compare different parts of states and population segments in order to more effectively govern territories and populations (Desrosières 1998; Porter 1995; Savage 2010). The modern sample survey is a child of the mid-twentieth century, and the basic properties of social surveys (theories of random sampling, inference, measurement, and statistical analysis) were established in the late 1950s, with the promise of providing the social sciences with a powerful instrument for objectively measuring social phenomena as well offering a powerful tool for social planning in the postwar period (Steinmetz 2007). In the same period, social surveys became the favored instrument for positivist-minded social scientists, so that social surveys together with variants of systems theory came to dominate US social science and were exported to Europe. Until the late 1970s, social surveys in Europe were primarily conducted within nation-states, but from the 1970s onward, survey research and political institutions began to launch transnational surveys. In 1973, the EU (led by Jacques-René Rabier, one of the founding members of the EVS) launched the Eurobarometer in order to measure "European attitudes toward European political issues," with the explicit purpose of using the knowledge thus generated to promote European integration to skeptical segments of the European population (Aldrin 2010). The ISSP (International Social Survey Program) launched in 1983 was closely linked to the US, German, and British general social surveys with a view to providing data to comparative social scientists working in political science and sociology, especially on issues close to Western welfare states, such as the role of government, social inequality, work, and the family (Smith 2012). The EVS was, in other words, not the only attempt of its time to mobilize survey knowledge for political purposes.

Four Social Currents in the European Values Study

In 1978, two scholars took the initiative and formed the European Value Systems Study Group, which eventually led to the EVS. The two scholars were Jan Kerkhofs, a Catholic priest and professor at the Katholieke Universiteit in Leuven, Belgium, and Ruud de Moor, a well-connected sociology professor at the Catholic University in Tilburg, the Netherlands. Both scholars were not only engaged in academic life but were also closely connected to the Catholic Church and to national and European political and bureaucratic circles. They gathered a group of scholars interested in changing values in Europe and with organizational and scientific resources to prepare and carry out a survey in Western Europe. Like Kerkhofs and de Moor, they were not only active academics but were also involved in politics and the private opinion polling industry. Central to the group was Jacques-René Rabier, former secretary of Jean Monnet and founder of the Eurobarometer, and an important connection to the European Communities; and Gordon Heald from the United Kingdom, head of Gallup Europe, which conducted the Eurobarometer that linked the EVS to the world's most renowned polling agency. Also in the group were people linking the social sciences, politics, and business. Among them was Elisabeth Noelle-Neumann, former president of the World Association for Public Opinion Research (WAPOR) (1979–80), and visiting professor at the University of Chicago, who alongside her academic career founded and ran the conservative German think tank and opinion-polling institution the Allensbach Institute, which was closely connected to the important German Christian Democratic political parties. Mediating between academia and public opinion polling was Professor Jean Stoetzel from the Sorbonne. As the first president of WAPOR (1947–48) and founder of the Gallup-inspired opinion polling institute, IFOP/Faits et Opinions, he too was simultaneously engaged in academic sociology and commercial opinion polling. Hence, the European Value Systems Study Group consisted of people who all possessed social and institutional connections and resources in the form of leading positions in firms and academic institutions as well as the symbolic merits of academia. In this way, the EVS was a product of academic, business, and political engagement whose founders drew on resources and epistemological approaches both from the social sciences and from more political realms in justifying and building it up.

The agents in the European Value Systems Study Group came together around concerns about the social changes arising from social movements ranging from European integration and secularization to changes in family patterns and political attitudes, which had characterized Western Europe since the mid-1960s. Conceptually, these changes were captured using concepts such as individualization and the corrosion of moral and social obligation in society in the 1960s and 1970s. Not only were these themes interesting and relevant from a social scientific point of view; they were also, and at the same time, concerns of church organizations and conservative political organizations, which were observing these social changes with both fear and anxiety (Arts and Halman 2014; Kerkhofs 1991). These concerns and outlook on the sociopolitical landscape influenced the themes taken up in the survey. One researcher who worked with the survey described the group's political concerns and commitments thus: "There was also a quite Catholic orientation to this. Gordon Heald was interested in Christian issues and Kerkhofs was a Catholic priest. . . . In general we were criticized a lot by other academics. They were dismissive of the EVS for not being grounded in sociological premises. Which was true, since the project consisted of different elements struggling to make sense."[1]

The quote here reveals the conjuncture of political and ethical concerns and the attempts to transform them into social science issues. For the group, the concept of values played an important role in tying together academic, political, and religious concerns, with multiple connotations attached to it both as an everyday concept and in its use in social science and theology. In postwar sociology Talcott Parsons had placed the concepts of values at the center of sociological research and theorizing. Here values were a fundamental moral arrangement that controlled "the structure of social action" and accounted for the functional integration of subsystems in modern societies. With its emphasis on moral obligations, this general assumption meshed well with the politically conservative and religious inclinations of the agents involved.

All in all, four political and social scientific currents shaped the EVS. The first was anxiety about changing values in Europe from the late 1960s, which stemmed from the Catholic Church and, linked to that, an ambition to use empirical sociological knowledge to inform the Catholic Church's response to these social changes. Second, the EVS was informed by a strong politically and socially conservative current whose advocates regarded the "corrosion" of morals and culture with fear and skepticism. In both cases, we find agents deeply concerned about the social changes taking place in the 1960s and 1970s. The third and fourth currents capture the ways in which societal concerns were conjoined with theoretical currents and epistemological positions in the social sciences. The third current was a sociological interest in values changes informed by modernization theory in its Parsonian version, which served as a way of formulating the concerns of Catholic and conservative agents in sociologically acceptable terminology. The fourth and last current was the widespread use of social survey techniques, here represented by commercial public opinion polling and only to a lesser extent by academic survey researchers. The four currents were, however, not separate "streams" but conjoined in several ways by agents and institutions and shared worldviews. Following these four interwoven currents that shaped the EVS, I show how these came together and how all four left a clear mark on the survey.

CATHOLIC UNIVERSITIES AND CATHOLIC SOCIOLOGY

Two Catholic universities, KU Leuven (KUL) and Tilburg University, were the institutional and intellectual cornerstones of the EVS, serving as the academic homes of the founders—Kerkhofs and de Moor. By looking at the institutional conditions of the two universities and the Catholic Church, and at how sociology—and modern social science more generally—was conceived of by Catholic scholars, we can gain a picture of the institutional framework of the EVS and the ambiguity with which Catholic scholars approached sociology—especially the sociology of moral and ethical questions (for another take on the relationship between science and religion, see Modern in this volume). Historically, the Belgian and Dutch higher education fields have been pillarized, and their universities have served as educational institutions for different religious, political, and language groups. However, despite the Catholic links of both KUL and Tilburg University, the two universities took up very different positions in their national higher education fields. KUL is one of the oldest universities in the region, with a history going back to 1425, and it occupies a central position as one of the largest and most prestigious universities in Belgium and Western Europe. Located outside Brussels, KUL has traditionally been positioned in opposition to the liberal university in Brussels that was established after the creation of Belgium in the 1830s, and until very recently it was headed by Catholic scholars who emphasized its close connections to the Catholic Church (Tollebeek and Nys 2006; Vanderstraeten and Louckx 2017). In important ways, Tilburg University differs from KUL despite both universities' explicit obligations and commitment to "Catholic scholarship." It was first established in 1927 as a Catholic business school, and it has expanded since then but remains focused on the social sciences. Thus, unlike KUL, Tilburg University occupies a subordinate position in the Dutch field of higher education, as the newcomer located outside the major cities and with only research and education in the social sciences. Despite the differences between the two universities' positions in their national fields, they both served as institutional linkages between the academic world and Catholic organizations, and Kerkhofs and de Moor used these linkages to mobilize resources and establish the foundation of the EVS.[2]

Since the early emergence of the social sciences, Catholic scholars had been inherently skeptical about, or directly hostile to, sociology, especially Durkheimian approaches that treated morals and ethics as "social facts" to be explained. The Catholic Church could see the use of the new techniques for producing knowledge about social issues, but it preferred empiricist approaches that recorded observational facts (Heilbron 2015). Around 1900, sociology drew some attention at the Higher Institute for Philosophy at KUL (Vanderstraeten and Louckx 2017, 39). Here sociological approaches were mobilized in order to describe both the "social problems" in Belgium and the "primitive societies" in the Congo Basin and thereby to govern social and clerical relations and institutions. Significant for the understanding of the EVS was the development of "religious sociology" in the middle of the twentieth century. Religious sociology was an explicit attempt to formulate and institutionalize a sociology that could service the Catholic Church and develop new instruments for evangelical work and that thus had a very different focus than the "sociology of religion" (Gerard and Wils 1999). Proponents of "religious sociology" argued that to study religious, moral, and ethical questions, one should be not only a devoted believer but also trained in theology and devoted to the Church—otherwise one would not be able to grasp the essential character of moral and clerical phenomena. Jan Kerkhofs (1924–2015) was trained in this tradition, and he brought this background into the EVS. In 1954 the Jesuit Kerkhofs defended the first sociological dissertation at KUL, titled "Religious Practices and Social Milieu: A Religious Sociological Study of the Province Limburg" (Gerard and Wils 1999, 55). In the foreword, Kerkhofs's bishop presented the dissertation as a premium example of "auxiliary science for pastoral work." As such, it presented a detailed overview of "religious practice in its social and economic setting" to guide the work of the Church "in critical times" (Vanderstraeten and Louckx 2017, 48). Looking at Kerkhofs's career, the use of sociology as a tool for the Church runs through it. Alongside his academic work, Kerkhofs was involved in a number of reports about the role and organization of the Catholic Church in societies undergoing change. These reports linked him not only to a national Belgian audience but also to a wider European one. Here he argued that the Catholic Church had to open up to the changes in values and social practices characteristic of the 1960s and 1970s in order to maintain its central societal position and authority on ethical and moral questions as a counter-movement to individualization and the expansion of secular values. In many ways the position and point of view that Kerkhofs represented captures the religious or Catholic current that informed not only him but also people like Gordon Heald, Jean Stoetzel, and Ruud de Moor. Their interest in values and moral questions was not an "academic interest," in other words, but rested on the firm belief that "European culture" was genuinely Christian and that the Catholic Church should play a central role in European societies as the authority on moral and ethical questions and as a central social institution, and that this position was threatened by social processes of modernization (Kerkhofs 1991). Kerkhofs argued that sociological knowledge could help with understanding society and hence assist the Church in formulating political strategies.

POLITICAL CONSERVATISM AND LINKS
TO THE CHRISTIAN DEMOCRATS

Just as the group had strong relations to the Catholic Church, it was also closely linked to right-of-center political parties, especially the Christian Democratic parties. Throughout the history of social science knowledge production, social scientists and their institutions have always been closely entangled with political institutions. Here I will focus on some of the more prominent participants with specific links to Christian Democratic parties and political projects in Europe. The connection to "the European integration project" was the French bureaucrat and social survey researcher J.-R. Rabier. After serving as head of Jean Monnet's cabinet, he was appointed head of the European Commission's information service in 1960. From this position, he promoted survey research as a political instrument (see the following section on social surveys as a political instrument), but just as importantly, he brought concerns about European integration as a modernization project to Brussels (Aldrin 2010). Carrying out political bridging from the academic side, we find Ruud de Moor. From early on in his career, de Moor participated in government commissions and working groups and served as adviser to the Dutch Ministry of Education (van de Kaa 2003). However, the most prominent agent mediating between conservative politics and social science in the EVS group is, without doubt, Elisabeth Noelle-Neumann. Noelle-Neumann grew up in a conservative upper-class milieu in Berlin in the 1920s and 1930s. In her dissertation from 1940, she analyzed the use of public opinion polling developed in the United States and its possible use for surveillance and propaganda in Nazi Germany. During the war she became a prominent writer for the Nazi newspapers *Deutsche Allgemeine Zeitung* and *Das Reich*.[3] After the war, she established what became one of the most important public opinion polling institutes in postwar West Germany—the Institut für Demoskopie Allensbach. Through her work as pollster for the Christian Democratic Union in the 1950s, she established close relations with other German Christian Democratic parties, served as adviser to Adenauer and later Kohl, and was known for her recurrent work as one of the most important national media commentators on elections and other political events, where she interpreted social survey results (Kruke 2007). In the early 1960s, she was appointed professor at the university in Mainz, where she established the departments of communication and journalism. In other words, Noelle-Neumann connected a number of different fields and effectively used these connections to promote her institutions and explicitly conservative worldview. Using Bourdieu's notion of homological positions (Bourdieu 1991), it becomes quite clear how the assumptions and implications of Noelle-Neumann's major scientific work, "The Spiral of Silence" (Noelle-Neumann 1984), reflect her conservative political perception and connect to her work in providing useful justifications and accounts for conservative politicians in the postwar era. The central assumption of Noelle-Neumann is that public opinions are not the results of rational discourses or representations of different interests but the products of fear of social isolation, which leads to pressure to conform. She further-more assumes that the "public sphere" is an institution for social control with elites in control who suppress or superimpose the "right" opinions on the people. However, this was not accompanied by a will to empower or include various societally marginalized groups or points of view; instead Noelle-Neumann argued that "public opinion" was a product of ill-informed masses and emotionally loaded stereotypes that made any kind of wider participa-tory democracy an illusion or even dangerous (Simpson 1996; Wendelin and Meyen 2009). In this way Noelle-Neumann's theoretical conceptualization of "mass societies" was in line with that of many other conservatives in the postwar years, those who reluctantly endorsed postwar democracy while still holding on to traditional values and institutions, all the while watching with great skepticism the growing welfare states, capitalist consumer societies, and new social movements' demands for participation. It was, in other words, a conservatism in opposition to the new left in the 1960s and 1970s, with its ideas about democratic participation in all social institutions and its critique of gender roles and established social hierarchies. Simultaneously, it opposed the rise of "neoliberalism," with its tendency to reject traditional values and institutions and its emphasis on the power of the market and money in place of the classical conservative critique of liberal capitalism.

MODERNIZATION THEORY AS FRAME FOR A
CONSERVATIVE UNDERSTANDING OF SOCIAL CHANGE

However, neither "religious sociology" nor Noelle-Neumann's conservative worldview could serve as the legitimate sociological point of reference or coherent sociological theory. Instead, the influence of modernization theory and Parsonian systems theory worked as a way of translating religious and political concerns into sociologically acceptable questions. In line with the theoretical winds blowing over the Atlantic, in 1961 Ruud de More wrote his doctoral thesis on "conflict sociology" following a Parsonian theoretical framework. Running through the EVS, and informing both its sociological conception and political concerns, was the discussion about modernization theory against the backdrop of Parsons's systems theory—not least because of the role Parsons ascribed to values in understanding social change and differ-entiation. What made these theoretical systems so attractive to the research-ers that came together to form the EVS? As has been argued, modernization theory was often taken up and used as a bundle of more or less implicit de-cisive assumptions that guided and linked empirical analysis (Gilman 2003).

For the EVS researchers, this approach had a number of features that fit well with their political, scientific, and religious habitus and also drew on some of the most prestigious work in postwar US sociology. As Knöbl points out, modernization theory represented a macro sociological theory that differed from Marxist theory but that also aimed to explain or at least conceptualize the relationship between economic and cultural changes using Parsons's pattern variable as a theoretical model. It expected societies to follow more or less similar development processes from traditional to modern societies, and its implicit telos consisted of US or Western societies characterized by secularism, individualism, rationalization, and functional differentiation, but also democracy and capitalism, which were seen as the "model" and as end goals for modern societies (Knöbl 2003). When modernization theory was first conceptualized in the early 1950s, the theory served to understand developing countries, and subsequently to guide development projects. In the two ensuing decades, it framed important theoretical discussions within political science and sociology in the pursuit of formulating real "scientific" theories, concepts, and explanatory models. From the late 1960s onward, many leading scholars abandoned the project, largely due to unfulfilled theoretical ambitions. However, to socially and scientifically conservative scholars like those in the EVS, the bundle "modernization theory" still served as an implicit reference in conceptualizing their concerns for Western societies during what appeared to be rapid social changes in the late 1960s and 1970s. The social changes that swept over Western societies from the late 1960s onward, and the sense of crisis that followed, were regarded with both anxiety and skeptical wonder (Arts and Halman 2014; Noelle-Neumann 2006, 186). Even though these events seemed to contradict modernization theory and its promises and predictions about stable welfare institutions in organized capitalist democracies, modernization theory still served to guide how the crisis was conceptualized. The researchers in the EVS asked whether the modernization processes of Western societies had led to an overemphasis on individual liberties, thereby eroding common moral and ethical values and creating an "ethical vacuum." In this way, they speculated whether stable modern societies were, in some ways, built on premodern institutions and values such as the Church and religion—a critique that obviously fit within the worldview of many of the agents setting up the EVS. The then-young US political scientist Ronald Inglehart's 1971 article and 1977 book in many ways encapsulate these concerns (Inglehart 1977, 1971). Inglehart and Rabier knew each other from the work on the Eurobarometer that Rabier ran in the European Commission, and Inglehart had used its data in his analysis of what he termed the change from "material" to "postmaterial" values in Western societies. Already, in the wording that emphasized values alongside the model explaining the shift from one social system to another, the heritage from Parsons and the discussions around modernization theory that informed Inglehart's work made it easy to fit into the scope of the coming EVS researchers. Even though modernization theory informed the EVS, as did the discussions that followed that linked it to Inglehart's theory on intergenerational value change, it was more in a post hoc way or as a bundle of ideas and theories than as a coherent set of theoretical propositions that would guide the empirical work.

OPINION POLLING AS AN ATHEORETICAL POLITICAL TOOL

Rather than strict theoretical conceptualizations, the EVS had a horizon of political and ethical concerns, theoretical concepts, and approaches. Nevertheless, the participants did gather around one epistemological mode of knowledge production—the social survey. At least three of the founding members had been driving forces for the import and proliferation of social survey methods after the war in Europe. As in most of Europe and the United States, the decades after the war witnessed a radical growth of social science, and social science techniques were taken up in all realms of society. The proliferation of social surveys happened at the intersection between academia, business, and the expanding welfare states, remaining close to political issues of the state and political parties but simultaneously rather detached from theoretically informed sociological research. In this intersection, we find Stoetzel as a front-runner in importing this form of survey research to Europe. After a visit to the United States in 1937, he established his public opinion survey bureau, IFOP/Faits et Opinions, in 1938, enabling him to secure a leading position in the Vichy regime's research institute led by eugenicist Alexis Carrel (Rosental 2006). From these beginnings, Stoetzel built a sociological career and became professor of social psychology at the Sorbonne in 1955. The other prominent Frenchman in the EVS group was Rabier. As the head of Monnet's cabinet, Rabier was one of the early "Eurocrats"—young, social science–trained civil servants engaged both professionally and politically in the European integration process. Working closely together with Stoetzel, Rabier became aware of the new possibilities that survey research provided and, drawing on Stoetzel, David Easton, and especially Paul Lazarsfeld, Rabier conducted a number of surveys in the 1960s to inform political processes in the European Economic Community by directing its information initiatives toward people with a positive attitude toward but little information about European integration, and thus strengthening their commitment to the political project (Aldrin 2010). Rabier collaborated with academics such as Stoetzel, and in 1973 he and Ronald Inglehart launched the Eurobarometer. He was thus not only the main proponent of "European" politics in the EVS group; he also brought the practical experience of conducting transnational social surveys in a political environment. The trajectories of Stoetzel and Rabier are parallel to Noelle-Neumann's, and it is likely that they met during the 1950s and 1960 at WAPOR or other public opinion polling meetings. Like their careers, their epistemological outlook was also rather similar and was, in a paradoxical way, caught between the high scientific ambitions of postwar social science and demands for the short-term political use of survey knowledge, which led to a rather empiricist practice of social science knowledge production. On the one hand, these figures mobilized the language of hypothetical deduction to legitimize their practices and what Steinmetz in the US case has called "methodological positivism" (Steinmetz 2005), discursively presenting their work as neutral empirical descriptions of the world. On the other hand, they constantly mobilized this knowledge, designed the research and presented the results in order to inform and support political action and the ambitions of, for example, the European Commission or the Christian Democratic parties, in lieu of meeting academic standards (Aldrin 2010; Kruke 2007).

The First Survey and What Followed

In 1981, the survey was launched in ten Western European countries, and in the following years more than a handful of books came out reporting on the results. Analyzing the different steps of the survey, we see how societal and social scientific currents clearly mark its epistemological and social configuration. In the late 1970s, the EVS group began meeting more regularly to develop a questionnaire. At the Allensback Institute, Noelle-Neumann put together a draft questionnaire that was field tested in a number of countries and led by Gallup UK researchers who carried out a number of roundtable interviews. Still, the enterprise was marked by the epistemological culture of marketing and public opinion polling. As a survey methodologist who joined the EVS in the late 1980s explained: "The main group of people working with them were the ones in the marketing area. This resulted in many isolated questions.... They never thought about scaling or reliable measurement.

They seemed to think that you could ask people about how religious they are the same way you would ask them about their butter in their fridge."[4]

And so they did. Seemingly lacking in any theoretical conceptualization or methodological operationalization of the central theoretical concepts and concerns of the project—values—the questionnaire was built from existing scales and items but also from questions informed very directly by the different interests of the group members. Hence, the questionnaire ended up including Inglehart's postmaterialism scale and twenty questions about the Ten Commandments, with little coherence in scales or consideration about the order or wording of the questions. When the survey was launched in 1981, the groups used their relationships to opinion polling institutes to carry out the survey. Relying largely on national Gallup institutes, the EVS depended on the methods used by Gallup in collecting the Eurobarometer data (Harding 1986). In other words, central agents in the EVS brought the empiricist and instrumental practices of public opinion polling with them into the EVS, in the way the questionnaire was put together, how the survey was carried out, and, as we will see, in how the data was analyzed.

The engaged Catholic and conservative starting point of the survey was, paradoxically, reflected in the books that came out of the survey. On the one hand, the books were presented by the authors as neutral academic analysis reporting on a major academic social survey of national or European "value systems," repeatedly emphasizing the scale of the project in respect of the number of countries included and the volume of data accumulated (e.g., Harding 1986, xii–xiii; Stoetzel 1983, 302; Noelle-Neumann 1988, 2:9–16; Abrams, Gerard, and Timms 1985, xix, 1). On the other hand, few of them meet the standards of contemporary survey research. The first book, Stoetzel's *Les valeurs du temps présent: Une enquête européenne*, came out in 1983 and was praised and discussed in the following books from the survey and in a review in Stoetzel's journal. But the book had a rough ride when it was reviewed in the first issue of the *European Sociological Review* (Husbands 1985). And in many ways, the review of Stoetzel's book captures common issues with a number of the books that came out of the project. The key concept—values—was not clearly defined or theoretically operationalized, and the book thus lacked a structuring concept that could tie together the various subjects treated, from attitudes toward morals and politics, to family and church attendance; neither did it compare the results with insights from existing literature in the field, the reviewer complained. Most of the books followed roughly the same pattern, devoting a chapter to each theme in the survey and commenting on descriptive tables. More sophisticated statistical techniques were rarely applied, and scarce information about data collection and analysis procedures made the results and claims hard to access.

Despite their apparently objective style, the books were written with the purpose of convening specific views on values and on the relationship between European values and social institutions. Throughout the books, the authors grappled to understand the position of religious institutions and relationships between attitudes toward, for example, the Ten Commandments and attempts to outline how these insights could be useful for the Church. In this way, the fundamental purpose was clearly linked to the position of the authors. The insights from the surveys were to be used by the Church, and theologians were given the role of writing introductions, wrapping up, and writing concluding chapters and thus providing the analytical conceptualization, the moral judgment, and the practical direction that could be deduced from more descriptive parts. Likewise, in Noelle-Neumann's *Die verletzte Nation*, a national conservative worldview was implicitly promoted via the argument that the Germans' lack of national pride was a social concern born from the loss of World War II. It further argued that German nationalism would not be a problem, since the majority of Germans alive in 1933 did not express pride in, or identify with, the Nazi regime when asked in a 1985 social survey (Noelle-Neumann 1988, 47, 390–93). Hence, reading through the books coming out of the EVS, it is clear that the authors' intention was not only to describe or analyze European values but also, maybe even more importantly, to construct European values and provide a social scientific analysis of them in accordance with specific political and religious principles of vision and division.

Among the participants in the EVS, the survey was seen as a success. The survey had accumulated a huge amount of data and resulted in more than a handful of books. However, looking at the surveys from the perspective of a survey methodologist, comparative sociologist, or political scientist in the mid-1980s, the enterprise looked very much like a marketing or public opinion polling project strongly guided by specific societal concerns and marked by empiricist practices.

Foregrounding Academic Properties: The EVS in the
1990s and 2000s

The EVS was the product of a number of different interests, and its trajectory was still not clear after the first wave. Was this primarily a survey driven by specific political and religious concerns with the intent to inform politics and shape public opinion? Or was it an academic enterprise guided by methodological standards and theoretical questions developed in the academic realm? As a participant in the two first rounds told me, "There was some confusion about what kind of creature the EVS was and who should look after the first wave. Ruud de Moor raised his hand and agreed to take it on. There was not really any competition over who wanted to take responsibility. . . . There were a few researchers from Tilburg, who . . . had the quantitative capability."[5] Placing the EVS in a university department defined the survey's trajectory. Despite the critique of its quality and the curious entanglement of interests and institutions involved, the survey still seems to be an attractive enterprise for survey methodologists due to its large scale and transnational character. And over the following thirty years, the EVS changed from being a survey guided primarily by political and religious concerns to becoming more of a "data-provider" or research infrastructure that concealed the original configuration of the survey and naturalized the reasons for including specific themes in it. The change was not simple and required changes in all aspects of the survey, from the composition of the questionnaire and sampling methods to the organization, funding, and social makeup of the EVS and the way the results were published (Kropp 2017). It also required a reconstruction of the data already collected and the social configuration of the survey in order to institutionalize the future use of the data or the symbolic recognition of the survey.

Thus, in the last three decades the EVS has put much work into "improving" the technical aspects of the survey. Looking at how the EVS changed its approach to sampling as well as at the survey's theoretical underpinning and data documentation, illustrates this point. The first survey relied on different national data collection practices with little documentation. It was not until the late 1990s that the huge heterogeneity and sparse documentation of the methods used became an issue and threatened to destabilize the EVS as a reliable source of comparative longitudinal data. Similarly, it became necessary for the EVS researchers to construct theoretical justifications for the survey and the specific items in it. One first step in this process is obvious when comparing the 1994 book reporting on the 1990 surveys with the books that came out of the 1981 survey. Unlike with the first books, the authors devoted the first two chapters of the 1994 book (*The Individualizing Society: Value Change in Europe and North America*) to establishing a common theoretical framework—ending up with four hypotheses—and to methodological operationalization of values and cross-national comparison (Ester, Halman, and de Moor 1994). Here the editors spelled out the legacy from modernization theory more explicitly than in any former publication. In the first sentence of the book they write: "One of the central hypotheses of this book is that as countries advance economically, the values of their population increasingly shift in the direction of individualization" (Ester, Halman, and de Moor 1994, 1). As the third survey was being prepared, this development was strengthened by the establishment of a working group tasked with accounting for the theoretical underpinnings of the survey, not least the different scales and items of the questionnaire. Efforts to ensure the symbolic recognition of the surveys had to be clearly displayed in order to fulfill its purpose, and in the 1990s the EVS started documenting all aspects of the survey. Working together with GESIS, researchers worked on documenting and accounting not only for the 1999 and 2008 surveys but also for the two earlier surveys in order to "enhance" the data and uphold the EVS as a high-quality cross-national longitudinal survey. Changes in the technical practices of the EVS were closely interrelated with social or organizational changes. Whereas institutions and agents from outside the academic field or in intermediary positions dominated the first surveys, during the 1990s the EVS began to recruit university researchers and especially survey methodologists, shifting its orientation toward a more scientific audience and evaluation criteria.

Despite the reconfiguration of the survey toward a more academic, "disentangled" position, the EVS maintained its historical relations to conservative political parties and the Catholic Church. Hence, national surveys were funded through Catholic Church organizations, especially in Eastern Europe. And in the 2003 book that presented results from the 1999 survey, three "eminent Europeans" presented their views on European values. The three Europeans in question were the Archbishop of Mechelen-Brussels, Godfried Daneels; a former Christian Democratic prime minister of the Netherlands, Ruud Lubbers; and a former CEO of RABO Bank, Herman Wijffels (Arts, Hagenaars, and Halman 2003).

Conclusion

The history of the EVS is a story of both change and continuity and of how social science instruments conceived as objective and neutral are deeply entangled with political, religious, and social concerns and institutions. As I have shown, the EVS is a very different academic enterprise today than it was forty years ago. Looking at the organization, we find university professors who publish academic books and articles and are engaged in "ordinary academic work," but no agents who replicate the position of a Noelle-Neumann or Rabier mediating between business, politics, and the social sciences. On the other hand, just by looking through publications from the official EVS series at Brill, the links to the Catholic Church and to Christian Democratic parties are clearly visible.

In the social sciences, the social survey and other quantitative methods are often presented as neutral measures disentangled from political and social engagement. This chapter tells a different story. It shows that surveys such as the EVS are constructed at the intersection of political and scientific interests. More concretely, the EVS came out of a configuration of conservative and Catholic-minded scholars who were concerned with social changes in the postwar arena and who commanded powerful institutions that enabled them to carry out a large-scale survey. The agents setting up the EVS brought to the survey not only specific political and religious worldviews but also an empiricist form of social science in which theoretical concepts and approaches were little used. The survey hence brought together a conservative and Catholic skepticism toward the social sciences and sociological theorizing, and demand-driven, short-sighted practices from public opinion polling. In the following thirty years, the EVS strove hard to reconfigure the survey, toning down its political orientations and turning it into a more academic configuration, thereby naturalizing its categories and concepts as the dominant approach to the study of European values.

This chapter analyzes a particular social survey that has become a reference point in European social survey milieus, one that constitutes a source widely used by numerous social scientists and serves as an infrastructure for international collaboration in European social science. And in addition to telling the story of the EVS and bringing to the forefront the curious historical conditions and currents that shaped it, my historical analysis serves another purpose. By laying out the historical configuration that shaped the EVS, the way it constructs European values, and how it was used to promote specific Catholic and conservative worldviews, the chapter invites us to critically analyze the use of consecrated transnational social scientific instruments (see also Morcillo Laiz and Pérez in this volume for discussions about the relationship between the content and social organization of social scientific knowledge production, politics, and funding). Only through such analyses are we as a scholarly community able to engage in qualified discussions about social scientific quality criteria and about the role of social science knowledge production and its relationship to other powerful social forces. The question is how the increasing international circulation of social science contributes to the naturalization, omission, and consecration of the political origins of ideas, concepts, and techniques.

Notes

1 Interview by the author with participant in EVS two, first round (November 26, 2012).
2 Interview by author with member of the steering committee in Tilburg (October 2012).
3 In the last thirty years Noelle-Neumann's Nazi past has been debated among critical scholars, herself, and her protégés (Becker 2013; Kepplinger 1997; Meyen 2010; Noelle-Neumann 2006; Simpson 1996; Wendelin and Meyen 2009). The debates first took off after her Nazi past was revealed prior to her stint as a visiting professor at the University of Chicago. As always in the history of social science, it is hard to establish the connection between lived experience, point of views held earlier, and later work. But without strong accusation it seems quite clear that throughout her career she was an opportunist with a strong conservative bent and a well-developed tendency to utilize her political connections for her own benefit.
4 Interview by the author with member of EVS methodology group from the 1990s (October 2012).
5 Interview by author with participants of the two first rounds (November 2012).

References

Abrams, Mark, David Gerard, and Noel Timms, eds. 1985. *Values and Social Change in Britain: Studies in the Contemporary Values of Modern Society*. Basingstoke, UK: Macmillan, in association with the European Value Systems Study Group.

Aldrin, Philippe. 2010. "From Instrument to Instrumentalisation of 'European Opinion': A Historical Sociology of the Measurement of Opinions and the Management of the Public Space." In *A Political Sociology of the European Union: Reassessing Constructivism*, edited by Jay Rowell and Michel Mangenot, 206–24. Manchester: Manchester University Press.

Arts, Wil, Jacques A. Hagenaars, and Loek Halman. 2003. *The Cultural Diversity of European Unity*. Leiden: Brill.

Arts, Wil, and Loek Halman. 2014. "Cross-National Values in Europe Today: Facts and Explanations." In *Value Contrasts and Consensus in Present-Day Europe*, edited by Wilhelmus Antonius Arts and Loek Halman, 1–18. Leiden: Brill.

Becker, Jörg. 2013. *Elisabeth Noelle-Neumann: Demoskopin zwischen NS-Ideologie und Konservatismus*. Paderborn: F. Schöningh.

Bourdieu, Pierre. 1988. *Homo Academicus*. Cambridge: Polity Press.

Bourdieu, Pierre. 1991. *The Political Ontology of Martin Heidegger*. Stanford, CA: Stanford University Press.

Bourdieu, Pierre. 2000. *Pascalian Meditations*. Cambridge: Polity Press.

Bourdieu, Pierre. 2015. *On the State: Lectures at the Collège de France, 1989–1992*. Oxford: Polity Press.

Bréchon, Pierre. 2012. "A Breakthrough in Comparative Social Research: The ISSP Compared with the Eurobarometer, EVS and ESS Surveys." In *The International Social Survey Program*, edited by Max Haller, Roger Jowell, and Tom W. Smith. London: Routledge.

Desrosières, Alain. 1998. *The Politics of Large Numbers*. Cambridge, MA: Harvard University Press.

Ester, Peter, Loek Halman, and Ruud de Moor, eds. 1994. *The Individualizing Society: Value Change in Europe and North America*. 2nd ed. Tilburg: Tilburg University Press.

Gerard, Emmanuel, and Kaat Wils. 1999. "Catholics and Sociology in Leuven from Desire Mercier to Jacques Laclercq: A Process of Appropriation." In *Sociology and Religions: An Ambiguous Relationship*, edited by Liliane Voyé and Jaak Billiet, 38–56. KADOC-Studies 23. Leuven: Leuven University Press.

Gilman, Nils. 2003. *Mandarins of the Future: Modernization Theory in Cold War America*. New Studies in American Intellectual and Cultural History. Baltimore, MD: Johns Hopkins University Press.

Harding, Stephen D. 1986. *Contrasting Values in Western Europe: Unity, Diversity and Change*. Basingstoke, UK: Macmillan in association with the European Value Systems Study Group.

Heath, Anthony, Stephen Fisher, and Shawna Smith. 2005. "The Globalization of Public Opinion Research." *Annual Review of Political Science* 8, no. 1: 297–333. https://doi.org/10.1146/annurev.polisci.8.090203.103000.

Heilbron, Johan. 2015. *French Sociology*. Ithaca, NY: Cornell University Press.

Heilbron, Johan, Nicolas Guilhot, and Laurent Jeanpierre. 2008. "Toward a Transnational History of the Social Sciences." *Journal of the History of the Behavioral Sciences* 44, no. 2: 146–60. https://doi.org/10.1002/jhbs.20302.

Husbands, Christopher T. 1985. Review of *Les valeurs du Temps present: Une enquête européenne*, by Jean Stoetzel. *European Sociological Review* 1, no. 1: 88–89.

Inglehart, Ronald. 1971. "The Silent Revolution in Europe: Intergenerational Change in Post-industrial Societies." *American Political Science Review* 65, no. 4: 991–1017. https://doi.org/10.2307/1953494.

Inglehart, Ronald. 1977. *The Silent Revolution: Changing Values and Political Styles among Western Publics*. Princeton, NJ: Princeton University Press.

Kepplinger, Hans Mathias. 1997. "Political Correctness and Academic Principles: A Reply to Simpson." *Journal of Communication* 47, no. 4: 102–17. https://doi.org/10.1111/j.1460-2466.1997.tb02728.x.

Kerkhofs, Jan. 1991. "Values and the Challenging of Europe's Identity." In *Eurobarometer: The Dynamics of European Public Opinion; Essays in Honour of Jacques-René Rabier*, edited by Karlheinz Reif and Ronald Inglehart, 377–84. Basingstoke, UK: Macmillan.

Knöbl, Wolfgang. 2003. "Theories That Won't Pass Away: The Never-Ending Story of Modernization Theory." In *Handbook of Historical Sociology*, edited by Gerard Delanty and Engin F. Isin, 96–107. London: Sage Publications Ltd. https://doi.org/10.4135/9781848608238.

Kropp, Kristoffer. 2017. "The Cases of the European Values Study and the European Social Survey–European Constellations of Social Science Knowledge Production." *Serendipities* 2, no. 1: 50–68.

Kruke, Anja. 2007. *Demoskopie in der Bundesrepublik Deutschland: Meinungsforschung, Parteien und Medien 1949–1990*. Beiträge zur Geschichte des Parlamentarismus und der politischen Parteien arteienhen, Bd. 149. Düsseldorf: Droste.

Meyen, Michael. 2010. "Noelle-Neumann, Elisabeth." In *The International Encyclopedia of Communication*. Hoboken, NJ: John Wiley and Sons. https://doi.org/10.1002/9781405186407.wbiecn042.

Noelle-Neumann, Elisabeth. 1984. *The Spiral of Silence: Public Opinion, Our Social Skin*. Chicago: University of Chicago Press.

Noelle-Neumann, Elisabeth. 1988. *Die verletzte Nation: Über den Versuch der Deutschen, ihren Charakter zu ändern*. 2 vols. Stuttgart: Deutsche Verlags-Anstalt.

Noelle-Neumann, Elisabeth. 2006. *Die Erinnerungen*. München: Herbig.

Porter, Theodore M. 1995. *Trust in Numbers: The Pursuit of Objectivity in Science and Public Life*. Princeton, NJ: Princeton University Press.

Rosental, Paul-André. 2006. "Jean Stoetzel, Demography and Public Opinion: For the Sixtieth Anniversary of *Population* 61 (1): 29–40.

Savage, Michael. 2010. *Identities and Social Change in Britain since 1940: The Politics of Method*. Oxford: Oxford University Press.

Simpson, Christopher. 1996. "Elisabeth Noelle-Neumann's 'Spiral of Silence' and the Historical Context of Communication Theory." *Journal of Communication* 46, no. 3: 149–71. https://doi.org/10.1111/j.1460-2466.1996.tb01494.x.

Smith, Tom W. 2012. "The ISSP: History, Organization and Members: Working Principles and Outcomes" In *The International Social Survey Program*, edited by Max Haller, Roger Jowell, and Tom W. Smith, 2–27. London: Routledge.

Steinmetz, George. 2005. "Scientific Authority and the Transition to Post-Fordism: The Plausibility of Positivism in U.S. Sociology since 1945." In *The Politics of Method in the Human Sciences*, edited by George Steinmetz, 275–323. Durham, NC: Duke University Press.

Steinmetz, George. 2007. "American Sociology before and after the World War I." In *Sociology in America: A History*, edited by Craig Calhoun, 314–66. Chicago: The University of Chicago Press.

Stoetzel, Jean. 1983. *Les valeurs du temps présent: Une enquête européenne*. Paris: Presses universitaires de France.

Tollebeek, Jo, and Liesbet Nys. 2006. *The City on the Hill: A History of Leuven University, 1968–2005*. Leuven University Press.

van de Kaa, Dirk J. 2003. "Levensbericht R.A. de Moor." In *Levensberichten en Herdenkingen*, 39–48. Amsterdam: Huygens Institute—Royal Netherlands Academy of Arts and Sciences (KNAW).

Vanderstraeten, Raf, and Kaat Louckx. 2017. *Sociology in Belgium: A Sociological History*. Berlin: Springer.

Wendelin, Manuel, and Michael Meyen. 2009. "Habermas vs. Noelle-Neumann." *Javnost—The Public* 16, no. 2: 25–40. https://doi.org/10.1080/13183222.2009.11009002.

Wright, James D., and Peter V. Marsden. 2010. "Survey Research and Social Sciences: History, Current Practice, and Future Prospects." In *Handbook of Survey Research*, edited by James D. Wright and Peter V. Marsden, 3–26. Bingley: Emerald.

10

making sense of globalizing social science

JOHAN HEILBRON

THE DEBATE ABOUT "global" or "world" social science, however important it is, has suffered from serious shortcomings. Like much of the broader literature on "globalization," it has been overly general and insufficiently grounded in historical, empirical, and comparative studies. Part of it, furthermore, has been ideologically driven. "Globalization" became a catchword of the neoliberal agenda that has ruled much of the policy-making in the West since the 1980s. But whatever the limitations and biases of the discourses on "globalization," the term also designates realities that cannot be ignored. In its most elementary meaning, globalization refers to processes of trans- or internationalization that take place on a world scale, involving relations between people and institutions from all continents.

With regard to the social sciences, these processes raise institutional as well as intellectual questions, the former related to organizational arrangements (journals, associations, conferences, funding), the latter to issues of overcoming "methodological nationalism" and Euro- and Western-centrism. Fundamentally concerned with the unequal international distribution of resources, the institutional questions are similar across the entire spectrum of the sciences and humanities; the intellectual issues, however, are not. Unlike elementary particles or chemical compounds, the objects of the social and human sciences change over time and vary greatly across space, and studying these objects is a more context-dependent endeavor as well. Objectifying, dissecting, and overcoming ethnocentric biases is therefore an essential component of inquiring into the global condition of the social and human sciences.[1]

A preliminary way to clarify the debate is by acknowledging the process character of the issues raised. Rather than discussing "global" social science statically, as a presumed state of affairs, the questions pertain to historical trends and tendencies, and the categories and approaches to address them are themselves historical products. "Global" and "globalizing" social science, for example, are recent expressions. Some of the terms for designating global connections have been around for a considerable length of time, but the vocabulary of "globalization" spread only during the 1990s, rapidly becoming a "global" debate itself (Lecler 2013, 7–29).

Leaving the general debate on globalization aside, in this chapter I will focus more specifically on the global dimension of the social sciences. Since processes on a global level have existed for some time, and science is itself often seen as intrinsically international, the first question concerns the historical background of the current debate. Is what is termed "globalization" something historically new, is it old wine in new bottles, or is it perhaps not radically, but relatively new? After arguing for the latter position, that "globalization" can be seen as a new stage in a historical process that is itself much older, I will discuss some empirical evidence of globalizing trends. Synthesizing work on contemporary developments, I will argue that globalizing tendencies have been quite limited; social scientists today probably find themselves in a very early stage of what may develop into a truly global social science.

For studying these processes a *field-theoretical approach* offers a fruitful theoretical framework. Rooted in a structural understanding of social differentiation, field theory avoids the pitfalls of homogenizing systemic approaches (world systems theory, Marxism, some forms of institutionalism) without lapsing into merely interactionist accounts of local transfers, which tend to ignore the structural constraints under which these occur.[2] If a *core-periphery* model seems an appropriate conceptualization of the patterns that the globalizing field of the social sciences displays, I will also argue that both field theory and core-periphery models cannot simply be applied to issues of globalization but are in need of substantive elaborations and refinements.[3]

A proper understanding of the globalizing field of the social sciences, finally, implies sustained attention to the heterogeneity as well as to the structural limitations of the process. Globalization, as I argue in the third section, is a conflictual process that plays out quite differently according to discipline and country. In addition to variations and internal contradictions, globalization is limited by structural factors that relate to the international power relations between nation-states. Both the heterogeneity and the limitations of globalizing processes, I maintain, have important theoretical implications. In the concluding section I propose a series of historical, empirical, and theoretical conclusions; some pertain specifically to the social sciences, while others have a more general meaning for theorizing about processes of transnationalization.

Historicizing "Global" Social Science

Any account of the social sciences at the global level should start with the observation that—contrary to Eurocentric visions of science and scholarship—a plurality of centers of higher learning has existed since at least antiquity. World historians have reminded us that only exceptionally and for short time spans have there been periods without significant circulation of people and ideas across the boundaries of cultures and societies. Migration and mobility, transfer and exchange—forced as well as voluntary—have been the rule in human history, not the exception. Very few of the earlier processes of circulation, however, were truly global.

According to Immanuel Wallerstein, systematic global connections emerged during the long sixteenth century with the development of long-distance trade and capitalist accumulation on a world scale (Wallerstein 2004). Although the "modern world-system" has been said to originate in this movement of European expansion, scholarly transfers had a more limited geographical reach. The early modern Republic of Letters, for example, represented a translocal universe of considerable geographical scope, characterized by high rates of mobility and exchange over long distances, while remaining—despite connections across the Mediterranean and the Atlantic—a primarily European phenomenon, not a *world* Republic of Letters.[4]

With the national and international expansion of competing nation-states and empires, furthermore, the European Republic of Letters disintegrated. The use of Latin declined and national institutions of higher learning came to the fore. The Royal Society (1660) and French national academies published their proceedings in the vernacular becoming leading institutions in what is conventionally described as the Scientific Revolution. From the late eighteenth and early nineteenth centuries onward, national academic systems replaced medieval universities and overshadowed the academies and other learned societies that began in the Renaissance.

The nationalization of higher learning and the uneven development of capitalism point to a problematic aspect of world systems theory. In these *systemic accounts* scholarly institutions and practices tend to be treated as a function of the system as a whole, in this case of the *geoculture* of the modern world system (Wallerstein 2004). Scholarly institutions, however, are not merely derivative of economic or political structures, and they do not simply *reflect* capitalist relations of production or state politics; rather, in Bourdieu's terms they constitute relatively autonomous social spaces that *refract* external forces according to their degree of autonomy and their specific dynamics (for the basic idea of fields, see Bourdieu and Wacquant 1992, 94–114; Sapiro 2015).

Analyzing transnational circulation on a global scale from a field perspective implies raising the question not only of cross-border transfers (Bourdieu 1991) but also, more generally, of the formation and functioning of a *global field*—that is, of a relatively autonomous social space with a specific stake and particular resources and institutions, related to, and in some cases built on, a variety of national social scientific fields (Bourdieu [2000] 2005, 223–32; Heilbron 2014). Such a perspective differs not only from systemic approaches, which tend to underestimate the relative autonomy of scholarly worlds and practices, but also from accounts that focus on localized transfers while abstracting from the structural conditions under which these transfers take place.

Organized social science in the West emerged historically within national systems of higher learning, initially in the form of national academies and other national scholarly associations, and somewhat later within national university systems. The institutionalization of the social sciences in national academic systems, which was related to expanding nation-states, was from the start accompanied by new modes of cross-border exchange. In addition to the older forms of circulation—correspondence, translation, travel, and migration—*international organizations* became the predominant institutional framework. Created or supported by national states, international organizations have since the mid-nineteenth century been the locus of a widening range of "international conferences" and "international" institutes and associations (Boli and Thomas 1999; Drori et al. 2003; Sluga and Clavin 2017). Conceived to bridge the cleavages between national academic systems, these forms of organized exchange and cooperation across national borders regulated and controlled transnational flows of knowledge (for a brief outline see Heilbron 2014). In this respect the development of the social sciences does not appear to be fundamentally different from that of the natural sciences.

Even in a well-established and purely formal discipline like mathematics, the institutional pattern is similar: the first disciplinary journals were national periodicals established in France and in Germany during the first half of the nineteenth century; *Acta Mathematica* (1882) was the first truly international journal, regular international congresses of mathematicians have been held since 1897, and the International Mathematical Union was established in 1920, dissolved in 1932 during a period of boycotts and counter-boycotts following World War I, and successfully reestablished in 1950 (Parshall and Rice 2002).

Against the background of this double process of the nationalization of teaching and research, on the one hand, and the formation of international disciplinary organizations, on the other, "globalization" could be seen as a relatively new phase in this long-term development. Patterns of international circulation in the second half of the twentieth century have gradually become more global in scope.[5] The initial impetus came from decolonization, which, among others, provoked a critique of Western social science and its Eurocentric biases while simultaneously promoting the search for alternative, "Indigenous" intellectual sources and traditions. Although the debates about the dominance of Western social science affected all social and human sciences, they were most vivid in anthropology (Asad 1973), which had been a colonial science, and, in the humanities, notably with Edward Said's *Orientalism* (1978) and its impact on postcolonial studies.[6]

During the 1990s, two major changes reinforced the breakdown of the international order as it had existed. The collapse of socialist regimes in the East and the rapid development of new communication technology (the World Wide Web in combination with the personal computer) formed the background of the terminological shift that can be observed from the *international* to the *global*. The older vocabulary of *international* exchange and cooperation, which had been promoted by and was associated with international organizations, was challenged by the slightly different idiom of the *transnational* and the *global*. The "international" order, which was routinely divided into three "worlds" (the First, Second, and Third Worlds), gave way to what was described and promoted as a more "global" constellation, in which the partition into three separate "worlds" didn't make sense anymore. Many international organizations, which had been the primary locus of "international" exchange and collaboration, reframed their mission.

UNESCO, which had been a key player in the process of internationalization, is a case in point. After 1945, UNESCO initiated and funded new, "international" associations in all major social science disciplines: the International Sociological Association (1948), International Political Science Association

(1948), the International Economic Association (1950). Similar to their nineteenth- and early twentieth-century predecessors, these organizations were restricted to a small elite from a limited number of Western countries. Over time, however, their membership not only increased, it also changed: through the inclusion of individual members, not merely official organizations, and through "research committees" international associations became less concerned with scholarly diplomacy and more with actual research. Proportionally Western Europe and North America still dominate membership, but the International Sociological Association (ISA) currently has members from 150 countries, the International Political Science Association (IPSA) from more than 100 countries (Boncourt 2018).

Typical for the shifting vocabulary from the "international" to the "global" is that UNESCO in 1999 started with the production of "world reports," two of which explicitly dealt with the social sciences at the global level (UNESCO 1999, 2010). In these reports the language of "global" or "world social science" refers to set of interconnected changes. As compared to the international order of the first decades after World War II, the social sciences are currently practiced in almost all countries and regions of the world. Aside from their global presence, the institutional structures are quite similar: they include the main social science disciplines (anthropology, political science, economics, sociology) that are practiced in comparable organizational settings (university departments, scholarly journals, professional associations). Traditionally centered on Europe and North America, international associations increased and geographically diversified their membership, in some cases actively pursuing a "global" agenda, as was the case of the International Sociological Association under the presidency of Immanuel Wallerstein (1998–2002) and Michael Burawoy (2014–18). Transnational exchange became more frequent and more significant in all regions, with English as the lingua franca of international social science (De Swaan 2001a, 2001b; Lillis and Curry 2010).

Since the trend toward more "global" arrangements indicates a historical change of considerable importance, prophets of "globalization" argued that the prevalence of globalizing forces would represent a new era. After the fall of the Berlin Wall in 1989 and the collapse of socialist regimes, a triumphalist political discourse spread in which the market economy and Western democracy would have definitively won the Cold War, inaugurating the "end of history" (Fukuyama 1992). The web of transnational exchange and new communication technology had not only become global, this interconnected world was also becoming "flat," as Thomas Friedman (2005) stated. Power relations and hierarchies between states and countries were dissolving into global flows of communication and worldwide exchanges on global markets. This ideology of "globalization," which became the official doctrine of organizations like the Work Bank and the International Monetary Fund (IMF), had a critical yet symmetric counterpart. In this view globalizing forces were depicted as no less far-reaching and transformative, albeit not in a liberating but in a destructive sense, threatening to dissolve the most valuable institutions in a state of liquidity and global insecurity, as Zygmunt Bauman (2000) has argued.

A Core-Periphery Structure

If one confronts these highly general views of globalization with the realities of transnational circulation, it is apparent that globalizing processes possess a structure that is neither one of *generalized liquidity*, as Bauman suggested, nor that of a *flattening universe*, as Friedman imagined. Emerging global structures are in all fields, first and foremost, characterized by uneven and hierarchical power relations, which can be conceived of as a *core-periphery structure*.

A first approximation of this global configuration can be obtained by considering basic indicators about the geographical distribution of the social science production. According to large databases such as the Social Science Citation Index (SSCI), the production of social science articles worldwide is still very much concentrated in North America and Europe. Over the past three decades, there has been a general increase in the article production worldwide, but growth was strongest in Europe, and together North America and Europe still produce roughly three-quarters of the registered articles— hardly less than thirty years earlier. Production in Asian countries has expanded, but it remains small as compared to North America and Europe (Gingras and Mosbah-Natanson 2010; Mosbah-Natanson and Gingras 2014). In addition to the production of articles, the geographical distribution of journals and their publishers has not changed dramatically either. Currently nine out of ten articles published in the journals included in the most widely used social science databases (Ulrich, SSCI) are in English. Of the journals registered in the Social Science Citation Index (SSCI), about two-thirds are published in four countries (the United States, the United Kingdom, Germany, the Netherlands). So there was and still is a massive concentration of the social science production in Western and especially in Anglo-American countries (Mosbah-Natanson and Gingras 2014).

The data and databases, however, cannot be taken for granted, as they are themselves an integral part of the structure they pretend to describe. What is represented as "global," and what is conversely classified as being merely "local" or "national," is itself part of the process. The most widely used databases do not simply register what is going on; they select according to specific principles, and the result of these selections shapes the reality that is registered, because the data and their interpretations are used in the strategies of various actors. Since representations of the social sciences based on the SSCI are biased in favor of English-language journals (journals in German, Spanish, and French are underrepresented, let alone journals in other languages), the dominant representation of the international article production referred to earlier is a representation that is itself produced in the dominant center. And there are no counter-images readily available, because there is no alternative database that is comparable to the SSCI in the information it contains.[7]

The biases of these databases, however, do not exclude a rational use of them, because as long as the selection bias has not changed dramatically over time, the data can provide a reasonably accurate indication of the changes that have occurred within the limited set of selected journals. Although the article production per country is obviously a crude indicator, various other bibliometric studies have also shown that social science disciplines have spread to many more countries and regions, but that beyond their global presence and general growth, globalization of research has mostly favored the already dominant regions of North America and Europe. Citation analysis, for example, shows that by becoming more integrated into global exchanges, the autonomy of non-Western regions has diminished, and their dependence on the dominant centers has increased.[8]

If, in addition to the distribution of articles, journals, and citations, prestige is taken into account, the global distribution becomes even more skewed. Among the approximately eighty laureates of the prize for the economic sciences of the Swedish central bank in honor of Alfred Nobel, only one, Amartya Sen, was born outside the Western Hemisphere, and his career has been largely in Western institutions. The most cited social scientists, more generally, are virtually all trained at, and affiliated with, elite institutions in the global North (Heilbron 2014). In communication studies, for example, it is almost impossible for scholars from the global South to gain international recognition without academic and social capital acquired in the global North (Demeter 2019). Leading scholars in postcolonial and subaltern studies like Said or Spivak are no exceptions (Brisson 2018).

If the social sciences can be said to form an *emerging global field*, including more countries and regions than before, it continues to be dominated by Western countries, their institutions and practitioners. The global constellation can, more specifically, be said to display a *duopolistic core*, consisting of North American and a number of West European countries, with a variety of semi-central or semi-peripheral countries, and multiple peripheral countries (Heilbron and Gingras 2018). Most countries occupy a peripheral or dominated position in the sense that they have a minor share in the most legitimate social science production worldwide, and an even smaller part in terms of recognition and prestige.

One way to specify the dynamics of this global structure is to consider transnational authorship. In 1980, only 4 percent of the SSCI articles were transnationally coauthored; that figure had gone up to 21 percent by 2014, indicating a marked growth of transnational collaboration (Heilbron and Gingras 2018). This trend is stronger in the social sciences than in the humanities (where the level of transnational coauthorship was a little over 5 percent in 2014), but lower than in the natural sciences. In terms of transnational collaboration, the social sciences occupy an intermediary position between the natural sciences and the humanities (Gingras 2002). In this sense and in others, the social sciences form a third culture (Lepenies 1988).

A closer look at the networks of transnational coauthorship confirms the existence of a Euro-US core, which has by far the largest number of transnational connections and which is closely linked to Canada, Australia, and other English-speaking countries. The cluster of Asian countries represents a smaller number of ties, occupying a semicentral or semiperipheral position, one that is probably comparable to that of some Latin American countries. Most countries, however, are peripheral in the sense that they have relatively few transnational links, most often only to the center and rarely to other countries. This is indeed a typical property of a core-periphery structure: the periphery depends on the center, even for links to other (semi)peripheries.

The development of coauthorship shows that although the proportion of transnationally coauthored articles has increased, the relative weight of countries and regions within these networks has not fundamentally changed. During the years 2006–14, two-thirds of the links in the global network of coauthorships were between Europe and North America. The position of the United States has slightly declined, but mainly in favor of other English-speaking countries (Australia, New Zealand, South Africa). China is the only country from the periphery that has clearly improved its position. It was virtually absent in 1980 and currently represents about 5 percent of the coauthored articles of European authors (Heilbron and Gingras 2018). In spite of these changes, the structure of the network of coauthorships has remained relatively stable since 1980.

From this brief summary it can be concluded that while a *globalizing* field of transnational relations of collaboration and exchange seems to be emerging, in which more researchers from more countries participate, there is no evidence that this "globalizing" tendency would have radically altered the power relations between countries and regions. Rather than consisting of unconstrained liquid flows of people and ideas on a global scale, or of a multiplicity of disparate, diverse, and highly flexible networks, the structure of this globalizing field is more accurately defined as a core-periphery structure. This enduring structure is based on unevenly distributed resources—that is, on the unequal volume of collective academic and scientific capital that countries have historically accumulated and that are obviously related to other global disparities.

But this core-periphery characteristic is only a first approximation; it needs to be specified and refined. First, the "core" itself is not a homogeneous unit, as terms like "the West" or "the global North" suggest, but a set of partly competitive and potentially conflictual relations among Western institutions and countries. According to the same database, the SSCI, the level of transnational authorship, for example, varies significantly among the dominant countries. US researchers are much less inclined to enter transnational coauthorships than their European counterparts are, and over time the difference has increased (Heilbron and Gingras 2018). This finding illustrates a general characteristic of internationally dominant powers: the more central or dominant their position in international scholarly or cultural relations, the higher the level of self-centeredness, and the lower the level of transnational orientation and cultural import (Heilbron 1999, 2002). This self-centeredness that is induced by international domination produces various types of ethnocentric biases. In the hegemonic center, there is a relatively strong neglect of other parts of the world, and if "foreign" cultures or societies are taken into account they tend to be perceived and understood according to American interests, categories, and norms. This typically happens without acknowledgment or questioning. Given the power and privilege of American social science, it is indeed easy "to imagine the world in American terms" (Kennedy and Centeno 2007, 668; Stevens, Miller-Idriss, and Shami 2018).

Euro-American relations have other intellectual components as well. Related to distinct intellectual traditions, these differences are not restricted to differentiations within the core but play out on a global scale as well. In Argentina, for example, and in Asian countries like Japan and Korea, the social sciences in France tend to be perceived as an alternative to North American social science (Sorá and Blanco 2018; Brisson 2018). A somewhat similar phenomenon exists within the United States, where the label "French theory" was invented for theories emanating from a Western yet somewhat exotic and intellectually more adventurous culture, different in any case from the American academic mainstream (Cusset 2008). These differentiations within the core and their *polycentric dynamics*, as it may be called, are an important dimension aspect of global power relations. Instead of essentializing power, Western dominance is located in an international field of power, a differentiated space of relations among the best-endowed institutions and countries.

Outside the core, similar differentiations exist. Countries that occupy a semicentral or, as Wallerstein calls it, a semiperipheral position tend to mediate between core and periphery by fulfilling a brokering role in international relations. They can function as *bridgeheads* of the core within the (semi)periphery, assuring the diffusion of dominant conceptions from the center. But the traffic is not necessarily one-way. In addition to imposition or diffusion from the core, these intermediary zones can be locations of *hybridization*. Under certain conditions they can also develop as *challengers* to the dominant centers. The dependency theories of Latin American scholars are a good example of a case where Western theories of modernization have been successfully challenged (Beigel 2010). One of the preconditions for such innovations is the existence of *peripheral centers*. The expression refers to cities or countries that play a central role in a region that is itself peripheral. Before the 1973 coup d'état in Chile, Santiago was such a peripheral center for the social sciences in Latin America (Beigel 2013).

Transnational Regionalization

Core-periphery relations of the globalizing field of the social sciences, should not only be refined along the lines suggested above; they also have to be analytically distinguished from other modes of internationalization. What is described as "globalization" is in reality often a more restrictive form of internationalization. The most significant other mode of international collaboration and circulation is that of *transnational regionalization*, a process that has been obscured in much of the globalization literature. In most regions of the world, for example, there are now social science research councils. The movement started in the periphery—in Latin America, Africa, and Asia— with, respectively, the Latin American Council of Social Sciences (founded in 1967), the Association of Asian Social Science Research Councils (1973), and the Council for the Development of Social Science Research in Africa (1973). Europe and the Arab countries followed with the European Research

Council (2007) and the Arab Council for the Social Sciences (2008). Regional organizations were usually created to help build national infrastructures, to "catch up" with the centers but also to stimulate countertraditions to Western dominance, as is exemplified by the debates about Arab, Asian, and Latin American traditions in the social sciences (Alatas 2006; Alatas and Sinha-Kerkoff 2010; Hanafi and Arvanitas 2016; Beigel 2013; Sorá and Blanco 2018). As the hegemonic region in the world, North America is typically absent from regional initiatives.

In this regionalization process, Europe is a particular case, because it has gone furthest and is—unlike many other regions—built on well-established national structures. Currently European funding bodies, European associations, and European journals exist in all research areas (Heilbron, Timans, and Boncourt 2017). After initial support from American foundations in the context of the Cold War, funding for European initiatives was taken over by European institutions. Since the 1980s a European Research Policy developed with the aim of strengthening the European economy and improving European competitiveness. With the so-called Lisbon Agenda of 2000, research and innovation became a European priority as Europe proclaimed the ambition of becoming the "most competitive knowledge economy" in the world. One of the consequences of the new policy was the establishment of the European Research Council (2007).

Aside from project-based research funding, more stable European social science institutions were established as well, among them "European" journals (Heilbron, Bedecarré, and Timans 2017). Most are disciplinary and subdisciplinary journals; others are in vocational fields (educational studies, European studies, communication studies) or are policy-related (aging, health, crime, security, etc.). Most troubling in this process of "Europeanization" is the absence of European journals with a clear-cut multidisciplinary and innovative intellectual program. Comparing "European" journals with their French counterparts, for example, it is striking that the most innovative, multidisciplinary French journals have no equivalent at the European level or, for that matter, at the global level. This applies to journals like the celebrated historical journal *Annales-SSH*; the journal *L'Homme*, which Claude Lévi-Strauss founded in 1960 with a linguist and a geographer; and Pierre Bourdieu's *Actes de la recherche en sciences sociales* (1975). Although Bourdieu has become the most cited sociologist in the world, the journal he founded and edited until his death in 2002 is hardly ever cited in the English-language journals that dominate the citation hierarchies. The same absence applies to other French interdisciplinary journals (*Politix, Genèses*). Although all of these periodicals are among the most prestigious ones in France, and there no doubt exist similar outlets in other countries, they are absent on the European and the global level. What circulates most easily across national borders are the best-established, mainstream forms of social science. With the French case in mind, it is no exaggeration to say that what is most needed intellectually has the greatest difficulty in circulating across national and linguistic borders.

As a specific mode of cross-border circulation, globalization thus needs to be distinguished from other forms of internationalization, particularly from transnational regionalization. In scrutinizing the meaning of these processes, variations need to be taken into account across different disciplines. Some disciplines have a pronounced international orientation in terms of references, methods, and other standards, whereas others are more strongly embedded in national contexts and traditions. The same can be said with respect to their openness or closure to other disciplines. Combining these two dimensions, the space of the social and human sciences appears to have a triangular structure. At least in France, disciplines like economics and management are very internationally oriented, referring very frequently to non-French journals, but the most-referenced journals tend to be other journals within economics and management. In other words, a high level of international openness is accompanied by an equally high level of closure with regard to other disciplines. In its reference pattern law tends to be highly monodisciplinary as well but, unlike economics and management, strongly oriented to national journals. Sociology represents the third pole, as it is most open to other disciplines but it too has a strong national orientation (Heilbron and Bokobza 2015; Heilbron and Gingras 2018).

With the global core-periphery structure in mind, the significance of these varying levels of transnational orientation can be assessed in a more precise manner. Although the *level* of transnational orientation varies greatly across disciplines, the *geographical orientation* is very similar. Among the non-French journals cited in France, American journals unambiguously dominate the hierarchy. The international profile of French social science journals is therefore very one-sided. None of the most-cited foreign journals, for instance, are called "international" or "European." None are German, Italian, or Spanish, and only a very small number are British. The reference pattern in French social science journals is, in fact, not international at all, let alone global. With hardly any exception, it is overwhelmingly *binational*, that is, Franco-American; other journals appear only exceptionally among the most-cited foreign journals (Heilbron and Bokobza 2015; Heilbron and Gingras 2018).

The binational orientation suggests that international reference patterns in the social sciences are structured like star networks in which all nodes are connected to the core but few if any relations exist among the periphery. In all countries the predominant international references are to US journals, whereas references to social science journals in other countries tends to be exceptional or nonexistent. The dominant orientation is toward the international center; links with semicentral countries are very infrequent, links with the (semi)periphery inexistent or insignificant. The need to differentiate and refine the core-periphery model—to speak of a duopolistic core, account for patterns of polycentricity, acknowledge hybridization, and reverse movements from the (semi)periphery to the center—should therefore not obscure the fact that on the highest level (most-cited journals, prizes, translations) the hegemony of the United States is overwhelming.

By Way of Conclusion—Eleven Theses

1 Transnational circulation of social science research is comparable to similar processes in the natural sciences in the sense that they are fundamentally dependent on unequally distributed resources, reflecting the cumulative advantage of Western countries. In intellectual terms, however, a significant difference needs to be taken into account. Unlike elementary particles, the objects of social science change over time and vary across borders. Inquiring into the principles of historical change and cross-cultural variation is the proper aim of social science research, not proposing ahistorical, decontextualized, and therefore pseudo-universal models.

2 The historical pattern of transnational circulation in the (social) sciences suggests that the emerging web of global connections may be seen as a relatively new phase in a much longer historical process. Beyond the modes of exchange that existed in the framework of *international organizations*, more global arrangements are based on the expansion of (social) scientific research to virtually all countries and regions of the world and are shaped by significantly higher levels of transnational communication and mobility.

3 Transnational circulation and cross-border mobility on a global scale do not constitute unstructured and unrestrained "liquid" flows of ideas and people, as some theorists of globalization (Bauman, Friedman) have imagined. Nor can they be properly understood as a mere function of a unified and homogeneous capitalist world system. Social science on

the global level is more fruitfully understood as constituting an *emerging global field*, that is, a relatively autonomous social universe with specific stakes, actors, and institutions. The structure of this particular universe is first and foremost determined by the unequal distribution of both material and symbolic resources of the agents and institutions involved.

4 Based on unevenly distributed forms of capital, the globalizing field can be conceived of as a *core-periphery* structure, which needs to be specified empirically and conceptualized beyond its initial formulations. For the social sciences, core-periphery relations can be said to consist of a *duopolistic*, Euro-American core, a variety of semicentral and semiperipheral countries, and a host of peripheral countries. Given that the core itself constitutes a differentiated space, a polycentric dynamics is an important feature of its functioning. As the traditional notion of "diffusion" merely captures one particular mode of cross-cultural transfer, the general process is more adequately captured as *uneven circulation* and *asymmetrical exchange* within global power relations.

Dominated by the core countries, semicentral or semiperipheral zones tend to function as *bridgeheads* of the core within the (semi)periphery, assuring forms of imposition, import, or selective appropriation from the center. They can also, however, be locations of *hybridization* of knowledge. Under certain conditions *peripheral centers* can develop into effective *challengers* to the hegemony of Western social science. In these last cases, *reverse flows* take place from the (semi)periphery to the core.

5 The functioning of this globalizing field is shaped not only by internal struggles but simultaneously by its relations to other levels of social science practice—that is, primarily to national and transnational regional fields. Since these distinct levels have a structure and dynamics of their own and are irreducible to a single mechanism or an all-encompassing system dynamics, a more accurate theoretical account is *multilevel field analysis*. This framework requires assessing the specificities of the various levels, their modes of separation as well as their interdependencies, and should include the *strategies of specialization and switching* that actors employ to deal with the multilevel structure.

6 Within the framework of multilevel field analysis, and unlike the assumptions of unilateral diffusion, a specific social category of *intermediary* actors (gatekeepers, brokers, import–export specialists, and other go-betweens) plays a critical role *between* and *within* these levels. Assessing their significance, which is well documented in reception studies (Sapiro, Santoro, and Baert 2020) and the analysis of cultural and intellectual

transfers (Werner and Zimmerman 2006), requires (a) specifying their particular position within the field structures that define the constraints and opportunities within which they function, and (b) assessing their specific trajectories (exile, migration, membership of cosmopolitan minorities) that predispose them for mediating between different (levels of) fields.

7 Considering transnational fields empirically, globalization in the social sciences has so far been quite limited. A variety of indicators (coauthorship, citations, prizes) shows that the more global presence of the social sciences has reproduced rather than undermined international hierarchies. In theoretical terms, both the transnational regional and the global level tend to be *weak fields* (Topalov 1999; Vauchez 2008). Despite having reached some level of institutionalization, many transnational fields remain structurally dependent on better-established national fields, on the one hand, and on the international hegemony of the United States, on the other.[9]

A rough indication of the relative strength of these levels may be obtained by comparing membership of professional associations. Sociological associations in France and Germany each have about fifteen hundred members, whereas the European association, rather than being much larger in membership, is of similar size. On the global level the disparities are even more telling, because the American Sociological Association (ASA) alone is about three times the size of the International Sociological Association (ISA), the world organization.

8 The mode of international domination of US social science is currently less that of *imperialism*, based on explicitly pursued policies of expansion beyond national borders, than that of *hegemony*, implying symbolic power and varying degrees of submission to global power relations.

9 Due to increasing internationalization, national scholarly fields tend to bifurcate in an internationally oriented elite, possessing transnational forms of academic and social capital, and a primarily nationally embedded elite that is often connected to national policy circuits. The relative weight of both poles and the modes of opposition between them vary across countries and disciplines.

In cases where the social sciences at the national level are weak, internationalization tends to lead to the imposition of internationally dominant models, risking an impoverishment of national knowledge production and a deterioration of public social science. Current evaluation regimes that privilege English-language articles over national publications reinforce such tendencies (Gingras 2016, 2019). In strongly internationally codified disciplines such as economics, the consequence is that in smaller and/or more peripheral countries certain topics are no longer properly researched, because they appear of merely national or local interest. This not only leads to *knowledge deficits*; it can also produce an impoverishment of the public debate and a *democratic deficit*.

In large countries where the social sciences are well established and national elites prevail over more internationally oriented groups, scholarly production can be more or less protected from foreign influences. Actively resisting international models or opposing certain of their features can lead to specific countertraditions as well as to regressive modes of isolation and parochialism.

Instead of imposing a uniform model on the social sciences globally, pretending to follow the universalism of the natural sciences, a more diversified, multilevel, multilingual, and multisupport publication system (favoring not only articles but also books for both peer and public audiences) should be promoted for scholarly as well as civic reasons.

10 Transnationalization through official international organizations tends to reinforce mainstream approaches, favoring standardized research, writing conventions, and publication practices. "European" journals in the social sciences, for example, tend to be restricted to mainstream research, lacking outlets for innovative, multidisciplinary research endeavors that exist in several national contexts but that are largely absent on the transnational level.

11 Innovative approaches in the social sciences develop and circulate less though official organizations, whether national or international, than through partly informal *networks* that are based on elective affinities. Shaped by varying forms of travel, migration, and punctual transfers, they may obtain a certain stability in organizational niches of the academic system. The (trans)national connections and transfers that these networks sustain offer the best chances for the "new combinations" that according to Schumpeter define innovation.

Notes

I would like to thank Louise and John Steffens, members of the Friends Founders' Circle, who assisted my stay at the Princeton Institute for Advanced Study in 2017–18, during which this chapter was written. Elaborating on earlier work (Heilbron 2014; Heilbron, Guilhot, and Jeanpierre 2008;

Heilbron, Timans, and Boncourt 2017; Heilbron, Bedecarré, and Timans 2017; Heilbron, Sorá, and Boncourt 2018; Heilbron, Boncourt, and Timans 2018), the text aims to synthesize the more salient findings and to propose theoretical conclusions that can be drawn from them.

1 Social scientists for whom research is universal "by definition" and who consider social science to have been "global" since its inception because it searches for "universal truths" tend to dismiss notions like Western domination and Eurocentrism as ideological constructs (Sztompka 2011). This particular claim to universalism is justified by distinguishing the "context of discovery" from the "context of justification." As was the case with Popper, the distinction is used to exclude contextual inquiries and avoid questions about their consequences for the knowledge that is produced. But how can the claim to scientific universalism be taken seriously when we are not prepared to confront issues of Eurocentrism and explore other, non-Western traditions of thought (see the debate between Sztompka [2011] and Burawoy [2011])? Much of the critique of Western-centrism and the quest for non-Western traditions is intended not to replace Western social science but to correct and complement it. Rather than rejecting universal aspirations, it objectifies these and opposes universalisms that are, in fact, ethnocentric projections. Much of this work ties in with questions that have been central to the historical and comparative social science traditions since at least Max Weber (an issue I have to leave aside in this chapter due to space limitations).

2 For discussions of field theory in this respect see Bourdieu 1991, [1989] 1999; Buchholz 2016; Dezalay and Garth 1996, 2002; Gingras 2002; Heilbron 2014; Krause 2016; Sapiro 2013, 2015; Steinmetz 2016; and Vauchez 2008.

3 The core-periphery model has been a central feature of world systems theory (Wallerstein 2004), but one can use it very well without subscribing to its systemic assumptions. For various uses of core-periphery models in this domain, see De Swaan 2002; Demeter 2017; Heilbron 1999, 2002, 2014; Keim 2010, 2011; Keim et al. 2014; and Medina 2014.

4 Exchanges of letters during the period of the Enlightenment, for example, were concentrated in the northwestern parts of Europe, branching out to the South, the East, and across the Atlantic, but it was a regional not a global network; see the Stanford project "Mapping the Republic of Letters," accessed July 6, 2022, http://republicofletters.stanford.edu.

5 Many chapters in this volume, especially those in the first two sections, are concerned with how the dialectic of national and international embeddedness has played out in particular research practices and disciplines.

6 In sociology see, for example, recent work by Alatas and Sinha-Kerkoff 2010; Brambra 2014; Connell 2007, 2018; Go 2016; and Steinmetz 2013. For economics see Fourcade 2006.

7 On the issue of indicators of internationalization, bibliometric and otherwise, see Gingras 2016; and Heilbron, Boncourt, et al. 2017.

8　The level of self-citation per region has gone down, whereas references to the production in the international centers has increased. This implies that the social science production in most regions has become more integrated into a hierarchical system, which has *itself* not fundamentally changed (Mosbah-Natanson and Gingras 2014). For an illuminating case study of publication patterns in the periphery, see Beigel 2014.

9　The notion of a "weak field" is not necessarily restricted to "interstitial spaces," as Christian Topalov (1999, 461–74) and Antoine Vauchez (2008) have proposed; it can also be fruitfully used in the framework of a multilevel field analysis, as proposed here.

References

Alatas, Syed Farid. 2006. *Alternative Discourses in Asian Social Science: Responses to Eurocentrism*. New Delhi: Sage.

Alatas, Syed Farid, and Kathinka Sinha-Kerkoff, eds. 2010. *Academic Dependency in the Social Sciences: Structural Reality and Intellectual Challenges*. New Delhi: Manohar.

Asad, Talal, ed. 1973. *Anthropology and the Colonial Encounter*. London: Ithaca Press.

Bauman, Zygmunt. 2000. *Liquid Modernity*. Cambridge: Polity.

Beigel, Fernanda. 2010. "Dependency Analysis: The Creation of a New Social Theory in Latin America." In *The International Handbook of Diverse Sociological Traditions*, edited by Sujata Patel, 189–200. London: Sage.

Beigel, Fernanda, ed. 2013. *The Politics of Academic Autonomy in Latin America*. London: Ashgate.

Beigel, Fernanda. 2014. "Publishing from the Periphery: Structural Heterogeneity and Segmented Circuits; the Evaluation of Scientific Publications for Tenure in Argentina's CONICET." *Current Sociology* 62: 743–65.

Bhambra, Gurminder K. 2014. *Connected Sociologies*. London: Bloomsbury Academic.

Boli, John, and George Thomas, eds. 1999. *Constructing World Culture: International Nongovernmental Organizations since 1875*. Stanford, CA: Stanford University Press.

Boncourt, Thibaud. 2018. "What 'Internationalization' Means in the Social Sciences: A Comparison of the International Political Science and Sociology Associations." In *The Social and Human Sciences in Global Power Relations*, edited by Johan Heilbron, Gustavo Sorá, and Thibaud Boncourt, 95–123. London: Palgrave Macmillan.

Bourdieu, Pierre. (1989) 1999. "The Social Conditions of the International Circulation of Ideas." In *Bourdieu: A Critical Reader*, edited by Richard Shusterman, 220–28. London: Blackwell.

Bourdieu, Pierre. 1991. "Epilogue: On the Possibility of a Field of World Sociology." In *Social Theory for a Changing Society*, edited by P. Bourdieu and James Coleman, 373–87. Boulder, CO: Westview Press/New York: Russell Sage Foundation.

Bourdieu, Pierre. (2000) 2005. *The Social Structures of the Economy*. Cambridge: Polity.

Bourdieu, Pierre, and Loïc Wacquant. 1992. *An Invitation to Reflexive Sociology*. Cambridge: Polity.

Brisson, Thomas. 2018. *Décentrer l'Occident: Les intellectuels postcoloniaux chinois, indiens et arabes, et la critique de la modernité*. Paris: La Découverte.

Buchholz, Larissa. 2016. "What Is a Global Field? Theorizing Fields beyond the Nation-State." In *Fielding Transnationalism*, edited by Julian Go and Monika Krause, 31–60. Sociological Review Monographs. Chichester: John Wiley and Sons.

Burawoy, Michael. 2011. "The Last Positivist." *Contemporary Sociology* 40, no. 4: 396–404.

Connell, Raewyn. 2007. *Southern Theory: The Global Dynamics of Knowledge in Social Science*. London: Allen and Unwin.

Connell, Raewyn. 2018. "Decolonizing Sociology." *Contemporary Sociology* 47, no. 4: 399–407.

Cusset, François. 2008. *French Theory: How Foucault, Derrida, Deleuze, and Co. Transformed the Intellectual Life of the United States*. Minneapolis: University of Minnesota Press.

De Swaan, Abram. 2001a. "English in the Social Sciences." In *The Dominance of English as a Language of Science*, edited by Ulrich Ammon. Berlin: Mouton de Gruyter.

De Swaan, Abram. 2001b. *Words of the World*. Cambridge: Polity.

De Swaan, Abram. 2002. "The Sociological Study of Transnational Society." In *Conflict in a Globalising World: Studies in Honour of Peter Kloos*, edited by Dick Kooiman, Adrianus Koster, Peer Smeets, and Bernhard Venema, 19–33. Assen: Royal Van Gorcum.

Demeter, Marton. 2017. "The Core-Periphery Problem in Communication Research: A Network Analysis of Leading Publications." *Publishing Research Quarterly* 33, no. 4: 402–21.

Demeter, Marton. 2019. "So Far, Yet So Close: International Career Paths of Communication Scholars from the Global South." *International Journal of Communication* 13: 578–602.

Dezalay, Yves, and B. Garth. 1996. *Dealing in Virtue: International Commercial Arbitration and the Construction of a Transnational Legal Order*. Chicago: University of Chicago Press.

Dezalay, Yves, and B. Garth. 2002. *The Internationalization of Palace Wars: Lawyers, Economists, and the Contest to Transform Latin American States*. Chicago: University of Chicago Press.

Drori, Gili, John Meyer, Francisco Ramirez, and Evan Schofer. 2003. *Science in the Modern World Polity: Institutionalization and Globalization*. Stanford, CA: Stanford University Press.

Fleck, Christian. 2011. *A Transatlantic History of the Social Sciences: Robber Barons, the Third Reich and the Invention of Empirical Social Research*. London: Bloomsbury.

Fourcade, Marion. 2006. "The Construction of a Global Profession: The Transnationalization of Economics." *American Journal of Sociology* 112, no. 1: 145–95.

Friedman, Thomas. 2005. *The World Is Flat*. New York: Farrar, Straus and Giroux.

Fukuyama, Francis. 1992. *The End of History and the Last Man*. New York: Free Press.

Gingras, Yves. 2002. "Les formes spécifiques de l'internationalité du champ scientifique." *Actes de la recherche en sciences sociales* 141–42: 31–45.

Gingras, Yves. 2016. *Bibliometrics and Research Evaluation: Uses and Abuses*. Cambridge, MA: MIT Press.

Gingras, Yves. 2019. "The Specificity of the Social Sciences and Humanities and Its Relation to Research Evaluation." In *Stay Tuned for the Future: Impact of the Research Infrastructures for Social Sciences and Humanities*, edited by B. Maegaard and R. Pozzo, 13–24. Florence: Leo S. Olschki.

Gingras, Yves, and Sébastien Mosbah-Natanson. 2010. "Where Are Social Sciences Produced?" In *World Social Science Report 2010*, 149–53. Paris: UNESCO Publishing.

Go, Julian. 2016. *Postcolonial Thought and Social Theory*. New York: Oxford University Press.

Go, Julian, and Monika Krause, eds. 2016. *Fielding Transnationalism*. The Sociological Review Monographs. Chichester, UK: John Wiley and Sons.

Hanafi, Sari, and Rigas Arvanitis. 2016. *Knowledge Production in the Arab World: The Impossible Promise*. London: Routledge.

Heilbron, Johan. 1999. "Toward a Sociology of Translation: Book Translations as a Cultural World-System." *European Journal of Social Theory* 2, no. 4: 429–44.

Heilbron, Johan. 2002. "Échanges culturels transnationaux et mondialisation." *Regards sociologiques* 22: 141–54.

Heilbron, Johan. 2014. "The Social Sciences as an Emerging Global Field." *Current Sociology* 62 (5): 685–703.

Heilbron, Johan, Madeline Bedecarré, and Rob Timans. 2017. "European Journals in the Social Sciences and Humanities." In Heilbron, Timans, and Boncourt 2017: 33–49.

Heilbron, Johan, and Anaïs Bokobza. 2015. "Transgresser les frontières en sciences humaines et sociales en France." *Actes de la recherche en sciences sociales* 210: 109–21.

Heilbron, Johan, Thibaud Boncourt, Gisèle Sapiro, Gustavo Sorá, Victor Karady, Thomas Brisson, Laurent Jeanpierre, and Kil-Ho Lee. 2017. "Indicators of the Internationalization of the Social Sciences and Humanities." In Heilbron, Timans, and Boncourt 2017: 129–45.

Heilbron, Johan, Thibaud Boncourt, and Rob Timans. 2018. "The Emerging European Research Area in the Social and Human Sciences." In *The Social and Human Sciences in Global Power Relations*, edited by Johan Heilbron, Gustavo Sorá, and Thibaud Boncourt, 153–81. London: Palgrave Macmillan.

Heilbron, Johan, and Yves Gingras. 2018. "The Globalization of European Research in the Social Sciences and Humanities (1980–2014): A Bibliometric

Study." In *The Social and Human Sciences in Global Power Relations*, edited by Johan Heilbron, Gustavo Sorá, and Thibaud Boncourt, 29-58. London: Palgrave Macmillan.

Heilbron, Johan, Nicolas Guilhot, and Laurent Jeanpierre. 2008. "Toward a Transnational History of the Social Sciences." *Journal of the History of the Behavioral Sciences* 44, no. 2: 146-60.

Heilbron, Johan, Gustavo Sorá, and Thibaud Boncourt, eds. 2018. *The Social and Human Sciences in Global Power Relations*. London: Palgrave Macmillan.

Heilbron, Johan, Rob Timans, and Thibaud Boncourt, eds. 2017. "Understanding the Social Sciences and Humanities in Europe." Special issue, *Serendipities: Journal for the Sociology and History of the Social Sciences* 2, no. 1. http://serendipities.uni-graz.at/index.php/serendipities/issue/view/5.

Keim, Wiebke. 2010. "Pour un modèle centre-périphérie dans les sciences sociales: Aspects problématiques des relations internationales en sciences sociales." *Revue d'anthropologie des connaissances* 4, no. 3: 570-98.

Keim, Wiebke. 2011. "Counterhegemonic Currents and Internationalization of Sociology: Theoretical Reflections and Empirical Example." *International Sociology* 26, no. 1: 123-45.

Keim, Wiebke, Ercüment Çelik, Christian Ersche, and Veronika Wöhrer, eds. 2014. *Global Knowledge Production in the Social Sciences: Made in Circulation*. Dorchester: Ashgate.

Kennedy, Michael, and Miguel Centeno. 2007. "Internationalism and Global Transformations in American Sociology." In *Sociology in America*, edited by Craig Calhoun, 666-712. Chicago: University of Chicago Press.

Krause, Monika. 2016. "'Western Hegemony' in the Social Sciences: Fields and Model Systems." In *Fielding Transnationalism*, edited by Julian Go and Monika Krause, 194-211. Sociological Review Monographs. Chichester: John Wiley and Sons.

Lecler, Romain. 2013. *Sociologie de la mondialisation*. Paris: La Découverte.

Lepenies, Wolf. 1988. *Between Literature and Science: The Rise of Sociology*. Cambridge: Cambridge University Press.

Lillis, Theresa, and Marie Jane Curry. 2010. *Academic Writing in a Global Context: The Politics and Practices of Publishing in English*. London: Routledge.

Medina, Leandro Rodriguez. 2014. *Centers and Peripheries in Knowledge Production*. New York: Routledge.

Mosbah-Natanson, Sébastien, and Yves Gingras. 2014. "The Globalization of Social Sciences? Evidence from a Quantitative Analysis of 30 Years of Production, Collaboration and Citations in the Social Sciences (1980-2009)." *Current Sociology* 62, no. 5: 626-46.

Parshall, Karen, and Adrian Rice, eds. 2002. *Mathematics Unbound: The Evolution of an International Mathematical Research Community, 1800-1945*. Providence, RI: American Mathematical Society.

Said, Edward. 1978. *Orientalism: Western Conceptions of the Orient*. New York: Pantheon Books, 1978.

Sapiro, Gisèle, ed. 2012. *Traduire la littérature et les sciences humaines: Conditions et obstacles*. Paris: DEPS. https://journals.openedition.org/traduire/502.

Sapiro, Gisèle. 2013. "Le champ est-il national?" *Actes de la recherche en sciences sociales* 200: 70–86.

Sapiro, Gisèle. 2015. "Field Theory." In *International Encyclopedia of the Social and Behavioral Sciences*, 2nd ed., 9:140–48. Oxford: Elsevier.

Sapiro, Gisèle. 2018. "What Factors Determine the International Circulation of Scholarly Books? The Example of Translations between English and French in the Era of Globalization." In *The Social and Human Sciences in Global Power Relations*, edited by Johan Heilbron, Gustavo Sorá, and Thibaud Boncourt, 50–93. London: Palgrave Macmillan.

Sapiro, Gisèle, Marco Santoro, and Patrick Baert, eds. 2020. *Ideas on the Move in the Social Sciences and Humanities. The International Circulation of Paradigms and Theorists*. London: Palgrave Macmillan.

Sluga, Glenda, and Patricia Clavin, eds. 2017. *Internationalisms: A Twentieth-Century History*. Cambridge: Cambridge University Press.

Sorá, Gustavo, and Alejandro Blanco. 2018. "Unity and Fragmentation in the Social and Human Sciences in Latin America." In *The Social and Human Sciences in Global Power Relations*, edited by Johan Heilbron, Gustavo Sorá, and Thibaud Boncourt, 127–52. London: Palgrave Macmillan.

Steinmetz, George, ed. 2013. *Sociology and Empire: The Imperial Entanglements of a Discipline*. Durham, NC: Duke University Press.

Steinmetz, George. 2016. "Social Fields, Subfields, and Social Spaces at the Scale of Empires: Explaining the Colonial State and Colonial Sociology." In *Fielding Transnationalism*, edited by Julian Go and Monika Krause, 98–123. The Sociological Review Monographs. Chichester: John Wiley and Sons.

Stevens, Mitchell, Cynthia Miller-Idriss, and Seteney Shami. 2018. *Seeing the World: How US Universities Make Knowledge in a Global Era*. Princeton, NJ: Princeton University Press.

Sztompka, Piotr. 2011. "Another Sociological Utopia." *Contemporary Sociology* 40, no. 4: 388–96.

Topalov, Christian, ed. 1999. *Laboratoires du nouveau siècle*. Paris: EHESS.

UNESCO. 1999. *World Social Science Report 1999*. Paris: UNESCO Publishing/Elsevier.

UNESCO. 2010. *World Social Science Report 2010*. Paris: UNESCO Publishing.

Vauchez, Antoine. 2008. "The Force of a Weak Field: Law and Lawyers in the Government of the European Union." *International Political Sociology* 2, no. 2: 128–44.

Wallerstein, Immanuel. 1999. *The End of the World as We Know It: Social Science for the Twenty-First Century*. Minneapolis: University of Minnesota Press.

Wallerstein, Immanuel. 2004. *World-Systems Analysis*. Durham, NC: Duke University Press.

Werner, Michael, and Bénédicte Zimmermann. 2006. "Beyond Comparison: *Histoire Croisée* and the Challenge of Reflexivity." *History and Theory* 45, no. 1: 30–50.

exploring borders and boundaries

PART THREE

critical humanities & the unsettling of the sociological field

Is There a
French Exception?

JEAN-LOUIS FABIANI

THE SEEMINGLY MOST settled institutional arrangements in an intellectual sphere of activity can be shaken by external forces as well as by internal morphological transformations. The conceptual unity and the project of sociology as an integrative science of the social have been seriously questioned since the end of the 1960s. Even if we consider, in a postpositivist way, that all scientific practices studying society are primarily defined by their historical character, the demise of the constructed past of our disciplines has been a major shock. The multiplication of approaches in the studies of social objects is not a threat per se. We can claim that a clear disciplinary zoning is always questionable in the social sciences due to multiple overlaps and permanent skirmishes at the borders. For instance, sociology and anthropology share the same object and, to a large extent, the same methods, owing their academic distinction to colonialism, but few would be ready to acknowledge the fact and opt for a unified knowledge. Many innovations in sociology and in anthropology that have appeared since the 1970s come from outside: think of Michel Foucault and governmentality, Judith Butler and performativity, Hardt and Negri and cognitariat, and so on. We constantly trade with our environment, risking every day to lose our formal disciplinary identity. Thomas Piketty's *Capital in the Twenty-First Century* is an attempt to reinscribe economics in the web of sociohistorical sciences, notwithstanding a constant interest for literature as a data provider (Piketty 2014). Jane Austen and Honoré de Balzac constitute a sort of database for Piketty, but they also provide sketches of analytical models. Severing our sciences from the myriad of humanist varieties of knowledge is thus an illusion. For instance, we, the social scientists, may declare that we have superseded philosophy, as Durkheim did, proposing sociology as the unifying science. Nevertheless, we still think through philosophy, often in a prereflexive manner. The great fortune of social theory in our curricula is a striking example of what Randall Collins once called a "rephilosophization of sociology," partly due to the contribution of Europeans in exile in the United States.

A *science de la société*, as programmed by Auguste Comte, will never come. It is not a horizon but a prescientific illusion, although many Comtean insights are still worth consideration. Science studies have taught us to raise serious doubts about the "external signs of scientificity," as Bourdieu would say, displayed by founders and refounders, particularly the rhetoric of breaking away from the humanities. The most interesting sociologies in Europe and the United States have often developed their most distinctive features against the mainstream scientific model, based on a false analogy with a totally consensual view of the natural sciences, that we consider now as a mere ideological construction with respect to their own mode of knowledge production. Sometimes the quest for disciplinary autonomy ends up in the illusion of a stable scholarly space disconnected from the sound and the fury of the social world. A large amount of "bricolage" or "montage" is at work in our disciplines. Science studies have freed us from the feeling of guilt that frequently stemmed from the epistemological frailty of our disciplines. The heterogeneous quality of our endeavors is not likely to disappear. Nevertheless, we must give an epistemological and sociographical account of the consequences of postpositivism and critical thinking in our day-to-day work. We have endured terrible attacks in the last forty years: what we considered as emancipatory and progressive sciences have been dismissed as sexist and colonial practices. This does not mean that mainstream social sciences have disappeared but they must live in a largely different environment.

In order to advance, we must distinguish between different stages of the structuration of the configurations of knowledge (*configurations de savoir*). This notion, borrowed from Norbert Elias and Michel Foucault, is much broader than the standard notion of field, which presupposes the joint action of habitus and capital as the constructive principle of a positional space, expressing through competitive interactions a set of acquired dispositions based on uneven resources. Some historical configurations may look like fields in Bourdieu's sense (such as the literary field in mid-nineteenth-century France), but this is not always the case, and most of the situations are less clear-cut. The term *configuration* allows me to account for the multidimensional aspects of positional spaces, the variability of their transposable elements, and sometimes the nonexistence of transpositions and homologies as well as the polysemous nature of competition, which is very often associated with alliances and cooperation in the real world (Fabiani 2010, [2016] 2021). In the social sciences and the humanities, our objects should not be limited to agents and positions but include material objects, spaces, and social practices. It implies that we envisage all types of reception, including the less orthodox. As with any other type of work, those objects presuppose different types of appropriation in space and time and exist only through the successive pacts of reception that constitute them as valued objects in a peculiar culture. In this respect, misreadings are as important as those authorized and protected by institutions. Concepts have a social life, as any other cultural objects. The sociology of the social sciences does not need what Louis Althusser called a "topique," that is, a systemic hierarchy between different levels of reality (Althusser [1965] 1969).

In his account of American sociology at midcentury, George Steinmetz brought in the important notion of a "relatively settled field" where positions can be considered as rather stable during a time span when new contenders can't get sufficient resources to challenge the incumbent positions (Steinmetz 2007). Fields can be settled and unsettled: their autonomy is never guaranteed, even in the academic sector, where established disciplines may oppose a strong resistance to external transformations. However, as Bourdieu showed in the *Rules of Art*, the most solid-looking fields remain fragile and can be deleted in a very short time. George Steinmetz draws an interesting opposition between US sociology before World War II and its situation in the 1950s. He recalls that, in order to be called a field, a collective space must be conditioned "by the multivocality of discourse, perception, and practice" (Steinmetz 2007, 321). A space totally dominated by a single voice is not a field, but an apparatus, like the philosophical "regiment" of Victor Cousin during the French Restoration (Fabiani 1988). However, multivocality may refer to two different orders of things: first, an anarchic situation, like the one that prevailed in Europe before the institutionalization of academic sociology. The word was used by totally different people in totally different contexts (mainly amateurs, novelists, and academics): Durkheim fought, not with total success, to establish a monopolistic use of the label based on the possession of certified capital, mainly philosophy credentials, since a formal training in the new science did not exist yet. Second, a field in Bourdieu's full meaning, where individuals and groups compete in an agonistic way while sharing the *illusio* and the implicit rules of the game, has never been entirely settled, since all agents do not agree on a cohesive definition of the field. This allows us, using Steinmetz's distinction, to isolate unsettled fields, as space with no full-fledged *illusio*, that is, the "feeling for the game" and no clear competitive logic. An unsettled field is, according to his definition, "an assemblage of practices in which no single definition of capital holds sway" (Fabiani 1988).

A settled field is governed by a common belief in the central stakes that characterize a particular configuration of knowledge, a form of epistemic definition of the situation. This settlement does not imply that the field is doomed to remain stable or to be devoted to simple reproduction. In certain conjunctures, there is a clear homology of conditions in different areas of social activity: Steinmetz shows the affinities between Fordism in the productive world and structuro-functionalism in the sociological one. Beliefs were shared about what Talcott Parsons called the "smooth functioning of society": he gave a central role to the sociologists as professionals in the construction and the control of that organizational principle. The stability of the structure of domination by the Harvard–Columbia alliance did not imply that the challengers were voiceless. One of the most acute critical analyses of the shortcomings of US sociology was not from the '68ers' unrest but from the trenchant *Sociological Imagination*, published in 1959 by C. Wright Mills, at the height of structuro-functionalism. However, this was not yet an unsettling force. The settled field was to be destabilized from inside by talented challengers, like Alvin Gouldner around 1970, by external endeavors that did not share the basic presuppositions that characterize ordinarily a field, and also by morphological changes, a fact analyzed both in *Canvasses and Careers* (White and White 1964) and in *Manet: A Symbolic Revolution* (Bourdieu [2013] 2017) with respect to the artistic sphere in the nineteenth century. In his book chapter, Steinmetz insists on the relative specificity of every department in US sociology, even in a time dominated by a seemingly consensual code. This is even more the case with national sociologies, which are rarely aligned along a same path of development. The comparison between France and the United States is striking in this respect. The sort of golden age of US sociology from the late 1940s to the mid-1960s, symbolized by the Capitoline triad Parsons-Merton-Lazarsfeld (Bourdieu [2004] 2008), never existed in France. Parsons accumulated enough capital, particularly political, to confer a regulating role to sociology in public affairs. In France, sociology kept a very low status in the hierarchy of disciplines, and its institutionalization was slow and, to a certain extent, incomplete until the 1960s (Heilbron 2015). This time lag accounts for the fact that the crisis of sociology did not take the same shape in France and the United States. In the former, a "real" discipline was yet to be constructed. In the latter, a dominating but exhausted paradigm had to be superseded. In other historical works, I tried to analyze the desynchronization of national sociologies, which could explain many transatlantic misunderstandings (Fabiani 2007). However, calendar clashes, due to the different paths of institutionalization and different disciplinary configurations are not the only key. France's colonial past, which also makes much of its present, sheds some light on the strong resistance against the reorientation brought about by postcolonial studies.

In the first part of my analysis, I will try to contrast the constructive mood of Bourdieu and his collaborators, who thought that a new science could be crafted, with the anti-institutional mood of '68ers at Nanterre University. In the second part, I will analyze the triple legacy of Georges Canguilhem, through both distinct and close trajectories of Louis Althusser, Michel Foucault, and Pierre Bourdieu. The subversive effort of the critical humanities, led by Foucault, unsettled the system of disciplines, blurring the lines of the established ways of constructing social objects. In the third part, I will take perhaps one of the most famous examples of a humanistic work put in the situation of questioning the ideological presuppositions of knowledge production: Edward Said's *Orientalism* divided its readers in France as in other countries, but along quite different lines. The analysis of the book reception will shed some light on the peculiar dimension of critical humanities in the French context. To conclude, one can ask whether, after a long *différance*, to speak like Derrida, France is slowly aligning itself along postpositivist and postcolonial lines. In the process, sociologists tend to lose sight of their original scientific ambition to embrace critique. Comte and Durkheim's ghosts vanish in the fog.

Building a New Science in 1968

In textbooks, Bourdieu and Lefebvre would both belong to what we today name critical sociology. However, if we look carefully at the history of French sociology in the late 1960s, the two men do not seem to belong to the same world. In 1968, Pierre Bourdieu, Jean-Claude Chamboredon, and Jean-Claude Passeron published the first French edition of *The Craft of Sociology*, which was to become both a successful textbook and an original epistemological manifesto. The trio aimed to construct a scientific sociology based on a specific form of craftsmanship that would associate, on the one hand, French theoretical stringency, largely borrowed from the tradition in the history of science developed by Gaston Bachelard and Georges Canguilhem in philosophy, and on the other hand, some technical know-how preexisting in US sociology. Although the critique of structuro-functionalism and of positivist methodology was quite harsh, the authors envisaged with some interest the capacity of US social sciences to be organized as a relatively unified field, a thing largely unknown in France: there the discipline conserved some amateurish characteristics. Bourdieu spoke regularly of a "refuge-discipline" and considered many of his colleagues with severity, as Durkheim had already done at the turn of the previous century. Trapped between the highly theoretic Althusserian Marxism that made fun of the so-called social sciences and the tedious positivism of newly institutionalized sociology, the three authors had to conquer the territory, quite improbable in the French intellectual world, of an empirical sociology oriented by epistemological questions borrowed from the Bachelardian philosophy of the scientific mind.

During the following decades, their manifesto became a sort of methodological scarecrow as relativism and epistemological anarchism found their way in the French academic landscape. Already in 1968, the position asserted in *The Craft of Sociology* was rather difficult to sustain. Following Durkheim's path, they contested the break between natural and social sciences. By refusing both a Diltheyan dualism and a flat positivism that is satisfied by a poor caricature of the exact sciences, it was easy to avoid engaging into an epistemological account of the differences that were empirically visible between the two types of knowledge. For our three authors, the difference was due to the fact that the social sciences encountered a lot of insidious obstacles, demanding an epistemic vigilance even more heroic than the dangers present everywhere, as for instance ethnocentrism, its virtuous denunciation being often the most perfect demonstration of its vice. The question of the scientific dimension of sociology was thus transported toward the sociology of sociology, in charge of defining the optimal rules for eliminating all sorts of social biases and "prenotions." At the same moment, in the United States, another form of critical sociology, developed by Harold Garfinkel and his disciples, rehabilitated the competencies at work in the ordinary operations of the commonsense and made indistinct the resources mobilized by social agents and by researchers. At least one of the members of the trio, Pierre Bourdieu, was perfectly aware of Garfinkel's pioneering work; he was the first to quote him in France. What is even more surprising is the fact that this very demanding epistemology, loaded with Max Weber and Ludwig Wittgenstein's concepts, remained trapped in the naturalistic frame that Durkheim had imposed to the discipline in a "scientistic" gesture.

Revisiting the *Craft of Sociology* more than twenty years later, Passeron acknowledged that their attitude was mainly the effect of the conjuncture, that is, the pressures of the field: reasserting the scientific dimension of sociology associated with its empirical basis allowed avoiding the hazards due to the antiscientific and anti-institutional mood that were expanding in the late 1960s. One might say, using Bourdieu's vocabulary, that it was a form of unconscious strategy, a prereflexive adaptation to the constraints of the field (Passeron [1991] 2013).

The three sociologists were far from being devoted '68ers. After the fact, Pierre Bourdieu and Jean-Claude Passeron's book *The Inheritors*, published in 1964, was regarded as the announcement of a big student crisis. Nevertheless, the careful rereading of their brilliant piece of work does not show any sign of a premonition. If the contradictions of the higher educational system are clearly stated, the potential social consequences of its critical state were not even evoked. The argument of the book did not allow any space for collective struggles against the selective effects of the system. More than that: after the events, the activists dismissed the structuralist theory of the educational system crafted by Bourdieu and Passeron as trapped in determinism, or worse in fatalism, a contemporary version of *amor fati*, the love of fate. Both sociologists did not take an active part in the movement. They stood in opposition to many of their colleagues, who saw in the events the occasion to put their discipline to the forefront.

When the movement started, sociology was celebrating the tenth anniversary of its full-size institutionalization (a bachelor's degree in sociology was created as late as 1958). Thus, almost all the sociologists who were teaching in French universities in May '68 did not have certified capital in their own discipline. Sociology was not fully professionalized. Many sociologists were philosophers by training, except Crozier, an outsider who came from a business school (Heilbron 2015). One can distinguish three main orientations in late 1960s French sociology. First, some sociologists imported US mainstream tools, an empirical functionalism that was not very attractive for students not really committed to what they saw as positivist and routine activities. This sociology was clearly hostile to the Durkheimian legacy, defined as a relic of a prescientific past. Raymond Boudon, who published a textbook with Paul Lazarsfeld (Boudon and Lazarsfeld 1966), offered a more sophisticated vision of the discipline but quickly abandoned "the empirical analysis of causality" to become the herald of methodological individualism. By contrast, the remains of the French school of sociology were still active in the very little community of anthropologists. Second, there was a Weberian orientation, embodied by Raymond Aron, who introduced the German thinker in France during the interwar period, and to a lesser extent by Julien Freund, a truly conservative political scientist. This trend was present at the Sorbonne and at Sciences-Po. Third, Henri Lefebvre, who started his career in the late twenties and launched the short-lived *Marxist Review*, dominated the Marxian orientation. Marxists were not that many, but they had the power to gather and unite students. The critical thinkers were more likely to be found in the University of Nanterre, where the prolegomena of the movement appeared in March '68. Nevertheless, sociology never played a major ideological role in the years preceding May '68. Philosophy, psychoanalysis, and even literary studies, particularly due to the aura of Roland Barthes, were at the center.

The University of Nanterre was the main place of sociological activities that were closer to student contestation. The movement started there: Dany Cohn-Bendit, who was to be its iconic leader, studied in the department, and sociology students took an active part. Within the Nanterre faculty, we can identify three instructors who were particularly in tune with social preoccupations. The first was the oldest: Henri Lefebvre, philosopher and sociologist, an early Marxist, was partly marginalized by the rise of Althusserian theoretical Marxism. In the '60s, Lefebvre played the role of a consciousness awakener and became the symbol of one of the most visible forms of critical thought. A professor in Strasbourg, Lefebvre joined Nanterre in '68, with the aura of his *Critique de la vie quotidienne*, first published in 1961. When he arrived, Nanterre was a very poor university, but sociologists played an active role in it. That was far from being the case at the Sorbonne. He defined himself as a "revolutionary romantic": he was quite close to literary and artistic movements, such as Cobra or early Situationism, before Guy Debord excluded him without appeal. The novelist Georges Perec was also Lefebvre's close friend, and his books bear the mark of the critique of everyday life developed by the sociologist. Lefebvre introduced a course titled Sexuality and Society in the curriculum. Nanterre sociology in the '60s was a tumultuous discipline. Pedagogical innovation was more important than conceptual innovation, but a new space of existential possibilities was sketched. Lefebvre's critical radicalism was concretely experienced. Dany Cohn-Bendit often recognized his debt to Lefebvre.

Two other sociological characters stood out in the Nanterre. Younger than Lefebvre, they did not have his aura, but they played a significant role in the post-'68 reorientation of French sociology. The first was Alain Touraine. He was a perfect representative of the French elite schools, an exceptional feature in Nanterre, where sociologists had mainly heterodox and poorly legitimate trajectories. Normalien from the rue d'Ulm, Touraine learned sociology from Parsons at Harvard University. His fieldwork on the French working class led him to orient his research toward more vivid examples of the theory of action. He developed the first elements of his method named "sociological intervention" in Nanterre. He aimed to restore their own speech to the actors and started collective fieldwork that would be central in French sociology during the following decades. During the movement, Touraine was an acute observer of the student revolt, both empathic and critical.

The second name was Jean Baudrillard. When the revolt started, he was still in his thirties and did not have Lefebvre or even Touraine's aura. His work was very solitary, but it attracted a lot of interest among students. Trained as a German scholar, Baudrillard turned to philosophy and defended his dissertation under Lefebvre's supervision in 1966: *The System of Objects* was a brilliant variation on the critique of everyday life. Baudrillard would never convert to sociology but would be the "thinker of post-'68" while keeping his relationship with Situationism and a taste for the study of simulacra. He kept away from the movement, as he did not like its belief in the possibility of another social world.

As we can see, *The Craft of Sociology* would have been rather unthinkable in the atmosphere of Nanterre, where science was not on the agenda: the space of possibilities was only existential. However, May '68 boosted French sociology, and everybody got the returns on investment generated by the event, particularly Bourdieu, who, although very skeptical about the "failed revolution," ousted his mentor Raymond Aron from the Centre de Sociologie Européenne that he had founded. How did French sociologists react to the events? The strength of the movement and its sudden backflow triggered many interpretations, quite different and often opposite. May '68 created long-lasting cleavages. Some senior academics rejected the movement as producing social disorder: they had been often humiliated during the movement. Raymond Aron wrote a book about a not-found revolution, and François Bourricaud, who would become Boudon's associate in proposing a new pedagogical supply, criticized the pedagogical heterodoxy of Nanterre. Social conservatism found new resources in the analysis of the movement. On the other side, Edgar Morin popularized his generational class struggle that would be highly successful in media circles. Claude Lefort and Cornelius Castoriadis, at the crossing of philosophy and sociology, insisted on the "breach" opened in the dominant representation of democratic societies, otherwise considered as incapable of revolutionary uprisings. More generally, particularly in the journal *Esprit*, the notion of "cultural revolution" took shape, severing the symbolic dimensions of May '68 from its radical political translation. May '68 gave a lot of weight to critical thought in society. It gave more strength and visibility to sociology. Sociologists appeared as the acute observers of a society that seemed unbearable to more and more citizens. In this respect, the legitimization of sociology was one of the unintended consequences of May '68 and went along with the considerable epistemological efforts of Bourdieu, Chamboredon, and Passeron. That conjunction allows for a partial reconsideration of the configuration of a field: it cannot be subsumed under the definition of a positional space made of competing individuals moving along structural lines of force, but of individuals and groups that contribute to restructuration (Sewell 2005).

Epistémè and Scientific Revolutions

When they wrote their book, the trio was not unaware of the huge success of another work, published in 1966, that brought about another kind of epistemological revolution, at least in the social conversation. *The Order of Things* followed *Madness and Civilization* (originally published in 1961) and helped establish the reputation of Michel Foucault as the gravedigger of previous intellectual trends (existentialism and Marxism mainly) and of the scientific pretense subjacent in the human sciences. There is an astonishing element in the fact that Foucault and Bourdieu shared the same epistemological background, as the former acknowledged in the last text he wrote in 1984 (Foucault 1985) and the latter recalled in his posthumous biographical piece (Bourdieu [2004] 2008). Georges Canguilhem was their common mentor, and their education owed much to the history of science "à la française" developed by Bachelard and Canguilhem from the late 1930s on. But they soon took quite opposite routes, since Bourdieu decided to build a new science, as the spectacle of the playful Nanterrois was an example of the miseries of the discipline, while Foucault experimented with new paths that he would never follow for too long, surprising his dedicated followers by unpredictable zigzags and U-turns. Canguilhem's totemic position, as Bourdieu put it, gave him a central position in the institutional philosophical field: he was the chairman of the jury of the Agrégation de Philosophie for years, and the dean of the Inspection Générale, the national bureau in charge of evaluating the philosophy teachers in Lycées and allocating them over the whole French territory. Althusser and his disciples paid tribute to the philosopher, although he was more on the conservative side of politics. Althusser's scientific vision of Marxism owed a lot to the French history of science, as the famous notion of "epistemological break"—originally a Bachelardian one, clearly shows. His reconceptualization of Marx's work made it acceptable in the most legitimate academic circles, as it was reloaded by epistemology, structuralism, and psychoanalysis. Thus, the author of *The Normal and the Pathological*, originally published in 1966, was the common reference to three endeavors, simultaneously close and very different. Canguilhem (1904–95), whom Bourdieu called the "exemplary prophet," played a major role in inspiring the postexistentialist renewal of French philosophy and also in offering fresh epistemological resources to a new generation of sociologists, namely Pierre Bourdieu, Robert Castel, and Jean-Claude Passeron. In his tribute to Canguilhem, Michel Foucault quoted their three names as an integrant part of the "philosophy of the concept" (Foucault 1985). He compared him with Sartre, the philosopher of the subject par excellence. He added a political tone to the comparison: Canguilhem joined the French Resistance very early, while Sartre had his works produced and published under the German occupation. There is a paradox here in the common admiration for a philosopher who was a great defender of the traditional institution (open neither to Marxism nor to the social sciences) and of the teaching mission inherent to the discipline. He was a disciple of Alain, who taught in a "classe préparatoire" at the Lycée Henri IV in Paris and represented a rather traditional view of the craft of philosophy, although he positioned himself as a pacifist and advocated the citizen's resistance against power.

Althusser, Bourdieu and Foucault invented radically new positions in the French academic field although they relied on the resources provided by Canguilhem's history of science. A rather "established" philosopher, and certainly not a member of the avant-garde, was used to subvert the state of things in philosophy and sociology. The three men took an explicit critical stance against the philosophical legacy of the French republican philosophy, which Canguilhem worshipped until his death (Fabiani 2020). Althusser despised the "miserable state of French philosophy" since the mid-nineteenth century (Althusser [1965] 1969). Bourdieu criticized relentlessly the scholasticism of the French *Homo academicus*, particularly in *Pascalian Meditations* (Bourdieu 2000), where he devoted one hundred pages to the topic. Foucault acknowledged in a famous radio show that he was a "minimal teacher" and that "institutional knowledge produced less than nothing before May 68" (Foucault 1975). Simultaneously they relied heavily on the established knowledge to promote their own transgression. Foreign readers could not see it, since they were not trained in the French way of schooling. Their prose sounded more familiar to Gallic ears: they could identify the system of stylistic gaps that made them both members of the academic family and elegant rebels. One of the features that they shared was a common hostility to Sartre, who was the French prominent postwar philosophical figure until the early 1960s. Existentialism was their common enemy; the aim of philosophical structuralism was to dislodge him from his dominant position as an "intellectual total," according to Bourdieu's definition. It happens that Canguilhem, who was Sartre's and Aron's classmate at the École Normale Supérieure in the mid-1920s, was extremely skeptical about the philosophical merits of existentialism. He doubted that the "engagement" of the intellectual was a new thing and mentioned the Dreyfus Affair as a starting point (Canguilhem 1991). He also made fun of the tendency to "philosophize while smoking cigarettes on a couch" rather than studying formal logic or probabilities (Canguilhem 1954). Althusser, Foucault, and Bourdieu shared the concern to make philosophy more technical, but with quite different relationships to science as such. Foucault proclaimed the end of human sciences along with the death of man. Bourdieu tried to found a full-fledged science of society that was very close to the model of natural sciences, at least in the first part of his life. Althusser recognized in Marx the founder of a science of history, analogous to the invention of mathematics in Greece and the invention of physics in the early classical age. Their use of the history of science "à la française" was thus quite different. Canguilhem, who appreciated both *Madness and Civilization* and *The Order of Things*, always considered Foucault as a part of his legacy, and after a few years of misunderstanding acknowledged the merits of Bourdieu's sociological approach. The conservative Canguilhem was appropriated by three different forms of intellectual leftism. This was allowed by the opening of the space of possibilities in the late 1950s. As existentialism was more and more estranged from its historical conditions of emergence, the beginnings of the de Gaulle's Fifth Republic opened a new range of positions for young and ambitious intellectuals in the public service. Foucault served the state as a cultural attaché for quite a few years. Bourdieu developed early links with the National Institute for Statistics and Economics Studies. The Algerian War was ending, and France was rapidly turning into a consumer society. The academic system expanded, and so did the readership for new and sophisticated products that would make Sartre and

Simone de Beauvoir look a little bit corny. The weekly *Nouvel observateur* was to be the main media vehicle for structuralism and its seductions. Althusser and Bourdieu were committed to science, but Foucault was closer to avant-garde literature, as his book on Raymond Roussel shows. Although Bourdieu was the only sociologist of the trio, Althusser and Foucault's were widely used by sociologists. The new Marxist sociologists were mainly Althusserian in a broad sense, like Nikos Poulantzas or sometimes even direct disciples, like Christian Baudelot and Roger Establet. A Foucauldian sociology prospered too, mainly in urban studies, most of the time led by nontenured scholars working on short-term contracts offered by the new state bureaucracy. Thus, in the post-'68 years, there was a great porosity between philosophy and sociology, and it would be absurd to reason in terms of an autonomous sociological field. Breaking away epistemologically from the humanities was very often more rhetorical than effective.

Nevertheless, many sociologists perceived a great danger in the success of Foucault's first book. The most interesting reaction to *The Order of Things* was written by a young sociologist at the Centre National de la Recherche Scientifique: Michel Amiot published his harsh criticism in Sartre's journal, *Les temps modernes*. The author of *Being and Nothingness* showed a steady hostility to Foucault, claiming that he was both the ideologist of the Gaullist regime and the undertaker of Marxism (Amiot [1967] 2009). Amiot's review was much more sophisticated. The key issue was Foucault's misuse of the notion of science in its relationship to *savoir* (knowledge). "The notion of science can't be articulated with the ruptures in knowledge proposed by Foucault" (Amiot [1967] 2009, 123). He is more of a juggler than an archeologist. His endeavor is characterized by a reduction of all natural sciences to a variety of savoir, among others. Accordingly, his philosophy is nothing more than a "variety of historicist skepticism," and he does not propose a theory of knowledge production, since "knowledge" is dissolved in the unruly successions of incommunicable structures, so one can claim rigorously that in Foucault's work there is neither concept nor notion (127). One can conclude that he is the bearer of a "new culturalist relativism." Foucault acknowledged the quality of the review in a manuscript letter that he sent to Amiot. He denied the fact that he was looking for a discontinuity without rules, but he said that he tried to define the whole set of transformations that constitute the rule of an empirical discontinuity (138). He recognized that the book lacked a methodological question that would have helped clarify the points raised by Amiot.

The young sociologist was visibly driven by epistemological concerns borrowed from Canguilhem and Althusser. His main criticism concerned the lack of trust in the very idea of science and of its demarcation with ideology. The blurring of the dividing line was a clear example of relativism or skepticism. Foucault did not answer the objection; rather, he insisted on the accuracy of his methodology to deal with empirical cases. To some extent, he rescientified his discourse for the occasion.

Later, Foucault always refused to be identified as a social scientist. He was greatly upset by the identification of his *Discipline and Punish* with Goffman's *Asylums*.

> I am not a researcher in the social sciences. I am not trying to do the same thing as Goffman. He is mainly interested in the functioning of a special type of institution: the total institution, the asylum, the school, the prison. As far as I am concerned, I try to show and to analyze the relationship that exists between a set of power techniques and some forms, political forms like the state and social forms. Goffman's problem is the institution in itself. Mine is the rationalization of the management of the individual. (Foucault [1994] 2001, 2:802).

In my previous work, I showed that Foucault's opposition to sociology was a constant feature of his work, despite some positive references to Max Weber (Fabiani 2018). Quite a few Foucauldians objected that I was hardening things excessively. Recent scholarly work on his relationship to history tends to strengthen my argument. Florence Hulak has shown that Foucault meant by archeology an operation intended to reduce to nothingness all the pretenses of human sciences, including history. She concluded by saying that the generalization of the Foucauldian project was incompatible with maintaining the idea of a historical science (Hulak 2013).

When Bourdieu tried to sketch a sociological analysis of his proximity to Foucault, he made an extremely interesting statement that dissociated scholarly training from social trajectory. Alumni from the École Normale Supérieure and philosophy majors, they shared the same starting point, as the common reference to Canguilhem and to the group of Clermont-Ferrand, organized by Jules Vuillemin, shows. The reading of Maurice Merleau-Ponty was also an element of their shared starting point. But two features opposed them according to Bourdieu: Foucault's bourgeois background and his homosexuality. Among resemblances in their work, Bourdieu mentioned the refusal of the social hierarchy of objects and the interest in historical sciences. Foucault, he added, tried to think the world "as it is" through the extension of the philosophical territory. He was also pioneering by reconciling scholarship and commitment. Where is the difference then? "Michel Foucault remained always within the philosophical field and paid constant attention to the expectations of the Parisian intellectual world" (Bourdieu [2004] 2008, 104). Bourdieu accounted for the large gap between their theoretical positions by referring to antagonistic social dispositions. One could say that this is a little bit rude, but this is totally in tune with the theory of fields.

What is the main difference? Foucault never spoke of Bourdieu's theory in his writings. Bourdieu developed an overall critique of his colleague's "internalism." In the *Rules of Art*, he claimed that there was no theory of practice in Foucault's work (Bourdieu [1992] 1996). Although the author of the *Archeology of Knowledge* is credited for having introduced relational thinking in the analysis of texts, insofar as no cultural work exists by itself, independently from the interdependencies that link it to other works, he was content with displacing the territory of the absolutization of a single text toward systems of intertextual relations. The "field of strategic possibilities" mentioned by Foucault is not at all a field of sociological forces, since it is entirely defined by the deployment of conceptual games. Bourdieu thus misses the main interest of the archaeology of knowledge, product of the paradoxical rapprochement between two intellectual streams, the history of the Annales school (particularly in its Braudelian version) and the French style of epistemology, developed by Bachelard and Canguilhem, which expressed itself as a history of science. Foucault tried to think together, at least in the first part of his work, the "longue durée" and the concept of discontinuity. This notion makes the constitution of a continuous chronology of reason quite impossible and paves the way for a general theory of discontinuity, including the analysis of series, of limits, of specific orders of autonomy, and of differentiated dependencies. Foucault never envisaged an autonomous world in which pure conceptual strategies would be deployed. It is true that the space delimited is more a logical space than a sociohistorical one and that the distinction between discursive practices and nondiscursive practices remains largely unexplored; but what differentiates Foucault from Bourdieu is much more the mode of construction of the object. If the former is mainly interested in documents, the latter develops his analysis out of the producers' strategies and the relationships they develop with each other (Fabiani 2018). In that respect, Foucault could help us refine the field analysis in disconnecting it from the sole agonistic game between dominant and dominated. The field should be a much more reticulated system, including not only competing agents' dispositions and positions but also the social life of texts and other cultural monuments.

One final remark concerns the strong and explicit relationship that Foucault developed very early with history of art (as shown in the fascinating analysis of Velasquez's *Las Meninas* at the beginning of the *Order of Things*) and avant-garde literature. He was particularly interested in transgressive forms. Bourdieu refused to mingle, at least before he turned late in his life into a major public intellectual who had to behave "à la Sartre" to be taken seriously. In his *Sketch for a Self-Analysis*, he insisted on the fact that he did not share his contemporaries' interest in Georges Bataille or Pierre Klossowski. He considered, as Durkheim did, that science had to break away from the seductions of humanities and liberal arts. Science demanded a form of anti-aesthetic asceticism.

After Orientalism

When Edward Said published the first edition of *Orientalism* in 1978, it was a shock, quite different from Foucault's reception. Readers were stunned by the *Order of Things*: it triggered a lot of debates among social scientists, as it threatened seriously the "scientistic" program of the social sciences of the 1960s. Although Michel Amiot and a few others criticized its cultural relativism, which would take on a much greater importance in the years to come, it did not shake the very basis of the social sciences. They were expanding quickly: great historians such as Georges Duby and Emmanuel Leroy-Ladurie became public intellectuals and wrote best sellers. If sociology remained, as Bourdieu used to say with some pessimism, something of a "refuge" discipline and failed to attract the best scholars, it finally became an established one precisely at that time (Heilbron 2015): Bourdieu's last lectures at the Collège de France were devoted to a strong defense of the scientific ambitions of the discipline, partly based on a positive reappraisal of Robert K. Merton's work against the postmodern mood prevailing in science studies. Claude Lévi-Strauss's structuralism had given anthropology the status of a rigorous science, as shown in the mathematical models used in the *Elementary Forms of Kinship*: his legacy was maintained through the positions held at the Collège de France. In many ways, in the post-'68 social atmosphere, Said had more disruptive ambitions. His book originated successive waves of dismissive accounts of Western humanities and social sciences. There was of course a significant relationship between Foucault's endeavor and Said's attempt to debunk the colonial unconscious of Orientalist studies. The latter played a major role in the introduction and adaptation of the former in the United States, before stating his disenchantment with his method of reading texts and with the ambiguities of his political purpose. One must recall that

Said had been cruelly disappointed by his encounter with Jean-Paul Sartre in order to note, with some irony, that a significant part of what is at stake in the harsh critique of French intellectuals, particularly philosophers, coming from radical academics in the United States, has much to do with the transfer of academic centrality from Europe to the American empire. The paradoxical success of the so-called French theory on US campuses should not hide the fact that the texts were fully decontextualized, largely reinterpreted and translated for other purposes in a new academic environment. One could think that the situation is close to what Horace said about the conquest of Greece by Rome: "Captive Greece conquered her savage victor and brought the arts to the Latium." However, it is quite different: French theory looks more like the post-Revolution aristocrats described by Karl Marx, condemned to become "the dancing masters of Europe," teaching good manners to the newly rich bourgeoisie. But that's another story.

Let's turn then to the reception of Said in France. *Orientalism* was translated into French two years after its original publication in English (1978). Maxime Rodinson, the leading Marxist historian and sociologist of Near East and Islam, evoked "something similar to a shock" when the book was out (Brahimi and Fordant 2017). Said, a professor of comparative literature, had an influence that went well beyond disciplinary borders and settlements. His argument was much stronger than Foucault's "death of man" and subsequent fading of the "human sciences." It attacked the very roots of knowledge production in the West. Orientalism was the example of a science based on false premises and of a knowledge loaded with ideological preconceptions. The book was bold enough to allow for some lack of historical precision and for hasty generalizations. Nevertheless, there was a force inherent to it that fitted perfectly the anti-institutional mood of the years following the late 1960s and that could be used by challengers entering different fields to get positions. Establishing the falsity of knowledge accumulated during many generations is a high-risk game, but in the meantime, gains can be huge. To a large extent, everybody knew the colonial origins of Orientalism. This was not a mystery. What Said brought to light (at least he believed so, and his many readers did too) were the functions of that type of discourse and imagery in a process of domination and dispossession. Oriental pictures were reloaded with ideological contents, although their users had mostly viewed them as pleasurable items. Aesthetics had to be repoliticized. Said's denunciative style was quite adapted to a deregulated competitive arena where agents fought against each other to get access to positions. Debunking the pretentions of a competitor with moral or political resources was becoming central in the daily life of academia. Said provided new challengers with a template that was to become dominant in the last years of the twentieth century.

In their fascinating research on Said's reception in the Francophone world ($n = 235$ authors: 88 women, 147 men), Mohamed Amine Brahimi and Clarisse Fordant have distinguished three types of attitude toward the book: positive, negative, and neutral. There is a significant difference between women and men: women "are more likely to use positive or indifferent citations, while men have the tendency to have a negative opinion of Said's works" (Brahimi and Fordant 2017, 12). Francophone authors from and living in North America at the time of publication "most often cite Said positively," unlike authors from and living in Western Europe, who "are more inclined to use negative or indifferent citations" (12). It seems clear that Said's most dedicated advocates are academics who give priority to interdisciplinarity as a way of deconstructing the settled practices in the social sciences. Literary studies or cultural studies constitute a weapon to change the order of things in their field. Comparative literature has played a major role in the process. A critical and anti-Eurocentric stance allows the reconquering of humanistic positions as opposed to the positivism and the imperialism of established social sciences. It offers the opportunity to combine a political commitment, albeit generally limited to the academic sphere, with a scholarly position. This is even truer in emerging countries, where the academic field is not settled yet. Brahimi and Fordant's survey illustrates that dimension. "The Saidian project offers a certain amount of balance between academic production and political commitment at a time when the expectations raised by the period of independence movements began to subside" (14). On the contrary, critical reviews of Said's work were more likely to appear in Western Europe (and, not quite surprisingly, largely from France). Very often, the controversial dimension of *Orientalism* lies in its "arbitrary vision of the West" (16). Within what the authors define as the critical pole, there are mostly men and a large proportion of political scientists, who were dominant in the field of Near East and Islam studies in the 1980s. This does not mean that there is a unified group of French Orientalists who defend their position by pointing out scholarly weaknesses and ideological standpoints in Said's book.

The post-1968 years saw a lot of change in the field of the Arab world studies: philologists and political scientists had to take into account the work of historians and sociologists. One can also notice a shift in recent years: as new challengers enter the field, junior scholars are more likely to introduce Said's ideas in the most legitimate academic field (Said 1978, 20).

Although the authors do not mention this point, the late positive reception of Orientalism is also due to the growing importance of the US academic norms in French universities. Importing American ways of thinking may be a powerful resource in constructing a new type of legitimacy. As some types of studies (notably, postcolonial studies and gender studies) do not seem to be spontaneously welcome in France, newcomers must rely on resources that are not inherent to the field, namely US references like Edward Said, Judith Butler, and Joan Scott, among many others. Nevertheless, the game has just started, and the end is not in sight. Paradoxically, what David Paul Haney aptly called the "Americanization of the social science" (Haney 2008) reached France not with structuro-functionalism but with postcolonialism and radical feminist studies. A large part of the resistance to those unsettling forces is very often viewed negatively by US prominent academics, who tend to interpret it as a colonial legacy. Things are undoubtedly not so clear. As the institutionalization of the social sciences is much more recent than in the United States, France occupies a different position in the long cycle of construction and deconstruction that affects knowledge production. Radical critique of disciplinary arrangements may generate a direct threat on the fragile autonomy of sociology and anthropology. Besides, the still dominant sociological paradigm, Bourdieu's genetic structuralism, has defended from the start the epistemological unity of the social sciences. The inevitable fragmentation induced by the proliferation of the specialized studies does not fit into the model.

Discussing *Orientalism* from a French point of view is not an easy task, as France was central in the colonizing process. Forty years after the first release of the book, it is possible to extirpate its contents from the overheated debate that characterized its reception. Contrary to Foucault's books that did not give any precise direction to the reader, and quite often lost her in a dead end, Said's prose was crystal clear. There were oppressors, and there were victims; there were bad people and good people. All the action was on the dominant side. Oppressed people seemed to have no agency. The oversimplification of the domination process was clear-cut. The affective dimension of the analysis was overwhelming and the simultaneous accession of the Palestinian to the status of paradigmatic victim helped construct a favorable environment to the reception of Said's theses. As the justification of the main ideas by careful empirical research was regularly submitted to the necessities of political engagement, the book was extremely vulnerable to erudite criticisms, but they in turn were dismissed a priori, since the critics were part and parcel of the colonial ideological system. In order to assess the value of critical humanities for the reflexivity of the social sciences, one has to turn to a more reflexive way of associating scholarship and commitment.

In their collective book *After Orientalism*, François Pouillon and Jean-Claude Vatin have tried to avoid the traps usually contained in the discussion of the book by reclaiming the rights of scholarship (Pouillon and Vatin 2013). This can be seen as a way back to a pre-postcolonial vision of the world. After all, the authors could be seen as sheer Orientalists. However, they have assimilated the main lesson of the postcolonial attitude: they aim to decenter the gaze and enlarge the scope. Perhaps Said gave too much importance to the Western world and became Eurocentric against his own will. Although the field of Orientalism extends significantly beyond this relatively brief period and the specific territory of the colonial regime, the authors write,

> We do not intend to provide an inventory of the criticisms that were leveled at this thesis. Nor do we claim that the link between Orientalism and Western imperialism is entirely false. Our goal here is instead to broaden the discussion. Until now, scholarship on Orientalism has focused on establishments located in the metropolis and on the agents of science and power that were involved in this enterprise of knowledge, representation, evocation or domination. This unilateral approach is inherently limited and should be corrected. (Pouillon and Vatin 2013, x)

Among the main criticisms addressed to Said was that the Orient was reduced to the passive status, while the Occident had a unilateral action on the dominated. One can find the analogous analytical scheme in many discourses where the dominated is simply silenced, made voiceless. That type of dichotomy rarely satisfies a historical or sociological eye. Besides, Orient and Occident can't be regarded as homogeneous entities. Colonial powers were different, and their exercise varied along time: the reactions of the dominated people could not be described in the same way. What is proposed here is the repatriation of an object in the frame of the social sciences. This is a way of denying the total disqualification of a false science while acknowledging that colonialism matters in terms of knowledge production.

In other terms, Said's revision was essential for the reflexivity of Oriental studies, but it did not lead to the end of a scientific project that could be detached from its historical conditions of production. In many ways, surviving the shock wave of *Orientalism* requires making the game more complex. For instance, the authors restore the agency of the dominated. The history of Orientalism "is neither uniform nor unequivocal," the authors note (Pouillon and Vatin 2013, xii). The end of the preface gives the key to the whole book.

It has nothing to do with a restoration of a "colonial" vision of the world expressed in terms of "civilizing mission." Claiming that there is a lot to do in the historical sciences after deconstruction does not mean that we must travel back to the status quo ante: François Pouillon notes in his own chapter that when it came out in 1980, Said's *Orientalism* went unnoticed in France, contrary to the shock experienced by Rodinson. Why? Since the decolonization a lot of work had appeared in the Francophone world, equally from the recently decolonized intellectuals (Anouar Abdel Malek, Mohamed Cherif Sahli, Abdelkebir Khatibi) and from the French "Orientalists" (most of the time ardent decolonizers, such as Jacques Berque, Jean Copans, and Charles-André Julien). To some extent, French historians and anthropologists did not seem to need to be cleaned up in a postcolonial bath. French scholars had largely the impression that they were ahead of Said, with respect to scholarship as well as anticolonial commitment that was besides quite overdue in the 1970s. The history of cultural and postcolonial studies remains to be done, but the authors of *After Orientalism* shed some light on the conjunction of circumstances that made them flourish: the rise of what I call "armchair radicalism," totally disconnected from any concrete engagement; the attraction of American campuses for new scholarly elites of the Third World; the growing identification of scholarly objects with a cause, the interpretation of the world as the permanent clash between perpetrators and victims.

Conclusion

Can we answer the inaugural question: Is there a French exception concerning the development of critical humanities? This text can be read as an experiment and should be completed by collective work. Gender studies and cultural studies were not considered in the argument, although one can think that they would strengthen it. There is undoubtedly a form of reluctance, even among the most critical scholars, to welcome disciplinary change through the identification of scholarship and activism. Attributing this sort of shyness to cultural factors such as colonialism and secularism is tempting. Some recent attempts to do so amount to a form of caricature, an academic brand of French-bashing. However, I do not want to automatically discard that type of explanation. Amiot's critique of Foucault and Pouillon and his colleagues' retrospective analysis of Orientalism can be compared. Both are based on an epistemological assumption: the production of knowledge about the social world is less vulnerable that it seems, although it is more difficult (and much longer) to establish than in the natural sciences. This can be seen in Althusser as well as in Bourdieu. The Comtean legacy that Foucault saw in the "philosophy of the concept" is still working in the French epistemological unconscious. Dismissing it as out of date is tempting, as the US model of scholarship is hegemonic. My suggestion is different: we should engage in comparative studies to see how we can disentangle morphological, structural, and ideological elements in the complex present configuration of knowledge. This text is just a way of launching a dispassionate debate.

References

Althusser, Louis. (1965) 1969. *For Marx*. London: Allen Lane.

Amiot, Michel (1967) 2009. "Le relativisme culturaliste de Michel Foucault," avec une réponse manuscrite de Michel Foucault, *Les temps modernes*, no. 248, 1271–98, reprinted in *Regards critiques: Les mots et les choses de Michel Foucault*, 91–143. Caen: Presses Universitaires de Caen.

Boudon, Raymond, and Paul Lazarsfeld 1966. *L'analyse empirique de la causalité*. Paris: Mouton.

Bourdieu, Pierre. (1992) 1996. *The Rules of Art: Genesis and Structure of the Literary Field*. Stanford, CA: Stanford University Press.

Bourdieu, Pierre. *Pascalian Meditations* (1997) 2000. Stanford, CA: Stanford University Press.

Bourdieu, Pierre. (2004) 2008. *Sketch for a Self-Analysis*. Chicago: University of Chicago Press.

Bourdieu, Pierre. (2013) 2017. *Manet: A Symbolic Revolution*. London: Polity.

Bourdieu, Pierre, Jean-Claude Chamboredon, and Jean-Claude Passeron. (1968) 1991. *The Craft of Sociology: Epistemological Preliminaries*. Berlin: Walter de Gruyter.

Brahimi, Mohamed Amine, and Clarisse Fordant. 2017. "The Controversial Receptions of Edward Said: A Sociological Analysis of Scientific Citations." *Sociologia* 1: 1–28.

Canguilhem, Georges. (1954) 2013. "De la philosophie comme débouché." *Œuvres Complètes*, vol. 4., 601–19. Paris: Vrin.

Canguilhem, Georges. (1966) 1991. *The Normal and the Pathological*. New York: Zone Books.

Canguilhem, Georges. 1991. "Qu'est-ce qu'un philosophe en France aujourd'hui, Vol 1 : 107 112.

Fabiani, Jean-Louis. 1988. *Les philosophes de la République*. Paris: Éditions de Minuit.

Fabiani, Jean-Louis. 2007. "L'ethnométhodologie, une affaire de coproduction?" In *Rapports ambivalents entre sciences sociales européennes et américaines*. Milan: Arcipelago Edizioni, 217–42.

Fabiani, Jean-Louis. 2010. *Qu'est-ce qu'un philosophe français? La vie sociale des concepts*. Paris: EHESS.

Fabiani, Jean-Louis. (2016) 2021. *Pierre Bourdieu: A Heroic Structuralism*. Leiden: Brill.

Fabiani, Jean-Louis. 2018. "Du discours à la pratique." *Cartografie Sociali* 2, no. 4: 31–50.

Fabiani, Jean-Louis. 2020. "Philosophes et professeurs de philosophie: Canguilhem, la discipline du couronnement et les 'hommes exemplaires.'" *Revue philosophique de la France et de l'Etranger* 1 (no. 145): 21–32.

Foucault, Michel. (1961) 2001. *Madness and Civilization*. London: Routledge.

Foucault, Michel. (1966) 1970. *The Order of Things: An Archaeology of the Human Sciences*. New York: Pantheon Books.

Foucault, Michel. 1975. Interview by Jacques Chancel. *Radioscopie*, March 10, 1975.

Foucault, Michel. 1985. "La vie, l'expérience et la science." *Revue de métaphysique et de morale* 90, no. 1 (January–March): 3–14.

Foucault, Michel. (1994) 2001. "Foucault Examines Reason in Service of State Power: Interview by M. Dillon." *Campus Report* 12, no. 6 (1979): 5–6. Translated in *Dits et écrits*, 2nd ed., vol. 2. Paris: Gallimard, Quarto. All the references to *Dits et écrits* are quoted from the second edition.

Haney, David Paul. 2008. *The Americanization of Social Science: Intellectuals and Public Responsibility in the Postwar United States*. Philadelphia: Temple University Press.

Heilbron, Johan. 2015. *French Sociology*. Ithaca, NY: Cornell University Press.

Hulak, Florence 2013. "Michel Foucault, la philosophie et les sciences humaines: Jusqu'où l'histoire peut-elle être foucaldienne?" *Tracés: Revue de sciences humaines* 13 (2013). https://doi.org/10.4000/traces.5718.

Passeron, Jean-Claude (1991) 2013. *Sociological Reasoning: A Non-Popperian Space of Argumentation*. London: Bardwell.

Piketty, Thomas 2014. *Capital in the Twenty-First Century*. Cambridge, MA: Harvard University Press.

Pouillon, François, and Jean-Claude Vatin, eds. 2013. *After Orientalism: Critical Perspectives on Western Agency and Eastern Re-appropriations*. Leiden: Brill.

Said, Edward. 1978. *Orientalism*. New York: Pantheon Books.

Sewell, William., Jr. 2005. *Logics of History: Social Theory and Social Transformation*. Chicago: University of Chicago Press.

Steinmetz, George. 2007. "American Sociology before and after World War II: The (Temporary) Settling of a Disciplinary Field." In *Sociology in America: A History*, edited by C. Calhoun, 314–66. Chicago: University of Chicago Press.

White, Cynthia, and Harrison White. 1964. *Canvases and Careers: Institutional Change in the French Painting World*. Chicago: University of Chicago Press.

recovering
subalternity in
the humanities
& social sciences   *PETER D. THOMAS*

SUBALTERN STUDIES EMERGED as a distinct field in the early 1980s with the pioneering works of the Subaltern Studies Collective in South Asian colonial history, under the leadership of Ranajit Guha. Its emphasis on recovering repressed but uneffaced traces of rebellious subaltern consciousness in colonial histories was soon recognized as one of the most provocatively productive research paradigms in the contemporary humanities and social sciences, and its organizing perspectives and methodological approaches were translated into a wide range of other geographical, linguistic, and historical contexts, from Latin America to Ireland to the United States (cf. Chaturvedi 2000; Ludden 2001; Rodríguez and López 2001). Stressing the subaltern as insurgent peasant, the Subaltern Studies Collective aimed to recover traditions of oppression and resistance that had hitherto been obscured not only in colonial and postcolonial contexts but also globally, insofar as the troubling questions that the experience of colonialism posed to political modernity's claims to universalism had been neglected or ignored.

While the early volumes of *Subaltern Studies* championed reading official histories against the grain and recovering the forms of subaltern consciousness silenced by and within archives, it would be reductive to regard this initiative as simply yet another iteration of a generic "history from below." One of the more specific and strongest claims of the early subaltern studies project was the insistence that subaltern classes and social groups should be understood not as a residue of the past but as fully modern phenomena. Objecting to Eric Hobsbawm's characterization of the peasant rebellions that marked both early political modernity and much of the experience of colonialism as "prepolitical," Ranajit Guha's intervention aimed to demonstrate the extent to which the practices of subaltern social groups in colonial India were instead already both fully "modern" and fully "political." For Guha, subaltern social groups in colonial India were not simply oppressed or subjugated by imperial state power. Rather, they constituted "an *autonomous* domain" defined by distinctive experiences that were irreducible to the determining coordinates of an ostensibly "normative" Western political modernity (1982, 4, 8). It was this emphasis on subalternity as a condition of colonial difference that constituted the basis for later creative developments of subaltern studies into different (and not always entirely compatible) directions, from Gayatri Spivak's influential theorization of the subaltern as a condition of incapacity (1988) and an "absolute limit" of the place where "history is narrativized into logic" (2012, 207), to Dipesh Chakrabarty's conception of those pluralized "life-worlds" and "subaltern pasts" that cannot be reduced to what he characterized as "History 1," or the "official" history of capital (2000).

Despite its growing international success throughout the 1980s and 1990s, however, key theorists in the development of the original subaltern studies project soon enough began to question its continuing relevance, or even to suggest its historical exhaustion. Chakrabarty (2005), for instance, suggested that the contradictory development of Indian democracy has fundamentally transformed the conditions originally theorized by Guha, while Partha Chatterjee argued that the subalterns excluded by the colonial and postcolonial order have been superseded by "populations" "governed" in "political society" (2004, 39; 2012, 44–49). In a related but distinct way, Gyanendra Pandey argued that the "peasant paradigm" of early subaltern studies needed to be recast in the twenty-first century in terms of the "deliberately paradoxical" figure of the "subaltern citizen," in order to comprehend the traces of subalternity that subsist even within the ongoing expansion of institutions of contemporary citizenship (2006).

Spivak, on the other hand, has argued that developments under neoliberalism since the 1990s have involved a transition to the figure of a (gendered) "new subaltern," now defined not by its removal from social mobility but by the invasive workings of globalization at social, political, and biopolitical levels. Such a new subaltern is depicted no longer in terms of opposition to or exclusion from citizenship but as representing a new mode of access to transformed conditions of citizenship, conditions that are conceived as lying "beyond" the hegemonic forms that defined the "classic" formulations of citizenship in political modernity (Spivak 2000).

Ironically, then, subaltern studies, at least in the now-"classical" formulation given to it in the volumes of *Subaltern Studies*, seems to have become precisely the type of "residue of the past" from which it took such pains at the moment of its inception to distance itself. Just as both the peasant rebellions of early modernity and their supposedly belated echoes in anticolonial insurgencies in the epoch of imperialism had been consigned to a mythical past from which an all-too-metropolitan present attempted to distinguish itself, so the moment of *Subaltern Studies* itself is now viewed as belonging to a "prehistory of the present," relevant to a colonial context that is no longer that of our "post-post-colonial condition."

Crisis and Foreclusion

The history of the development of subaltern studies thus confronts us with a curious paradox: on the one hand, the incredible international success of an interdisciplinary research program, spanning the humanities and the social sciences and inspiring new projects around the globe; and on the other hand, precisely at the moment of this success, a steadily increasing skepticism culminating in a crisis of confidence regarding the original program's ongoing theoretical and analytical force—a crisis felt not simply by those already critical of its fundamental propositions but also, even more remarkably, by some of its most distinguished practitioners. This paradox has a broader significance, beyond the history of subaltern studies in a narrow or broad sense, and helps us to pose a more general question regarding the production of knowledge and the emergence, expansion, and decline of research paradigms in the humanities and social sciences: What is to be done when a tradition feels itself to be in crisis? How should one attempt to rebuild after a "concept-quake" (Steinmetz, this volume) seems to have compromised a research project's very foundations?

The responses to the perceived crisis of subaltern studies are instructive regarding potential ways in which such a challenge might be confronted. On the one hand, former participants in the original Subaltern Studies Collective have engaged in a periodizing gesture, arguing that while the collective's original initiative may have been highly relevant to its own time and context (in the post-Emergency debates in South Asian history and social theory), the changed conditions of the present call for a different style of project and analysis (Chakrabarty 2005; Chatterjee 2012). On the other hand, scholars already critical of the original subaltern studies project have argued that its exhaustion is not merely one of temporal superannuation but reflects deeper theoretical flaws in its fundamental theoretical presuppositions (Chibber 2013; Kaiwar 2014). In both cases, subaltern studies in a broader sense—that is, not merely the original collective's intervention in South Asian history but the wider international research program that it inspired—is thought to be inextricably tied to, and perhaps compromised by a fatal flaw in, its original constitution and formulation.

In this chapter, I want to propose another mode of response to a crisis in a paradigm of knowledge production: namely, a genealogical consideration of that which was "foreclosed" in a research program's originary moment of institution. My use here of the notion of foreclosure, rather than repression, aims to indicate not those elements that were more or less knowingly excluded from a research program and which thereby might be open to recuperation by an act of Benjaminian *rettende Kritik*. In the case of subaltern studies, such an unexpected "return of the repressed" might be found, for instance, in the neglect by the South Asian historians of an earlier discussion of the notion of subaltern social groups among scholars of the contradictions of southern Italy, including Ernesto de Martino, Cesare Luporini, and Franco Fortini, in a debate about the political meaning of the "national-popular" in the early years of the so-called first Italian postwar republic (Pasquinelli 1977). My interest here is instead directed to those elements that a research program constitutively disavows, unwittingly and frequently productively: the necessary silences and silencings from which its speech emerges, and which in turn might continue to determine its development, dissolution, and potential revival in often unforeseen ways.

The development of subaltern studies provides an almost paradigmatic case study of the role that such a process of foreclosure can play in the development of a research program, both in its (presumed) success and its (perceived) crisis. For although it remains the great merit of Guha and the early Subaltern Studies Collective to have forcefully directed international attention to the theme of subalternity in the *Prison Notebooks*, their readings of it foreclosed just as much as they disclosed. The Subaltern Studies Collective's references to the partial English translation of Gramsci's carceral writings then available (Gramsci 1971) were highly suggestive but also decidedly occasional (the few textual references to the *Prison Notebooks* in the early volumes of *Subaltern Studies* do not extend far beyond Guha's preface to the initial volume in the series). Rather than a "meticulous recuperation of Antonio Gramsci's thought," as Rosalind Morris has suggested (2010, 10), the development of the notion of subalternity within subaltern studies (in both a narrower and broader sense) is more accurately characterized as a contextually overdetermined and therefore necessarily limited interpretation of it. As subsequent scholarship based on the full critical edition of Gramsci's writings (Gramsci 1975) has demonstrated, however, the notion of subalternity developed in the *Prison Notebooks* contains a wider range of critical perspectives than those that were valorized in the earlier or later stages of *Subaltern Studies* (Liguori 2016). In the following section, I aim to highlight how these foreclosed themes might today be reactivated in a reflexive relationship to the "crisis" of subaltern studies, in the broadest sense of the term: as moment of dissolution but also, potentially, of critical renewal.

Subalternity in the *Prison Notebooks*

The theme of subalternity was not present in Gramsci's earliest writings and was not included in his various plans for the carceral research project that later become his *Prison Notebooks*, written between 1929 and 1935. The theme suddenly became theoretically significant and central to all of his subsequent writing in the space of a few months in the summer of 1930. He argued that "the history of the subaltern classes is necessarily disaggregated and episodic: there is in the activity of these classes a tendency to unification, even if on provisional levels; but it is the less apparent part that only appears when victory is achieved. The subaltern classes suffer the initiative of the dominant class, even when they rebel; they are in a state of alarmed defense" (Q3, §14, 299–300).[1]

Gramsci made very clear that he regarded subalternity as a fully "modern" phenomena—not a residue of previous sociopolitical organizations but a distinctive dynamic that was only fully affirmed in the process of the consolidation of the modern state. In the ancient and medieval worlds, he argued, the "subaltern classes had a separate life, their own institutions." The modern state, however,

> abolishes many autonomies of the subaltern classes—it abolishes the state as a federation of classes—but certain forms of the internal life of the subaltern classes are reborn as parties, trade unions, cultural associations.

The modern dictatorship abolishes these forms of class autonomy as well, and it tries hard to incorporate them into the activity of the state: in other words, the centralization of the whole life of the nation in the hands of the dominant class becomes frenetic and all-consuming. (Q 3, §18, 303)

In later notes he argued that the disaggregation and reconfiguration of the life of the subaltern classes constitutes a general process in political modernity, the dynamic of which he dated back to at least the French Revolution. Rather than a supposed transformation of "subjects" into "citizens," or the affirmation of principles of popular sovereignty or autonomy, Gramsci's narrative instead focused on the "enclosure" of the life of the subaltern classes in a process of simultaneous mobilization and domestication. Political modernity, in both metropolitan and colonial variants, is in this view distinguished by the contradictory forms in which "private" energies released on the terrain of consolidating capitalist market relations are immediately overcoded by the extension of "public"' administrative power. The unity of the ruling classes is found in the state and its history, or what Gramsci called the "result of relations between the state and civil society." For the subaltern classes, on the other hand, such "unification does not occur: their history is intertwined with that of 'civil society,' it is a disaggregated fraction of it" (Q 3, §90, 372–73).

Central to Gramsci's subsequent development of this theme was the insight that there is no opposition between the hegemonic and the subaltern but rather a relation of mutual coconstitution; it is precisely because hegemony is already at work within subalternity itself, as a condition and consequence of the subaltern classes' disaggregation, that a potential transition from the subaltern to the hegemonic is conceivable. This perspective of the hegemonic constitution of subalternity was developed across a series of notes and themes, between 1930 and 1935, in complex ways that both shape and reflect the fundamental coordinates of the overall political theory developed in the *Prison Notebooks*. It is a perspective that flowed into Gramsci's 25th Notebook, titled "On the Margins of History," followed by the parenthetical subtitle "(History of Subaltern Social Groups)." The first note in this notebook (Q 25, §1, 2280) recounts the curious case of the literally unarmed prophet Davide Lazzaretti, the leader of a "tendentially republican" movement in Tuscany in post-Risorgimento Italy that was "bizarrely mixed" with religious and prophetic elements. Gramsci drew attention to the emergence of Lazzaretti's only seemingly "spontaneous" movement in a period when the Catholic Church's abstention from official politics in the post-Risorgimento state, alongside popular delusions in a newly installed government of the left, had released subaltern energies from containment within established political structures.

Pace Guha, subaltern social classes are not here considered as autonomous, or as excluded, from the modern state. Nor, contra Spivak, are they simply oppressed or subjugated by it, vanishing points of a prehistory narrativized away by the logic of modern state formation. Rather, they are represented as continually transformed and reconstituted by the expansive logic of the modern state conceived in the broadest sense—that is, not as a normative ideal but as a complex historical process. Subaltern social groups have been mobilized to participate in the political projects that have marked this process of state formation in contradictory and frequently passive forms, imposed forms that overdetermine even moments of rebellion against them.

This political conception of subalternity was elaborated in the context of Gramsci's distinctive understanding of the modern state as a dialectical unity in distinction of "political" and "civil society." Against what were effectively the neo-Kantian revisions of Marxist state theory by dominant currents in both the Second and Third Internationals, the *Prison Notebooks* undertook a critical return to the Hegelian theory of the state. Like Hegel (and in opposition to the various caricatures of the state theory of the *Philosophy of Right*, within and outside the Marxist tradition), Gramsci insisted on the mutually constitutive relation between "civil society" and what he called "political society" or "state," a relation that he characterized as the formation of an "integral state" (Gramsci's reformulation of the Italian neo-idealist reading of Hegel's theory of the state as an "ethical state").

Civil society and political society here are not conceived as separate geographical or institutional terrains, or as "autonomous domains" (in Guha's sense), but as forms of imbricated sociopolitical relationality. Rather than characterized by "consent" and opposed to the "coercion" of the state, or as a terrain of equality and formalized rights and responsibilities, civil society is instead theorized much more expansively. It includes all those practices in which the state's rationality is realized and affirmed, frequently unknowingly and often in associative or communal forms that may appear to be autonomous from or even opposed to it. Civil society, that is, does not stand in an external relationship to political society or the state, such as to make possible the "assimilation" of the former by the latter (or civil society's "nonassimilation," in the case of the "colonial state"). Civil society, far from being a terrain of freedom before or beyond the state (a central tenant of classical and contemporary liberalism), is thus depicted instead as a mode of relationality characteristic of the disaggregated subalterns, who remain subaltern precisely to the extent that they remain confined within this relationality of hegemonic subordination. The tendency toward unification of the subaltern social groups in civil society is continually fractured by the interventions of the political society that constitutes them as the subaltern "raw material" for its directive operations. Rather than outside of or opposed to the hegemonic, the subaltern in this sense is integrally and immanently related to it, as simultaneously the presupposition and the product of its operations. Subalternity was thus for Gramsci not merely not "prepolitical"; in a strict sense, the process of subalternization is coincident with the nature of politics within the modern integral state as such.

Recovering the full complexity of Gramsci's theory of subalternity provides us with a very different conception of the nature of subaltern social groups than those characterizations that were so productively explored by the early *Subaltern Studies* volumes but that also played a decisive role in the later perception of its crisis or exhaustion. In the following sections, I outline three ways in which reopening some of the perspectives that *Subaltern Studies* had constitutively foreclosed can provide resources not only for relaunching a new phase of subaltern studies "beyond *Subaltern Studies*" but also for engaging with some of the central concerns of contemporary critical theory and practice. These are the notions of subaltern capacity; of the integral relation between subalternity and hegemony even and especially within colonial difference; and of the nature of modern citizenship as a process of subalternization.

Subaltern Capacity

The conception of subalternity in the *Prison Notebooks* is radically different from the widely diffused notion that the subaltern is a figure of undifferentiated destitution, consigned to a zone beyond expressive capacity or purposive political agency. Spivak's influential text "Can the Subaltern Speak?" undoubtedly laid the foundations for this approach (1988). Originally written as reflection on debates regarding the status of intellectuals' politics, without reference to the subaltern in either *Subaltern Studies* or Gramsci (cf. Morris 2010), the later prominent insertion of this figure in the essay's title has led to its themes assuming almost paradigmatic status in the wider discussion of subalternity. Spivak's subsequent interventions have reinforced this general tendency of defining the subaltern primarily in terms of incapacity. In some of her more provocative formulations, for instance, the subaltern becomes an almost mystical concept in a Wittgensteinian sense: the subaltern not only cannot speak but is also that figure of whom one should not speak, lest one falls into the trap of speaking for the subaltern, thus dominating it. In Spivak's words, "If the subaltern can speak then, thank God, the subaltern is not a subaltern any more" (1990, 158; for an analysis of the development of this "perspective" in Veena Das's work, see Chitralekha's chapter in this volume). The subaltern is here represented, paradoxically, as that which is not representable in any given order; the entrance into (self-)representation is immediately the exit from subalternity.

For Gramsci, on the other hand, subaltern social groups are continually expressive and self-representing, albeit in ways that are not easily comprehended within the existing political or intellectual orders—or even by themselves in the initial phases of their rebellions. Gramsci's example of Lazzaretti's prophetic-republican movement, for instance, is composed of layer upon layer of subaltern expressions and representative containments. On the one hand, his note is framed by considerations of the way in which Italian social commentators and theorists, including Domenico Bulferetti, Giovanni Verga, Cesare Lombroso, and Giacomo Barzellotti, had represented this and other similar movements in post-Risorgimento Italy in terms of a "pathological biography," giving "restrictive, individual, folkloric explanations" of movements that called for broader contextual and political analysis (Q 25, § 1, 2279–80). On the other hand, Gramsci argues that representative dynamics are discernible within Lazzaretti's movement itself. One of the reasons for Lazzaretti's popular appeal, he argues, was that Lazzaretti reformulated peasant discontent with previous manifestations of republicanism in Tuscany, particularly in 1848, in a prophetic direction. Rather than a negation of subalternity, this form of attempted self-representation constituted one of the ways in which the movement's subaltern status was performed, even and especially in the attempt to overcome it.

The parenthetical subtitle of Notebook 25 is perhaps most telling indication of the extent to which a dialectic between expression and representation is inscribed within Gramsci's conception of subalternity. Subaltern classes or social groups are "on the margins of history," that is, "history" conceived in the sense of historiography, as a text written almost invariably by the victors (Q 25, 2277). This does not mean, however, that they are "without" or "outside" history, in the sense of the real historical events that the dominant forms of historiography seek to narrativize and, by so doing, to domesticate. Subalterns are fully present actors on the stage of history, though reduced to minor and fleeting roles in the official script. Extra- or paradiscursive forms of subaltern expression jostle alongside inchoate and often discordant attempts to develop forms of self-representation. It is the role of what Gramsci calls the "integral historian" to recover and valorize the full range of these forms of expression within and beyond the dominant narrative (Q 25, § 2, 2284).

Furthermore, rather than an amorphous mass of the indifferently oppressed, Gramsci's conception emphasizes the varying degrees of subalternity within the subaltern social groups. There are many subalterns within the subaltern relationality of civil society, structured by their relation to the organizing instances of political society. As Marcus Green has emphasized, Gramsci's conception of subalternity is not limited to class understood in an economistic sense; it includes a wider range of relations, including gender, ethnicity, and regionality (2011). Just as significantly, the fact that subaltern social groups are actively and differentially incorporated into historically specific systems of hegemonic power, in forms of passive citizenship just as much as by practices of pacification, also means that there are different potential stages in the emergence from subalternity. There is no Rubicon lying between subalternity and hegemony, just as civil society and political society are not conceived as spatially distinct zones. Rather, there are degrees of subalternity, and degrees of emergence from it, ranging from inchoate rebellion, co-optation, partial or merely asserted autonomy, to complete autonomy. Were there no degrees of subalternity, were civil society a terrain of total domination instead of a continually renewed hegemonic relation of subordination, hegemony, conceived as a practice of pedagogical leadership that encourages the emergence of capacities for self-direction of previously subaltern social groups, would not be a realistic political strategy.

Subalternity, Hegemony, and Colonial Difference

The emphasis in the early volumes *of Subaltern Studies* on the "autonomous domain" of the subalterns, or the people, has frequently been interpreted to imply an externality of the subaltern to the hegemonic, or as a key marker of its colonial difference. Guha's analysis of colonial (and even more pointedly, postcolonial) South Asia, for instance, depicted a sociopolitical formation composed of "subjects," "vast areas in the life and consciousness" of whom "were never integrated into [the colonial or Indian bourgeoisie's] hegemony." In other words, it was not a society populated by the "citizens" that Guha held to be the "normal" inhabitants of political modernity and its hegemonic constitution in Western Europe (1982, 5–6; 2009, 368). Chatterjee has extended this perspective to argue that the failure of the Indian bourgeoisie to stabilize a normal hegemonic order had left the majority of the population in a perennial hegemonic "outside," first in the form of the subalternity of the insurgent peasant in colonial times, and more recently in the form of the populations subjected to a logic of governmentality in the "political society" of the postcolonial state. Political society is here defined by Chatterjee in an antinomic rather than a dialectical relation to civil society, which he conceives, following classical liberal political theory, as the terrain of "rights-bearing citizens" (2004, 8–9).[2]

In the *Prison Notebooks*, however, the subaltern is not opposed to the hegemonic but instead constitutes its necessary complement. The type of subalternity that interests Gramsci is already "enclosed" or constituted within the hegemonic relations of the passive revolutionary processes condensed in the bourgeois integral state. These subaltern classes or social groups do not simply exist as such, in a supposedly "natural" or "prepolitical" (as opposed to "historical" or "political") dimension before or beyond the state, as Guha rightly insisted. Precisely insofar as they are both fully "modern" and fully "political," however, subaltern classes or social groups, whether in the metropolitan "centers" or their colonial "peripheries," fully participate in hegemonic—that is, fully political—relations in varying forms. The diverse ways in which these relations are expressed are not signs of an irreducible difference between "colonial and metropolitan theatres," as Gyan Prakash has suggested (1994, 1480), but are constituted by their differential participation in the general dynamic of political modernity as a process of subalternization.

The preponderance of coercion over persuasion does not indicate the absence or diminution of hegemonic relations, or what Guha characterized as the "dominance without hegemony" of the "nonhegemonic" South Asian "colonial state" (1998, xii).[3] Rather, it points to the differential articulation of those hegemonic relations, to the shifting balance between mobilization and domestication, between private and public initiatives of state power, in different concrete contexts. Gramsci's notion of "passive revolution," in its complex development and implications, registers precisely this potential for such a form of "hegemony without hegemony," whether produced by a crisis of the "normal" exercise of hegemony on the "classic terrain" of the parliamentary regime in Western Europe, or the supposed "failures" of revolutionary or national liberation movements to establish it elsewhere (Q 1, §48, 59). The type of modern subalternity on which Gramsci's analyses focus is both index and expression of the efficacy of such passive revolutionary processes.

This understanding of the hegemonic constitution of subalternity also has implications for understanding the hegemonic constitution of the ruling classes. Just as the subalterns are not merely the excluded, so too are the ruling classes not simply oppressors or dominators. In late 1934, in Notebook 25, Gramsci transcribed the previously cited note from August 1930 in which he had first linked the fate of subaltern classes to civil society. He introduces some significant specifications in his revisions that emphasize that the formation of the ruling classes is also determined by the hegemonic relations within the integral state. He argues that

> the historical unity of the ruling classes occurs in the state and their story is essentially the history of states and of groups of states. But we shouldn't think that such unity is purely juridical and political, even if this form of unity has its importance, and not merely a formal importance: the fundamental historical unity, in its concrete nature, is the result of the organic relations between state or political society and "civil society." (Q 25, §5, 2287)

Insofar as the historical unity of the ruling classes results from the organic relations between political society and civil society, such unity presupposes just as much as it imposes the production of subalternity. Ruling classes in political modernity need to produce—and to reproduce continually—subaltern social groups in order to become and to maintain themselves as ruling classes. Whether in the extreme forms of fascist dictatorship or colonial administration, or in the seemingly more benign forms of liberal representative regimes with their systems of political elites and passive citizenries, the need for the continual production and reproduction of subaltern social groups constitutes a fragile and tenuous basis of enduring political power. It remains always dependent on the ongoing subjugation of its interpellated antagonist, or on the hegemonic relations of force that constitute it in both a material and formal sense. It is precisely here, in the midst of a hegemonic relationship, constitutively open to contestation, that the potential political power of the subaltern lies.

Citizenship *sive* Subalternization

One of the fundamental perspectives of the early volumes of *Subaltern Studies* was a distinction between "subjecthood" and "citizenship." While the latter was conceived as hegemonically constituted in the imperial centers, the former was the condition of the subalterns in their colonial peripheries, an exclusion from full participation in the normal or even normative institutions of political modernity that has been held to continue, in the case of the Indian Republic or even "most of the world," long into the postcolonial period (Chatterjee 2004). In one of the most innovative attempts to update or "to sublate" the legacy of *Subaltern Studies* after the exhaustion of its classical "peasant paradigm," Pandey has urged the adoption of the "deliberately paradoxical . . . category of the subaltern citizen" (2006, 4736). These "subaltern citizens" are conceived as those "who have been granted the status of citizen (rights-holders, inhabitants, subjects of the state) without becoming quite 'mainstream.'" In a dual move, the "traditional" subaltern is thus reconceived, on the one hand, as a "potential citizen," a potential now still only partially fulfilled for some social groups; and on the other, subalternity comes to be seen as an enduring "trace" or latent threat of exclusion, even and perhaps especially within the achievement of citizenship (2010, 5–6). Subalternization, conceived in terms of "minoritarization," continues to represent a primary experience of exclusion, oppression and marginalization. It both precedes (historically and logically) the affirmation of citizenship, and continuously threatens to reemerge within it, frustrating the full realization of citizenship's promises.

In the *Prison Notebooks*, however, the type of modern subalternity generated within the hegemonic dynamics between civil society and political society in the integral state does not precede citizenship or subsist within it as trace or threat. Citizenship is conceived not as a supplement or corrective to the subaltern's "otherness" but as one of the forms of the political expression of subalternity. In other words, citizenship and subalternity in the *Prison Notebooks* are in a relationship of simultaneous coconstitution. The two concepts can be regarded as different vocabularies for describing (and in so doing validating or challenging) the same historical process: on the one hand, the narrative of political modernity as the consolidation of juridical forms guaranteeing individual rights and responsibilities within an homogenous political community; on the other hand, the history of the constitution of hegemonic relations of subordination between classes and groups, with dominance by one group in political society depriving other groups of the capacity for self-direction and autonomous political initiative in civil society. Conceived as two sides of the same coin, the two vocabularies can thus be seen as developing in parallel, reinforcing or subverting each other. Rather than the "citizen subaltern" or the "subaltern citizen," in which one of the terms qualifies the other, I argue that this relation is more adequately characterized by the figure of the coterminous "citizen-subaltern," or "citizen *sive* subaltern." Gramsci's theory of subalternity can therefore be regarded as an attempt to theorize the constitutive relationship between freedom and unfreedom in political modernity, conceived in terms comparable to those with which Étienne Balibar has more recently proposed to comprehend with the figure of the "citizen subject" (2011).

Thus, just as subaltern classes or social groups are never completely deprived of expressive or representative capacities, and just as subalternity is not exterior to hegemony but a product of it, so is subalternity not a relation of exclusion from citizenship, but rather, one of the forms of its realization. This does not mean, however, that it should be thought in the specular terms of an inclusion of what was originally excluded, or even as the type of "inclusive exclusion" theorized by Giorgio Agamben under the heading of the "relation of exception." For Agamben, "the juridico-political order has the structure of an inclusion of what is simultaneously pushed outside," and the "relation of exception" is the "extreme form of relation by which something is included solely through its exclusion" (1998, 18). For Gramsci, on the contrary, it is not such an exclusion (whether conceived in the begin forms of marginalization or minoritorization, or the extreme forms of expulsion) that encloses the subalterns within the integral state. Rather, it is their active mobilization within hegemonic relations in civil society, especially in the dynamic of passive revolutionary processes, from "transformist" integration of them into other social groups' political organizations, to the constitution of their own economic corporative associations and even partially autonomous political organizations. This enclosure is constitutive and productive of subaltern classes and social groups. "The end" of subalternity is conceived not in terms of an exit from this condition, but as the internal transformation of the hegemonic relations that structure it. For this reason, the type of citizenship that early *Subaltern Studies* held to distinguish the normative West from its colonial East does not represent an escape from relations of subalternity; on the contrary, it can in this perspective be regarded as subalternity's temporal consolidation and institutional intensification.

Conclusion

A study of Gramsci's integral development of the notion of subalternity reveals a much richer field of reflection on the contradictions and forms of political modernity than became apparent during the first season of engagement with his texts. Subalternity for Gramsci is an experience of marginality, in terms of the subalterns' relations to the centers of political power, but it is not a marginal experience, in terms of the political relations and forms to which the majority of the inhabitants of modern political communities are subjected, in the West and North just as much as the East and South. The

Prison Notebooks provide a general characterization of political modernity as a process of subalternization. It is a process in which the disaggregation of subaltern classes and social groups in civil society, or associative forms, constitutes them as the objects of the directive instances of political society, or of instances of political organization and administration.

Beyond questions of historical or philological accuracy, such a perspective might also suggest ways in which the crisis of confidence in the utility and relevance of subaltern studies as a research program might be productively resolved in a critical analysis on the present. Far from being exhausted by recent political transformations, the more expansive understanding of subalternity that can be found in Gramsci's full *Prison Notebooks* seems particularly well placed to comprehend significant developments in a wide variety of contemporary political contexts. For example, Gramsci's emphasis on the irrepressibility of the subaltern, continually engaged in struggle, has been used to rethink the consequences of the extension of biopolitical and governmental logics and in contemporary India. As Nilsen and Roy argue, rather than the negation of an "autonomous domain" of subaltern politics, these developments can be productively analyzed in terms of transformed "entanglements" between civil and political societies, which have been shaped by subaltern resistance and have also helped to produce new forms of subaltern agency (2015). Similarly, the notion of subalternity as a hegemonic relation, constitutive not only of subaltern social classes and groups but also of the ruling classes qua "subalternizers" can help to understand both the flood and ebb of the "pink tide" of "progressive" governments in Latin America in the early twenty-first century. As Massimo Modonesi argues, the "pacification" of popular movements in Latin America in recent years might be understood in terms of a process "re-subalternization," or of the ways in which subaltern rebellions have been compromised by longer-term transformist and passive revolutionary strategies (2017). In another context, Gramsci's analysis of subalternity and citizenship as coconstitutive rather than opposed can also provide a critical perspective on what Wendy Brown has characterized as an "undoing" of democracy by neoliberal rationality, which she argues to have characterized politics in the "Euro-Atlantic world" over the last three decades (2015). Rather than a recent and conjunctural negation of the promises of inclusion within democratic citizenship, Gramsci's theorization suggests that such processes have emerged from longer-term, structural conditions of subalternization inscribed within the general dynamic of political modernity, even and especially when it is realized in the contradictory forms of citizenship.

The "de-foreclusion" of the texts and themes that provided the initial inspiration for the institution of subaltern studies as an expansive research program thus ultimately not only constitutes an act of recovery of a significant critical tradition in the history of twentieth-century social and political thought. It can also be understood as a critical perspective onto some of the central debates in contemporary political theory in an international perspective. Ultimately, such a response to the crisis of subaltern studies offers the initiation of a new phase of subaltern studies "beyond *Subaltern Studies*," a type of subaltern studies that would be both global and contemporary, capable of inheriting the project of reading archives of dominant historiography against the grain, and of intervening into the struggles of the present, in "postcolonial" and "metropolitan" realities alike.

Notes

1   References to Gramsci's *Prison Notebooks* are given according to the Italian critical edition of the *Quaderni del carcere* (Gramsci 1975), following the internationally established standard of notebook number (Q), number of note (§), and page number.

2   Later inheritors of this approach have emphasized in more strongly normative terms the opposition of the subaltern and the hegemonic. In a formulation representative of an important tendency in Latin American subaltern studies, for example, Alberto Moreiras argues that the subaltern should be understood as a "perspective from the constitutive outside of hegemony," or as "the remainder of the hegemonic relation" (2001, 53, 296).

3   As a number of critics have argued, Guha's characterization of the condition of colonial India as one of "dominance without hegemony" underestimates the extent to which the supposedly more hegemonic constitution of the state in Western Europe was and remains itself reliant on an excess of dominance over "consent" at decisive instances. Even more pointedly, this perspective not only posits qualitative rather than quantitative differences between the functioning of state power in Western centers and their supposedly colonial peripheries, thereby neglecting that ways in which the historical experience of colonialism was central and not incidental to the emergence of the modern state as a distinctive, geographically located concentration of military capability, administrative violence and temporal ordering (Anievas and Nişancioğlu 2015). It also underestimates the extent to which state power in those Western centers themselves was itself constituted as a "colonial power," in the sense of exercising an often brutal governance of populations conceived less as rights-bearing subjects than as objects of the exercise of state power. The experience of coloniality is in this sense not something that lies before, beyond, or outside the modern

Western state, but is something that is central to its originary and continuously reproduced constitution. Normative principles argued by Guha and Chatterjee to be lacking or weaker in colonial or postcolonial societies—the rule of law, respect for the rights of citizenship, or the pacific functioning of an "unruly" and decidedly "civil" civil society—were, after all, often more honored in the breach than the observance in the history of Western political modernity, as the massacre of the Communards, widespread restrictions on the franchise up to and including the twentieth century, or suppression and restriction of autonomous popular organizations such as trade unions (in the twenty-first century just as much as the nineteenth) amply attest.

References

Agamben, Giorgio. 1998. *Homo Sacer: Sovereign Power and Bare Life*. Stanford, CA: Stanford University Press.

Anievas, Alexander, and Kerem Nişancioğlu. 2015. *How the West Came to Rule: The Geopolitical Origins of Capitalism*. London: Pluto Press.

Balibar, Étienne. 2011. *Citoyen sujet et autres essais d'anthropologie philosophique*. Paris: PUF.

Brown, Wendy. 2015. *Undoing the Demos: Neoliberalism's Stealth Revolution*. New York: Zone Books.

Chakrabarty, Dipesh. 2000. *Provincializing Europe: Postcolonial Thought and Historical Difference*. Princeton, NJ: Princeton University Press.

Chakrabarty, Dipesh. 2005. "Subaltern Studies in Retrospect and Reminiscence." *South Asia: Journal of South Asian Studies* 38, no. 1: 10–18.

Chatterjee, Partha. 2004. *The Politics of the Governed: Reflections on Popular Politics in Most of the World*. New York: Columbia University Press.

Chatterjee, Partha. 2012. "After Subaltern Studies." *Economic and Political Weekly* 47, no. 35: 44–49.

Chaturvedi, Vinayak, ed. 2000. *Mapping Subaltern Studies and the Postcolonial*. London: Verso.

Chibber, Vivek. 2013. *Postcolonial Theory and the Specter of Capital*. London: Verso.

Gramsci, Antonio. 1971. *Selections from the Prison Notebooks*. Edited and translated by Quintin Hoare and Geoffrey Nowell-Smith. New York: International Publishers.

Gramsci, Antonio. 1975. *Quaderni del carcere*. Edited by Valentino Gerratana. Turin: Einaudi.

Green, Marcus. 2011. "Rethinking the Subaltern and the Question of Censorship in Gramsci's *Prison Notebooks*." *Postcolonial Studies* 14, no. 4: 387–404.

Guha, Ranajit. 1982. "On Some Aspects of the Historiography of Colonial India." In *Subaltern Studies I: Writings on South Asian History and Society*, edited by Ranajit Guha, 37–44. Delhi: Oxford University Press.

Guha, Ranajit. 1998. *Dominance without Hegemony: History and Power in Colonial India*. Oxford: Oxford University Press.

Guha, Ranajit. 2009. *The Small Voice of History: Collected Essays*. Ranikhet: Permanent Black.

Kaiwar, Vasant. 2014. *The Postcolonial Orient: The Politics of Difference and the Project of Provincialising Europe*. Leiden: Brill.

Liguori, Guido. 2016. "Subalterno e subalterni nei 'Quaderni del carcere.'" *International Gramsci Journal* 2, no. 1: 89–125.

Ludden, David, ed. 2001. *Reading Subaltern Studies: Critical History, Contested Meaning and the Globalization of South Asia*. London: Anthem.

Modonesi, Massimo. 2017. *Revoluciones pasivas en América*. Mexico City: Itaca.

Moreiras, Alberto. 2001. *The Exhaustion of Difference: The Politics of Latin American Cultural Studies*. Durham, NC: Duke University Press.

Morris, Rosalind, ed. 2010. *Can the Subaltern Speak: Reflections on the History of an Idea*. New York: Columbia University Press.

Nilsen, Alf Gunvald, and Srila Roy, eds. 2015. *New Subaltern Politics: Reconceptualizing Hegemony and Resistance in Contemporary India*. New Delhi: Oxford University Press.

Pandey, Gyanendra. 2006. "The Subaltern as Subaltern Citizen." *Economic and Political Weekly* 41, no. 46 (November 18–24): 4735–41.

Pandey, Gyanendra, ed. 2010. *Subaltern Citizens and Their Histories: Investigations from India and the USA*. New York: Routledge.

Pasquinelli, Carla, ed. 1977. *Antropologia culturale e questione meridionale: Ernesto De Martino e il dibattito sul mondo popolare subalterno negli anni 1948–1955*. Florence: La Nuova Italia Editrice.

Prakash, Gyan. 1994. "Subaltern Studies as Postcolonial Criticism." *American Historical Review* 99, no. 5: 1475–90.

Rodríguez, Ileana, and María Milagros López, eds. 2001. *The Latin American Subaltern Studies Reader*. Durham, NC: Duke University Press.

Spivak, Gayatri Chakravorty. 1988. "Can the Subaltern Speak?" In *Marxism and the Interpretation of Culture*, edited by Cary Nelson and Lawrence Grossberg, 271–313. Urbana: University of Illinois Press.

Spivak, Gayatri Chakravorty. 1990. *The Postcolonial Critic: Interviews, Strategies, Dialogues*. New York: Routledge.

Spivak, Gayatri Chakravorty. 2000. "Discussion: An Afterword on the New Subaltern." In *Subaltern Studies XI: Community, Gender and Violence*, edited by Partha Chatterjee and Pradeep Jeganathan, 305–34. Delhi: Permanent Black.

Spivak, Gayatri Chakravorty. 2012. *In Other Worlds: Essays in Cultural Politics*. New York: Routledge.

13

thinking about cognitive scientists thinking about religion

JOHN LARDAS MODERN

OVER THE PAST TWENTY YEARS the concept of a hyperactive agency detection device (HADD) has become a central component in the cognitive
study of religion. Cognitive scientists use this felicitous phrase to discuss
the bundle of cognitive processes that prime humans to scan for and believe
in supernatural agents. HADD is, and has always been, the source of our
overdeterminations—from the worship of animal spirits to the actions of
suicide bombers to contemporary conspiracy theorists. As Ilkka Pyysiäinen
summarizes recent trends concerning HADD,

> This mechanism is triggered by very minimal cues. We see faces in the
> clouds and detect predators in rustling bushes because such ambiguous
> perceptions easily trigger the postulations of agency. . . . A normally func-
> tioning HADD is hyperactive by its very nature—hyperactivity is not some-
> thing special. From an evolutionary point of view, this is plausible, insofar
> as the costs of false positives that an overreacting detector produces are
> lower than the benefits it brings. (Pyysiäinen 2009, 13)[1]

To be clear, the hyperactive agency detection device is not part of a crass claim about where religion is located à la phrenology but a more subtle attempt to understand the consequential integration of scanning and computational capacities of the brain (Boyer 2003). Different parts of the brain come together to form a sustained statistical stare. The accumulation of statistics allows the stare to surveil. The eye is kept relatively mobile amid a swirl of information and data stimulations, tracking patterns across the surface of things.

Since the 1940s there has been an abundance of work on "the precise stimulus conditions that give rise to these percepts [of agency] [and] the perceptual 'grammar' of causality" (Scholl and Tremoulet 2000). Religion, however, as a misguided form of agency detection—that is, animism—has a rich anthropology behind it: think Ludwig Feuerbach, Karl Marx, E. B. Tylor, and Sigmund Freud. It was not until 1980, however, that the anthropologist Stewart Guthrie made the explicit case for a cognitive theory of religion as agency detection (Guthrie 1980), arguing that religion could be explained as an efficacious anthropomorphism—the process by which humans projected their own humanity upon the world, for better or for worse. Guthrie's question was essentially this: If animism is a conceptual mistake (for who among us believes in ghosts?), how then to explain the situation in which many people still detect agents when in fact they have not?

Guthrie's *answer*?

Such detections, asserts Guthrie, "arise inevitably, as by-products—namely, as false positives—of our scanning an uncertain world for what matters most. What matters most is agency" (2007, 37). The question of why agency matters is, of course, assumed. According to Guthrie and other cognitive scientists, the category of agency and their interest in it is a natural by-product of evolutionary history.

One marvels at the lack of reflexivity when the analytic of agency detection is naturalized amid a culture dense with measures of "attention regulation," "attentional expertise," and "attention disorders." And then there is the academic industry of "Error Management Theory" in which evolutionary insight is disseminated in business school classrooms and workshops. There the theory of hyperactive detection is used to frame good and bad decisions, risk management, and acts of deception among businessmen, pilots, doctors, and economists (Linder, Foss, and Stea 2016; Johnson, Blumstein, et al. 2013).[2] More ominously, the question of agency detection implies a concept of religion as mental error or, at the sociological level, an excessive collective investment of cognitive resources.

IN WHAT FOLLOWS I seek to contextualize the conceptual present of the Cognitive Science of Religion (CSR), to tend, as any empirically minded scientist would, to ecological confounds, cultural artifacts, and the conditions that make possible (and increasingly legible) cognitive investigations into religion.

I lead with a discussion of the cognitive revolution within the human sciences that began at midcentury with the integration of information theory and the study of neural networks. Along the way I offer a prehistory of CSR, its emergence vis-à-vis trends with Cold War social science, and the particular stakes involved in its framing of religion as a matter of natural cognition. After considering the epistemology and politics embedded in the concept of hyperactive agency detection, I revisit Fritz Heider and Marianne Simmel's "An Experimental Study of Apparent Behavior" (1944). This seminal article serves as an origin story of hyperactive agency detection and illuminates both its ambition and limitations. Heider and Simmel claimed to have demonstrated how humans ascribed human characteristics, motives, and narrative to situations that were anything but. Through a close reading of this experiment I want to call attention to the degree to which CSR has uncritically drawn inspiration from Heider and Simmel's style of science.

I argue that CSR not only is part and parcel of a contemporary secular imaginary but also serves as a significant gear in what might be called a religion machine (Modern 2021). CSR is emblematic, in other words, of the discursive mechanics involved in naturalizing the concept of religion that one is in the process of studying. Drawing on notions that the "whole function of the brain [can be] summed up in error correction," CSR emerges in the wake of cybernetics and its formative paradigm of the brain as a self-organizing information-processing device (Ashby, cited in Clark 2013). Consequently, CSR is part of a contemporary secular imaginary not because of its scientific pose vis-à-vis the religious but, rather, because of the kind of human it assumes and instantiates with every pronouncement it makes about human religiosity—a human hard-wired to believe in supernatural agents but capable, at the end of the day, of overcoming this proclivity.

The Brain and the Human Sciences

As the twenty-first century dawns ... neuroscientists, cognitive scientists, and social scientists are placing less emphasis on the arbitrary division between the social and the biological sciences and are moving beyond simplifying assumptions toward developing more comprehensive theories of mind, brain, biology, and behavior.—J. T. CACIOPPO AND G. G. BERNSTEIN, *ESSAYS IN SOCIAL NEUROSCIENCE*

The language of systems and self-organization proliferated in the human sciences over the course of the twentieth century. Since midcentury there has been an "abiding interest in the means by which systems *store, process, and communicate information* about themselves and their environments" (Heyck 2015, 11). Key to this cybernetic revolution was the conception of the brain as an information-processing device—a cognitive script rehearsed in the key of Claude E. Shannon's "Mathematical Theory of Communication" (1948).

Shannon witnessed the rapid uptake of information theory across numerous disciplines over the next decade. As Shannon's friend at Bell Labs, J. R. Pierce, later commented, information theory "came as a bomb, and something of a delayed-action bomb" (Slepian 1973). By 1956 Shannon was already complaining that information theory had become "something of a scientific bandwagon" (Shannon 1956, 3). Part of this midcentury bandwagon was the emergence of a brain ever in relationship to its environment that was, itself, continuously processing information. As it was read alongside emerging theories of neural nets, information theory gained much of its cognitive traction and soon came to mark, in statistical terms, the predictability of neuronal firing (and not the meaning of that process). In their groundbreaking work of 1943, "A Logical Calculus of the Ideas Immanent in Nervous Activity," Warren McCulloch and Walter Pitts investigated the "macro effects displayed by nervous systems." The "Logical Calculus" was initially received with little fanfare among biologists and psychologists. It would soon, however, gain significant traction in those fields and beyond as it was read in dialogue with Shannon and featured prominently in Norbert Wiener's *Cybernetics* and in John von Neumann's "The General and Logical Theory of Automata."[3]

Soon neurophysiologists were utilizing information theory to probe normal and abnormal brains and their respective relationships to their environments. They were also setting a research agenda for large swaths of the human sciences in the postwar years. As Nikolas Rose and Joelle M. Abi-Rached have pointed out, the disciplinary formation of neuroscience, officially nominated in 1962, achieved intellectual currency through rapid institutionalization, streams of money, and an abiding enthusiasm for all things neuro (2013, 5, 30). A burgeoning neuroscience at midcentury provided theoretical and methodological inspiration for all manner of approaches to human interactions with their environment. As a site where different disciplinary concerns could be put in dialogue with one another, the study of the brain, the human nervous system, and the processing of information were taken up far afield from the neuroscience laboratory and used to make new and often bracing sense of personality, culture, society, politics, and the economy:[4] *a new vision of the human*. This human processed information. This human was, at the end of the day, primarily and paradigmatically, a brain.

The humanism that laced the cognitive revolution at midcentury continues to present itself as a brain-centered approach, which is adopted across different disciplinary spaces—neuropsychiatry (Martin 2002), neurolaw (Picozza 2016), neuroethics, neuroeconomics,[5] neuroaesthetics (Pearce et al. 2016), neuroergonomics (Mehta and Parasuraman 2013), neuroanthropology (Turner 1986; Domínguez et al. 2009), neurosociology (TenHouten 2013; Kalkhoff, Thye, and Pollock 2016), and neurotheology (Newberg 2013). Such "neuromania" has served, among other things, to generate hope in a future state of interdisciplinarity in which scholars from all backgrounds investigate their specific areas by privileging the neural processing of information.

In light of scholars who have demonstrated both the institutional and conceptual reach of the neurosciences into the world at large, I will now turn to a single case study in which cognition becomes the central axis for evaluating the human and measuring its normative status. For the remainder of this essay I will dig down into a local manifestation of our brain-obsessed present and consider the Cognitive Science of Religion as a singular example of the cognitive revolution within the human sciences.

The Cognitive Science of Religion

The Cognitive Science of Religion (CSR) is a burgeoning and highly interdisciplinary enterprise.... What unites these researchers is a shared focus on the role of human cognition in religious thought and behaviour, which they study by importing axiomatic assumptions from the cognitive revolution and their respective disciplines. The rich array of culturally postulated supernatural agents and supernatural realms, and the associated diversity of culturally prescribed and proscribed behaviours, are assumed to be constrained and canalized by genetically endowed cognitive capacities and structures shared by all typically developing humans. These structures are assumed to govern the types of information that is attended to, the contexts in which information is attended to, and the manner in which information is

stored, processed and acted upon.—DIMITRIS XYGALATAS AND
RYAN MCKAY, "ANNOUNCING THE *JOURNAL FOR THE COGNITIVE
SCIENCE OF RELIGION*"

The Cognitive Science of Religion (CSR) is a garden-variety yet exemplary subfield of the neuro turn in the human sciences. CSR—with its phalanx of journals[6] and seemingly endless funding opportunities—claims to have instituted a paradigm shift in the study of religion.[7] Pascal Boyer, one of the most visible figures in the cognitive science of religion, bluntly states that past theorizing in the field of religious studies has consisted "in the half-hearted adoption of particular academic fads." Most scholars of religion, he writes, pay "lip-service to the current fad, while carrying on with the[ir] erudition projects" of mere cataloguing. Boyer, who is considered something of an architect of CSR with the publication of *Religion Explained* in 2001 (a book E. O. Wilson blurbs as written "in the spirit of the French Enlightenment"), pulls no punches when it comes to describing the descriptive mode of contemporary religious studies: "As a consequence of this lackadaisical approach to explaining religious thought and behavior, the field has become theoretically amorphous, and unresponsive to actual scientific proposals" (Boyer 2013, 168). The solution, according to Boyer and his colleagues (who describe themselves as "empirically responsible" intellectuals) is to take up the calling of the brain to explain itself to itself, that is, to offer an explanation of human cognition that conforms to the social mechanics of cognitive processing (McCauley 2004, 60).

CSR is an international and self-consciously interdisciplinary subfield with competing claims about its object of study. But differences in opinion about the origins of religion or arguments about whether, for example, religion is an evolutionary adaption or an evolutionary effect, betray an underlying epistemic coherence. A style of reasoning is present and practiced among those who might disagree about the primacy of belief or ritual, the exact relationship between cognition and culture, or the preferred means of measuring that relationship. One point of substantive agreement across the various corners of CSR is that whatever religion is, it involves the superimposition of intentional agency on natural entities, events, or even groups (Ma-Kellams 2015; Bloom and Veres 1999). Put another way, CSR is motivated by an interest in explaining the cognitive mechanics of religion. But CSR is also fueled by a bemused and perhaps even benevolent concern for those subjects "prone to self-induced spiritual experiences [because they] *under* perceive the extent of their *own* agency in the world" (McKay 2014, 94).

The Hyperactive Agency Detection Device

The hyperactive agency detection device, or something like it, has been historicized and popularized and tested in the laboratory using, more often than not, two-dimensional simulations—TV screens, essentially, used to stimulate responses in experimental subjects (Dennett 2006, 109, 116, 151; Dawkins 2008, 214; Shermer 2009). Indeed, the "proper evolutionary domain" of agency "encompasses animate objects relevant to hominid survival"—such as predators, protectors, and prey—"but which actually extends (as an inadvertently but spontaneously activated evolutionary by-product) to moving dots on computer screens, voices in wind, and faces on clouds." Just as pornographic pictures or drawings can arouse measurable sexual pleasure, humans are easily fooled and mistake signs for reality when it comes to staring at a flat surface (Atran 2006b, 305).

The hyperactive agency detection device is a machine of sorts, inside your head right now, *no matter who you are*. It is a screening mechanism. All "typically developing humans" possess one. It is the machine that is at the base of religion. It scans the horizon for movement and pattern and alerts us to forces of otherness, variously construed. It is on all of the time, a form of troubleshooting the lines of transmission between you and what is on the other side of the screen (*Television* 1948, 197).

I use the word *screen* deliberately to mark the particularity of mechanical metaphor that is being used to designate a universal a subject who witnesses from afar, seeing in terms of physical laws, expectation, and counterintuition. For scanning yields incredibly detailed knowledge but is always at one remove. Scanning is a privileged form of vision that assumes a state of immunity, or at the very least, idealizes it, from the beginning. And it is precisely because the scanner does not get involved, physically, in that which it scans, there is much room for error correction above the fray. Scanning is said to be scientific. And it is said to be natural. Improvement and growth are built in. Self-correction is premised on the scanner keeping *his* distance (Haraway 1997, 32). Scanning is said to be liberated vision, a process of seeing without categories or preexisting taxonomies. Vision becoming "an algorithmic process for pattern extraction" (Halpern 2014, 204).

By 1980, at the dawn of the cable age and the twenty-four-hour news cycle (and the same year in which the American Psychiatric Association renamed the disorder of hyperkinesis Attention Deficit Disorder), scanning was becoming a thing (Spitzer 1980, 41–45). It was the logic of television. And it was how we detected the agency of others and exercised our own. Scanning also became part and parcel to a conception of the human, particularly a cognitive conception of the human bent on pattern recognition.[8] For whereas agency has become the end of religion for CSR, scanning is now thought to be the primary means. Scanning, as the bass line of cognition, is precision incarnate. As a physiological process, scanning serves to evacuate everything that weighs down the present save for its mathematical truth. Better living through scanning is sensing the numerical truth of present conditions and continually producing probabilistic scenarios that may stem from those conditions. *Better, stronger, faster*.[9]

According to the cognitive psychologist Justin Barrett (who coined the term), the hyperactive agency detection device was an evolutionary advantage in a hostile climate (Barrett and Keil 1996; Barrett 2000). Our ancestors were those individuals whose vigilance bordered on paranoia. They "scanned" the horizon for potential threats and predators and, in the process, attributed agency and purpose to trees, rocks, the wind, and whatever else struck their fancy as alive. "We constantly scan our environment for the presence of other people and nonhuman agents," argues Barrett. "If you bet that something is an agent and it isn't, not much is lost. But if you bet that something is not an agent and it turns out to be one, you could be lunch" (Barrett and Johnson 2003; Barrett 2004b, 31).

Anthropologist Pascal Boyer has recently offered a friendly amendment to Barrett's argument, writing that it makes sense to "over-detect" agents only if you can quickly "discard false positives." "Otherwise," notes Boyer, "you would spend all your time recoiling in fear, which is certainly not adaptive." Like Guthrie and Barrett, Boyer insists that religion is a natural attribute of the human that demands explanation. According to Boyer, humans are expert at scanning the horizon in order to produce as many inferences as possible. They are always computing, learning from their mistakes, and maximizing inferences for the sake of future efficiency, survival, and sociality (Boyer 2001, 147).[10]

Boyer writes that religion is bound up in this complex process of computational scanning and pattern recognition. Perception becomes disembodied. In the hands of CSR, this lends itself to a conception of religion as bloodless belief, or, more precisely, as a matter of looking at the sacred from a distance but doing little else by way of interaction.

Devoted Actors

As part of a complex predictive apparatus, HADD serves the ongoing process of secularization in which the passions of religion subside, its disciplines forgotten, and its traditions recede into memory. The secularization thesis embedded in Boyer's explanation of religion, a story of cognitive progress, shares much in common with nineteenth-century anthropologists such as E. B. Tylor. As with Tylor, a subtle strain of paranoia laces Boyer's prose, a strain that is familiar, particularly among new atheists writing in an age of simmering Islamophobia (Greenwald 2013). Not only do religious concepts and activities impinge on our agentive potential but, to quote Boyer, they also "hijack our cognitive resources" (2008b).[11] For religion, in Boyer's scheme, may have had its local advantages, but at the end of the day it is a form of laziness or obsessive-compulsive pathology or both. Scientific atheism, on the other hand, is a hard job: unlike religion, argues Boyer, "disbelief is generally the result of deliberate, effortful work against our natural cognitive dispositions—hardly the easiest ideology to propagate" (2008b). Cognitive scientists, Boyer triumphantly claims, can scan and see more clearly than anybody else. Accordingly, cognitive inquiry has the power to disenchant, to transform religion from a mystery into a problem to be solved.

The notion of a religion as a naturally occurring pathology has assumed a central place in what might be called the metaphysics of the war on global terrorism. Scott Atran, for example, is a leading cognitive scientist and founder of Artis International, a nonprofit group "that uses social science research to help resolve seemingly intractable political and cultural conflicts." Atran and his team of researchers have recently addressed the problem of "devoted actors" who "adhere to sacred, transcendental values that generate actions disassociated from rationally expected risks and rewards." Such actors are dangerous and unpredictable precisely because they have failed to achieve their own version of agentive reason. Having failed to negotiate the communal pressures on them, the identity of such actors is a product of insufficient detection of their own agency and overinvestment in the agency of divinities that define the coherence of their local communities. Rather than being an effect of calculating costs and consequences, the actions of terrorists have been the result of "costly commitment to idiosyncratic and apparently absurd beliefs and associated values, cued by sartorial and corporeal markers (e.g., veils, beards, and especially more indelible marks, such as the *zabiba* on the forehead of pious Muslims generated by repeated friction with the prayer mat" (Atran 2016).[12]

As Boyer declared shortly after the publication of *Religion Explained*, "Atran's work is a brilliant exposition of the evolutionary by-product interpretation [of religion] as well as a mine of references for empirical research into the psychology of religion" (Atran 2002, frontmatter). Drawing inspiration equally from the current clash of civilizations and the evolutionary refinement of our hyperactive agency detection devices, Boyer insists on the pressing need "to establish why and how religious thought is so pervasive in human societies." This "understanding," he adds, "is especially relevant in the current climate of religious fundamentalism." Boyer insists that this close-mindedness can be resisted through clear thinking about the brain and its by-products. Here is a place where politics has been transcended. Having arrived at the deep fundament of the human, Boyer is calculating the odds, just like the brains he studies are doing: all in the service of instantiating a secular imaginary of a particular kind (Foucault 1994, 57); all for the possibility of "hazard[ing] a guess at what the realistic prospects are for atheism" (Boyer 2008b).

From Boyer's post-Protestant perch, atheism becomes the most heroic, the most agentive, the most human position one can assume in a universe that has only begun to be properly understood (Lienard and Boyer 2006). Boyer's evolutionary frame assumes that humans in general, and Boyer in particular, have gotten better at detecting agency and more accurate in their capacity to discard false positives. Boyer, for example, claims to be getting beyond the "surface of religious concepts" and "moving from the table to the kitchen and observing how the concepts are concocted in human minds." Religion is not special, nor should it be protected. Subsequently, Boyer calls for a recovery of "scientific ambition" in order to move beyond mere, but necessary, "description of those aspects of human nature that lead people to adopt certain ideas or beliefs rather than others" (2001, 57, 172, 48, 31). Boyer seems to be playing a zero-sum game here, for the more accurate and less hyperactive your detection device becomes, the more agency that will be attributed to you and the less agency that will be attributed to entities that, *for God's sake*, are not agents after all is said and done.[13]

As our evolutionary inheritance, the hyperactive agency detection device offers necessary leverage on the future. Rest assured, the hyperactive agency detection device is strategically diminishing its own hyperactivity, *becoming its true, even-tempered detection device self.* And the more it checks its own excess, the more we become the only agents deserving of the designation. Yet even as Boyer and others make the case for the fact that the hyperactive agency detection device contains the seeds of its own refinement, they do so in such a way that begs a question that has little to do with the time of evolution but instead inquires into the artifactual, and perhaps even confounding pressures of our secular age.

Distinguishing Marks on a Screen

In the midst of World War II our natural penchant for anthropomorphism was discovered in Northampton, Massachusetts. An experiment was conducted, facts were gathered, and questions were asked: "What kind of person is the big triangle? . . . Why did the two triangles fight? . . . Why did the circle go into the house? . . . What did the big circle do when it was in the house with the big triangle? . . . Why did the big triangle break the house?"

In 1944, at Smith College in Northampton, Professor Fritz Heider and his student Marianne Simmel published their foundational study, "An Experimental Study of Apparent Behavior." In it they explored the discrepancy between the laws of physics and the misperception and mischaracterization of these laws by human observers (Heider and Simmel 1944).[14] Heider and Simmel demonstrated that there were common biases in which our perception was consistently at odds with the way things were in essence. References to Heider and Simmel are pervasive in the scientific literature on religious cognition and agency detection, and Boyer himself claims to be updating their study when he identifies the neural networks involved in hyperactive agency detection.[15]

In "An Experimental Study of Apparent Behavior," Heider and Simmel demonstrated, among other things, how different perceptual cues catalyzed different degrees of agency attribution. They conducted their anatomy of agency detection—on a flat screen—by exposing test subjects to a "moving picture-film . . . in which geometrical figures (a large triangle, a small triangle and . . . a circle) were shown moving in various directions at various speeds."

The Heider and Simmel film had no sound, only animated geometry and the errant noise of a 16mm projector in a room (see fig. 1 in Heider and Simmel 1944). Heider's laboratory surveyed the reactions of 114 undergraduates attending college in Northampton. The students were divided into three groups and shown the film twice. The first group of thirty-four was given a specific command: "Write down what happened in the picture." The second group of thirty-six was given the anthropomorphic prompt and "instructed to interpret the movements of the figures as actions of persons." A narrative pattern emerged among this group: The big triangle was typecast male—"aggressive, warlike, belligerent, pugnacious, quarrelsome, troublesome, mean, angry, bad-tempered . . . bully, villain, taking advantage of his size . . . dominating, power-loving, possessive." Two-thirds of this group attributed femininity to the circle, describing "her" as "frightened, afraid, fearful,

cowardly, shy, timid, meek, not too sure of herself...helpless, dependent."
Leaving aside the fact that of the gendered ecology in which this film was
screened and meaning attributed to it, students here were becoming ac-
customed to living vicariously through a screen. *A way of seeing was becoming
increasingly compatible with a way of being in the world.*

The third group of forty-four was shown the film in reverse. Although
each student's interpretation was in and of itself, coherent, the variety of
narratives in group 3 did not reveal an overarching pattern as happened with
group 2.

Looking back on the experiment that made his career, Heider cannot
help but signal the universality of the truth that he had discovered. "It has
been impressive," he writes, "the way almost everybody who has watched it
has perceived the picture in terms of human action and human feelings."
This, of course, is not surprising given that Heider and Simmel had rigged
the system. In their composition and editing they produced a film that drew
from narrative expectations, domestic hierarchies, and gendered conventions
of the time (Heider and Simmel 1944, 252). They had infused drama into the
flatness of lines and arcs. It was, indeed, a story about humans. For as Heider
later admitted, he loaded his film with all kinds of anthropomorphic cues—
"As I planned the action of the film," Heider recalled, "I thought of the small
triangle and the circle as a pair of lovers or friends, and I thought of the big
triangle as a bully who intruded on them. The rectangle served as a room with
a door, which could be opened or closed. The movements of the three characters were such that the two smaller ones in the end defeated and eluded
the bully." Geometry, here, was meant to be alive. And, indeed, geometry
was manifest—in "apparently" conscious shapes and movements, gendered
prompts, and scenes of domestic conflict. Despite his tampering, Heider
concluded that "movements or behavior, if you like, of even unchanging
forms can produce an impelling impression of a network of interpersonal
events and relations involving love, hate, power connections, fights, and
happy reunions" (Heider 1983, 148–49).

And the elephant in the room—the cognitive dissonance experienced by
those primed to humanize cardboard shapes moving around a pull-down
screen, according to Heider's script, in a small room. At least one Smith
undergraduate noted these artificial constraints (and the possibility that
the results of this experiment were present from the very beginning): "The
first thing we see in this little episode," she remarked, "is triangle number-
one closing the door of his square. Let's insist that the action of the play is

on a two-dimensional surface (not that it makes much difference) and we will undoubtedly start calling the square in which the triangle number-one seems to make his dwelling, a house, which infers three dimensions. But we are not sticking to the theme of our story." The words of the anonymous Smith undergraduate hint at a pressing demand to narrativize what has been unnaturally internalized. For in the extended riff and hesitation of this particular undergraduate one detects a recognition on her part of the power of mediation, that is, the capacity for an image on the screen to exceed the frame and make its way in (Heider and Simmel 1944, 247).

It is telling, then, that the Heider and Simmel film was screened by researchers and an audience ostensibly captivated by site-specific yet undetected norms of masculinity, femininity, and sexual power structures. It is even more telling when someone like Stewart Guthrie displays the same captivated subjectivity when he cites the Heider and Simmel study a half century later, without question, as indirect evidence for religion being a mode of agency detection *from a distance*. "We do not need to interact," assured Guthrie,

> with a mechanical process to anthropomorphize it. Fritz Heider and Marianne Simmel showed viewers a short animated film in which two triangles and a circle move on a surface. The figures "bump into" each other, "follow" each other, and "enter" and "leave" a rectangular enclosure through a swinging line "door." The experimenters asked the viewers to write what happened. Virtually all saw figures as persons. One wrote, for example,
>
>> A man has planned to meet a girl and the girl comes along with another man. The first man tells the second to go; the second tells the first, and he shakes his head. Then the two men have a fight, and the girl starts to go into the room to get out of the way and hesitates and finally goes in. She apparently does not want to be with the first man. The first man follows her into the room after having left the second in a rather weakened condition leaning on the wall outside the room.
>
> Here, flat geometrical figures on a flat surface suffice to evoke humans in sexual rivalry and conflict. (Guthrie 1993, 95–96)

In jeremiadic mode, Heider and Simmel lamented the lack of attention paid by their contemporaries to those processes involved in perceiving "other individuals and their personal qualities" in public. Citing their desire to move beyond representational models of perception as motivation for their research, they wrote that "experiments on the perception of the behavior of others" have been stalled by an overemphasis on facial recognition. There is a deeper layer, they suggested, not readily accessible, but nonetheless where our shared humanity occurred. Consequently, in order to access this level, "we have presented situations and activities without the face." The individuality of individuals, in other words, had a formal essence. And it was precisely this formal essence that conditioned its recognition (Heider and Simmel 1944, 243-44).

Conclusion

The alignment of HADD with a definitional essence of religion conjures a specific religious past and situates CSR at the cutting edge of Protestant, albeit nonspecific, reform.[16] CSR, in other words, is an integral part of a contemporary secular imaginary. In its implicit framing of ritual as meaningless without the brain being involved, in its sanctification of interiority in the key of information, in its drift away from the structures that bind both scientist and subject alike in a cloud of mass-mediated unknowing, in its retreat into the space of agency that is, from the outset, immunized from the world around—all of these moves set the stage for a machine, or in this case, device, that originates from the inside, always already, waiting to correspond with the world around. And it is this framing of the brain in terms of information processing rather than meaning-making that haunts the long making of the hyperactive agency detection device. For HADD is the machine that is able to commit and correct its own errors for evolutionary advantage. HADD trades in and, regrettably, sometimes wallows in uncertainty in order to arrive at certainty in the long run (Boyer 2001, 42, 286).

CSR is part of a wave of recent interest in and funding of studies that explore predictive processing—that the "brain is a sophisticated hypothesis-testing mechanism, which is constantly involved in minimizing the error of its predictions of the sensory input it receives from the world."[17] In contrast to consciousness being the simple transfer of content, a scientist like Boyer insists that the brain is an information-processing system comprising myriad subsystems such as HADD. Cognition is not about casual chains but about accumulation and intensity and the ongoing coordination of those subsystems (Boyer 2001, 30, 319). As I have demonstrated, the most distinguishing mark of CSR is its wholesale internalization of information theory and biological processes of data-driven communication. "Every bit of information is fodder for the mental machinery," reminds Boyer (2001, 30).

In its rush to naturalize religion, CSR betrays its agenda of normalizing the human, of taming its excesses, of offering a cure for "irrational and dysfunctional cognition" (Boyer and Bergstrom 2010). As Boyer notes, HADD is bound up in a Precaution System that is designed to detect and to react to potential danger (and not part of the great system that is geared to respond to manifest danger) (Lienard and Boyer 2006). The screens that saturate our existence now blurt out breaking news of mass shootings and terrorist threats, economic collapse, and impending global catastrophes. We scan the signs looking for leverage. Luckily for us, Boyer has recently turned from explaining religion to framing the brain's predictive power as a mode of risk assessment—useful information as more and more resources are allocated to lessen our collective risk. When the brain encounters information, argues Boyer, it scans for cues that signal as a threat—and the more threatening the message, the more we tend to trust it. Individuals achieve a sense of security, then, within group settings because they come to detect, evaluate, rate, and react to potential threats (Boyer, Firat, and van Leeuwen 2015). In an age of global insecurity, Boyer has discovered that our brains are hardwired to manage risk, to assume the worst, to act accordingly, and to learn from the consequences of those actions.

Like all the other machines that fill our days with the joy of social mediation, the hyperactive agency detection device is engaged in perpetual prediction. It is calculating how to act in an information-rich environment, that is, an environment made up of "statistical structures."[18] Detecting agency, in persons or in other places or things, comes naturally to us according to CSR. At the root of all belief, CSR has detected an innate capacity to make statistical inferences and continually refine them. We come to anticipate agents (or not) based on snippets of perception—the quality or substance or personality of the agents we detect is secondary to the fact that they exhibit formal characteristics of volition, intentionality, or counterintuitive behavior. Scanning, here, becomes the base mechanics of probability theorizing—the fact that our agency detection devices are bent toward hyperactivity, of erring on the side of overestimating the presence of agents, is for our long-term evolutionary good (Boyer and Bergstrom 2010). Tamping down such hyperactivity comes at a price, however—for reason, rightly arrived at, portends the jettisoning of our illusions of comfort and divine connection, of being watched over, of seeing the world straight and mean and just as it is.

Setting aside the fact that the concept of hyperactive agency detection has taken hold amid an all but overwhelming saturation of screens, the cognitive revolution within the human sciences on display in CSR ropes religion into a particular argument about the human who scans the horizon, recognizes patterns, learns from those patterns, and becomes better and more efficient in scanning the horizon (Lutz et al. 2008; Brefczynski et al. 2007). This is the kind of humanism that creeps up, that is embedded in the products that we consume, the media through which we socialize, and the devices that we find ourselves in front of at any given time. And let us not forget that scanning is also an ideal of scientific sight. Scanning is to perceive as an information-processing machine, without bias or subjective inflection. As in a telephone wire or a computer. Scanning is to aspire to a vision whittled down to form, striving to live in the future tense when (and where) one need not be bothered by questions of substance. Scanning is to repeat without difference. Scanning is to draw from the differential between present and past, every moment, to ever be producing the future.

The claim that the brain is involved in processes of scanning, statistical inference, and prediction may well be true, but that truth (and our arrival at it) is not unrelated to the desire for that claim to be true (not to mention the cultures and histories that fuel that desire). What kinds of worlds are being validated when such a brain is assumed to be self-evident? This brain may scan the horizon for a deviation in pattern and it may then anthropomorphize that deviation into a fully realized agent, but what other machines and what other conventions also make this possible? But rather than grapple with the complexities of life as it is lived—or, for that matter, the contingencies of science as it is practiced—CSR investigators adopt a rather clean (and rather unified) picture of cognition (of their test subjects as well as their own). Despite acknowledging the role that culture plays in the evolution of cognition, there is very little attention paid to history, mediation, ideology, discourse, and so on. This is what positivism looks like after the cybernetic moment, when information becomes both physical and metaphysical horizon. In a delicious irony that is, perhaps, worthy of further study by social and cognitive scientists alike, much authority is invested into the prime mover of this story—"selective pressures over evolutionary history" that facilitate the ever more efficient processing of information (Boyer 2008a, 2015). Perhaps, like any "cosmic law, or sharia," the evolutionary paradigm encompasses for cognitive scientists what Atran has referred to in the context of studying jihadists, "the Everywhen." To use the words of cognitive scientists, then, to describe the function of this episteme is neither unfounded nor ironic, for "it provides 'an explanation of nature, establishes a social code, creates a basis for prestige and political status . . . acts as a religious philosophy and forms the psychological basis for life'" (Atran 2016, S193).[19]

Notes

1 On the insistence on evolving mechanisms of cost-benefit analysis, see Atran 2006a and 2006b.

2 For an explicit application of HADD in terms of optimizing efficiency within the workplace, see Johnson 2009.

3 The cross-fertilization of information theory and neural nets began in earnest at the Hixon Symposium of 1948 (Jeffress 1951) and was vividly on display in articles collected in (Shannon and McCarthy 1956).

4 Anthropologists drawn to cybernetics at midcentury include Margaret Mead, Gregory Bateson, Lawrence Frank, Paul Lazarsfeld, Klyde Kluckhohn, and Claude Lévi-Strauss. For iterations of anthropological systematicity that anticipated cybernetic holism, see Modern 2014, 2011.

5 See, for example, the *Journal of Neuroscience, Psychology, and Economics* published by the American Psychological Association.

6 Leading journals in the cognitive science of religion include *Journal of Cognition and Culture* (Brill), *Religion, Brain and Behavior* (Taylor and Francis), *Journal for the Cognitive Science of Religion* (Equinox), and *Journal of Cognitive Historiography* (Equinox). *Method and Theory in the Study of Religion* (Brill) is a general journal devoted to methodological and theoretical issues that includes many articles (and entire issues) devoted to questions of cognition.

7 For a triumphal summary of the revolution, see Pinker 2006.

8 For a slightly earlier iteration of this humanism, see Uhr 1966.

9 The prospect is broached in Abed 1991.

10 HADD, for example, is composed, in part, by an algorithm of fear. As Boyer writes, "Fear is not just what we experience about it; it is also a *program*, in some ways comparable to a computer program" (2001, 22).

11 Boyer (2008b) notes that unlike art or politics, religious concepts have immediate and deleterious effects precisely because of their sociality, for "hijacking also occurs because religions facilitate the expression of certain behaviours. This is the case for commitment to a group, which is made all the more credible when it is phrased as the acceptance of bizarre or non-obvious beliefs."

12 On how the insights of CSR are used to gain explicit leverage on terrorism, see Ramakrishna 2014.

13 This is also a fair characterization of a scientist like Barrett, a committed evangelical who, unlike Boyer, has no grudge with what he identifies as religion. For Barrett, "believing in other minds and believing in God are comparably natural beliefs. One is not markedly more strange or bizarre than the other" (Barrett 2004b, 95–105). In naturalizing religion for different political agendas, Barrett and Boyer share the same secular imaginary. For both, religion comes easy for us because believing in God is a natural inheritance, a fundament that is neurological. For Barrett it should be privileged site of exploration, for Boyer a privileged site of evacuation.

14 See also Michotte (1946) 1963; and Gruber, Fink, and Damn 1957.

15 Guthrie 1993, 95; Barrett 2004a. Boyer draws on the self-evident authority of Heider and Simmel in articles published concurrently with *Religion
Explained*. In these coauthored studies, Boyer used fMRI and manipulated
visual stimuli to investigate the neural networks involved in agency detection (Blakemore and Boyer 2001, 2003). Similarly, fMRI was used to localize
neural functioning while viewing animations based on the Heider and Simmel film (Osaka, Ikeda, and Osaka 2012).

   In addition to Boyer, Guthrie, and Barrett, a sampling of citations of
Heider and Simmel by scientists of cognition and agency detection include
Pyysiäinen 2012; Epley, Waytz, and Cacioppo 2007; and Bloom and Veres
1999. On the use of the Heider and Simmel film to diagnose cognitive ab-
normality, see Klin 2000; and Bowler and Thommen 2000.

16 On the nonspecificity of Protestantism within secular modernity, see Fessenden 2007.

17 According to this position, the brain is continually "testing hypotheses" and
engaged in "optimizing the rich tapestry of statistic processes" (Hohwy 2013,
1, 3, 59). See also Clark 2016.

18 Andy Clark argues that nature speaks in terms of mathematical
probability—despite the fact that the world "does not *look* as if it is encoded
as an intertwined set of probability density distributions!" (Clark 2013, 196).

19 Atran is quoting Bird et al. 2016, who in turn are quoting Cane 2002.

References

Abed, Farough. 1991. "What Are the Cultural Influences on [Visual] Scanning Pat-
   terns?" *Journal of Cross-Cultural Psychology* 22, no. 4: 25–34.
Ashby, W. Ross. *Aphorisms*. http://www.rossashby.info/aphorisms.html.
Atran, Scott. 2002. *In Gods We Trust: The Evolutionary Landscape of Religion*. New
   York: Oxford University Press.
Atran, Scott. 2006a. "The Cognitive and Evolutionary Roots of Religion." In
   Where God and Science Meet, edited by Patrick McNamara, 181–208. Westport,
   CT: Praeger.
Atran, Scott. 2006b. "Religion's Innate Origins and Evolutionary Background."
   In *The Innate Mind*, vol. 2: *Culture and Cognition*, edited by Peter Carruthers,
   Stephen Laurence, and Stephen Stich, 302–17. New York: Oxford University
   Press.
Atran, Scott. 2016. "The Devoted Actor: Unconditional Commitment and Intrac-
   table Conflict across Cultures." *Current Anthropology* 57 (June): S192–S203.
Barrett, Justin L. 2000. "Exploring the Natural Foundations of Religion." *Trends in
   Cognitive Sciences* 4: 29–34.
Barrett, Justin L. 2004a. "The Naturalness of Religious Concepts: An Emerging
   Cognitive Science of Religion." In *New Approaches to the Study of Religion*,
   edited by Peter Antes, Armin W. Geertz, and Randi Ruth Warne, 401–18.
   Berlin: Walter de Gruyter.

Barrett, Justin L. 2004b. *Why Would Anyone Believe in God?* Lanham, MD: Alta Mira Press.

Barrett, Justin L., and Amanda Hankes Johnson. 2003. "The Role of Control in Attributing Intentional Agency to Inanimate Objects." *Journal of Cognition and Culture* 3, no. 3: 208–17.

Barrett, Justin L., and Frank C. Keil. 1996. "Conceptualizing a Nonnatural Entity: Anthropomorphism in God Concepts." *Cognitive Psychology* 31: 219–47.

Bird, Douglas W., Rebecca B. Bird, Brian F. Codding, and Nyalangka Taylor. 2016. "A Landscape Architecture of Fire: Cultural Emergence and Ecological Pyrodiversity in Australia's Western Desert." *Current Anthropology* 57: S65–S79.

Blakemore, Sarah-Jayne, Pierre Fonlupt, Mathilde Pachot-Clouard, Céline Darmon, Pascal Boyer, Andrew N. Meltzoff, Christoph Segebarth, and Jean Decety. 2001. "How the Brain Perceives Causality: An Event-Related fMRI Study." *Brain Imaging* 12, no. 17: 3741–46.

Blakemore, Sarah-Jayne, Pascal Boyer, Mathilde Pachot-Clouard, Andrew Meltzoff, Cristoph Segebarth, and Jean Decety. 2003. "The Detection of Contingency and Animacy from Simple Animations in the Human Brain." *Cerebral Cortex* 13, no. 8: 837–44.

Bloom, Paul, and Csaba Veres. 1999. "The Perceived Intentionality of Groups." *Cognition* 71: B1–B9.

Bowler, Dermot M., and Evelynne Thommen. 2000. "Attribution of Mechanical and Social Causality to Animated Displays by Children with Autism." *Autism* 4, no. 2: 147–71.

Boyer, Pascal. 2001. *Religion Explained: The Evolutionary Origins of Religious Thought.* New York: Basic Books.

Boyer, Pascal. 2003. "Religious Thought and Behavior as By-products of Brain Function." *Trends in Cognitive Science* 7, no. 3: 119–24.

Boyer, Pascal. 2008a. "Evolutionary Perspectives on Religion." *Annual Review of Anthropology* 37: 111–30.

Boyer, Pascal. 2008b. "Religion: Bound to Believe?" *Nature* 455: 1038–39.

Boyer, Pascal. 2013. "Explaining Religious Concepts: Lévi-Strauss the Brilliant and Problematic Ancestor." In *Mental Culture: Classical Social Theory and the Cognitive Science of Religion*, edited by Dimitris Xygalatas and William W. McCorkle Jr., 164–75. Durham, NC: Acumen.

Boyer, Pascal. 2015. "How Natural Selection Shapes Conceptual Structure: Human Intuitions and Concepts of Ownership." In *The Conceptual Mind: New Directions in the Study of Concepts*, edited by Eric Margolis and Stephen Laurence, 185–200. Cambridge, MA: MIT Press.

Boyer, Pascal, and Brian Bergstrom. 2010. "Threat-Detection in Child Development: An Evolutionary Perspective." *Neuroscience and Biobehavioral Reviews* 35: 1034–41.

Boyer, Pascal, Rengin Firat, and Florian van Leeuwen. 2015. "Safety, Threat, and Stress in Intergroup Relations: A Coalitional Index Model." *Perspectives in Psychological Science* 10, no. 4: 434–50.

Brefczynski-Lewis, Julie A., Antoine Lutz, Hillary S. Schaefer, Daniel B. Levinson, and Richard J. Davidson. 2007. "Neural Correlates of Attentional Expertise in Long-Term Meditation Practitioners." *National Academy of Sciences* 104, no. 27: 11483–88.

Cane, S. 2002. *Pila Nguru: The Spiniflex People.* Freemantle, MA: Fremantle.

Clark, Andy. 2013. "Whatever Next? Predictive Brains, Situated Agents, and the Future of Cognitive Science." *Behavioral and Brain Sciences* 36, no. 3: 181–204.

Clark, Andy. 2016. *Surfing Uncertainty: Prediction, Action, and the Embodied Mind.* New York: Oxford University Press.

Dawkins, Richard. 2008. *The God Delusion.* New York: Houghton Mifflin Harcourt.

Dennett, Daniel. 2006. *Breaking the Spell: Religion as a Natural Phenomenon.* New York: Penguin.

Domínguez, Juan F., E. Douglas Lewis, Robert Turner, and Gary F. Egan. 2009. "The Brain in Culture and Culture in the Brain: A Review of Core Issues in Neuroanthropology." *Progress in Brain Research* 178: 43–46.

Epley, Nicholas, Adam Waytz, and John T. Cacioppo. 2007. "On Seeing Human: A Three-Factor Theory of Anthropomorphism." *Psychological Review* 114, no. 4: 864–86.

Fessenden, Tracy. 2007. *Culture and Redemption: Religion, the Secular, and American Literature.* Princeton, NJ: Princeton University Press.

Foucault, Michel. 1994. *The Order of Things: An Archaeology of the Human Sciences.* New York: Vintage Books.

Greenwald, Glenn. 2013. "Sam Harris, the New Atheists, and Anti-Muslim Animus." *The Guardian*, April 3, 2013. https://www.theguardian.com /commentisfree/2013/apr/03/sam-harris-muslim-animus.

Gruber, Howard E., Charles D. Fink, and Vernon Damn. 1957. "Effects of Experience on Perception of Causality." *Journal of Experimental Psychology* 53, no. 2: 89–93.

Guthrie, Stewart E. 1980. "A Cognitive Theory of Religion." *Current Anthropology* 21, no. 2: 181–203.

Guthrie, Stewart E. 1993. *Faces in the Cloud: A New Theory of Religion.* New York: Oxford University Press.

Guthrie, Stewart E. 2007. "Anthropology and Anthropomorphism in Religion." In *Religion, Anthropology, and Cognitive Science*, edited by Harvey Whitehouse and James Laidlaw, 37–62. Durham, NC: Carolina Academic Press.

Halpern, Orit. 2014. *Beautiful Data: A History of Vision and Reason since 1945.* Durham, NC: Duke University Press.

Haraway, Donna J. 1997. *Modest_Witness@SecondMillennium: FemaleMan_Meets_ OncoMouse: Feminism and Science.* New York: Routledge.

Heider, Fritz. 1983. *The Life of a Psychologist: An Autobiography.* Lawrence: University Press of Kansas.

Heider, Fritz, and Marianne Simmel. 1944. "An Experimental Study of Apparent Behavior." *American Journal of Psychology* 57, no. 2: 243–59.

Heyck, Hunter. 2015. *The Age of System: Understanding the Development of Modern Social Science*. Baltimore, MD: Johns Hopkins University Press.

Hohwy, Jacob. 2013. *The Predictive Mind*. New York: Oxford University Press.

Jeffress, L. A., ed. 1951. *Cerebral Mechanisms in Behavior: The Hixon Symposium*. New York: Wiley and Sons.

Johnson, Dominic D. P. 2009. "The Error of God: Error Management Theory, Religion, and the Evolution of Cooperation." In *Games, Groups, and the Global Good*, edited by S. A. Levin, 169–80. Berlin: Springer.

Johnson, Dominic D. P., Daniel T. Blumstein, James H. Fowler, and Martie G. Haselton. 2013. "The Evolution of Error: Error Management, Cognitive Constraints, and Adaptive Decision-Making Biases." *Trends in Ecology and Evolution* 28, no. 8: 474–81.

Kalkhoff, Will, Shane R. Thye, and Joshua Pollock. 2016. "Developments in Neurosociology." *Sociology Compass* 10, no. 3: 242–58.

Klin, Ami. 2000. "Attributing Social Meaning to Ambiguous Visual Stimuli in Higher-Functioning Autism and Asperger Syndrome: The Social Attribution Task." *Journal of Psychology and Psychiatry and Allied Disciplines* 41, no. 7: 831–46.

Lienard, Pierre, and Pascal Boyer. 2006. "Whence Collective Rituals: A Cultural Selection Model of Ritualized Behaviors." *American Anthropologist* 108, no. 4: 814–27.

Linder, Stefan, Nicolai J. Foss, and Diego Stea. 2016. "Epistemics at Work: The Theory of Mind in Principal-Agent Relations." *Oxford Handbooks Online*. http://www.oxfordhandbooks.com /view/10.1093/oxfordhb/9780199935406.001.0001/oxfordhb-9780199935406-e-8.

Lutz, Antoine, Heleen A. Slagter, John D. Dunne, and Richard J. Davidson. 2008. "Attention Regulation and Monitoring in Meditation." *Trends in Cognitive Sciences* 12, no. 4: 163–69.

Ma-Kellams, Christine. 2015. "When Perceiving the Supernatural Changes the Natural: Religion and Agency Detection." *Journal of Cognition and Culture* 15: 337–43.

Martin, J. B. 2002. "The Integration of Neurology, Psychiatry, and Neuroscience in the 21st Century." *American Journal of Psychiatry* 159, no. 5: 695–704.

McCauley, Robert N. 2004. "Is Religion a Rube Goldberg Device, or, Oh, What a Difference a Theory Makes." In *Religion as a Human Capacity: A Festschrift in Honour of E. Thomas Lawson*, edited by Timothy Light and Brian C. Wilson, 45–64. Leiden: Brill.

McCulloch, Warren, and Walter Pitts. 1943. "A Logical Calculus of the Ideas Immanent in Nervous Activity." *Bulletin of Mathematical Biophysics* 5: 115–33.

McKay, Ryan. 2014. "Religion and Agency." *Journal for the Cognitive Science of Religion* 2, no. 2: 93–96.

Mehta, Ranjana K., and Raja Parasuraman. 2013. "Neuroergonomics: A Review of Applications to Physical and Cognitive Work." *Frontiers of Human Neuroscience* 7: 889.

Michotte, Albert. (1946) 1963. *The Perception of Causality*. Translated by T. R. Miles and E. Miles. London: Methuen.

Modern, John Lardas. 2011. *Secularism in Antebellum America*. Chicago: University of Chicago Press.

Modern, John Lardas. 2014. "In the Men's Room: E. B. Tylor and the Will to Systematize." *Social Text* 120: 87–107.

Modern, John Lardas. 2021. *Neuromatic; or, A Particular History of Religion and the Brain*. Chicago: University of Chicago Press.

Neumann, John von. 1951. "The General and Logical Theory of Automata." In *Cerebral Mechanisms in Behavior: The Hixon Symposium*, edited by L. A. Jeffress, 1–31. New York: Wiley and Sons.

Newberg, Andrew B. 2013. *Principles of Neurotheology*. Burlington, VT: Ashgate.

Osaka, Naoyuki, Takashi Ikeda, and Marioko Osaka. 2012. "Effect of Intentional Bias on Agency Attribution of Animated Motion: An Event-Related fMRI Study." *PLOS One* 7, no. 11: 1–6.

Pearce, Marcus T., Dahlia W. Zaidel, Oshin Vartanian, Martin Skov, Helmut Leder, Anjan Chatterjee, and Marcos Nadal. 2016. "Neuroaesthetics: The Cognitive Neuroscience of Aesthetic Experience." *Perspectives on Psychological Science* 11, no. 2: 265–79.

Picozza, Eugenio, ed. 2016. *Neurolaw: An Introduction*. Berlin: Springer.

Pinker, Stephen. 2006. "The Evolutionary Psychology of Religion." In *Where God and Science Meet: How Brain and Evolutionary Studies Alter Our Understanding of Religion*, edited by Patrick McNamara, 1–9. Westport, CT: Praeger.

Pyysiäinen, Ilkka. 2009. *Supernatural Agents: Why We Believe in Souls, Gods, and Buddhas*. New York: Oxford University Press.

Pyysiäinen, Ilkka. 2012. "Cognitive Science of Religion: State-of-the-Art." *Journal for the Cognitive Science of Religion* 1, no. 1: 5–28.

Ramakrishna, Kumar. 2014. *Islamist Terrorism and Militancy in Indonesia: The Power of the Manichean Mindset*. New York: Springer.

Rose, Nikolas, and Joelle M. Abi-Rached. 2013. *Neuro: The New Brain Sciences and the Management of Mind*. Princeton, NJ: Princeton University Press.

Scholl, Brian J., and Patrice D. Tremoulet. 2000. "Perceptual Causality and Animacy." *Trends in Cognitive Sciences* 4, no. 8: 299–309.

Shannon, C[laude] E. 1948. "A Mathematical Theory of Communication." *Bell System Technical Journal* 27: 379–423.

Shannon, Claude E. 1956. "The Bandwagon." *IRE Transactions—Information Theory*: 3.

Shannon, C. E., and J. McCarthy, eds. 1956. *Automata Studies*. Princeton, NJ: Princeton University Press.

Shermer, Michael. 2009. "Why People Believe Invisible Agents Control the World." *Scientific American*, June 1, 2009.

Slepian, D. 1973. "Information Theory in the 1950s." *IEEE Transactions on Information Theory* 19, no. 2: 145–48.

Spitzer, Robert L., Kurt Kroenke, and Janet B. W. Williams, eds. 1980. *Diagnostic and Statistical Manual of Mental Disorders*. 3rd ed. American Psychiatric Association.

Television: How It Works. 1948. New York: John F. Rider.

TenHouten, W. D. 2013. "A Neurosociological Model of Weberian, Instrumental Rationality: Its Cognitive, Conative, and Neurobiological Foundations." In *Handbook of Neurosociology*, edited by D. D. Franks and J. H. Turner. Dordrecht: Springer.

Turner, Victor. 1986. "Body, Brain, and Culture." *Performing Arts Journal* 10, no. 2: 26–34.

Uhr, Leonard, ed. 1966. *Pattern Recognition: Theory, Experiment, Computer Simulations, and Dynamic Models of Form Perception and Discovery*. New York: John Wiley and Sons.

Wiener, Norbert. 1948. *Cybernetics: or, Control and Communication in the Animal and the Machine*. Oxford: Wiley.

Xygalatas, Dimitris, and Ryan McKay. 2013. "Announcing the *Journal for the Cognitive Science of Religion*." *Journal for the Cognitive Science of Religion* 1, no. 1: 1–4.

cooperative primates & competitive primatologists

Prosociality &
Polemics in a
Nonhuman
Social Science

NICOLAS LANGLITZ

EVOLUTIONARY THEORY HAS ITS reflexive moments. For example, in 2010, when the journal *Nature* published a comment on a resurfacing controversy over how selfless behavior could have evolved, the philosopher of science Samir Okasha (2010, 653) demanded that "altruism researchers must cooperate." Instead they once again fought over whether natural selection only worked on individuals and their kin or whether it also operated on the group level, where even help to non-kin would benefit all group members, including the generous helper. *Nature* illustrated this state of affairs with a picture of a honeycomb, each cell inhabited by a bee in a white lab coat, either sulking or suspiciously eyeing its coworkers. Okasha warned that by descending into tribalism the warring camps risked causing serious damage to evolutionary biology. Financial support would be cut if funding agencies perceived the field to be in massive disarray. And, as had already happened during the "sociobiology wars" of the 1970s and 1980s, once more creationists might seize on and exaggerate the differences in opinion between biologists for their own ends. Okasha's evolutionary anthropology of science clearly favored group selection theory and suggested that altruism researchers would be selected against unless they worked *with* rather than *against* each other.

This chapter examines the social behavior of behavioral researchers who contributed to the surge of interest in prosociality during the past three decades. It focuses on a primatological controversy over cooperation in humans and chimpanzees between two codirectors of the Max Planck Institute for Evolutionary Anthropology in Leipzig, Germany. As they jointly ran this international center for the study of our natural history, the American comparative psychologist Michael Tomasello and the Swiss-French field biologist Christophe Boesch did not cooperate but instead argued over the question of whether the ability to cooperate set apart or united *Homo sapiens* and *Pan troglodytes*. Thus primatologists reanimated an old philosophical quarrel, imagined as a debate between two Enlightenment thinkers. "So is the devilish Hobbes or the angelic Rousseau correct?" asked Tomasello (2009b, 44). "Are humans by nature kind or mean-spirited?" The debate between the experimenter and the fieldworker was as much about primate behavior as it was about primatological methods. And it was about the ethos of science: Should it be an essentially collaborative or a competitive endeavor?

My essay contributes to the social science of social science a study of primate sociology in a broad sense (neither Boesch nor Tomasello self-identifies as a primate sociologist, but both have studied the social behavior and cognition of primates, and Boesch [2012] describes his approach to chimpanzee societies as ethnographic). I take Okasha's intervention as an incentive to examine a rarely vocalized reflexive dimension in primatology as research that primates conduct on primates. Qualified by socio-cognitive differences between primate species, conceptions of competition and cooperation among primates should also affect how primatologists understand their own behavior, including their scientific research. Thus far, I don't practice reflexivity but make it an object of social scientific observation and reconstruction.

Yet findings in primate sociology also pertain to research on human sociality, even if sociologists rarely compare and contrast their subjects or themselves with members of other species. One exception that proves the rule is the use that Bruno Latour made of Shirley Strum's primatological research on baboons, which led me to interpret his early actor-network theory as a "primatology of science" (Langlitz 2019; Strum and Latour 1987). At a time when a growing number of social researchers have discarded the opposition of nature and society and consider the two-cultures divide between the natural and the social sciences an anachronism that new interdisciplinary methodologies should overcome, the social science of primate social science can facilitate a conversation about what both sides share and what keeps them apart. In this essay, I focus on issues that both students of human and primate societies have struggled with: whether or not to think of humans and other primates as primarily cooperative or competitive and whether cooperation or competition is the better behavioral strategy to advance knowledge and understanding in our respective fields of scholarship. So the essay will conclude with the question of what ethos would be appropriate to a reflexive social science beyond the human.

Primate Sociology

Since its inception in the early nineteenth century, social science had never been an exclusively human science. Although Auguste Comte, who had given sociology its name, had still speculated that only humans formed societies, the first doctoral thesis in sociology, defended in 1877 at the Sorbonne, took animal societies as its object (Heilbron 2015, 63). Critics of Alfred Espinas's *Des sociétés animales* (1877) dismissed it as a mere zoology, but the *soutenance de thèse* took place at the Faculté des Lettres rather than the Faculté des Sciences (D'Hombres and Mehdaoui 2012, 33–34). By the 1870s, Charles Darwin and Herbert Spencer had sufficiently established the continuity between human and animal societies for a reviewer of Espinas's book to curtail the author's claim to a new science: the ground of "animal sociology" was "all but unoccupied" (Collier 1878, 105). The controversial question was not whether animals lived in societies but what that meant for "the limits of the Social Science." "How far down the animal scale are we to go?" asked the reviewer. "Are not plants societies too? . . . If animals and plants are societies, are not masses of inorganic matter also societies?" (108). What was the scope of a sociology beyond the human?

Émile Durkheim referred to the literature on animal societies to compare them with human society. To be sure, the gulf was vast. But the differences in kind had grown out of a difference in degree: human groups tended to be larger. "Even the smallest we know are more extensive than the majority of animal societies," Durkheim (1964, 345) claimed. "The more people there are in association, and the more they react upon one another, the more also does the product of these reactions pass beyond the bounds of the organism." This quantitative difference gave rise to a qualitative difference. Colonies of lower animals could act collectively only by doing the same thing at the same time. But social evolution had created more complex and differentiated societies. Modern humans, especially, practiced a division of labor in which individuals acted independently while also depending more on each other to get by. Based on such cooperation, their "organic solidarity" contrasted with the "mechanical solidarity" of more primitive forms of life (Durkheim 1964, 283–84).

Sociological studies of primate groups constituted a core component of primatology as the discipline began to emerge in the 1930s. Solly Zuckerman (1932) argued for a divorce of human and animal sociology. Describing the social lives of nonhuman primates in the same vocabulary as that of humans amounted to a variety of anthropomorphism known as sociomorphism, which was anathema to many European and American primatologists (Asquith 1986; Daston 2005). He pleaded for a description in purely ecological and physiological terms. However, at a time before long-term field observations (Zuckerman only knew wild monkeys from shooting them on hunting expeditions), little was known about primate ecology, so Zuckerman presented primate sociality as "determined primarily by the mechanisms of reproductive physiology" (1932, 29). Since this behavior was "blind" and "reflex in character," what had appeared to observers as cooperation, mutual aid, and altruism could only be superficially and misleadingly cast in such anthropomorphic terms (Zuckerman 1932, 304–5).

This short essay is not the place for a history of primate sociology, which gradually shifted from physiological to ecological and genetic explanations (for a brief sketch, see Rees 2006). Suffice it to say that the controversy over whether human and nonhuman social behavior could be explained in the same conceptual framework did not come to an end. Nor did disagreements about how exceptional the human capacity for cooperation and altruism was. The evolution of behaviors that benefit other individuals or the group has been debated and politicized ever since, in the late nineteenth century, the English naturalist Charles Darwin and the Russian geographer and anarcho-communist Pyotr Kropotkin provided two very different images of nature: Was it primarily shaped by competition over scarce resources or by mutual aid? Since the sociobiology debate of the 1970s, interest in prosocial behaviors has flared up again as a wide range of disciplines—from anthropology, economics, and population genetics to developmental psychology and primatology—have challenged the idea that humans naturally behave in predominantly selfish ways and can only be brought to care for and collaborate with others through a precarious process of enculturation.

Since the mid-twentieth century, these debates have received important impulses from Japan (Asquith 2000; Asquith 1981; Langlitz 2020, chaps. 1, 5, and 6; for a historical account of the human sciences in Japan, see Kingsberg Kadia, this volume; regarding the globalization of the social sciences in general, see Heilbron, this volume). From the 1940s onward, Kinji Imanishi's Kyoto School developed an anti-Darwinist biosociology that emphasized harmonious coexistence in a hierarchically organized world of living things (Imanishi 2002). His student Jun'ichirō Itani (1985) developed his mentor's evolutionary theory into a research program for a comparative primate sociology. The Buddhist tradition, which held that souls transmigrated between humans and other animal species, helped monkey and ape researchers to overcome "anthropodenial," the false negation of humanlike traits in animals, which the Dutch primatologist Frans de Waal (1999) considered as grave an epistemological error as anthropomorphism. He spoke of a "silent invasion" of Japanese primatology, which helped the discipline at large to put into perspective the cultural biases of free-market capitalism that had informed primatology's overemphasis of competition (de Waal 2003, 2001).

Historically de Waal's claims are questionable, since many European and American animal sociologists, from Espinas (1877) to Carpenter (1942) and Kummer (1971), had also highlighted the importance of solidarity, cooperation, and a peaceful and well-coordinated coexistence for the survival of nonhuman primate groups. But more than anyone else in late twentieth-century primatology, de Waal (1997, 1990, 1982) moved to center stage the idea that so-called prosocial behaviors such as cooperation, helping, reconciliation, consolation, empathy, and so on, are no thin culturally learned veneer under which nature is red in tooth and claw.

The bottom line of the historical narrative of a prosocial turn in the behavioral sciences, which de Waal and others have spun, is that, for at least four centuries, Western thought has been led astray in presupposing an essentially egoistic human nature that needs to be restrained by the state or let loose to serve the common good on free markets—or, I might add, in academic controversies (Benkler 2011; de Waal 2010; for a historical sketch of this development, see Milam 2012; Sennett 2012). This somber human self-conception is currently brightened up by researchers showing prosocial behavior to be as deeply rooted in our biological constitution as purely self-serving and aggressive conduct. That man was a wolf to man now appeared as a politically consequential misunderstanding of the behavior of both canine packs and primate groups.

Cooperation Controversy

The comparative psychologist Michael Tomasello and the field primatologist Christophe Boesch would both fit into the narrative of a prosocial turn. As far as human nature is concerned, they share some common ground. As codirectors of the Max Planck Institute for Evolutionary Anthropology in Leipzig, both understood our social behavior as shaped by natural history, and neither of them doubted that we were born with the cognitive capacity for cooperation, mutual aid, and altruism.

Experiments in Tomasello's laboratory painted a sympathetic portrait of *Homo sapiens* that bears little resemblance with the Hobbesian *Homo homini lupus*. Even one-year-old human infants Tomasello's group had tested were eager to help without having learned to be so. Later considerations of reciprocity, reputations, norms, and so on would mediate their cooperativeness (usually based on mutualism rather than altruism; Tomasello 2009b, 4, 45, 52). By and large, this mediation even increased the human potential for collective action.

Tomasello's French Swiss colleague Boesch did not deny our ability to cooperate. As a former rugby player, he had learned that a team could only win if everybody followed the motto of the Three Musketeers: "All for one and one for all." Yet Boesch (2012, 92) had also experienced the limits of human cooperation: "The demon of selfishness lurked around every corner and whenever one player had the impression that he could succeed alone, he would invariably forget the team and sadly be knocked to the ground."

Tomasello had also experienced the dark side of human prosociality. Having grown up in the American South in the 1950s and '60s, which he conceived of as an apartheid system, he knew firsthand how the group-mindedness in cooperation could lead to aggression against other groups, corroding the social integration of multiethnic societies. In the face of an increasingly globalized world inhabited by a fast-growing human population of unprecedented size, he wondered whether our evolved capacities for cooperation in small groups scaled up successfully to large-scale modern civilization: "We are still here. But of course we are only a few nuclear bombs or a few more decades of rampant environmental degradation away from not being here" (Tomasello 2009a).

At the height of the Obama era, however, Tomasello spun a surprisingly optimistic narrative. He drew political hope from natural history. While evolutionary psychologists had worried that our modern skulls housed a Stone Age mind, which had not evolved to cope with the exigencies of a globalized industrial world that was home to more than 7 billion people, Tomasello's antireductionist account of cultural inheritance and social coordination suggested that *Homo sapiens* had acquired mechanisms of behavioral adaptation many orders of magnitude faster than organic evolution (Tomasello 1999). This made him confident that the very capacities that had led to the problems humanity was now facing also enabled the political practices and institutions that would solve them: "New prosocial norms for being careful with our environment and for recognizing the dignity and value of all peoples from all ethnic groups seem to be spreading in influence, not receding, and we are continually finding new ways for creating more cooperative and open arrangements for communication and coalition-building in large-scale societies," Tomasello (2009a) claimed a few years before a surge of right-wing populism in Europe and the United States put his belief in historical progress to the test.

Tomasello considered the socio-cognitive capacities underlying such progress the prerogative of *Homo sapiens*, while his experiments with apes in the Leipzig zoo suggested that they could not cooperate with each other, nor did they altruistically teach or assist others to get food, even if such help came at no cost to themselves. Their egocentrism went so far that mothers competed and refused to share food with their own children (Tomasello 2009b, 21–28). "Great apes are all about cognition for competition," Tomasello (2014, 31) claimed. "Human beings, in contrast, are all about (or mostly about) cooperation."

The field primatologist Boesch (2012, 2002, 1994), on the other hand, had described how wild chimpanzees in Taï Forest, Ivory Coast, cooperated when they hunted monkeys. A sophisticated division of labor between a driver, a blocker, a chaser, and an ambusher increased their chances to make a catch. He had not been able to observe such a division of labor when he visited Gombe Stream National Park in Tanzania. Boesch (2012, 86, 91) interpreted this geographical difference in behavior as a difference between two hunting cultures. Its cultural nature did not free hunting from ecological constraints: while the open woodland of Gombe enabled lone hunters to capture a monkey in an isolated tree, the continuous forest canopy of Taï provided ample escape routes and forced the chimpanzees to hunt in a well-coordinated team. He took this evidence to be compatible with Tomasello's demanding definition of collaboration as based on shared goals and intentions (Boesch 2005, 692). Of course, such cooperation would only be sustained if the captor did not keep all meat to himself but shared it with the other hunters—not based on each individual's place in the group hierarchy but on their contribution to the joint endeavor. That was exactly what the chimpanzees of Taï Forest did, Boesch claimed. Thereby, he directly contradicted Tomasello, whose experiments in the Leipzig Zoo suggested that chimpanzees did not cooperate or voluntarily share with each other (Tomasello 2014, 35; Tomasello et al. 2005).

Laboratory versus Fieldwork

This disagreement about whether cooperation distinguished humans from other apes led to a heated methodological controversy over controlled experiments and field observations. Boesch (2005, 693) accused Tomasello of ignoring forty-five years of field studies on wild chimpanzees: "Observational data are dismissed as mere anecdotes or are discredited as not conclusive because alternative scenarios could always be constructed." Comparative psychologists of Tomasello's ilk reminded Boesch of "the old philosophers" who pronounced on what made humans unique based on their personal convictions and intuitions rather than experience and empirical data (2005, 691).

Tomasello and colleagues (2005, 722) countered that his group knew the field data that Boesch sought to leverage against them but that these data "have many interpretations in terms of the cognitive processes involved." On the basis of mere observations Boesch could not rule out leaner and less anthropomorphic interpretations of chimpanzee behavior. For example, what appeared to Boesch like a collaborative activity with a shared goal might have been a motley of opportunistic tactical choices. An individual might respond to the relative positions of prey and other hunters without coordinating with the latter: maybe everybody just hoped to "get lucky" (Tomasello et al. 2005, 722). And if the hunt was really collaborative, why did the captor still get to keep a larger chunk of the meat instead of handing out equal shares to all participants? Only controlled experiments could determine the underlying cognitive processes.

Thus Tomasello proposed scientific cooperation based on a division of labor between experimental psychologists and field biologists: fieldworkers reported *what* animals did in their natural habitat; experimenters revealed *how* exactly the animals did it cognitively (Tomasello and Call 2008, 451). As far as Boesch's observations of cooperation among chimpanzees was concerned, Tomasello's lab had provided evidence that the animals did not share intentions and adopt different roles. Pace Boesch, they did not collaborate with each other to achieve a common end, experiments by Tomasello and colleagues (2005) suggested.

Boesch, however, called into question whether these experiments actually allowed Tomasello to make valid claims about the difference between how humans and chimpanzees thought. Since the early days of comparative psychology when, in the 1910s Louis Boutan tested human children against his gibbon Pepée, the validity of cross-species comparisons rested on the similarity of the respective experimental and psychological conditions (Thomas

2005, 443). But Tomasello tested human children and adult chimpanzees under different conditions. While the children were "free-ranging," as Boesch (2008, 453) put it, and came to Tomasello's laboratory at the Max Planck Institute in the company of a parent, the chimpanzees lived in captivity and, for most experiments, they were isolated from their group. The children were tested by conspecifics, chimpanzees by another primate species. Since the experimenters did not want to take the risk of entering into an experimental booth with a potentially violent chimpanzee, they interacted with test animals through a thick Plexiglas wall, while no such wall separated experimenters and children. While toddlers were told what to do in their native language, verbal instruction could not be given to the apes. Such differences between experimental conditions allowed critics to call into question the proposed causal relationship between experimentally manipulated variable and observed effect. Every uncontrolled variable enabled alternative explanations and compromised the so-called internal validity of the experiments. As a consequence, laboratory data turned out to have as many interpretations as field data.

Boesch also challenged the external validity of Tomasello's findings by calling into question whether they applied beyond the walls of his laboratory. "The ability to care for the welfare of others has been denied to chimpanzees by some authors on the basis of experimental results obtained from captive chimpanzees," he wrote. "This difference should not come as a surprise as we should not expect that individuals would care for others without any prior experience of group solidarity, and such solidarity will develop only if external pressures favoring it exist" (Boesch 2012, 102). Living in the Leipzig Zoo, Tomasello's test subjects did not have to fend off predators, nor did they have to cooperate to obtain meat. They relied on keepers to provide the necessities of life. In Taï Forest, by contrast, the chimpanzees were regularly attacked by leopards or neighboring chimpanzee groups competing over scarce resources. In such situations of life and death, they would rush to each other's defense (Boesch 2012, 96–97). If an infant lost its mother, Boesch and colleagues (2010) had observed, the orphan frequently got adopted by a genetically unrelated foster mother or father who extended group solidarity to children even though they could not reciprocate. Considering that such adoptions had been observed less frequently at East African field sites where leopards had either been eradicated or did not attack chimpanzees, Boesch (2012, 100–102) presented the altruism of the Taï chimpanzees as cultural. "Well-tuned captive experiments incorporating socio-ecological circumstances equivalent to those seen in nature might elicit cooperation more readily in animals,"

Boesch (2012, 105) concluded. "Sadly, though[,] captive conditions are not ideal for this and engineering experimental situations mimicking group hunting, predator attacks, or territory defense are probably not possible."

Even if the Leipzig chimpanzees could be tested under more natural conditions, Boesch doubted that they would behave like their wild conspecifics. Many had been obtained from a Dutch biomedical research institute. To provide a sense of how abnormal Tomasello's test subjects were, Boesch recounted that when they first arrived at the zoo, these chimpanzees did not dare to enter the outdoor compound because they had never seen any grass. "Now it's more than fifteen years and the zoo director has just told me that some individuals still don't go on the grass," he said to me in an interview in 2013. "Can you imagine what these chimpanzees must have gone through?" (see also Boesch 2012, 203–4).

Underneath Boesch and Tomasello's methodological disagreements loomed the old theoretical rift between universalism and particularism, which primatologists had inherited from anthropologists. Against the background of what Boesch (2007, 233) considered the single most important finding of the last two decades of chimpanzee fieldwork, namely the behavioral diversity within the species, he asked how the behavior of psychologically deformed animals could represent *the* chimpanzee while Leipzig kindergarten children represented humankind. In a bellicose tone, Boesch (2012, 41) alleged that "such captive studies would be akin to studying the culture of the Aka Pygmies in Central Africa with Nigerian prisoners in German prisons!"

Science: Cooperation or War?

Although neither Boesch nor Tomasello wrote in a reflexive key, the distinctive ways in which they engaged in this controversy reflected their anthropological positions. While Tomasello highlighted the exceptional place of *Homo sapiens* in natural history by painting an almost black-and-white picture of cooperative humans and competitive apes, Boesch argued for human–animal continuity by presenting humans as less cooperative and chimpanzees as more cooperative than his opponent would admit. In their debate, Tomasello fashioned himself as a highly cooperative human, while Boesch adopted the persona of a competitive hominoid.

When Boesch accused him of disdain for observational data, Tomasello pushed back in a cool tone that betrayed nothing of Boesch's thymotic anger. He denied that there even was a "debate on the relative importance of field observations versus controlled captive experiments," as Boesch (2007, 227) had claimed: "Both are necessary, and their functions are complementary" (Tomasello and Call 2008, 451). Why not work together?

In an interview with me, on the other hand, Boesch paraphrased the French philosopher Bernard-Henri Lévy (2010, 33–56) as saying: "Philosophy is war. When I discuss with another philosopher my goal is not to compromise, my goal is to convince him that he is wrong and should accept my opinion." Boesch added:

> I feel science should be like that. Science should not be about doing politics. It should not be about reaching compromises, but about finding the one solution to go forward. Some people in the field of cognition say we need all the different approaches to understand culture and cognition. I disagree. . . . If some people argue that field and captivity are complementary, that's wrong. Removing animals from the wild and putting them into totally artificial situations, sometimes for generations, and then to test them in equally artificial experiments to claim that this was representative of what they could do in the wild is wrong.[1]

Boesch doubted that *Homo academicus* should generally comport himself as a cooperative primate.

This bellicose vision of science can be traced back to the eighteenth-century philosopher Pierre Bayle, who had imagined the Republic of Letters as torn by a Hobbesian *bellum omnium contra omnes*: scholars would fight until all contradictions would perish and only incontrovertible truths would survive, with no Leviathan assembled from the multitude of conflicting researchers to trade academic freedom for security (Daston 1991; Koselleck 1988, 108–13). Throughout the nineteenth and twentieth centuries, the pendulum swung back and forth between combative and collaborative conceptions of knowledge production. Most relevant to a social science of primate social science is the fact that the sociological framework in which we are currently thinking about science was created by a generation of scholars who would have concurred with Boesch rather than Tomasello. In the 1970s, Pierre Bourdieu (2004, 45) turned against Robert Merton's "irenic image" of a "scientific community" as a "world of generous exchanges in which all scientists collaborate towards the same end" (see also Bourdieu 1999, 31). Instead he sociologized Bayles's vision of "a truth that has undergone the test of discussion in a field where antagonistic interests, and even opposing power strategies, have battled over it" (Bourdieu 2004, 84). Harry Collins (1983) regarded the analysis of such controversies as the royal road to understanding the social construction of scientific knowledge. Bruno Latour's (1987) account of science in action was teeming with war metaphors: only facts constructed so robustly that no scientific adversary had the resources to unscrew them could pacify select domains of research as they congealed into textbook knowledge. Despite all their internal differences, the social studies of science coalesced around their opposition to the positivist ideal of a unified science.

Many scientists perceived these social scientific descriptions of their work as hostile and struck back. The Science Wars of the 1990s broke out over many things—epistemology, ethics, politics, style—but they were also about what some scientists perceived as the sociologists' overemphasis on competition and controversy. The Cambridge primatologist Robert Hinde (2000, 105, 115), for example, complained about an exaggeration of the differences between schools of thought that failed to present these different approaches against a background of their commonalities and the common goal of unifying knowledge.

The Hungarian philosopher of science György Márkus (1987, 36–37) noted that the natural sciences developed practices to contain dissent and establish a widely shared background understanding. These normalizing practices make challenges to the conceptual and practical foundations of scientific research in open polemics and controversies the exception, not the norm. By contrast, Márkus argued, the humanities and social sciences came to be articulated in a "polemic-dissensive manner" (34–35). Different traditions have been organized around theoretical alternatives, which can be traced back to texts considered classical because each provides a paradigmatic formulation to one or another of these alternatives.

If we followed this account of the two epistemic cultures, Boesch's scientific warrior ethic rearticulated the ethnography of chimpanzee societies in the polemogenic manner that Márkus presented as the modus operandi of the human and social sciences. Although the primatologist opted for polemics to triumph over competitors, the history of knowledge seems to suggest that dissensive approaches are more likely to add perspectives than to eliminate them. Whatever the actors intend, the result is rarely a cognitive monoculture; rather, it tends to be an epistemically disunified intellectual space.

Conclusion

Bourdieu (2004, 91) sought to institute and collectivize reflexivity as the common law of the social scientific field, in which a "sociological critique of all by all" would intensify the truth-producing effects of the "epistemological critique of all by all." This conception of science contrasts sharply with the ideal of a cooperation of all with all, which inspired Okasha's plea for less controversy and more esprit de corps among altruism researchers. If I end this essay on a reflexive note, it is not to second Bourdieu's rationale for a social science of social science or to warn that such calls for total critique might have self-defeating consequences for a scientific field, as Okasha prophesied. Instead of making any such spirited appeal, I would like to raise some genuine questions.

As research on social cognition and behavior extends beyond the human (Fassin, this volume), it creates an ontological borderland in which social and natural scientists encounter one another more frequently again. Calls for interdisciplinary cooperation abound. Both sides largely agree that the epistemic divide between the two cultures is an anachronism that owes more to the social organization of the nineteenth-century university than to the makeup of the world (although we saw that even in the nineteenth century, animals had been objects of sociological study). What natural scientists and posthumanities scholars disagree over is whether research practices should be hybridized under the sign of the natural or interpretive social sciences. While the sociobiologist Edward O. Wilson (1998) called for consilience between the two great branches of learning within the epistemological and ontological framework of the natural sciences, as he understood them, multispecies ethnographers tried to model the study of nature and our place in it on the humanities, replacing naturalistic observation by morally engaged witnessing and controlled trials in the laboratory by artistic experiments in exhibition spaces (Kirksey 2014; Kirksey et al. 2016; Kirksey and Helmreich 2010; van Dooren, Kirksey, and Münster 2016). But the dividing lines are not always clear-cut. The case of Christophe Boesch, a staunch natural scientist who operates in the polemic-dissensive manner of many humanists and social researchers, suggests that epistemic virtues and practices from both sides can be remixed in numerous ways and to different ends (Langlitz 2020, chap. 3; see also 2015).[2]

As the social sciences return to their animal origins, they need to decide which elements to adopt from the natural and the human sciences and how to assemble them. Do they want to collaborate on a shared vision of human and nonhuman sociality or engage in a pluralization of available alternatives? Do they want to implement and maybe collectivize reflexivity? If so, would it amount to a critique of all by all, or would less agonistic forms of scholarly life enable more consensus-oriented forms of knowledge? Should a reflexive sociology beyond the human bridge the gap between social and natural sciences by inventing new prosocial norms and forms for science or by fostering controversy over the hominoid condition, which great ape researchers share with the great apes?

Notes

1 For an ethnographic and historical case study of the integration of laboratory experiments, field experiments, and naturalistic field observations, see my article "Synthetic Primatology" on Tetsuro Matsuzawa's chimpanzee research in Japan and Guinea (Langlitz 2020, chaps. 5–6; 2017b). In the human sciences, field experiments have also come to serve as a bridge between bench- and fieldwork. Behavioral economists, for example, use experimental games to study prosocial behaviors across cultures and species, both in the laboratory and in the field (Camerer and Fehr 2004; Henrich et al. 2005; Henrich and Henrich 2007; Jensen, Call, and Tomasello 2007).

2 A similar point could be made about Michael Tomasello, but it would require more space than is available here. See Langlitz 2020, chap. 4.

References

Asquith, Pamela J. 1981. "Some Aspects of Anthropomorphism in the Terminology and Philosophy Underlying Western and Japanese Studies of the Social Behaviour of Non-human Primates." PhD diss., University of Oxford.

Asquith, Pamela J. 1986. "Anthropomorphism and the Japanese and Western Traditions in Primatology." In *Primate Ontogeny, Cognition and Social Behavior*, edited by J. G. Else and P. C. Lee, 61–71. Cambridge: Cambridge University Press.

Asquith, Pamela J. 2000. "Negotiating Science: Internationalization and Japanese Primatology." In *Primate Encounters: Models of Science, Gender, and Society*, edited by S. C. Strum and L. M. Fedigan, 165–83. Chicago: University of Chicago Press.

Benkler, Yochai. 2011. *The Penguin and the Leviathan: How Cooperation Triumphs over Self-Interest*. New York: Crown Business.

Boesch, Christophe. 1994. "Cooperative Hunting in Wild Chimpanzees." *Animal Behaviour* 48: 653–67. https://doi.org/10.1006/anbe.1994.1285.

Boesch, Christophe. 2002. "Cooperative Hunting Roles among Taï Chimpanzees." *Human Nature* 13: 27–46. https://doi.org/10.1007/s12110-002-1013-6.

Boesch, Christophe. 2005. "Joint Cooperative Hunting among Wild Chimpanzees: Taking Natural Observations Seriously." *Behavioral and Brain Sciences* 28: 692–93.

Boesch, Christophe. 2007. "What Makes Us Human (Homo Sapiens)? The Challenge of Cognitive Cross-Species Comparison." *Journal of Comparative Psychology* 121: 227–40.

Boesch, Christophe. 2008. "Taking Development and Ecology Seriously When Comparing Cognition: Reply to Tomasello and Call." *Journal of Comparative Psychology* 122: 453–55. https://doi.org/10.1037/0735-7036.122.4.453.

Boesch, Christophe. 2012. *Wild Cultures*. New York: Cambridge University Press.

Boesch, Christophe, Camille Bolé, Nadin Eckhardt, and Hedwige Boesch. 2010. "Altruism in Forest Chimpanzees: The Case of Adoption." *PLOS One* 5: e8901. https://doi.org/10.1371/journal.pone.0008901.s.

Bourdieu, Pierre. 1999. "The Specificity of the Scientific Field and the Social Conditions of the Progress of Reason." In *The Science Studies Reader*, edited by Mario Biagioli, 31–50. New York: Routledge.

Bourdieu, Pierre. 2004. *The Science of Science and Reflexivity*. Chicago: University of Chicago Press.

Camerer, Colin F., and Ernst Fehr. 2004. "Measuring Social Norms and Preferences Using Experimental Games: A Guide for Social Scientists." In *Foundations of Human Sociality: Economic Experiments and Ethnographic Evidence from Fifteen Small-Scale Societies*, edited by J. Henrich, R. Boyd, S. Bowles, C. F. Camerer, E. Fehr, and H. Gintis, 55–95. Oxford: Oxford University Press.

Carpenter, Clarence R. 1942. "Characteristics of Social Behavior in Non-human Primates." *Transactions of the New York Academy of Sciences* 4: 248–58. https://doi.org/10.1111/j.2164-0947.1942.tb00856.x.

Collier, J. 1878. "Book Review of Espinas, *Des sociétés animales*." *Mind* 3: 105–12.

Collins, Harry M. 1983. "The Sociology of Scientific Knowledge: Studies of Contemporary Science." *Annual Review of Sociology* 9: 265–85.

Daston, Lorraine. 1991. "The Ideal and Reality of the Republic of Letters in the Enlightenment." *Science in Context* 4: 367–86. https://doi.org/10.1017/S0269889700001010.

Daston, Lorraine. 2005. "Intelligences: Angelic, Animal, Human." In *Thinking with Animals: New Perspectives on Anthropomorphism*, edited by L. Daston and G. Mitman, 37–58. New York: Columbia University Press.

Daston, Lorraine. 1991. "The Ideal and Reality of the Republic of Letters in the Enlightenment." *Science in Context* 4: 367–86. https://doi.org/10.1017/S0269889700001010.

de Waal, Frans B. M. 1982. *Chimpanzee Politics: Power and Sex among Apes*. New York: Harper and Row.

de Waal, Frans B. M. 1990. *Peacemaking among Primates*. Cambridge, MA: Harvard University Press.

de Waal, Frans B. M. 1997. *Good Natured: The Origins of Right and Wrong in Humans and Other Animals*. Cambridge, MA: Harvard University Press.

de Waal, Frans B. M. 1999. "Anthropomorphism and Anthropodenial: Consistency in Our Thinking about Humans and Animals." *Philosophical Topics* 27: 255–80.

de Waal, Frans B. M. 2001. *The Ape and the Sushi Master: Cultural Reflections by a Primatologist*. New York: Basic Books.

de Waal, Frans B. M. 2003. "Silent Invasion: Imanishi's Primatology and Cultural Bias in Science." *Animal Cognition* 6: 293–99. https://doi.org/10.1007/s10071-003-0197-4.

de Waal, Frans B. M. 2010. *The Age of Empathy: Nature's Lessons for a Kinder Society*. New York: Broadway Books.

D'Hombres, Emmanuel, and Soraya Mehdaoui. 2012. "'On What Condition Is the Equation Organism–Society Valid?': Cell Theory and Organicist Sociology in the Works of Alfred Espinas (1870s–80s)." *History of the Human Sciences* 25: 32–51.

Durkheim, Émile. 1964. *The Division of Labor in Society*. New York: Free Press.

Espinas, Alfred. 1877. *Des sociétés animales: Étude de psychologie comparée*. Paris: Germer Baillière.

Heilbron, Johann. 2015. *French Sociology*. Ithaca, NY: Cornell University Press.

Henrich, Joseph, Richard Boyd, Samuel Bowles, Colin Camerer, Ernst Fehr, Herbert Gintis, Richard McElreath, et al. 2005. "'Economic Man' in Cross-Cultural Perspective: Behavioral Experiments in 15 Small-Scale Societies." *Behavioral and Brain Sciences* 28: 795–815.

Henrich, Joseph, and Natalie Henrich. 2007. *Why Humans Cooperate: A Cultural and Evolutionary Explanation*. Oxford: Oxford University Press.

Hinde, Robert A. 2000. "Some Reflections on Primatology at Cambridge and the Science Studies Debate." In *Primate Encounters: Models of Science, Gender, and Society*, edited by S. C. Strum and L. M. Fedigan, 104–15. Chicago: University of Chicago Press.

Imanishi, Kinji. 2002. *A Japanese View of Nature: The World of Living Things*. London: Routledge.

Itani, Junichiro. 1985. "The Evolution of Primate Social Structures." *Man* 20: 593–611. https://doi.org/10.2307/2802752.

Jensen, Keith, Joseph Call, and Michael Tomasello. 2007. "Chimpanzees Are Rational Maximizers in an Ultimatum Game." *Science* 318: 107–9.

Kirksey, Eben, ed. 2014. *The Multispecies Salon*. Durham, NC: Duke University Press.

Kirksey, Eben, Dehlia Hannah, Charlie Lotterman, and Lisa J. Moore. 2016. "The Xenopus Pregnancy Test: A Performative Experiment." *Environmental Humanities* 8: 37–56. https://doi.org/10.1215/22011919-3527713.

Kirksey, Eben, and Stefan Helmreich. 2010. "The Emergence of Multispecies Ethnography." *Cultural Anthropology* 25: 545–76.

Koselleck, Reinhart. 1988. *Critique and Crisis: Enlightenment and the Pathogenesis of Modern Society*. Cambridge, MA: MIT Press.

Kummer, Hans. 1971. *Primate Societies: Group Techniques of Ecological Adaptation*. Chicago: Aldine.

Langlitz, Nicolas. 2015. "On a Not So Chance Encounter between Neurophilosophy and Science Studies in a Sleep Laboratory." *History of the Human Sciences* 28: 3–24. https://doi.org/10.1177/0952695115581576.

Langlitz, Nicolas. 2019. "Primatology of Science on the Birth of Actor-Network Theory from Baboon Field Observations." *Theory, Culture and Society* 36, no. 1: 83–105. https://doi.org/10.1177/0263276417740409.

Langlitz, N. 2017b. "Synthetic Primatology: What Humans and Chimpanzees Do in a Japanese Laboratory and the African Field." *British Journal for the History of Science Themes*: 101–25.

Langlitz, Nicolas. 2020. *Chimpanzee Culture Wars: Rethinking Human Nature alongside Japanese, European, and American Cultural Primatologists*. Princeton, NJ: Princeton University Press.

Latour, Bruno. 1987. *Science in Action: How to Follow Scientists and Engineers through Society*. Cambridge, MA: Harvard University Press.

Lévy, Bernard-Henri. 2010. *De la guerre en philosophie*. Paris: Éditions Grasset and Fasquelle.

Márkus, György. 1987. "Why Is There No Hermeneutics of Natural Sciences? Some Preliminary Theses." *Science in Context* 1: 5–51.

Milam, Erika L. 2012. "On Playing Well with Others." *BioSocieties* 7: 93–97.

Okasha, Samir. 2010. "Altruism Researchers Must Cooperate." *Nature* 467: 653–55. https://doi.org/10.1038/467653a.

Rees, Amanda. 2006. "Ecology, Biology and Social Life: Explaining the Origins of Primate Sociality." *History of Science* 44: 409–34. https://doi.org/10.1177 /007327530604400402.

Sennett, Richard. 2012. *Together: The Rituals, Pleasures, and Politics of Cooperation*. New Haven, CT: Yale University Press.

Strum, Shirley C., and Bruno Latour. 1987. "Redefining the Social Link: From Baboons to Humans." *Social Science Information* 26: 783–802.

Thomas, Marion. 2005. "Are Animals Just Noisy Machines? Louis Boutan and the Co-invention of Animal and Child Psychology in the French Third Republic." *Journal of the History of Biology* 38: 425–60. https://doi.org/10.1007/s10739 -005-0555-y.

Tomasello, Michael. 1999. *The Cultural Origins of Human Cognition*. Cambridge, MA: Harvard University Press.

Tomasello, Michael. 2009a. *Rede, gehalten anlässlich der Verleihung des Hegel-Preises*. [English]. Accessed December 29, 2012. http://www.stuttgart.de/img/mdb /item/383875/51641.pdf.

Tomasello, Michael. 2009b. *Why We Cooperate*. Cambridge, MA: MIT Press.

Tomasello, Michael. 2014. *A Natural History of Human Thinking*. Cambridge, MA: Harvard University Press.

Tomasello, Michael, and Joseph Call. 2008. "Assessing the Validity of Ape-Human Comparisons: A Reply to Boesch (2007)." *Journal of Comparative Psychology* 122: 449–52. https://doi.org/10.1037/0735-7036.122.4.449.

Tomasello, Michael, Malinda Carpenter, Joseph Call, Tanya Behne, and Henrike Moll. 2005. "Understanding and Sharing Intentions: The Origins of Cultural Cognition." *Behavioral and Brain Sciences* 28: 675–735.

van Dooren, Thom, Eben Kirksey, and Ursula Münster. 2016. "Multispecies Studies: Cultivating Arts of Attentiveness." *Environmental Humanities* 8: 1–23. https://doi.org/10.1215/22011919-3527695.

Wilson, Edward O. 1998. *Consilience: The Unity of Knowledge*. New York: Alfred A. Knopf.

Zuckerman, Solly. 1932. *The Social Life of Monkeys and Apes*. London: Kegan Paul, Trench, Trubner, and Company.

15

the rise & rise of posthumanism

Will It Spell
the End of the
Human Sciences?

DIDIER FASSIN

THE HUMAN SCIENCES are a recent human invention. As Roger Smith (1997, 4) wrote in the introduction of his one-thousand-page history of these disciplines, although the interest in "human nature" goes far back in time, the denomination "human sciences"—a category that for him includes "psychology, sociology, anthropology, linguistics, economics and political science," while "history, geography, jurisprudence, business management, literary criticism and art history are also possible"—is "an anachronistic label when applied to any area of scholarship before the twentieth century." In fact, Claude Blanckaert (1999, 27) observes that, although in French the wording *sciences de l'homme* dates back to the seventeenth century, its less sexist reformulation, *sciences humaines*, only gained currency in the mid-twentieth century, when Georges Canguilhem and Georges Gusdorf used the phrase polemically to contrast it with the growing technicist and utilitarian trend in the study of human beings, particularly through psychometry and behaviorism. Today both locutions remain in use in France, with the Institut des Sciences Humaines et Sociales administering these disciplines at the National Center for Scientific Research and numerous researchers of these domains working in the Maison des Sciences de l'Homme et de la Société of their university. But as Theodore Porter and Dorothy Ross (2003, 3) note, the irony is that at the same time the human sciences were advocated for their humanistic connotation more than their scientific denotation, a formidable attack was launched against them, most notably by Michel Foucault (1970), who foretold their extinction and, simultaneously, what he called the death of man. But paradoxically, it is this very prediction that ensured the success of the expression *human sciences* in English within the academic humanities, albeit as an object of inquiry rather than a field of research.

If we therefore follow this succinct chronology, not only were the human sciences recently invented, but they were also short-lived. Soon after they were born, they fell victims of structuralism and poststructuralism, and Claude Lévi-Strauss (1966, 247) declared that "the ultimate goal of the human sciences to be not to constitute but to dissolve man," while Jacques Lacan (2006, 732) asserted that "there is no such thing as a science of man because science's man does not exist." Like Lichtenberg's proverbial knife without a blade that has no handle, the human sciences had therefore a dual problem, since they had no subject and their object was vanishing. They received the coup de grâce with *The Order of Things* (Foucault 1970, 386–87): "Man is neither the oldest nor the most constant problem that has been posed for human knowledge.... As the archeology of our thought easily shows, man is an invention of recent date. And one perhaps nearing its end." However, the social sciences and the humanities, as they are commonly named, survived the antihumanist offensive of the 1960s and 1970s. But a new wave of contestation has recently emerged, claiming to be not so much against but beyond the human. The question therefore becomes: Will they also survive the posthumanist assault of the early twenty-first century?

Indeed, whereas structuralists and poststructuralists had challenged both the human and the sciences in the human sciences, fifty years later, an influential current in the social sciences and the humanities adopts a no less disruptive approach to the human sciences, which consists in diminishing, marginalizing, or simply eliminating the human so as to invent a new science, or, more accurately, a new episteme. The point of departure of most of these posthumanist theories is a critique of the way the centrality of the human in Western modern sciences, with their focus on language, discourse, meaning, and representation, has not only deprived our understanding of the world from other forms of knowing but has also overdetermined it by a series of preconceptions socially induced. The corpus that these theories constitute is anything but homogeneous or coherent, and even the term *posthumanism* does not necessarily reflect the way some of these authors designate themselves. However, I want to suggest that the existence of correspondences and convergences within the movement makes possible an analysis of its various strands under a shared umbrella. Moreover, its impact across disciplines as well as continents—with many scholars being seduced by its powerful critique, in anthropology as well as philosophy, from Brazil to Australia—makes it necessary to take seriously the epistemological as well as political challenge it entails. In the following pages, I will first provide a general view of posthumanism and trace its multiple intellectual genealogies, then analyze its anthropological avatar and question its consistency, and finally discuss the issues raised by their approaches to the world. Ultimately, the point is to consider whether posthumanism—inasmuch as there is such thing—represents a significant advance, a potential danger, or a passing fad, which would have only added one more turn in a domain where there is no shortage of them.

Let a Hundred Posthumanisms Blossom: A Cultural Revolution

What do Peter Singer's antispeciesism, Bruno Latour's actor-network theory, Donna Haraway's cyborg feminism, Jane Bennett's new materialism, Rosi Braidotti's nomadic theory, William Connolly's immanent naturalism, Quentin Meillassoux's speculative realism, Ray Brassier's transcendental nihilism, and Graham Harman's object-oriented ontology—to mention only a few labels under which posthumanism is known—have in common? And what do they share with transhumanism, initially conceived by Julian Huxley and today decomposed in multiple branches—democratic and libertarian, immortalist and technogaianist, postpoliticist and postgenderist—with their imagined or actual enhancement of the human condition via technologies? Posthumanism and transhumanism certainly never run out of "isms," but this nominal creativity, in which the sociologist cannot avoid seeing ways of defining boundaries and defending territories in a competitive field, does reflect important theoretical variations. The question is whether there is a minimal core to these various strands.

Connecting fiction and reality around the posthuman, Pramod Nayar (2014, 3–4) establishes a primary distinction between posthumanism as "ontological condition" and critical posthumanism as "new conceptualization of the human." In the first case, posthumanism simply refers to biological mutations, bodily prostheses, and organ replacements as well as social interactions with a variety of devices and machines, most notably computers, which redefines the limit of the human and draws on earlier works on robotics, such as that of Hans Moravec (1988), who argued that artificial intelligence would lead to a new species of beings. In a classic interpretive reading of this ontology, Katherine Hayles (1999, 2–3) explains "how we became posthuman" by producing a hybrid form in which "there are no essential differences or absolute demarcations between bodily existence and computer simulation, cybernetic mechanism and biological organism, robot teleology and human goals." For her, "the posthuman view privileges informational pattern over material instantiation, so that embodiment in a biological substrate is seen as an accident of history rather than an inevitability of life." In the second case, critical posthumanism stands against the traditional view, which consists in positioning the human on top of a moral and political hierarchy ordering the multitude of entities that compose the world, which is often named speciesism, and which Peter Singer (1975) considers equivalent to racism or sexism. This hierarchical view is widely regarded as the legacy of Cartesianism, which, according to Cary Wolfe (2010, 40 and xviii), "rests on two fundamental points: (1) the assertion that animals, however sophisticated they may be, can only 'react' but not 'respond' to what goes around them; and this is so because (2) the capacity to respond depends on the ability to wield concepts or representations, which is in turn possible only on the basis of language." He opposes this approach by referring to "Jeremy Bentham's famous assertion that the question is not 'can they talk?' or 'can they reason?' but 'can they suffer?'" In fact, the English philosopher used the argument by establishing a comparison between an animal and a newborn.

There is thus a dual tension in this presentation of posthumanism: in terms of approach, between the interpretive and the critical; in terms of boundary, with the machine and with the animal. On the one hand, one analyzes the existence of a new being that is more than human, since it is augmented by technology: this is an enriched description of humans. On the other hand, one denounces the ideology of human supremacy, which leads to the mistreatment of other living creatures: this is a strong prescription for humans. In fact, Donna Haraway's (1985) seminal essay "A Manifesto for Cyborgs," which she wittily described as a political fiction, already included but connected these two dualisms: "My cyborg myth is about transgressed boundaries," she writes, adding to those with animals and with machines a third boundary "between physical and non-physical" that refers to signals, waves, numbers, codes, and other invisible objects that have densified and expanded human lives but also taken control them.

Yet if posthumanism was only a redefinition of the human in order to include its transformations by ever more advanced technology and a contestation of its prominence so as to reinscribe it in the animal kingdom, the gesture would undoubtedly be significant but not terribly problematic for the social sciences and the humanities. Some would resist the idea of the cyborgs as substitutes to the sovereign human, and others might deplore his fall from his pedestal dominating the natural world. But most would accept this posthumanist turn, probably noting that the two criticisms are not on the same plane and do not have the same stakes. The question is, in the first case, whether we should fear that machines might replace humans, and in the second case, whether one should consider it more important to avoid the suffering of humans than of animals. Yet in both cases, with some accommodations, the humanist edifice would remain in place for the most part, simply populated with fairly enhanced and more modest humans.

However, for some, especially among philosophers, the project is more extreme, although different again from one author and theory to the next. In the view of the most radical thinkers, the target is not merely Descartes and his alleged human supremacism; it is Kant and his anthropocentrism. The problem is not only that human beings have been placed at the top of the pyramid of living beings but also that they have been placed at the center of the knowable or even conceivable universe. All modern philosophy, from Hegel to Husserl, and from Heidegger to Wittgenstein, can therefore be reduced to what Quentin Meillassoux (2010), a student of Alain Badiou, calls "correlationism," that is, the idea that it is not possible to think of the world without humans and humans without the world or, said otherwise, that we can only know what is given to our thinking, but not what exists out of it. If we reject this claim, he says, then we are left with a cosmos dating a few billion years and full of contingencies—a world needing no humans, a world where human presence is a mere accident with no future. This is of course an abyssal challenge for the social sciences and the humanities, since it excludes humans not only as objects of study, since their existence becomes anecdotal and doomed to destruction, but also as subjects involved in the process of studying, since there is no longer any reason to do so, as he writes. Such a view leads Ray Brassier (2007), who belongs to the same current of thought named speculative realism, although he takes some distance with his predecessors, to embrace a form "nihilism" explicitly borrowed from Nietzsche as the only way to confront the perspective of the extinction of humankind and the inanity of a search for any meaning in front of this annihilation foretold.

A more social sciences–and humanities-friendly approach to the posthuman, although sometimes influenced by speculative realism, is that of the quite prominent new materialism, which again has multiple subdivisions and alternative labels, including material feminism, material ecocriticism, and panpsychism. Although it has diverse sources, notably science studies and cultural theory, its most determining impulse comes from critical feminism. The general idea of the new materialism is to acknowledge the material dimension of the world that idealism has neglected, to contest the hierarchy of values that recognizes a nobler status to the mind than to the body, and to rehabilitate the status of things and objects as active contributors to the composition of the universe. The influence of Judith Butler's early works insisting on the materiality of sex is notable, but most new materialists acknowledge above all the influence of Gilles Deleuze, although the legacy of Marx and Nietzsche is also present. Among the most preeminent figures, Rosi Braidotti (2006) focuses on the role of biotechnologies in the becoming of new posthuman subjectivities and on the embodied and affective interconnections across both human and nonhuman entities, while Jane Bennett (2010) extends the vibrancy of life to stem cells, fish oils, electricity, metal, and trash to form posthuman assemblages with specific agency. While appearing under various forms, this theory presents a series of common features. First, rather than being inert, matter forms complexes with energy as shown by physics. Second, no epistemological privilege is granted to the human over the nonhuman, whether an organism or a thing. Third, the understanding of the processes at work implies distinct methods such as speculation, experimentation, and artistic imagination. Fourth, this approach has a political and ethical dimension, the former manifesting itself via a critique of capitalism and its reification of the relations between humans and nonhumans, the latter expressing itself through care for the world and the entities that compose it in the context of climate change. Thus, William Connolly (2013, 410–11) speaks of "the fragility of things" calling for a particular attentiveness to them and of "democratic militancy" developed outside traditional electoral politics.

But the expansion of the social sciences and humanities beyond the human and the integration of nonhumans in their intellectual landscape is obviously not new. In particular, it was at the heart of the actor-network theory, proposed in the 1980s by Michel Callon and Bruno Latour as well as by John Law and Peter Lodge, which also exercised an influence on the new materialisms. The central argument, initially developed within the field of science and technology studies but later extended to various other fields, is that in a given context multiple entities are simultaneously to be taken into account on an equal basis, whether humans, animals, organisms, objects, ideas, or even problems. As is well-known, Bruno Latour (2005, 9, 16) speaks of actants rather than actors, suspects that they often have relations

THE RISE AND RISE OF POSTHUMANISM   373

without forming real networks, and regards his program as more a method than a theory proper, which would ironically make the very designation of his contribution to the social sciences as actor-network theory somewhat inadequate on the three counts of the three parts of its name. But his main point is, of course, the decentering of the social sciences away from the centrality of humans, be they scientists or more generally social agents. Using a geographical metaphor, he writes that the objective is "to render the social world as flat as possible in order to ensure that the establishment of any new link is clearly visible." Opposing both Durkheimian and Weberian traditions in sociology, he rejects society and the social, which he deems human, all too human, as well as their potential for critique as being humanistic, all too humanistic—hence his recurrent attacks on Pierre Bourdieu.

Instead, his expanded relational approach opens the way to not only give a place to nonhuman entities, particularly the indefinite realm of things, but to also rethink the concept of human agency, once it has been rid of its dimension of intentionality. If things have agency as individuals do, then intention becomes irrelevant. This affirmation leads Latour (2013, 453, 457) to logically infer that all entities have politics and moralities, from ticks and glaciers to the pope, to mention his own examples. It is thus not surprising that he would have belatedly rediscovered and rehabilitated, as many others in recent years, the metaphysics of Alfred North Whitehead ([1927] 1958, 44–45), for whom "primitive living organisms have a sense for the fate from which they have emerged, and for the fate towards which they go," a sense also experienced by human beings when they feel "anger, hatred, fear, terror, attraction, love, hunger, eagerness, massive enjoyment." Such a statement is definitely a radical way of saying that "the humanities are not just about humans," which Graham Harman (2016) describes as Latour's "primary lesson" in a special issue of a journal dedicated to "recomposing the humanities" through his critique of modernity.

In light of this space travel across the territories of its numerous avatars, posthumanism seems to resort more to intellectual ufology than to the traditional history of ideas. It is not sure that there is much in common between theories inspired by Badiou, Deleuze, and Whitehead, between calls for extending the human boundaries so as to include computers and demands to redefine them so as to respect other species, between paying more attention to the material world and emphasizing the immateriality of information, between care for nature and anticipation of the extinction of life, all elements that lead to considerable differences and even contradictions in terms of the politics and ethics implied. Some strands are clearly normative, either politically, with a critique of capitalism and a call for emancipation, or ethically, with a demand for more attentiveness toward animals and the planet. Others are mostly analytical, reconfiguring the importance of the body, from the perspective of gender and sexuality or in terms of hybridization by machines and biotechnologies, or reconsidering the place of the human among living species or within geological epochs. In sum, one would have to be very imaginative—or strategic—to depict posthumanism as a simple coherent intellectual move.

Yet one cannot dismiss the fact that posthumanists cite each other and declare to be inspired by each other, and that many of them claim the label. Is it therefore possible to reconstitute a core of elementary theoretical principles that characterize many of its expressions? The rejection of anthropocentrism is certainly central. It comprises an epistemological and a moral dimension. The epistemological critique insists on the equal importance of humans and nonhumans for the understanding of the world; it can even go as far as to suppose some form of agency not only for all living beings but also for all things. The moral critique rejects the superiority of humans over other beings; it has concrete consequences on both the treatment of animals and the protection of the planet. In its extreme form, this dual critique goes as far as to contest the very significance of the human. The other crucial element of posthumanism concerns a series of dichotomies that have been formative of the modern mode of thinking, particularly the distinctions between the knowing subject and the object to be known, with its corollary self/other, culture/nature, mind/body, intellectual/material. These dichotomies are narrowly related to anthropocentrism, either epistemologically, when the perspective is that of the person as subject or self, or morally, when a hierarchy is established in favor of culture, mind, and intellectual over nature, body, and material.

Remarkably, however, what had been an important incentive of many in critical feminism as well as cultural critique at the inception of the posthuman movement, that is, the contestation of anthropocentrism as socially and historically situated, has sometimes disappeared in the later developments of the various forms of posthumanism. And initially that was indeed the strong bias of anthropocentrism, since the supposedly universalist vision of the human was actually that of Western white males. As the focus of posthumanism moved away from everyday life to privilege the macroscopic perspective of the universe and microscopic lenses on organisms, the ontology of things and the metaphysics of everything, consequently, the concern for the legacies of colonialism and Orientalism, the problems of androcentrism and reification, the issues of embodiment and intersectionality tended to vanish, despite the efforts of some to keep them alive. The level of abstraction of certain forms of posthumanism had for counterpart a disinvestment from the concrete social condition of human beings and the historical processes accounting for it. This was no accident. It was the logical consequence of the invention of a new politics and a new ethics, in which the treatment of humans did not matter more than that of insects, machines, or rocks.

The Eleventh-Hour Posthumanists: The Last Shall Be First

Anthropology is a latecomer in the posthumanist circles, but its entrance has been spectacular in terms of visibility of publications, intensity of debates, and international impact. To be fair, the anthropologists who have engaged this battle have not spared their efforts to nurture and fertilize their collective bold enterprise—they claim no less than a refoundation of the discipline—and, contrary to the rest of the posthuman movement, they have used a single brand name to include their significantly different approaches: the ontological turn. Anthropologists certainly have been fond of the appellation *turn* in the past decades: their discipline has gone through an interpretive turn, a linguistic turn, a textualist turn, an affective turn, and an ethical turn, to name a few. James Laidlaw and Paolo Heywood (2013) make this ironic comment about the ontological turn: "One more turn and you're there." In fact, one could argue that, with the disappearance of general theories, such as evolutionism, diffusionism, functionalism, structuralism, Marxism, and even the discredit of the very possibility of a grand theory, the more modest designation of turns has become the normal way of challenging the common theoretical frameworks of anthropology via more or less significant inflexions. For instance, the ethical turn reappraises the Durkheimian tradition based on the approach to morality through the study of local moral codes defining the values to be adopted and rules to be followed by the members of a given society or group, and draws instead from the Foucauldian legacy to take into account the individuals' free ethical decisions, or more precisely the formation of ethical subjectivities independent of moral codes. It therefore works as an enrichment of anthropology.

But in the case of the ontological turn, it is not an inflection; it is allegedly a revolution. For Eduardo Viveiros de Castro (2014, 40, 43), who has played a major pioneering role in this new approach:

> If we are all more or less agreed that anthropology, even if colonialism was one of its historical *a prioris*, is today nearing the end of its karmic

cycle, then we should also accept that the time has come to radicalize the reconstitution of the discipline by forcing the process to its completion. Anthropology is ready to fully assume its new mission of being the theory/practice of the permanent decolonization of thought.

The ambition could not be clearer. To achieve this project, Viveiros de Castro finds his original inspiration in *Anti-Oedipus*, to which he ironically alludes by titling the first part of his book "Anti-Narcissus" in a form of homage to Gilles Deleuze and Félix Guattari (1983). A decolonization of thought implies for him to replace the habitual ways of practicing anthropology using preconceived categories, such as representation or kinship, by "descriptions of the conditions of the ontological self-determination of the collectives studied." Such a reformulation of the anthropological project entails the possibility of understanding the world as it is apprehended by diverse societies or groups, for instance when they consider, as some Amerindian peoples do, that "peccaries are humans," thus disrupting the delimitation of humanity. For him, it must be anthropology's project to describe these ontologies.

Yet such project, which he never explicitly inscribes in a posthumanist program, is certainly not new. One could indeed revisit the pioneering but forgotten work of Ernesto De Martino (1948) on magic in Italy, using a method he later defines as "critical ethnocentrism" to apprehend local worldviews, with the crucial difference that he insists on the importance of history and therefore never thinks in terms of ontology. More obvious is the precedence of Claude Lévi-Strauss (1981, 588) who, attempting to account for the fact that the Kayapo "said that the jaguar's wife was a human," explains that "in mythic times, humans were indistinguishable from animals, but between the non-differentiated beings who were to give birth to mankind on the one hand and the animal kingdom on the other, certain qualitative relationships pre-existed, anticipating specific characteristics that were still in a latent state." However, Viveiros de Castro (2014, 69, 71) goes further than the father of structuralism in two ways: by affirming that "animals see themselves as humans" because "we humans see them as animals, while seeing ourselves as humans"; and by arguing that "all beings see ('represent') the world in the same way" but "what changes is the world they see." Two undoubtedly remarkable, albeit literally irrefutable, assumptions: in the first case, ontologies are projected not only onto other societies but also onto other living beings; in the second one, a conjecture is formulated according to which the world rather than its representation is what accounts for different ontologies among humans as well as among nonhumans. Affirming that

Amerindians see one culture and many natures when we, moderns, have one nature and many cultures, this radical speculative reasoning is meant to disrupt both positivist and interpretive traditions in anthropology. Yet one can wonder whether the claim that non-Western Indigenous people have their own theory of the world, which he coins, in the emblematic case of the Amerindians, multinaturalist perspectivism, has not in fact been accepted as self-evident for a long time by most anthropologists, even when they draw different conclusions. Is it not a foundational tentative principle of ethnography since Malinowski? But of course, the application of such principle does not presume the existence of ontologies.

It is in the same vein, and moreover within the same Amerindian universe, that Eduardo Kohn (2013, 1, 7–8) engages his celebrated ethnographic research in Ecuador. His premises are almost similar, and he also takes the example of the jaguar. A Quechua woman explains to him that he should sleep face up because in this way the feline will see that he can look back at it and therefore go away, whereas if he sleeps face down it would assimilate him with meat and consequently attack him. "How other kinds of beings see us matters," Kohn observes, since "if jaguars represent us, then anthropology cannot limit itself just to exploring how people from different societies might happen to represent them as doing so." For him, nonhumans also have ontologies. To infer from the relatively obvious observation that animals see and represent humans the confident assertion that they have ontologies can certainly be disputed. Indeed, ethologists have long established that predators make an estimation of their chance of being successful when they attack their prey, and National Park rangers have used such scientific work and perhaps their personal experience to establish recommendations helping human beings to avoid delicate issues in natural environments. Thus, for an encounter with a black bear, one should face the animal, stand tall and make oneself large, but never play dead. In that respect, the National Park ranger does not reason very differently from the Quechua woman. However, it is unlikely that there will be an anthropologist to study the ontology of the rangers.

Besides jaguars, Kohn also considers hybrid creatures named "runa puma" which people believe to be present in the forest and that have predatory instincts like jaguars. The role of the anthropologist, he argues, is to include these other entities of the natural world in his ontological account. Indeed, "social science's greatest contribution—the recognition and delimitation of a separate domain of socially constructed reality—is also its greatest curse," he writes. And while the "posthumanities," to which he acknowledges his debt, particularly the "Deleuze-influenced scholarship" and Donna Haraway's work, have opened our understanding of the world to nonhumans, he maintains that they have not gone far enough on this path by not developing a critique of representation. For him, whereas humanists were captive of their reduction of representation to the human realm, posthumanists are captive of their conflation of representation with language. The provocative phrase "how forests think," which gives the book its title, invites us to consider that "non-human life-forms also represent the world," a statement that only makes sense if one expands the meaning of representation to its "iconic" and "indexical" modalities, as proposed by Charles Peirce. This is what Kohn calls "an anthropology beyond the human." There is an obvious connection here with multispecies ethnography, as discussed by Eben Kirksey and Stefan Helmreich (2010, 551). This growing field of anthropology is interested in "the lives of animals in labs, on farms, in agricultural production, as food, in rapidly changing ecosystems," as well as in the presence of plants, mushrooms, microbes in our environment. Such ethnographies, beyond their specificity, can induce a profound transformation of our worldview. If we think with Anna Tsing (2012, 141) that "human nature is an interspecies relationship," it is possible to consider, as she does, the role of fungi "as protagonists for histories of the world," which would be read from the perspective of the interdependencies between humans and other species. Instead of stories of domestication, she says, such reconstitutions would be stories of companionship.

Up to this point, the expansion of the exploration of the territory beyond the human proposed by anthropologists has concerned living beings, did they belong to the animal, vegetal, fungal or even supernatural kingdom. But what about nonliving entities? This is the program proposed by Amiria Henare, Martin Holbraad, and Sari Wastell (2007, 3): "thinking through things." Again, the project is formidable: "What would an artefact-oriented anthropology look like if it were not about material culture? And could such a project develop, not as a new subgenre within the discipline, but as a means of reconfiguring anthropology's analytic methods more generally?" Clearly, the intention seems more in line with Graham Harman's object-oriented theory than with Rosi Braidotti's and Jane Bennett's new materialism. It is not a rehabilitation of the corporeal and the biological; it is a reconceptualization of things. Whereas the study of material culture is a well-established domain of anthropology that explores the characteristics, properties, usages, and ultimately meanings of objects in various cultural contexts, the idea of an artefact-oriented anthropology is quite different, since, following Marilyn Strathern (1990), it is to view things not as exemplars of a culture but as meanings as such. "The starting point is to treat meaning and things as an identity," explain the three anthropologists. Speaking of "things" rather than objects or even artefacts, as they initially suggested, has the advantage that "they carry minimal theoretical baggage." Regarding this assumption, it is necessary to recall that Martin Heidegger (1971) has formulated a distinction between objects, which are connected with human beings, and things, which exist in their absence. The distinction has contributed to giving birth to a field of research that Bill Brown (2001) refers to as "thing theory," which has many ramifications in the humanities and arts.

To the notion of "thing-as-analytic" as understood in what Henare, Holbraad, and Wastell view as classic anthropology, they oppose that of "thing-as-heuristic," which they describe thus: "Rather than going into the field armed with a set of pre-determined theoretical criteria against which to measure the 'things' one already anticipates might be encountered, it is proposed that the 'things' that present themselves be allowed to serve as a heuristic with which a particular field of phenomena can be identified, which only then engender theory." It is probable that many ethnographers would again recognize their own way of doing research in this method and, like Monsieur Jourdain, would discover that they have long been practicing inquiry into things-as-heuristic without knowing it. Conversely, many ontologists working on things do not seem to explore them in a way that is very distinct from the majority of their colleagues who are not ontologists, and titling an article "How Drones Think," as Grégory Delaplace (2017) does, may not lead to more than an interesting description of the work of the military who pilot these devices and of the fear of the people on the ground who represent them as nefarious agents.

In fact, the fascinating case studies presented in the volume edited by Henare, Holbraad, and Wastell would not have seemed incongruous among those gathered, two decades earlier, by Arjun Appadurai (1986), despite his insistence on the commodification of things, and even more, a few years later, among those assembled by Jean Bazin and Alban Bensa (1994), who were precisely calling for a shift "from objects to things." In that respect, it is interesting to note that the synthesis more recently produced by Martin Holbraad and Morten Axel Petersen (2017) insists more than previous publications on the historical continuities in the interest for things within anthropology, from Marcel Mauss and E. E. Evans-Pritchard to Clifford Geertz and Marshall Sahlins, even if they add that the ontological turn is distinctive because "it fundamentally recasts and radicalizes" the challenge of ethnocentrism: "The epistemological problem of how one sees things is turned into the ontological question of what there is to be seen in the first place." The distinction is important, indeed, since, on the one hand, it affirms that the true nature of things can ultimately be apprehended by anthropologists, and on the other hand, it grants them the power not only to think through things but also to speak in their stead.

A quite different anthropological approach to ontology from those presented until now is that of Philippe Descola (2013). Considering the dualism nature/culture—which is central not only to our world vision but also to the division of labor among the sciences—to be ethnocentric, he proposes a radical revision of the way to apprehend the "schemas" underlying societies across the world. Human experiences, he explains, involve two major processes—"modes of identification," by which analogies and contrasts are established between humans and nonhumans, and "modes of relation," by which these entities are engaged in various forms of action. Modes of identification are defined by the distribution of interiority, or subjective existence, and physicality, or external form, according to whether individuals see resemblances or dissimilarities. The two-by-two table thus constructed generates four types of society based on animism, naturalism, totemism, or analogism. For instance, animists, who are for the most part Amerindians, believe that humans and nonhumans are persons but that their appearance varies, whereas naturalists, who correspond to modern Westerners, hold that individuals and cultures differ but nature is one. Modes of relation can be reversible or nonreversible. In the first category, one finds gift, exchange, and predation, whereas the second one comprises production, protection, and transmission. This classification of societies according to their modes of identification and of practices according to their modes of relation is meant to be exhaustive. It explicitly follows Claude Lévi-Strauss's way of producing definitive atemporal classifications defined by cognitive as well as social structures, and reconnects with older conceptions of anthropology as producing a systematic order in the world.

It is clear that the various theories of the ontological turn—and the authors evoked represent only part of it—have less in common than their single designation would invite us to think. In particular, Viveiros de Castro opposes Amerindian multinaturalism to Western multiculturalism, arguing that it is the world that is different, whereas Descola more traditionally characterizes the Amerindians as animists and the Westerners as naturalists, establishing his four-term typology on the basis of how human beings see the world. In other words, in the former approach, the ontology characterizes the world, while in the second one, it refers to the representation of the world. Although both share common premises about the importance of bringing nonhumans into the anthropological picture, the perspectivism of one is not only distinct from the taxonomy of the other, but incompatible with it. Similarly, there is probably as much conceptual distance between Kohn's semiosis and the multispecies ethnographies as there is between Holbraad's thing theory and the anthropology of material culture. And whereas all these approaches, in coherence with their intellectual project, dismiss history and politics, the theory developed by Elizabeth Povinelli (2016) under the label *geontologies* attempt to reinscribe them via deep history and the politics of recognition of Australian Aborigines. In other words, to paraphrase its champions, the ontological turn is one phrase and many meanings.

Ignoring the connections between these authors and their works would however be a mistake. They write about each other and sometimes together, appear in conferences together all over the world, and ultimately recognize themselves under the label *ontological turn*, while often relating their approach with posthumanism, even if it is to readily claim that they go further than their predecessors in their radical understanding of the world. Beyond their rejection of anthropocentrism, which is common to all posthumanists, what do they share? Borrowing from one of their sources of inspiration, actor-network theory, I suggest sociologically exploring their connections from the three perspectives of theories, forests, and anthropologists. First, there is an intellectual genealogy, with the influence of Lévi-Strauss's structuralist thinking for the French lineage and Strathern's multiple ontologies for the British strand, although other less direct influences have already been noted, particularly Whitehead and Deleuze. Thus, Descola studied with Lévi-Strauss and Holbraad acknowledges his debt to Strathern. Albeit trained and teaching in Brazil, Viveiros de Castro, who has occupied positions in France and Britain, is a sort of bridge between the two traditions radicalizing Lévi-Strauss's reading of the human/nonhuman worlds and developing Strathern's theory into his own perspectivism. This genealogy is clearly distinct from and even opposed to that of critical approaches, which are influenced by Marx, Arendt, Foucault, or Wittgenstein; have inherited from the lessons of Max Gluckman, Eric Wolf, Georges Balandier, or Talal Asad; and take seriously history and politics as part of their anthropology. Second, they have a field site in common, which is Amazonia and the Amerindians, at least for three of the major figures, Viveiros de Castro on the Brazilian side, and Descola and Kohn on the Ecuadorian one, although not in the same region. This specific ecology with its particular ethnic groups and their long history of ethnological representation as the purest-from-Western-influence groups has for its only equivalent in the discipline that of Papua New Guinea, which is precisely where Strathern conducted her studies. Their forests are the natural environment of their uncorrupted natives. By contrast, it is remarkable that the ontological turn has almost no echo on the African continent. Third, there has been an obvious entrepreneurial dimension to the scientific enterprise, with the multiplication of performances on the global scene through panels and lectures and the pronouncement of provocative statements giving agency to trees, rocks, and things. In this public relations process, Latour himself has been instrumental, developing theatrical shows such as the Gaïa Global Circus, establishing a connection with the climate change cause via the Anthropocene, and humorously transforming a debate between Descola and Viveiros de Castro into a *disputatio* evocative of that of Valladolid's theologians.

The Report of the End of the Social Sciences and the Humanities: Greatly Exaggerated

The tentative depiction of the posthumanist universe probably leaves the reader with a certain dizziness as the theoretical ground is in perpetual movement, inventive labels appear at a frantic pace, and conceptual turns proliferate. The topography seems undecipherable; the territory has disputed frontiers; the terrain is full of formidable pitfalls; the landscape is stridden across by strange creatures. Undoubtedly, traveling in posthuman dominions is not an easy journey. But the effort is worthwhile, and even if we end up with a blurred picture of them, it offers important insights for social scientists as well as problematic issues.

Before examining both these insights and these issues, it is useful to reflect on what have been the conditions of possibility of posthumanism. Because of its multiple dimensions and heterogeneous claims, it certainly cannot be reduced to a single genesis. There must have been a *Zeitgeist*, an *air du temps*, a cultural context that has made these various theoretical moves emerge and, at least partially, converge. I will discuss three factors, which I do not claim to be the only ones involved—technological, moral, and religious.

First, the development of technologies, both on the side of computer science and artificial intelligence and on the side of life sciences and bioengineering, have broadened the limits of the body, enhanced the potentialities of the mind, contested the distinction between nature and culture, and raised new expectations about the future of human beings beyond what had until then been thought as their human condition. This beyond-the-human world has been a matter of prolific discursive, literary, and artistic production, through catastrophist or enthusiastic statements, science fiction novels and films, performances, and exhibits, thus creating a powerful imaginary of robots and cyborgs that questioned the human sciences.

Second, the nonhuman world, from the perspective of both the treatment of animals and the future of the planet, has become an object of increasing awareness and concern. Not only the occasional killing of scores of animals to limit the dissemination to human beings of epidemics such as the bovine spongiform encephalopathy and the avian influenza has shocked many observers, but even more the revelation of the ordinary modes of industrially raising and slaughtering animals, whether chicken or bovines, for human consumption has created emotional reactions and political responses. In parallel, the growing evidence of the dramatic progression of global warming, the mobilizations it has generated, the international resolutions that have been taken, and again the literary and artistic production to which it has given birth have led to the consciousness of the deleterious effect human beings have on their sole habitat. The other-than-human world appeared in need of recognition of its dignity and protection of its future.

Third, the transcendence of the human has an important, albeit rarely discussed, religious component. In a time when scientific knowledge seems to be opposed to beliefs in supernatural entities and when the demiurgic power deployed by humans appears to be challenging, posthumanism, which has both this scientific knowledge and this demiurgic power for foundation, can paradoxically be viewed as postsecular. It is indeed promoted by authors who often have a religious background and/or a religious project: Latour is a Catholic who recalls his church attendance on Sundays and gave the Gifford Lectures on natural theology; Jane Bennett speaks of being raised in a liberation-theology-inflected Catholicism in which the world was regarded as a divine creation that had to be cared for; and Quentin Meillassoux tries to conceive a solution to the perennial contradiction between the belief in a benevolent God and the existence of human suffering by inventing what he calls a virtual God. Moreover, the new materialism proposes to reconsider religion on novel grounds by integrating physics, neuroscience, and digital culture against earlier anthropological or sociological approaches; while surprising for anthropologists depicted as naturalists, the ontological turn reinvents animism by attributing human features to animals, thinking to plants, and agency to objects. More broadly, posthumanism appears to be a metaphysics haunted by the disappearance of the human species, which could only be avoided, at least for some, by a better care of the nonhuman world.

These three explicative factors being discussed, we can examine the present scope of posthumanism. A preliminary observation must be done regarding its location and extension within the social sciences and the humanities. To envisage the impact of the posthumanist project on these disciplines, it is, indeed, necessary to circumscribe its domain of influence. Drawing a precise cartography is impossible, but some indications may be provided. Within the social sciences, posthuman approaches are mostly limited to science and technology studies, from which they partially stem, as well as to anthropology, where they have made a late but noted appearance, and also to part of the field of international relations. History, sociology, economics, and political science are hardly affected, as they continue to see human relations and human behavior as the core of their interest, and many scholars in these disciplines might probably not even be aware of the existence of such phrases as "posthuman studies" or "ontological turn." Within the humanities, the posthuman trend is more salient, notably within feminist studies, which have been the cradle of several original interventions, starting with Donna Haraway and Rosi Braidotti, and it is present in various departments of cultural theory and literary studies, in relation with the critique of humanism, and in marginal segments of philosophy, a discipline dominated by analytic philosophy in North America and Britain, and Continental philosophy, critically oriented or not, in a good part of Europe. Postcolonial and race studies seem to have sometimes found inspiration in posthumanist projects, although they are mostly remote from their epistemological and political preoccupations. Beyond the social sciences and humanities, interactions are natural with certain multidisciplinary fields, notably animal studies and environmental studies as well as cybernetics.

This outline is of course reductive on several counts: the panorama is definitely dynamic and cannot be rendered by a fixed image; the geography of the circulation of theories needs to be refined; the very categories *posthuman*, *posthumanism*, and *posthumanities*, which are commonly used, are vague, changing in their content and uncertain for their contours. Anthropology is a case in point: the advocates of the ontological turn occupy a growing space within the discipline; the initial Amazonian nucleus now has numerous ramifications across the world; the reference to posthumanism is intermittent, and the connection with posthuman studies depends on schools of thought. Despite its limits, this cartography shows the selective permeability of the social sciences and humanities to the posthuman wave.

To refine the understanding of the footprint of the latter on the former, I will distinguish two sorts of posthuman assumptions—soft ones and hard ones.

Soft posthumanism provides a critique of humanism as anthropocentrism on a dual basis: humans have been wrongly placed at the top of the pyramid of life and at the center of the universe. The first element—top of the pyramid—has consequences in terms of how we consider and treat other living beings and, more broadly, nature. It invites us to a more ethically responsible conduct toward nonhumans, and by extension the planet. The second element—center of the universe—has consequences in terms of knowledge about, and comprehension of, the world we inhabit. It incites us to look at this world and the multiple entities that compose it with new lenses. In terms of impact on the social sciences and humanities, those working in animal studies or environmental studies have not waited for the posthumanists to engage in both these directions, but they have been able to build with them alliances leading to mutual intellectual enrichment and greater power to intervene in public debates. Soft posthumanism will have thus opened new horizons for research as well as for action. Although it is critical of a certain strand of humanism for its Western-centrism, blindness and arrogance, it remains human-friendly, so to speak. It rather questions its boundaries with nonhumans, demonstrating that they are more problematic than the traditional image of the self implies, whether these redefined boundaries involve great apes or computers.

Hard posthumanism, by contrast, engages in a critique of humanism that is not only more radical but also eminently speculative. It takes two main configurations. In its philosophical avatar, it imagines a dehumanized world, in the sense of claiming no necessity for humanity, a world resulting from endless contingencies and facing its programmed extinction. In its anthropological variation, it conceives its method in terms of discovery of ontologies for which history, culture, and society are superfluous. In the first case, philosophy has to be entirely rebuilt, since its foundations are irremediably corrupt. In the second case, anthropology has to be completely reinvented since its presuppositions are inadequate to its project. Both come with abstract theories and hermetic language that limit their accessibility not only for general audiences but also for cognate disciplines. Yet although they tend to produce an intellectual closure, it would be imprudent to predict whether this will lead to a lesser impact on the social sciences and humanities. The obscurity of hard posthumanism combined with its novelty has, indeed, an indisputable seductive power. So far, however, the foretold revolution of hard posthumanism has not taken place.

A crucial question posed by posthumanism—soft and hard—in its latest developments is that of the future of the planet in the Anthropocene. It has two main dimensions: one political, the other cognitive. On the political side, it is an invitation to protect the environment and limit global warming by caring for nature and reducing greenhouse gas. On the cognitive side, it is a call to rethink the place of humans in their relation to nature as well as the idea of history in light of a dangerous and even mortiferous geologic epoch. The paradox is, however, that both dimensions are discussed within a posthuman paradigm, when the very idea of the Anthropocene presupposes the deleterious presence of humans and their role as a "geological force," in Dipesh Chakrabarty's (2009, 207) words. The Anthropocene is definitely not posthuman; on the contrary, it is uniquely human—terribly human. Considering the number of publications unrelated to posthuman studies that have long established the reality and seriousness of the problem and have discussed its implications for the social science and the humanities, it would not be legitimate to attribute the merit of its recognition to posthumanism. In fact, one could even advance the opposite idea that the attentiveness to climate change and the invention of the new geologic era involve a critical form of humanism, which brings the humans back into the middle of the picture, this time not with the heroic garments of the Enlightenment but, rather, with the tragic costume of the Anthropocene. It might even be the case that the concern for the planet will have saved radical posthuman studies from its demons—in particular, their reification, otherization, and depoliticization of the world. The ontological turn is once more a revealing illustration, even if the variations among its proponents do not necessarily produce a consistent theoretical framework. I will therefore focus my analysis on this anthropological trend.

First demon: reification. With the concept of representations being rejected, ontological differences are substituted for cultural differences. It is not that we see the same thing differently but that things themselves are different. For these anthropologists, "what 'is' has no external point of reference, which means that its meaning should not be sought outside itself but essentially in the thing itself," write Henrik Erdmann Vigh and David Brehm Sausdal (2014, 50, 58). They underline the empirical impasse of this approach: it presupposes that this "post-social radical essentialism is to be taken as face value," since fieldwork is of no help for lack of possible communication between nonhumans and humans. Indeed, the strength of such speculative approach resides in the fact that it does not need any empirical verification and that any ethnographic refutation is merely discarded as irrelevant. One has to merely believe the anthropologists when they tell their readers that forests or drones think.

Second demon: otherization. The radical alterity that underlies the ontological approach is epitomized by the encounter between Westerners and Amerindians, which is at the foundations of its first champions' work. Whether in the dualist we/they model of perspectivism or in the quadripartite table of the structuralist taxonomy, it presupposes not only an incommunicability of cultures but also their homogeneity on each side of some grand divide. Yet all Amazonian natives are obviously no more alike than all European urbanites are. As Alcida Rita Ramos (2012, 481) remarks, "By reducing ethnographic complexity to a single model, it virtually refuses to acknowledge indigenous creativity." According to her, the anthropologist should instead "extinguish the ventriloquist and make room for the voices of the Indians themselves, thus reducing intermediacy and transforming the puppet into a co-thinker and 'symmetrical' interlocutor." Otherization therefore tends to essentialize differences, ignore shared understandings, and deny each one's right to identify oneself in multiple ways.

Third demon: depoliticization. Since the ontological reading of the world dismisses society as a fallacy and history as irrelevant, politics has no place—or, rather, it is reinterpreted in a completely different manner. As Martin Holbraad, Morten Axel Petersen, and Eduardo Viveiros de Castro (2014) express it, "The ontological turn is not so much a means to externally defined political ends, but a political end in its own right." Yet while anthropologists professing this new creed try to imagine how Natives see peccaries and jaguars, they miss the facts that these Amerindians are displaced from their homes and dispossessed of their territories by oil companies and other extractivist activities, that they witness the damage or destruction of their environment, that they protest with their Indigenous organizations, and that they endure the state's harsh repression. For lack of an "ethnography of the actual," write Lucas Bessire and David Bond (2014), this approach "diverts from the actually existing politics of nature and culture," disregarding in particular the "increasingly sharp forms and active processes of inequality and marginalization." Such depoliticization eludes, indeed, the hardships that people experience in their everyday life and the struggles in which they are engaged. To be fair, however, it must be acknowledged that Amerindians can find tools in the ontological turn and champions among its promoters in their fights against the political and economic forces threatening their natural resources.

Although its house has many mansions, which calls for caution with general interpretation, posthumanism meets various forms of these three challenges, notably in its radical form and recent developments. To address them, the principle of reality and the sense of urgency generated by the recognition of the Anthropocene should serve as a reminder that society is not an illusion, that history weighs heavily on the shoulders of its members as they confront this imminent danger, and that politics is about conflict even in the alliance between humans and nonhumans. When Michael Fischer (2014, 349), having lashed out at the ontological turn, states that we need "a new humanistic politics, open also to the posthuman with its human components, the cyberhuman and companion species, that will allow us to survive, to live after whatever catastrophes lie in store, and that will counter the widening inequalities and devastations of our current cannibal economies, consuming the lives of some for the luxury of others," he expresses in dramatic terms both the achievements and the limits of the posthuman moment—its probably indelible trace in the development of the social sciences and humanities, and the necessity to move beyond its excessive pretentions when human beings and the world they inhabit are facing such pressing issues.

Note

I am grateful to the scholars who have participated in this project and made comments on an earlier version of this chapter, especially to Nicolas Langlitz for having drawn my attention to the religious dimension of posthumanism and suggested readings of it.

References

Appadurai, Arjun. 1986. "Introduction: Commodities and the Politics of Value." In *The Social Life of Things: Commodities in Cultural Perspective,* edited by Arjun Appadurai, 3–63. Cambridge: Cambridge University Press.

Bazin, Jean, and Alban Bensa. 1994. "Des objets à 'la chose.'" In "Les objets et les choses," special issue, *Genèses* 17: 4–7.

Bennett, Jane. 2010. *Vibrant Matter: A Political Ecology of Things.* Durham, NC: Duke University Press.

Bessire, Lucas, and David Bond. 2014. "Ontological Anthropology and the Deferral of Critique." *American Ethnologist* 41, no. 3: 440–56.

Blanckaert, Claude. 1999. "L'histoire générale des sciences de l'homme: Principes et périodisation." In *L'Histoire des sciences de l'homme,* edited by Claude Blanckaert, Loïc Blondiaux, Laurent Loty, Marc Renneville, and Nathalie Richard, 23–60. Paris: L'Harmattan.

Braidotti, Rosi. 2006. *Transpositions: On Nomadic Ethics.* Cambridge: Polity.

Brassier, Ray. 2007. *Nihil Unbound: Enlightenment and Extinction.* Basingstoke, UK: Palgrave Macmillan.

Brown, Bill. 2001. "Thing Theory." In "Things," special issue, *Critical Inquiry* 28, no. 1: 1–22.

Chakrabarty, Dipesh. 2009. "The Climate of History: Four Theses." *Critical Inquiry* 35, no. 2: 197–222.

Connolly, William. 2013. "The New Materialism and the Fragility of Things." *Millennium: The Journal of International Studies* 41, no. 3: 399–412.

Delaplace, Grégory. 2017. "Comment pensent les drones: La détection et l'identification de cibles invisibles." *L'Homme* 222: 91–118.

Deleuze, Gilles, and Félix Guattari. 1983. *Anti-Oedipus: Capitalism and Schizophrenia.* Minneapolis: University of Minnesota Press.

De Martino, Ernesto. 1948. *Il mondo magico: Prolegomeni a una storia del magismo.* Turin: Einaudi.

Descola, Philippe. 2013. *Beyond Nature and Culture.* Chicago: University of Chicago Press.

Fischer, Michael. 2014. "The Lightness of Existence and the Origami of 'French' Anthropology." *Hau: Journal of Ethnographic Theory* 4, no. 1: 331–55.

Foucault, Michel. 1970. *The Order of Things: An Archeology of the Human Sciences.* New York: Vintage Books.

Haraway, Donna. 1985. "A Manifesto for Cyborgs: Science, Technology, and Socialist Feminism in the 1980s." *Socialist Review* 80: 65–107.

Harman, Graham. 2016. "Demodernizing the Humanities with Latour." *New Literary History* 47, nos. 2–3: 249–74.

Hayles, Katherine. 1999. *How We Became Posthuman: Virtual Bodies in Cybernetics, Literature, and Informatics.* Chicago: University of Chicago Press.

Heidegger, Martin. 1971. "The Thing." In *Poetry, Language, Thought*, translated by Albert Hofstadter, 163–80. New York: Harper and Row.

Henare, Amiria, Martin Holbraad, and Sari Wastell, eds. 2007. *Thinking through Things.* London: Routledge.

Holbraad, Martin, and Morten Axel Pedersen. 2017. *The Ontological Turn: An Anthropological Exposition.* Cambridge: Cambridge University Press.

Holbraad, Martin, Morten Axel Petersen, and Eduardo Viveiros de Castro. 2014. "The Politics of Ontology: Anthropological Positions." *Fieldsights* (blog), Society for Cultural Anthropology, January 13. https://culanth.org/fieldsights/462-the-politics-of-ontology-anthropological-positions.

Kirksey, Eben, and Stefan Helmreich. 2010. "The Emergence of Multispecies Ethnography." *Cultural Anthropology* 25, no. 4: 545–76.

Kohn, Eduardo. 2013. *How Forests Think: Toward an Anthropology beyond the Human.* Berkeley: University of California Press.

Lacan, Jacques. 2006. *Écrits.* Translated by Bruce Fink. New York: W. W. Norton and Company.

Laidlaw, James, and Paolo Heywood. 2013. "One More Turn and You're There." *Anthropology of This Century*, 7. http://aotcpress.com/articles/turn/.

Latour, Bruno. 2005. *Reassembling the Social: An Introduction to Actor-Network-Theory.* Oxford: Oxford University Press.

Latour, Bruno. 2013. *An Inquiry into Modes of Existence: An Anthropology of the Moderns.* Translated by Catherine Porter. Cambridge, MA: Harvard University Press.

Lévi-Strauss, Claude. 1966. *The Savage Mind.* Anonymous translation. Chicago: University of Chicago Press.

Lévi-Strauss, Claude. 1981. *Mythologiques*, vol. 4: *The Naked Man*. Translated by John and Doreen Weightman. Chicago: University of Chicago Press.

Meillassoux, Quentin. 2010. *After Finitude: An Essay of the Necessity of Contingency*. Translated by Ray Brassier. London: Continuum International.

Moravec, Hans. 1988. *Mind Children: The Future of Robot and Human Intelligence*. Cambridge, MA: Harvard University Press.

Nayar, Pramod. 2014. *Posthumanism*. Cambridge: Polity.

Porter, Theodore, and Dorothy Ross. 2003. *The Cambridge History of Science*, vol. 7: *The Modern Social Sciences*. Cambridge: Cambridge University Press.

Povinelli, Elizabeth. 2016. *Geontologies: A Requiem to Late Liberalism*. Durham, NC: Duke University Press.

Ramos, Alcida Rita. 2012. "The Politics of Perspectivism." *Annual Review of Anthropology* 41: 481–94.

Singer, Peter. 1975. *Animal Liberation: A New Ethics for the Treatment of Animals*. New York: HarperCollins.

Smith, Roger. 1997. *The Norton History of the Human Sciences*. New York: W. W. Norton and Company.

Strathern, Marilyn. 1990. "Artifacts of History: Events and the Interpretation of Images." In *Culture and History in the Pacific*, edited by Jukka Siikala, 25–44. Helsinki: Finnish Anthropological Society.

Tsing, Anna. 2012. "Unruly Edges: Mushrooms as Companion Species." *Environmental Humanities* 1, no. 1: 141–54.

Vigh, Henrik Erdman, and David Brehm Sausdal. 2014. "From Essence Back to Existence: Anthropology beyond the Ontological Turn." *Anthropological Theory* 14, no. 1: 49–73.

Viveiros de Castro, Eduardo. 2014. *Cannibal Metaphysics*. Translated by Peter Skafish. Minneapolis: Univocal.

Whitehead, Alfred North. 1927. *Symbolism, Its Meaning and Effect*. New York: Fordham University Press.

Wolfe, Cary. 2010. *What Is Posthumanism?* Minneapolis: University of Minnesota Press.

CONTRIBUTORS

DIDIER FASSIN is the James D. Wolfensohn Professor at the Institute for Advanced Study at Princeton University and Director of Studies at the École des Hautes Études en Sciences Sociales in Paris. He has conducted research on political and moral issues, notably on public health, humanitarianism, immigration, asylum, policing, and prison. He has authored twenty books that have been translated into eight languages, including *The Will to Punish* (2018), *Life: A Critical User's Manual* (2018), and *Death of a Traveler: A Counter Investigation* (2021).

GEORGE STEINMETZ is the Charles Tilly Professor of Sociology at the University of Michigan. His research interests include the sociology of empires, states, and cities; social theory; and the history and philosophy of the social sciences. His publications include *The Devil's Handwriting: Precoloniality and the German Colonial State in Qingdao, Samoa, and Southwest Africa* (2007); *Sociology and Empire: The Imperial Entanglements of a Discipline* (2013); and *The Colonial Origins of Modern Social Thought: French Sociology and the Overseas Empire* (2022).

CHITRALEKHA is an assistant professor at Jawaharlal Nehru University, Delhi. She is an anthropologist working on the remembered work of history and time on constitutions of resistance and the dreamwork of freedom. She is the author of *Ordinary People, Extraordinary Violence: Naxalites and Hindu Extremists in India* (2012), which was based on ethnographic fieldwork with armed cadres in India's long-running Maoist insurgency and with perpetrators in the 2002 pogrom against Muslims in Gujarat.

JEAN-LOUIS FABIANI is a professor of sociology at Central European University in Vienna. He has recently published *Bourdieu: A Heroic Structuralism* (2020) and *Clint Eastwood* (2021). He is currently writing a book on the uses of the concept of charisma.

JOHAN HEILBRON is a historical sociologist at Uppsala University and the Centre Européen de Sociologie et de Science Politique (CESSP-CNRS-EHESS) in Paris. His research is in economic sociology and the sociology of culture, knowledge, and science. Book publications in the latter category include *The Social and Human Sciences in Global Power Relations* (coedited, 2018), and *Pierre Bourdieu et l'art de l'invention scientifique* (coedited, 2022).

MIRIAM KINGSBERG KADIA is a professor of modern Japanese history at the University of Colorado Boulder. She is the author of *Moral Nation: Modern Japan and Narcotics in Global History* (2014) and *Into the Field: Human Scientists of Transwar Japan* (2020). She is currently working on a book on the history of time-use surveys.

KRISTOFFER KROPP is an associate professor at Roskilde University, Denmark. He has specialized in the history of sociology, European social surveys, and the relation between social science knowledge production and processes of Europeanization. He recently authored *A Historical Account of Danish Sociology: A Troubled Sociology* (2015).

NICOLAS LANGLITZ is an associate professor and chair of the Department of Anthropology at the New School for Social Research in New York. He is the author of *Chimpanzee Culture Wars: Rethinking Human Nature alongside Japanese, European, and American Cultural Primatologists* (2020). At present, he studies behavioral sciences that examine moral behavior and is working on a book of microessays and aphorisms on the psychedelic experience.

JOHN LARDAS MODERN is a professor of religious studies at Franklin and Marshall College, where he teaches classes on American religious history, literature, technology, and aesthetics. Modern recently published *Neuromatic: Or, a Particular History of Religion and the Brain* (2021). He is currently working on *The Book of Akron*, a project that explores the end of the world through the global history of rubber.

ÁLVARO MORCILLO LAIZ is a research fellow in the Cluster of Excellence research consortium "Contestations of the Liberal Script" at the Free University Berlin. His research focuses on problems of power and domination around donor-recipient relations in the social sciences and in transnational activism. He is the author of *Contentious Regions in the European Union: Nationalist Parties and the Coordination of European Policies in Federal Member States* (2009). He is currently working on a book on philanthropic domination.

AMÍN PÉREZ is an assistant professor of sociology at the Université du Québec à Montréal. His research is focused on migration, colonialism, and intellectual history in the Caribbean and in Europe. He has edited and authored the forewords to three books by Pierre Bourdieu and Abdelmalek Sayad. He recently published *Combattre en sociologues, Pierre Bourdieu et Abdelmalek Sayad dans une guerre de libération (Algérie, 1958–1964)* (2022).

CAREL SMITH is an associate professor at Leiden University in the Netherlands. His research focuses on legal methodology and the rhetorical analysis of law and legal theory. He coedited *The Rhetoric of Sincerity* (2009) and *Legal Argumentation and the Rule of Law* (2016).

PETER D. THOMAS teaches the history of political thought at Brunel University London. Among other works, he is the author of *The Gramscian Moment* (2009) and *Radical Politics: On the Causes of Contemporary Emancipation* (2022). He serves on the editorial boards of *Historical Materialism* and the *International Gramsci Journal*.

BREGJE VAN EEKELEN is Professor of Design, Culture, and Society at the Delft University of Technology. She uses a combination of historical and anthropological approaches to the study of knowledge concepts, most notably concepts that are situated in the contact zone of design, economy, and society (e.g., creativity, failure, interdisciplinarity, knowledge economy, design thinking, and complexity). Her NSF VENI project *Brainstorms: A Cultural History of Undisciplined Thought* traces the history of creative thinking in military and industrial settings from 1935 to 1965. Through an analysis of how the notion of creativity emerged and transformed in response to military and managerial rationalities, the standardization and disciplining of work, and the incorporation of social scientists in corporate America, she seeks to show that the employment of unstructured thought as a productive tool is more than an accident of history.

AGATA ZYSIAK is a historical sociologist working at the University of Vienna and the University of Łódź. Her research interests include state socialism and working-class history. She is the author of an award-winning book about the socialist university and upward mobility in postwar Poland, *Punkty za pochodzenie* (Points for social origin, 2016), and coauthor of *From Cotton and Smoke: Industrial City and Discourses of Asynchronous Modernity 1897–1994* (2019).

INDEX

categorization (legal adjudication): Alexander Aleinikoff and, 137, 139, 141; balancing and, 139–41; nature of, 137, 139; proportionality test and, 139; Stephen Gottlieb on, 140

Catholic Church, 243–47, 256

Catholic scholars and scholarship, 245, 246

Catholic sociology: Catholic universities and, 245–47; European Values Study (EVS) and, 245–47, 253, 257 (*see also* European Values Study)

Centro de Estudios de Asia y África (CEAA), 93, 94

Centro de Estudios Internacionales (CEI) at El Colegio de México, 93, 94; two counterfactuals to study CEI negotiation, 95–98

Centro de Estudios Sociales (CES), 91, 92, 96

Chałasiński, Józef: academia and, 180, 183; background and early life, 180; criticism of, 180; on intelligentsia, 180, 183; overview and characterizations of, 180, 183, 185, 189, 190, 191n9; personality, 185, 186; on science, 185; on sociology, 175, 183; University of Łódź and, 186–88; writings, 180, 183

Chall, Leo P., 40, 49

Chatterjee, Partha, 311, 319–20

Chiapello, Eve, 120

China, 37

Christian Democrats: conservatism and, 247–49

citizenship: *sive* subalternization, 321–23; vs. subjecthood, 315, 319, 321

citizen subject, 323

civil societies and political societies, 316, 317, 319–22, 324

class relations. *See* social class relations

cognition, 341–43; scientific, 36

Cognitive Science of Religion (CSR), 332–35; Pascal Boyer and, 333, 335–38, 341–43, 344n11, 344n13, 345n15

cognitive scientists, 328–30, 336, 343

Cohen, I. B., 51

Cohen-Eliya, Moshe, 138

Cohn-Bendit, Dany, 294, 295

Cold War, 38–40, 122, 221

Colegio de México, El, 91, 93, 97, 100; Alfonso Reyes and, 91, 95–97; archives, 95, 96; Centro de Estudios Internacionales (CEI), 93–98; Centro de Estudios Sociales (CES), 91, 92, 96; Daniel Cosío Villegas and, 91, 95–100; finances, 93, 98, 99; history, 91; international relations (IR) and, 83, 92, 95, 97, 98; library, 91, 98; overview and nature of, 83, 91; Rockefeller Foundation (RF) and, 82–83, 91–100; social sciences and, 83, 91, 92, 96, 97, 99

collective intellectual, 164

collective violence, 196–98, 213

colonial peripheries, 320, 321

communism: opposition to, 93, 188. *See also* Maoists; Marxism

Communist Party of India (Marxist-Leninist) (CPI[M-L]), 199, 207–8, 210

competition, 179; apes and, 357; chimpanzees and, 359; vs. cooperation/collaboration, 354 (*see also* cooperation/collaboration); primatology and, 355; science, sociologists, and, 352, 360, 362

Comte, Auguste, 26–27, 288, 353

Conant, James Bryant, 40

concept-quake, 22, 219, 312; first, 27–32; second, 32–42; third, 42–48

concepts, 108, 109, 289; creativity and, 110, 116–18 (*see also* creativity); history of, 107, 117–19; scientization and, 114; shifts in the meaning of, 108–9; social life of, 108, 116, 122–23; Teflon, 107–9, 118; traveling, 108, 109, 111

Condorcet, Marquis de, 25

configurations of knowledge, 288–91

consilience, 30, 363

cooperation/collaboration, 351, 357, 358; Christophe Boesch on, 352, 355–63; limits of, 356; Michael Tomasello on, 355–61; science as cooperation vs. war, 360–62

cooperation controversy, 355–57

core-periphery model, 263, 275, 279n3

core-periphery relations, 272, 276

core-periphery structure, 268–72, 274, 276

École Normale Supérieure (ENS), 149

Eiichirō, Ishida, 224

El Colegio de México. *See* Colegio de México

Elias, Nobert, 2, 14n1, 288

empiricism, 53; abstracted, 43

Engels, Friedrich, 30–32

Enlightenment, Age of, 25, 29

epistémè, 343, 369; scientific revolutions and, 296–302

epistemological break, 45, 46, 297

epistemological crises in legal theory, 129–30, 135, 143. *See also* balancing

epistemological revolutions, 296

epistemological shift. *See* concept-quake

epistemologie française (historical school of epistemology), 45, 52

epistemology, 292–93, 362–63, 375; assumptions regarding, 219; critical, 3; Foucault and, 45, 46, 296, 299, 308; French historical school of, 23; Gaston Bachelard and, 45, 46, 292, 297, 301; Georges Canguilhem and, 297, 299, 301; ontology and, 363, 380–81; power and, 235. *See also* European Values Study

Escuela Nacional de Ciencias Políticas y Sociales (ENCYPyS), 92, 97

Espinas, Alfred, 353

Ester, Peter, 255–56

ethical and moral questions, 245–47

ethics and morality, 244, 373–76

ethnocentrism, 263, 271, 380, 381; critical, 377

European integration, 243, 244, 248, 251

European Values Study (EVS), 240–41, 256–57; in 1990s and 2000s, 254–56; Catholic universities, Catholic sociology, and, 245–47, 257; the first survey and what followed, 252–54; a generic sociological approach, 241–42; Jacques-René Rabier and, 243, 248, 250–52; modernization theory and, 249–51; and opinion polling as an atheoretical political tool, 251–52; political conservatism and links to Christian Democrats, 247–49; social currents in, 243–52; statistics, science, and social engagement, 242–43

evolutionary anthropology of science, 351–52

evolutionary theory, 351, 355

exact sciences, 3, 25, 33, 34

exceptionalism, 233–34

existential ideology, 208–13

existentialism, 294–98

exuberant counterfactuals, 89–91

Fabiani, Jean-Louis, 46, 290

feminism, critical, 373, 375

Fichte, Johann Gottlieb, 29

field analysis, multilevel, 276

fields, 290; George Steinmetz on, 289, 290; settled vs. unsettled, 289, 290; weak, 277, 280n9

field theory (sociology), 263, 265; Bourdieu and, 23, 47, 63n24, 242, 263, 289, 290. *See also* social fields

fieldwork, revelations of, 152; how and what to observe?, 152–55; in search of social transformation, 159–61; for whom and for what?, 155–59. *See also* Bourdieu, Pierre; laboratory vs. fieldwork; Sayad, Abdelmalek

Fischer, Michael, 389

flattening universe, 268

Fleck, Ludwik, 38–39

Fordant, Clarisse, 304

formalism, 135; balancing and the turn toward, 136–39, 141; culture of, 139

Forman, Paul, 33

Foucault, Michel, 46, 296–301, 307, 308; Bourdieu and, 296–301; discontinuist approach to history, 46, 53, 299, 301; Edward Said and, 302, 303, 305; Georges Canguilhem and, 45, 297–99, 301; historical school of epistemology and, 45; Karl Mannheim and, 35; Louis Althusser and, 297–99; opposition to sociology, 300; writings, 299, 305, 369

France: Algeria and, 150–52, 155, 165, 166; sociology in, 291

Frängsmyr, Tore, 27

Franklin, Sarah, 117

free decision, method of, 134. *See also* sociological method

Freirechtsbewegung (Free Law Movement), 132; Legal Realism and, 132, 135, 140

French history of science. *See under* history of science

French theoretical stringency, 292

French theory, 272, 303

Freudenthal, Gideon, 36, 37

Friedman, Thomas, 267, 268

Fuller, Steve, 42, 54, 55, 64n30

gakujutsu, 219, 235

Garfinkel, Harold, 292–93

generalized liquidity, 268

Geny, Francois, 132–35

geoculture of the modern world system, 265

geographical orientation, 274

geometry, 338, 339

geontologies, 382

George, Stefan, 33

German sociologists, 41-42, 44

Germany, 29, 31, 33, 44; postwar, 34, 41, 50–52, 58, 222, 244, 248, 254; Weimar, 33, 40, 41. *See also* Nazi Germany

Giddens, Anthony, 59, 108, 118, 124n11

Gillispie, Charles C., 38

global connections, 263, 264

global field, 265; emerging, 269, 276

globalization, 263, 266–68, 271; meanings and use of the term, 262, 263, 272; vs. other forms of internationalization, 272, 274; in the social sciences, 263–64, 272, 277n7; sociology in the era of, 175. *See also* transnationalization

"global" social science, historicizing, 264–68

Gmelin, Johann G., 133, 134

Goffman, Erving, 300

Gottlieb, Stephen E., 140

Gough, Kathleen, 223

Gouldner, Alvin, 23, 44-45, 51

Graham, Loren R., 35, 36, 38, 185

Gramsci, Antonio, 58; on passive revolution, 320; *Prison Notebooks*, 198, 313, 314, 320, 322–24; on subalternity, 313–24

Grossman, Henryk, 37

group solidarity. *See* solidarity

Guha, Ranajit, 198, 199, 310, 311, 316, 319, 320

Gupta, Dipankar, 198, 204-6; Veena Das and, 197, 198, 204, 213

Guthrie, Stewart E., 329, 340

Hacking, Ian, 141

Halman, Loek, 255-56

Haney, David Paul, 305

Haraway, Donna Jeanne, 371

Harding, Harold Friend, 113

Harman, Graham, 370, 374, 379

Hayles, Katherine, 371

Hegel, Georg Wilhelm Friedrich, 28, 46; contextual readings of science by, 27–32; Gramsci and, 316; Marx and, 29–32, 42–43; overview, 28

Heider, Fritz, 330, 338-41, 345n15

Hessen, Boris, 36-39

heurematography, 24

Heyck, Hunter, 331

Heywood, Paolo, 376

historical science, 300

historical sociology, 21; of natural science, 38

historical sociology of social science, 46, 60–61; emergence, 21, 23, 33, 48, 50; science studies and, 52–54; as social scientific reflexivity, 54–58, 60–61; from social studies of science to the, 42–48; theoretical and methodological programs for a, 47

histories and the present, 117–23

historiography of science, 24, 35

history, Marx's theory of, 29–30

history of science, 40, 45–46, 50, 51, 53, 81–82, 298, 301; books on, 26t; development of, 24–27; explaining variations in interest in the, 48–52; France and, 45, 292, 297, 298, 301; Gaston Bachelard and, 32, 45–46, 292, 296, 297, 301; Georges Canguilhem and, 292, 296–98, 301; German, 29; Marx, Marxism, and, 35, 37, 38, 297; Soviet Union and, 35-36, 38. *See also* sociology of science

history of social science: explaining variations in interest in the, 48-52; justifications for the, 55; uses of the, 58–60. *See also specific topics*

history of sociology, 48, 50–52, 87; Alvin Gouldner and, 23, 44–45, 51; Heinz Maus on, 63n16; postwar, 190; writings on, 47, 51

Hulak, Florence, 300

human, transcendence of the, 384

humanism: secular, 206; socialist, 186. *See also* anthropocentrism; posthumanism

humanities: report of the end of the, 383–89; social science of the, 4

human sciences, 27, 46, 368, 369; the brain and the, 330–33; history of the term, 368; Lévi-Strauss on ultimate goal of, 369; scope of the term, 368. *See also specific topics*

hybridization (of knowledge), 272, 276

hyperactive agency detection device (HADD), 328–30, 334–35, 337, 338, 341, 342; distinguishing marks on a screen, 338–41; Pascal Boyer and, 335, 337, 338, 341, 342, 344n10

hysteresis, 167n7

identification, modes of, 381

ideology: academic intellectuals are mainly producers of, 30–31

Ienaga Saburō, 224, 226–27

imagination, 110, 115, 120

imperialism, 234, 277

imperialist origins of social science, 225–26

India, anthropology of violence in, 195–99, 212–14; nation-state and secular humanism, 204–7; revolution, university, and (existential) ideology, 207–12; speech of the survivor and anthropological listening, 199–203

Indian bourgeoisie, 319–20

individual rights. *See* rights

information theory, 331

Inglehart, Ronald, 250–53

innovation, 278

integral historians, 319

integral state, 316, 317, 320–23

intelligentsia, 179, 180, 183, 184, 191n3, 210

internalism, 37, 132, 301; vs. externalism, 38–39, 47, 82

internationalization, 272, 274, 277. *See also* globalization

international organizations, 265, 266, 275; transnationalization through, 278

international relations (IR): Colegio de México and, 83, 92, 95, 97, 98; in Mexico around 1960, 91–95; Rockefeller Foundation (RF) and, 83, 92, 95, 97, 99. *See also* Centro de Estudios Internacionales (CEI)

involvement and detachment, 2–3

irrationality and creativity, 110, 111

Itani, Junichiro, 230, 355

Izumi, Seiichi, 225, 230–31

Izumi, Takura, 230

Japan, 218; rethinking objectivity, 223–26; studying diversity (after 1968) in, 232–35

Japanese exceptionalism (*Nihonjinron*), 233–35

Japanese transwar generation: in crisis, 229–32; worldview of the, 219–23

Japanese university protests (1968–1969), 217–18; the student struggle, 226–29. *See also* University of Tokyo

jouissance, 205

justice: Aristotle on, 134; defined, 134

Kabylia, Algeria, 158, 159

Kant, Immanuel, 28, 50, 372

Katō, Ichirō, 231, 232

Kawakita, Jirō, 224

Kerkhofs, Jan, 244–47

Kleinman, Daniel Lee, 54

Kłoskowska, Antonina, 187

Knobl, Wolfgang, 250

knowledge: archeology of, 301; configurations of, 288–91; flourishing of, 58–59; hybridization of, 272, 276

knowledge deficits, 278

Kohn, Eduardo, 378, 379, 382

Koselleck, Reinhart, 123n4

Koskenniemi, Martti, 136, 139

Koyré, 45, 46

Krzywicki, Ludwik, 178–80, 182, 183

modernization theory, 57, 245; as frame for a conservative understanding of social change, 249–51

Modonesi, Massimo, 324

Moore, F. J., 62n8

moral and ethical questions, 245–47

morality and ethics, 244, 373–76

multilevel field analysis, 276

Nakao Katsumi, 234–35

Nakazawa, Miyori, 227, 228, 230

Nanbara Shigeru, 222

nation-state: Dipankar Gupta on, 204–6; secular humanism and, 206

naturalism, 381

natural sciences: human sciences and, 2, 30, 34; (historical) sociology of, 35, 38; ways they are socially determined, 29–30

nature/culture dualism, 381

Naxalbari, 209, 211

Naxalbari uprising, 207, 208

Naxalism: Rabindra Ray on, 209; scholarship on, 199, 207, 211

Naxalite ideology, 207–9, 211, 213

Naxalite movement: Bela Bhatia and, 211–13; Rabindra Ray and, 208–11, 213

Naxalites, 213–14; Rabindra Ray and, 207–9, 211

Nayar, Pramod, 370

Nazi Germany, 41, 42, 52, 58, 222, 229, 254

Needham, Joseph, 37–38

neoliberalism, 164, 249, 311

neoliberal rationality, 324

neopositivism, 4

neuroscience and human sciences, 330–33

Nietzsche, Friedrich, 21, 32, 34, 372, 373

nihilism, 209–11; Rabindra Ray and, 209–11; Ray Brassier and, 370, 372

Nihonjinron, 233–35

Nilsen, Alf Gunvald, 324

Noelle-Neumann, Elisabeth, 248

Nouschi, André, 150, 151

objectivity, 219, 220, 230, 235; rethinking, 34, 223–26, 228; transwar, 228, 233, 234; World War II, American ideals, and, 221, 222

objects and things, 379–80

observation. See fieldwork

Okamoto Tarō, 225

Okasha, Samir, 351–52

ontological differences substituted for cultural differences., 387

ontological emergence, 53

ontological turn, 382; Africa and, 383; animism and, 381, 384; anthropology and, 376–77, 380, 382, 384, 385, 387; ethnocentrism and, 380–81; Michael Fischer and, 389; politics, depoliticization, and, 388; posthumanism and, 376, 382, 384, 385; as a revolution, 376–77; theories of, 381

ontologists, 380

ontology, 363, 388; of animals, 377, 378; anthropological approaches to, 381; anthropology and, 377–78, 386; collapse of, 209; epistemology and, 363, 380–81; otherization, alterity, and, 387–88; posthumanism and, 370, 371, 375, 386

opinion polling as an atheoretical political tool, 251–52

Orientalism (Said), 266, 291, 302–7

Ossowski, Stanisław, 186

otherization, 387–88

Pandey, Gyanendra, 311, 322

paradigms, 141, 142

Parsons, Talcott, 250, 251, 291; on smooth functioning of society, 290; systems theory, 249; on values, 244–45, 249

Passeron, Jean-Claude, 292, 293, 296, 297

Payne, Christine A., 32

peripheral centers, 272, 276

personal involvement. See involvement and detachment

perspectivism, 378, 382, 388

philanthropic foundations. See science patronage and of philanthropic foundations

philosophy, 31, 361; history of, 27–28

philosophy of science, 361; Marx and, 30; vs. sociology of science, 34

Piketty, Thomas, 288

Pitts, Walter, 331

Plato, 44–45

Platt, Jennifer, 87, 88

Polish Sociological Association, 178, 188

Polish sociologists, 175, 188

Polish sociology, 175–78, 183, 184, 189–90; and the agenda of tomorrow, 181–83; bourgeoisie out, 183–87; interwar institutionalization, 177–81; Stalinist consolidation, 187–89

political conservatism and Christian Democrats, 247–49

political modernity, 310–12, 315, 319–24

political societies, 311, 319, 320; civil societies and, 316, 317, 319–22, 324

Pollak, Michael, 50

polycentric dynamics, 272, 276

Porat, Iddo, 138

positivism, 4, 9, 10, 61, 177, 291–93; meanings and uses of the term, 191n5; methodological, 178, 191n5, 252. See also antipositivism; neopositivism; postpositivism

posthumanism, 13, 369–70; challenges related to, 388–89; components, 13; conditions of possibility of, 383–84; critiques of humanism, 385–87; definitions and meanings of the term, 369–70; and the future of Earth in the Anthropocene, 386–87; hard vs. soft, 385–86; humanities and, 372–73, 385–87, 389; Michael Fischer and, 389; nature of, 371–72; terminology, 369–70, 385

posthumanists, 375; eleventh-hour, 376–89

posthumanities, 378–79, 385

posthuman studies, 385

postpositivism, 287, 288

Pouillon, François, 306–7

Poupeau, Franck, 158

power, 190; epistemology and, 235

practice, theory of, 148, 160–61

Priestley, Joseph, 25

primate social science, social science of, 352–53, 361

primate sociology, 353–55

Prison Notebooks (Gramsci), 198, 313, 314, 320, 322–24; subalternity in, 314–17. See also Gramsci, Antonio

production: modes of, 31, 120

productive forces, 29–31, 36; primacy of, 29

proportionality test, 134–40

protoi heuretai, study of, 24, 25

Punjab, 205

Puritanism, 39

Pyysiäinen, Ilkka, 328

Rabier, Jacques-René, 243, 248, 250–52

Raphael, Lutz, 52

rationality, 129, 137, 141–43

Ray, Rabindra, 199, 209–12; death, 211; Naxalism, Naxalites, and, 207–11, 213; nihilism and, 209–11; writings, 207, 210, 213

realist international relations (IR) scholars, 94, 95

reasoning methods, 142

reflexive sociology, 161. See also critical sociology

reflexivity, social scientific, 164–65, 306, 329, 352; historical reflexivities, 196, 197, 200; historical sociology of social science as, 54–58, 60–61; Pierre Bourdieu and, 1, 55, 56, 161, 165, 362. See also critical reflexivity

reification, 387

Reischauer, Edwin O., 221

relatively settled field, 289

relativism, 39, 292, 299, 300

religion: nature of, 329; and transcendence of the human, 384. See also Cognitive Science of Religion

religious sociology, 246–47, 249

Republic of Letters, 264, 361

research methodology. See methodology

resentment, 33

restrained counterfactuals, 88, 90

reverse flows, 276

revisionism, 209, 210

revolutionism, 209

Reyes, Alfonso, 91, 96; Colegio de México and, 91, 95–97; Daniel Cosío Villegas and, 91, 95–96, 99–100; Rockefeller Foundation (RF) and, 95–96, 99–100

rights: fundamental, 139, 140; policies and, 139; protection of individual, 138–39; vs. social interests, 138–39

Rockefeller, John D., 85

Rockefeller Foundation (RF), 91, 92, 95; Alfonso Reyes and, 95–96, 99–100; background and history, 83, 85, 100; César Sepúlveda and, 97; Colegio de México and, 82–83, 91–100; Daniel Cosío Villegas and, 95–100; Dean Rusk and, 93, 98; Division of Social Science (DSS), 93–95, 97, 99; fellowships, 98, 99; Francisco Cuevas Cancino and, 97; health and, 86; international relations (IR) and, 83, 92, 95, 97, 99; Lucio Mendieta y Núñez and, 92; Manuel Tello and, 97–99; nature of, 85; political science and, 99; science and, 86; social sciences and, 87, 92; Universidad Nacional Autónoma de México (UNAM) and, 92, 97

Rodinson, Maxime, 303

Roscher, Wilhelm, 29

Rosenberg, Bernard, 41

Roy, Srila, 324

Rueschemeyer, Dietrich, 41–42

Rusk, Dean, 93, 97, 98

Said, Edward, 302–4, 307; Foucault and, 302, 303, 305; *Orientalism*, 266, 291, 302–7

Sarton, George, 27

Saverien, M., 25

Sayad, Abdelmalek: Algeria and, 152, 154–60, 162; background and overview, 152; Bourdieu and, 151–67; on colonial system, 162; fieldwork, 151–53, 155, 157–58, 160, 161, 163, 164, 166; writings, 153, 155

scanning (cognition), 328, 329, 334–36, 342–43

Scheler, Max, 33

Scheper-Hughes, Nancy, 195, 196

science: as cooperation vs. war, 360–62; nature of, 36; origins, 33. *See also* history of science; *specific topics*

science and technology studies (STS), 52–55, 63n24

science patronage and of philanthropic foundations, 83–88, 90–91, 100

science wars, 362

scientific cognition, 36

scientificity, 51, 288

scientific revolutions, 45–46, 264; epistémè and, 296–302

scientization, 114

screens, 334

Secret Army Organization (OAS), 155

secular humanism and nation-state, 206

Sepúlveda, César, 97

settled vs. unsettled fields, 289, 290

Shannon, Claude E., 331

Sica, Alan, 39–40

Sikhs: 1984 anti-Sikh riots, 197–98, 202, 203, 207; Dipankar Gupta and, 204, 205; Veena Das and, 197–98, 203

Simmel, Marianne, 330, 338–41, 345n15

skepticism, 32, 299, 300

Smith, Carel E., 142

Smith, Roger, 368

Smith College in Northampton, MA, 338–40

smooth functioning of society, 290

social classes, 31, 33; subaltern, 316

social class relations, 30, 31, 36

social etymologies, 108–9

social evolution, 353

social fields, 54. *See also* field theory

socialist humanism, 186

social science: goals, 43; greatest contribution and greatest curse, 378; multisited histories of, 116–17; permeation of reality by, 59. *See also specific topics*

social science concepts, 108, 114, 116–18, 122, 123. *See also* concepts

social sciences, report of the end of the, 383–89

social scientific knowledge, how political commitment delineates, 240–41; a generic sociological approach, 241–42; statistics, science, and social engagement, 242–43

social surveys. *See* surveys

societies: types of, 381

sociobiology, 351, 354

Sociological Imagination (Mills), 21, 23, 43, 290

sociological method, 134; balancing of interests as quintessence of, 134–36 sociologists, 177; definitions, 176; role of, 163

sociology: characterizations of, 177, 184–85, 187; defining, 176–78, 184; rephilosophization of, 288. *See also* history of sociology; *specific topics*

sociology journals, 273–74

sociology of knowledge (*Wissenssoziologie*), 43, 44, 62n9; aim of, 33–34; Bourdieusian, 55; as concept-quake, 22, 32–42; in Germany, 44, 48–50, 52; Karl Mannheim and, 33–34, 39–41, 48, 59, 62n9; reasons for the backlash against, 22; Robert Merton and, 22, 23, 33, 34, 39, 40, 48; science and, 34, 53; transition to sociology of science, 22, 39–42

sociology of science, 34, 51; Bourdieu and, 52–55; vs. philosophy of science, 34; Robert Merton and, 22, 23, 34, 39, 40, 43, 44, 48–49, 51, 52, 55, 82; transition from the sociology of knowledge to, 22, 39–42

solidarity, 355, 359; organic vs. mechanical, 354. *See also* cooperation/collaboration

specialization and switching, strategies of, 276

speciesism, 371

Spivak, Gayatri Chakravorty, 311, 316–18

"split public," 197

Stalinist consolidation, 187–89

Stalinization, 177, 190

Steinmetz, George, 290; on concept-quake, 219; on fields, 289, 290; on methodological positivism, 252

Stocking, George W., Jr., 42

Stoetzel, Jean, 244, 251–53

strategies of specialization and switching, 276

Strathern, Marilyn, 379–80, 382–83

structuralism, 35, 297–99, 302; Bourdieu and, 56, 293, 305

Struik, Dirk J., 37

subalternity: citizenship *sive* subalternization, 317, 321–23; crisis and foreclusion, 312–14; hegemony, colonial difference, and, 319–21; terminology, 322; Veena Das and, 198–201. See also *Prison Notebooks*

subaltern(s): autonomous domain of, 319; new, 311–12; subaltern capacity, 317–19; subaltern social groups, 311, 313, 316–19, 321

Subaltern Studies, 200, 310–12, 314, 317, 319, 321–23; beyond, 317, 325

Subaltern Studies Collective, 198–99, 310, 312–13

subjecthood vs. citizenship, 315, 319, 321

Subsumption Formula, 138

Sundar, Nandini, 213, 214n8

Supreme Court, U.S., 133, 137–39

surveys, social, 248, 251–52. *See also* European Values Study (EVS)

systemic accounts, 265

Szczepański, Jan, 181

Tangerman, E. J., 118

Tannery, Paul, 27

technologies, development of, 383–84

technology, 35, 36; and the body, 383; Marx and, 29–30; vs. science, 30, 53. *See also* machines; science and technology studies

Teflon concepts, 107–9, 118

Tello, Manuel, 97–99

Temporary Measures concerning University Management, Law for, 232–33

terrorism, 208–10

Therborn, Göran, 175

thing-as-analytic vs. thing-as-heuristic, 380

things, 379–81, 387; objects and, 379–80

thing theory, 380, 382

Thompson, Kenneth W., 93–95, 97–99

thought collective, 38, 39

thought experiments. *See* counterfactuals

thought style, 38

Three Stages, Law of, 26

Tilburg University, 245, 246

Tōdai. *See* University of Tokyo

Tomasello, Michael, 352, 355–60; chimpanzees and, 357–60; vs. Christophe Boesch, 352, 356–61; Christophe Boesch compared with, 355–56; on cooperation/collaboration, 355–61; research methodology and, 358–61

topique, 289

Torrance, E. Paul, 112

"trained judgment," 129, 142

transnational authorship and coauthorship, 270, 271

transnational circulation, 265, 268, 275–76

transnational collaboration, 270

transnational fields, 277n7

transnationalization, 262, 270, 271, 278n10. *See also* globalization

transnational orientation, levels of, 274

transnational regionalization, 272–74

traveling concepts, 108, 109, 111

Tsing, Anna, 379

unconscious (and history), Bourdieu on, 21, 241–42, 293

UNESCO (United Nations Educational, Scientific and Cultural Organization), 266–67

Universidad Nacional Autónoma de México (UNAM), 92, 97

university autonomy, 226, 231. *See also* autonomy

University of Łódź, 176, 181–84, 186; Department of Sociology, 182, 187, 188; Józef Chałasiński and, 186–88

University of Tokyo (Tōdai), 222, 227–33; activists and protesters at, 227–33 (*see also* Japanese university protests)

unsettled field, defined, 290

Uprooting: The Crisis of Traditional Agriculture in Algeria (Bourdieu and Sayad), 153, 162, 165

Vatin, Jean-Claude, 306–7

violence. *See* India, anthropology of violence in Viveiros de Castro, Eduardo, 376–77, 381–83

Wacquant, Loïc, 158

Wagner, Peter B., 47, 50, 60

Wallerstein, Immanuel, 264

weak fields, 277, 280n9

Weber, Max, 88, 89

Weimar Republic, 33, 40, 41

Whewell, William, 26

Whitehead, Alfred North, 25, 374

Williams, Raymond, 107, 109

Wilson, Edward O., 30, 333, 363

Wissenssoziologie. *See* sociology of knowledge

Wittrock, Björn, 46, 47, 60

Wolfe, Cary, 371

Work and Workers in Algeria (Bourdieu), 153, 156, 165

world systems theory, 265, 279n3

Wurzel, Karl-Georg, 129

Yasuda Hall, occupation of, 227, 232

Zilsel, Edgar, 37

Znaniecki, Florian, 178–81, 184

Zuckerman, Solly, 354